STORY & ART BY

Maki Enjoji

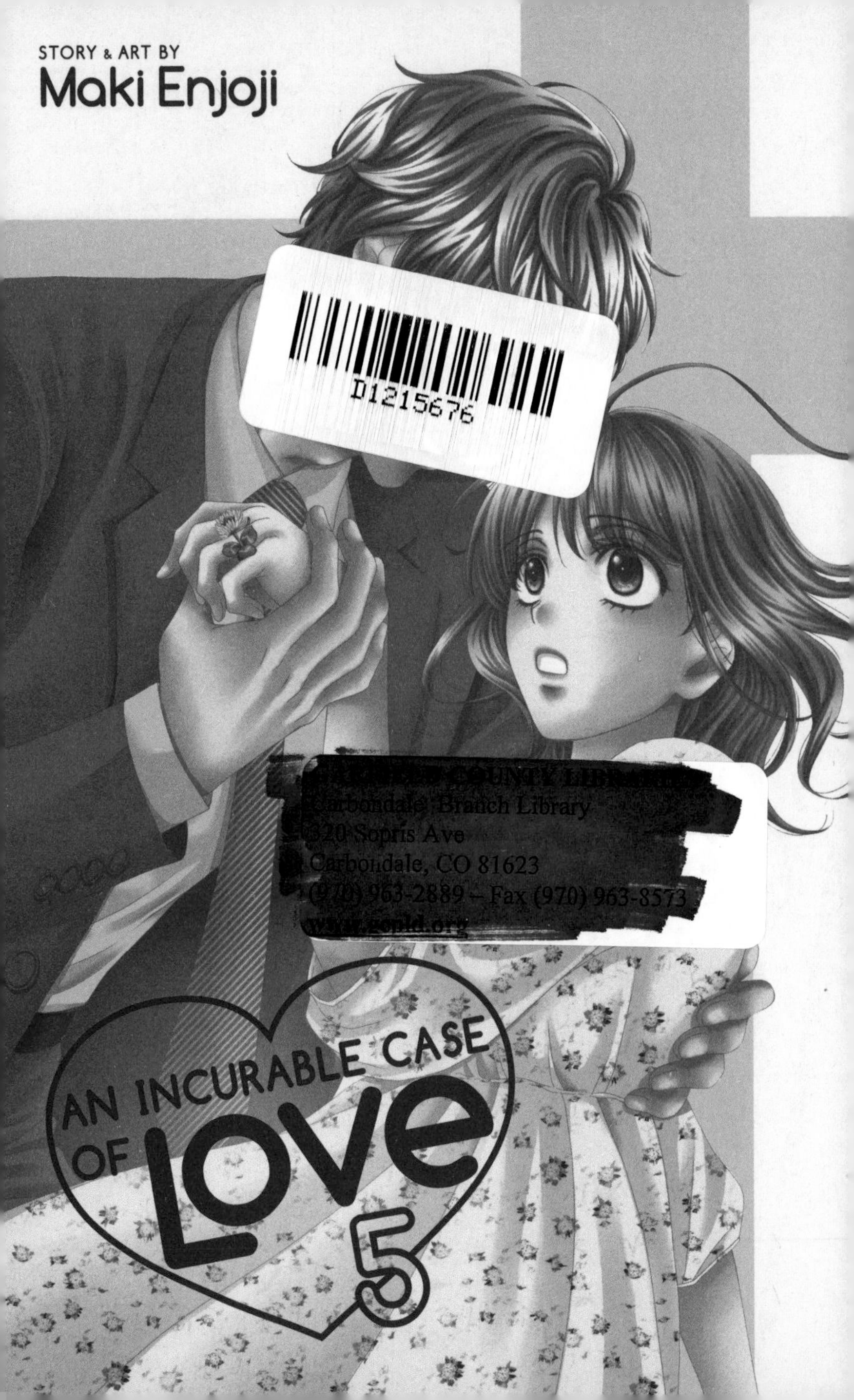



# AN INCURABLE CASE OF LOVE 5

# Characters

Narimiya Central General Hospital

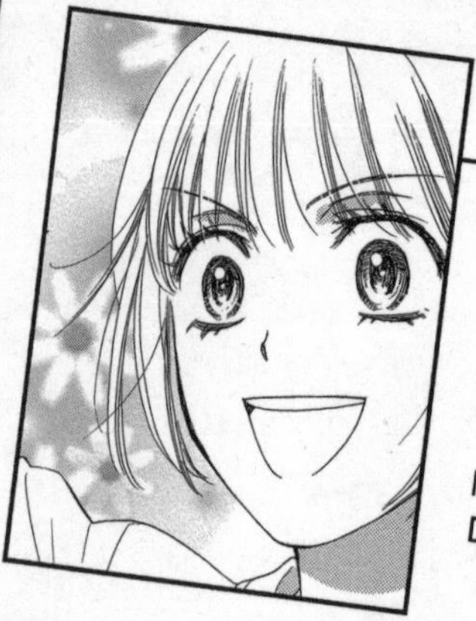

## Nanase Sakura

**Occupation: Nurse**
**Department: Pulmonology**
**Nickname: Valiant One**

She went into medicine because she admired Kairi Tendo. She confesses her love for him and is brutally rejected. Despite that, she requests to be placed in Pulmonology, the department where he works.

Narimiya Central General Hospital

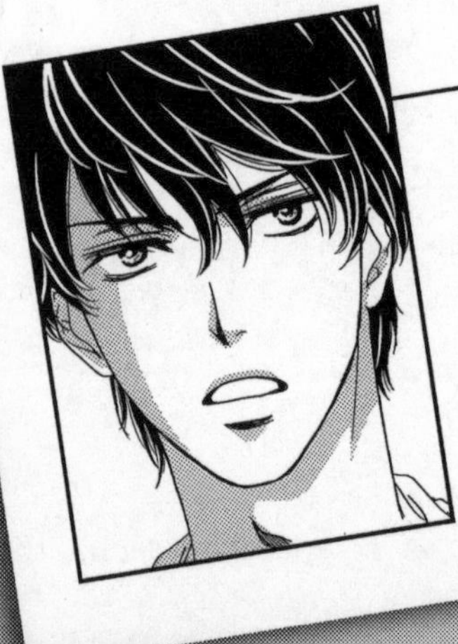

## Kairi Tendo

**Occupation: Doctor**
**Department: Pulmonology**
**Nickname: Dark Lord**

He is unpopular with the nurses in the hospital because of his abrasive attitude. Despite his rough treatment of Nanase Sakura, he still cares for her?

# Kisugi

## Department: Pulmonology

He is Kairi's classmate from college, but the two of them don't get along. He is loved by the nurses for his gentle personality.

# Minori Wakabayashi

Kairi and Kisugi's college classmate and Kairi's ex-girlfriend. She passed away from a disease.

# Ryuko Tendo

## Occupation: Apartment Building Manager

Kairi's older sister. She is carefree and loves alcohol. She's quite fond of Nanase.

# Story Thus Far

Five years ago, Nanase Sakura worked with Kairi Tendo to save an old lady who had suddenly collapsed in the street. Nanase instantly falls in love with Kairi when she sees his smile, and she decides then to become a nurse. She believes he is the prince she's been waiting for, but upon meeting Kairi again, she discovers he's not at all like she thought he was! He's strict and unyielding with the nurses in his department. Though she resents Kairi's tyranny, she doesn't leave his side. She takes on impossible tasks though sheer willpower, and everyone starts referring to her as the "Valiant One." Since Kairi's plans to study abroad have been canceled, Nanase is overjoyed that they can be together. They slowly start acting more like lovers and become united in mind and body. Our couple is more affectionate than ever before!

# CONTENTS

## Twenty-First Love

# The Second Act of Love: The Appearance of a Rival! Huh? Does That Mean—?!

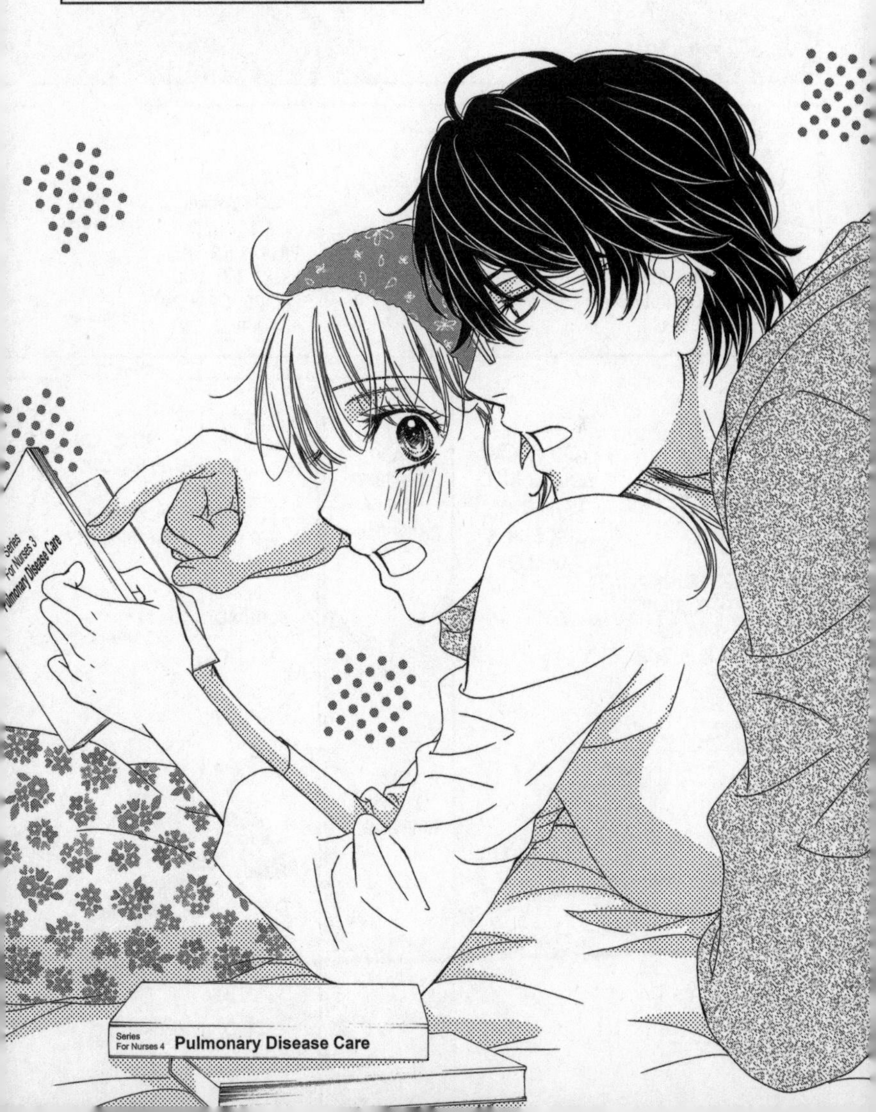
Series
For Nurses 3
Pulmonary Disease Care
Series
For Nurses 4
Pulmonary Disease Care

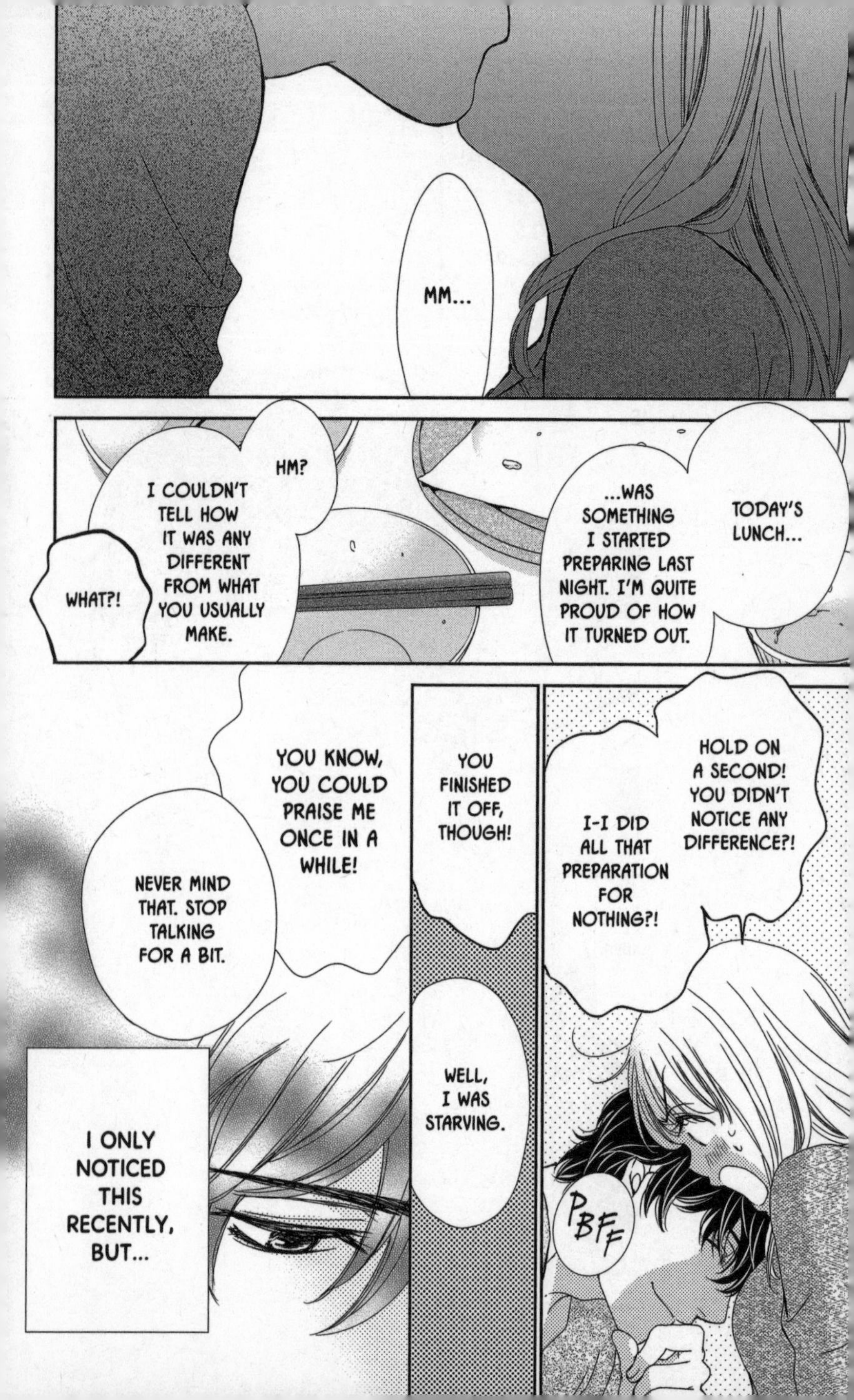
MM...
TODAY'S LUNCH...
...WAS SOMETHING I STARTED PREPARING LAST NIGHT. I'M QUITE PROUD OF HOW IT TURNED OUT.
HM?
I COULDN'T TELL HOW IT WAS ANY DIFFERENT FROM WHAT YOU USUALLY MAKE.
WHAT?!
HOLD ON A SECOND! YOU DIDN'T NOTICE ANY DIFFERENCE?!
I-I DID ALL THAT PREPARATION FOR NOTHING?!
PBFF
YOU FINISHED IT OFF, THOUGH!
WELL, I WAS STARVING.
YOU KNOW, YOU COULD PRAISE ME ONCE IN A WHILE!
NEVER MIND THAT. STOP TALKING FOR A BIT.
I ONLY NOTICED THIS RECENTLY, BUT...

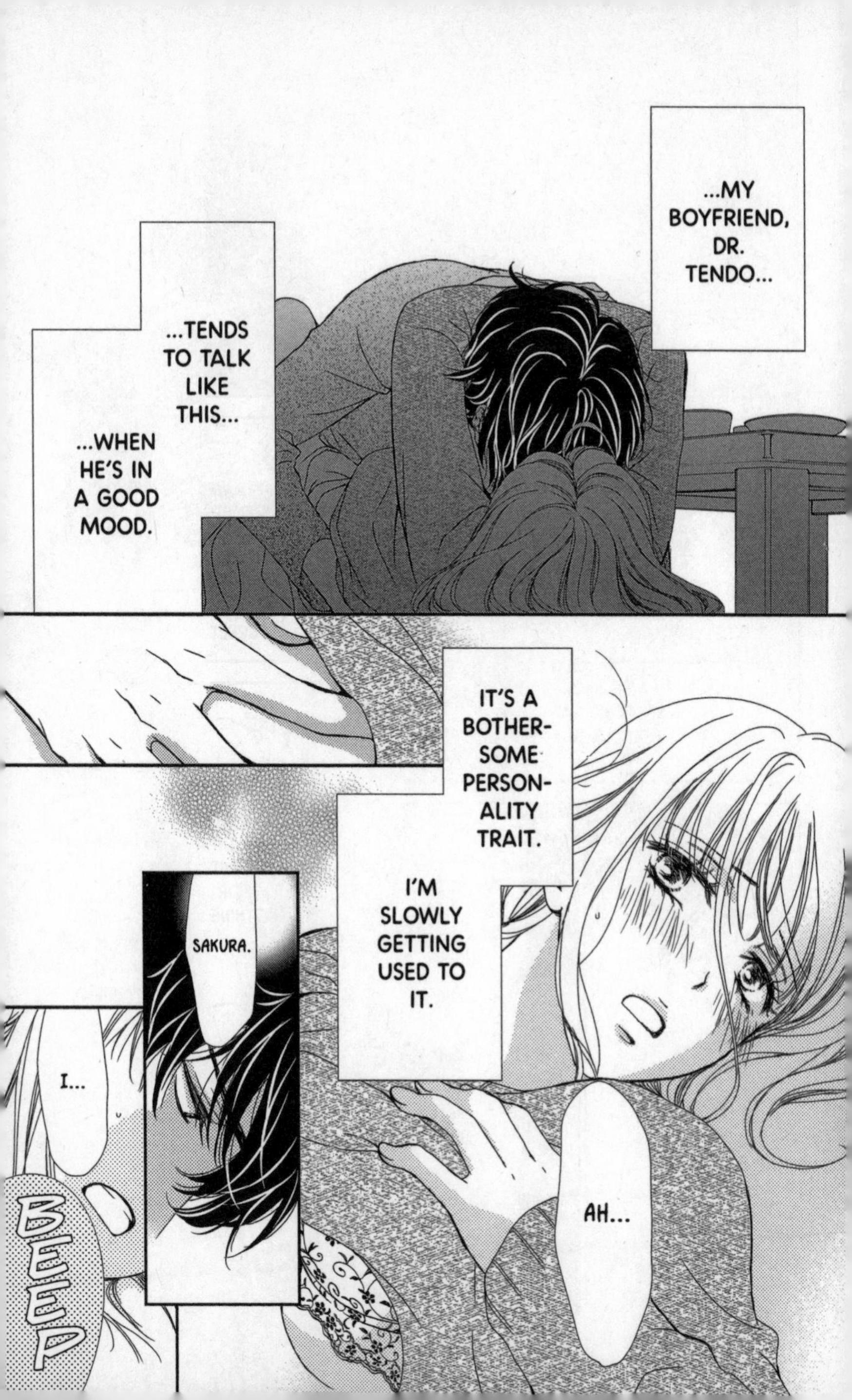
...MY BOYFRIEND, DR. TENDO...
...TENDS TO TALK LIKE THIS...
...WHEN HE'S IN A GOOD MOOD.
IT'S A BOTHER-SOME PERSON-ALITY TRAIT.
I'M SLOWLY GETTING USED TO IT.
AH...
SAKURA.
I...
BEEP

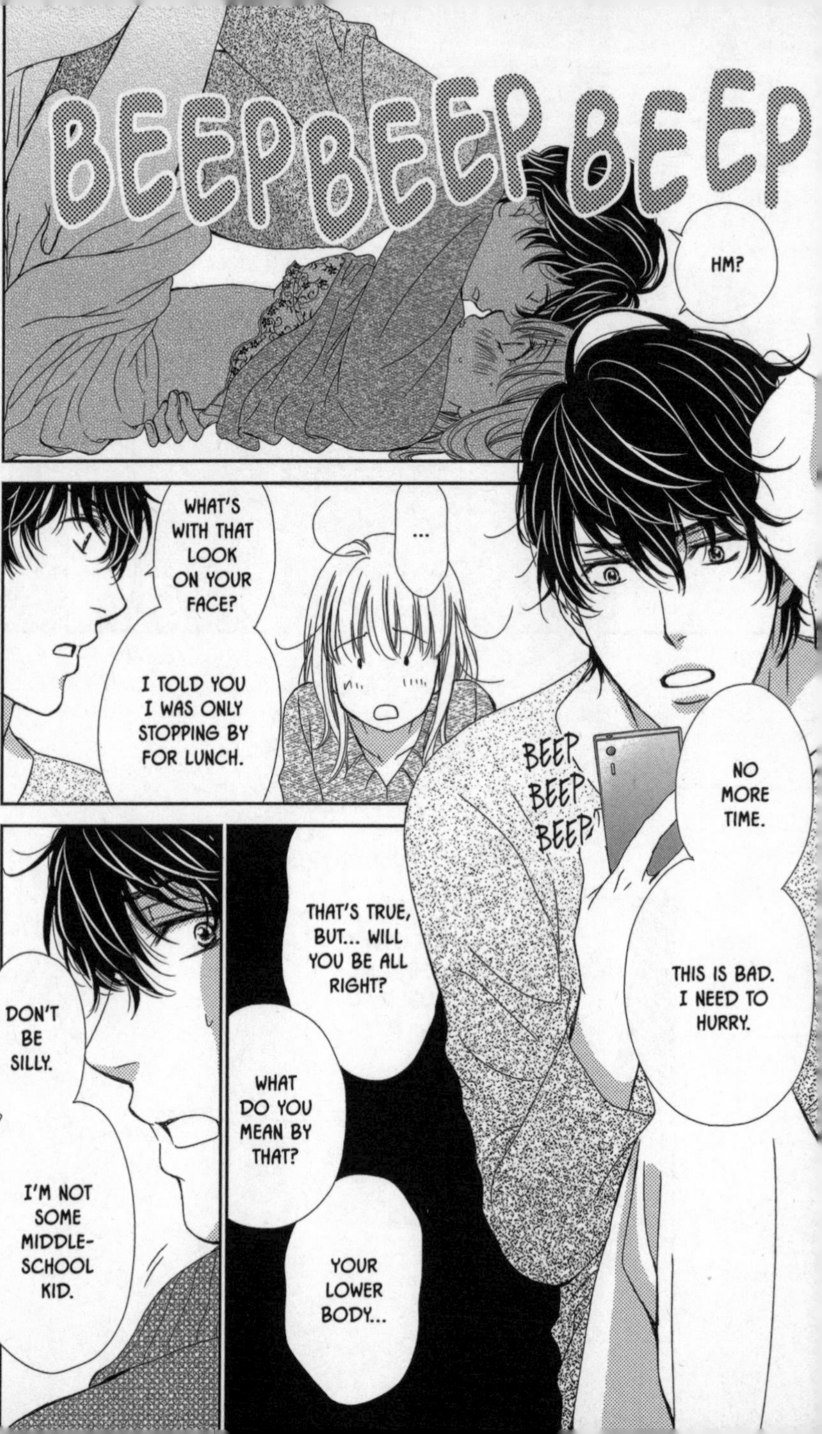
BEEP BEEP BEEP
HM?
BEEP BEEP BEEP
NO MORE TIME.
THIS IS BAD. I NEED TO HURRY.
...
WHAT'S WITH THAT LOOK ON YOUR FACE?
I TOLD YOU I WAS ONLY STOPPING BY FOR LUNCH.
THAT'S TRUE, BUT... WILL YOU BE ALL RIGHT?
WHAT DO YOU MEAN BY THAT?
YOUR LOWER BODY...
DON'T BE SILLY.
I'M NOT SOME MIDDLE-SCHOOL KID.

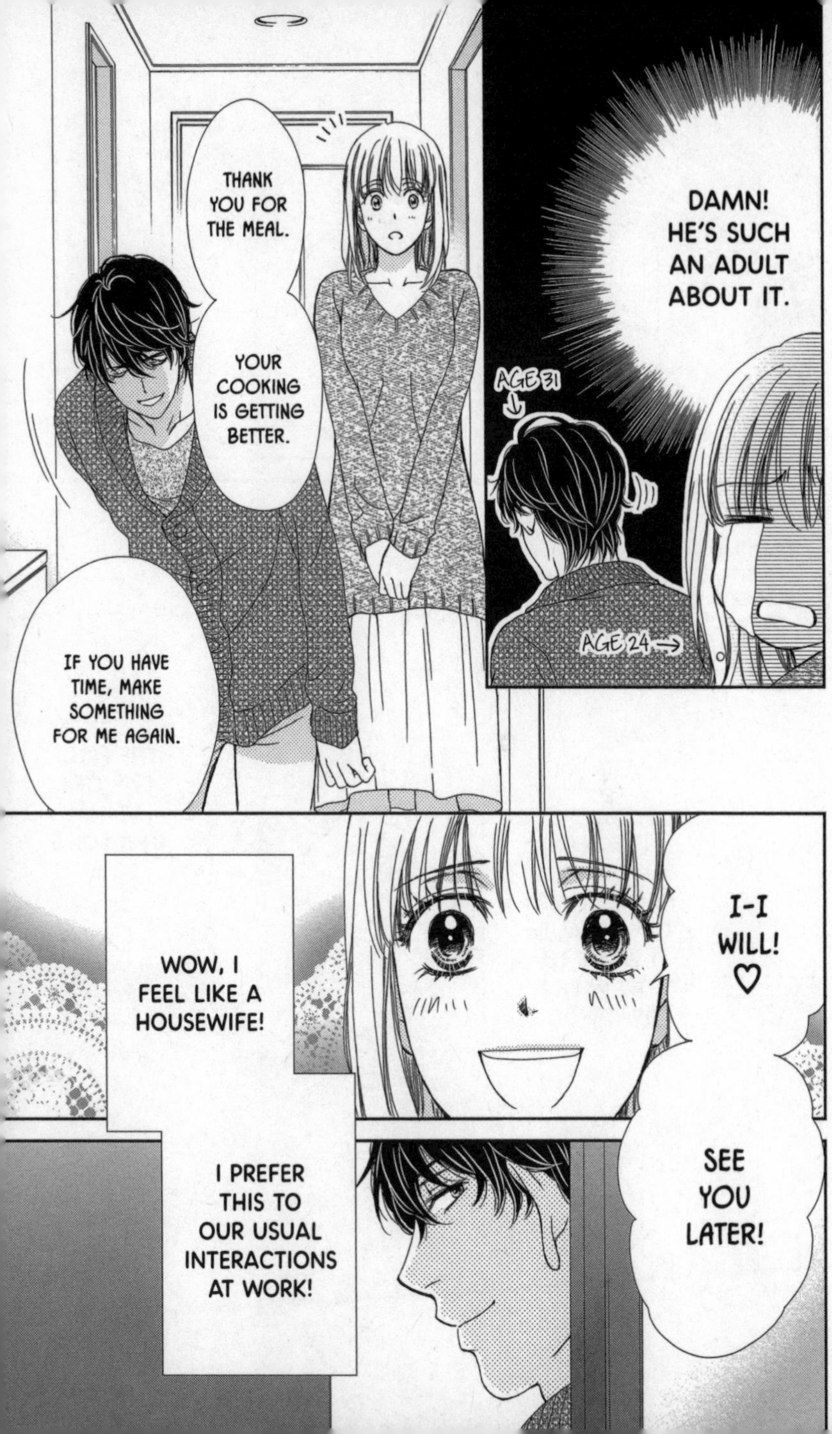
DAMN! HE'S SUCH AN ADULT ABOUT IT.
AGE 31
AGE 24
THANK YOU FOR THE MEAL.
YOUR COOKING IS GETTING BETTER.
IF YOU HAVE TIME, MAKE SOMETHING FOR ME AGAIN.
I-I WILL! ♡
WOW, I FEEL LIKE A HOUSEWIFE!
SEE YOU LATER!
I PREFER THIS TO OUR USUAL INTERACTIONS AT WORK!

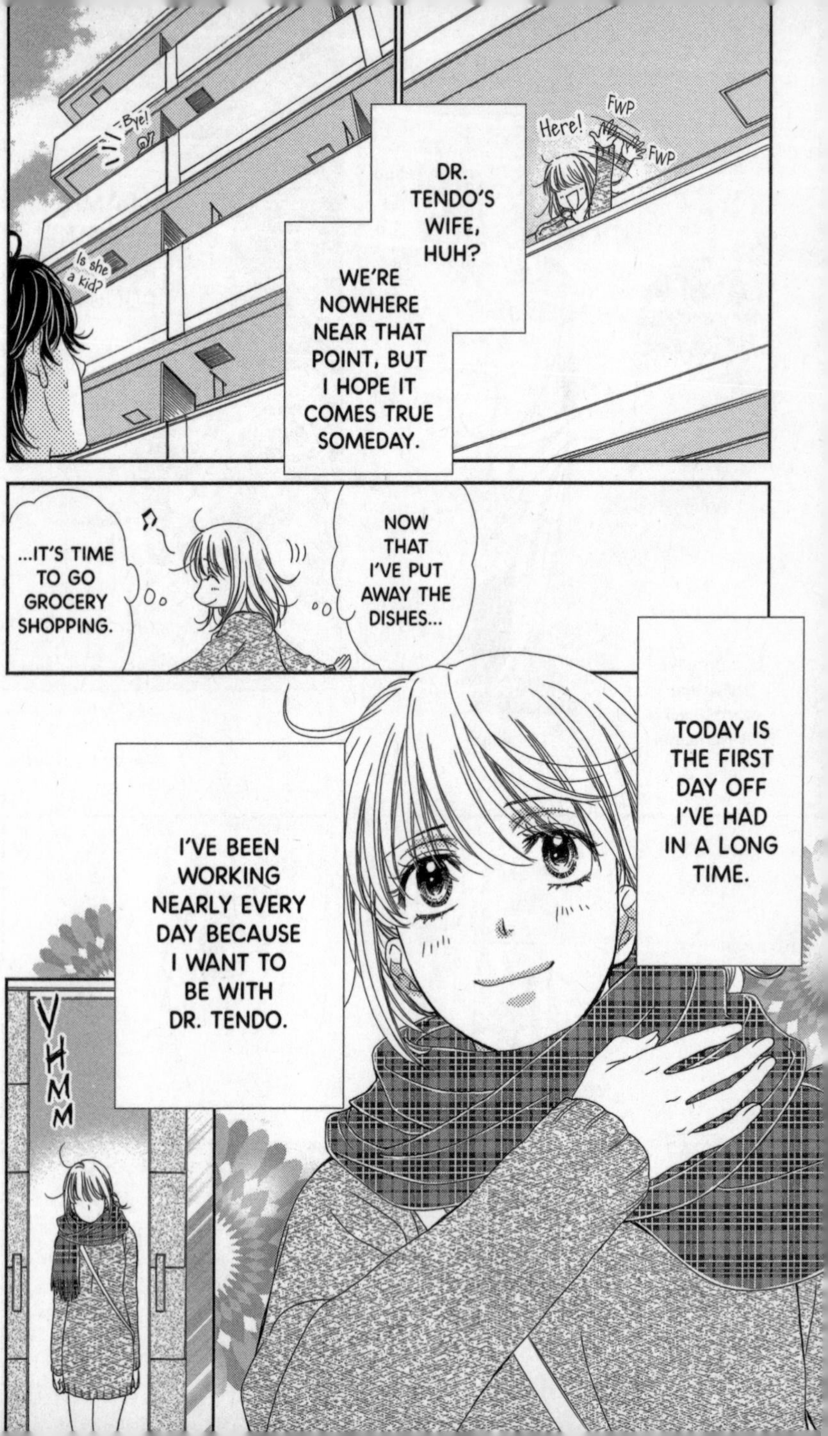
FWP
Here!
FWP
DR. TENDO'S WIFE, HUH?
WE'RE NOWHERE NEAR THAT POINT, BUT I HOPE IT COMES TRUE SOMEDAY.
Bye!
Is she a kid?
NOW THAT I'VE PUT AWAY THE DISHES...
...IT'S TIME TO GO GROCERY SHOPPING.
TODAY IS THE FIRST DAY OFF I'VE HAD IN A LONG TIME.
I'VE BEEN WORKING NEARLY EVERY DAY BECAUSE I WANT TO BE WITH DR. TENDO.
VHMM

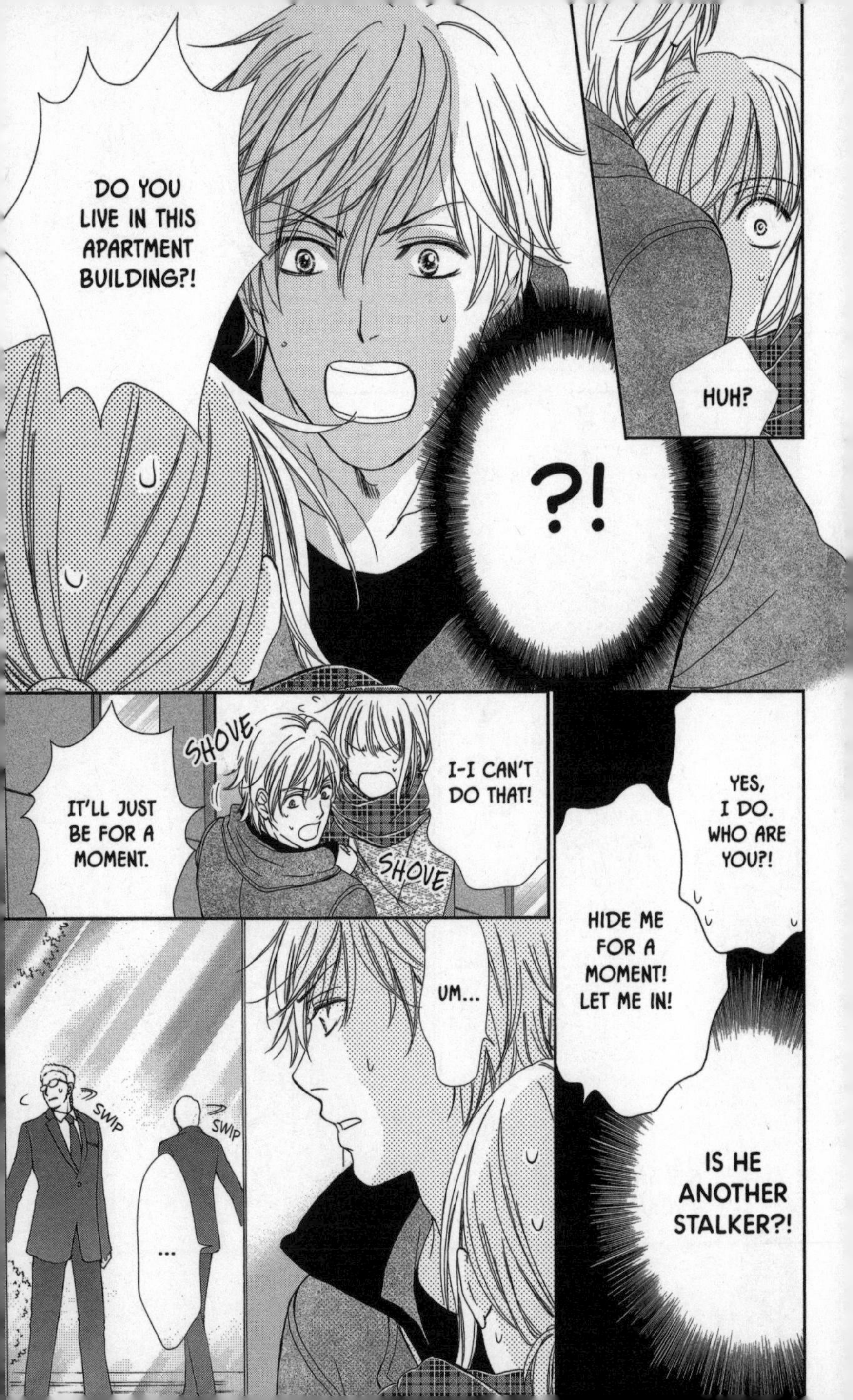
DO YOU LIVE IN THIS APARTMENT BUILDING?!
HUH?
?!
YES, I DO. WHO ARE YOU?!
HIDE ME FOR A MOMENT! LET ME IN!
IS HE ANOTHER STALKER?!
I-I CAN'T DO THAT!
SHOVE
SHOVE
IT'LL JUST BE FOR A MOMENT.
UM...
SWIP
SWIP
...

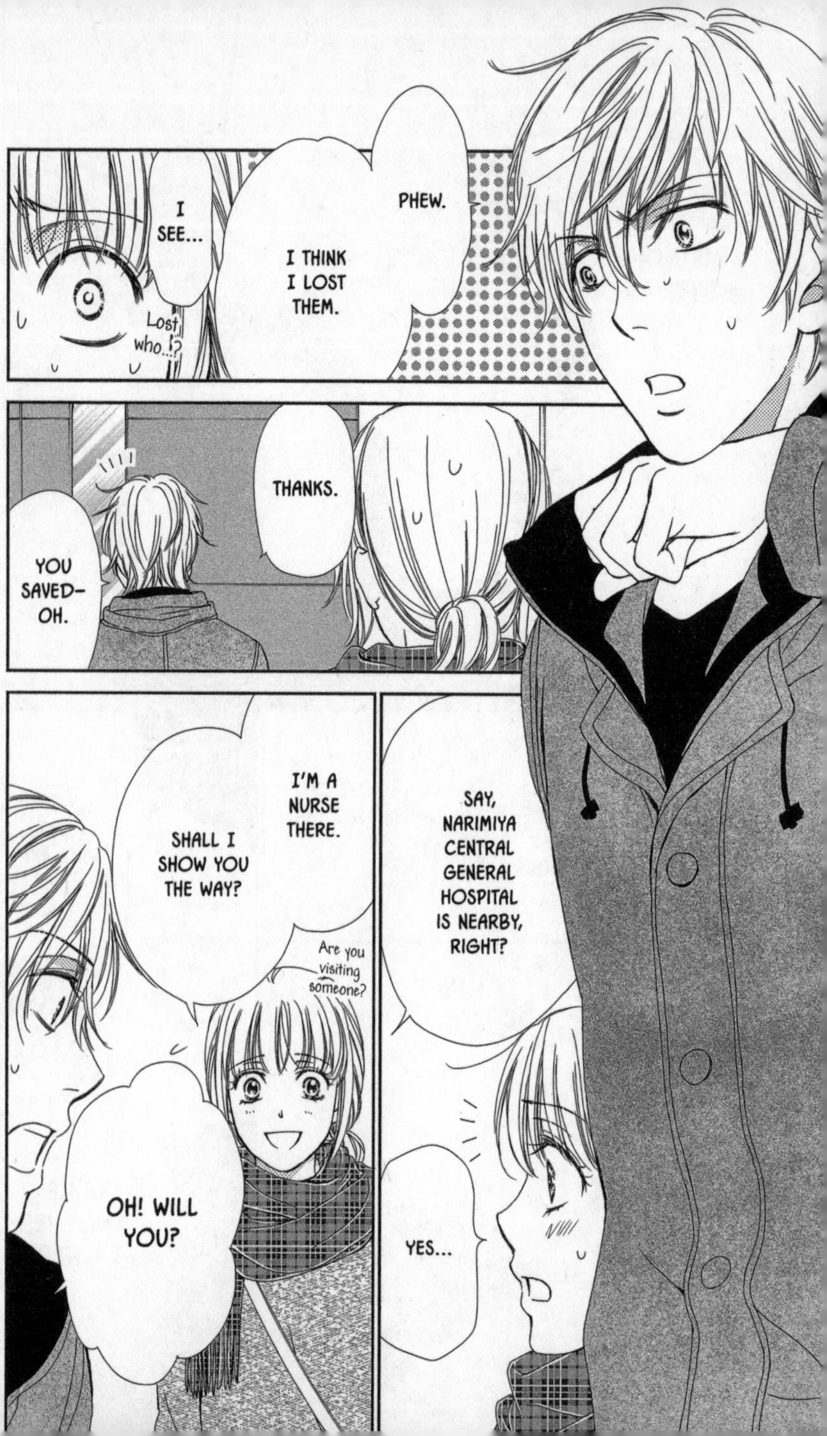
PHEW.
I THINK I LOST THEM.
I SEE...
Lost who...!?
THANKS.
YOU SAVED—OH.
SAY, NARIMIYA CENTRAL GENERAL HOSPITAL IS NEARBY, RIGHT?
YES...
I'M A NURSE THERE.
SHALL I SHOW YOU THE WAY?
Are you visiting someone?
OH! WILL YOU?

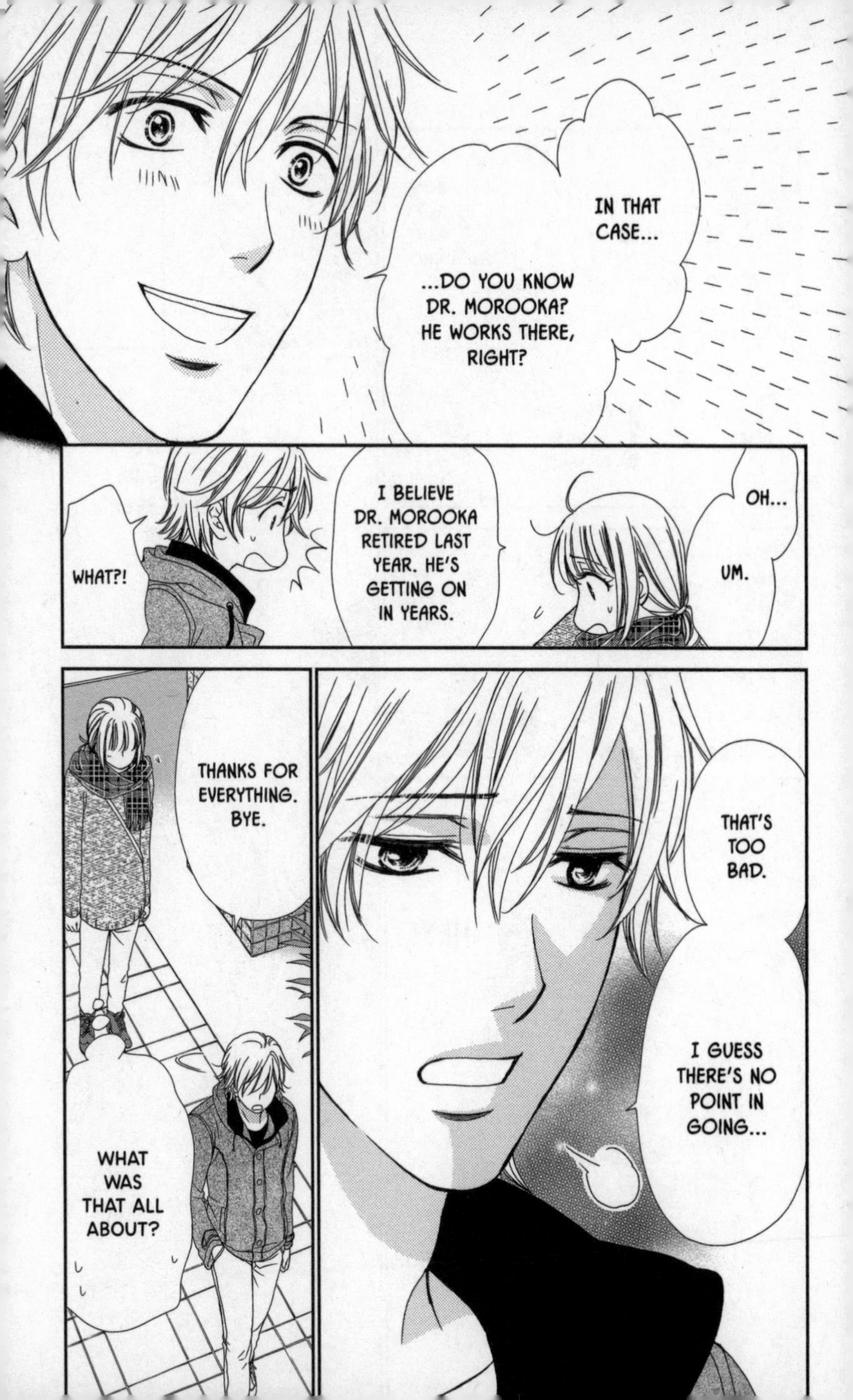
IN THAT CASE...
...DO YOU KNOW DR. MOROOKA? HE WORKS THERE, RIGHT?
OH...
UM.
I BELIEVE DR. MOROOKA RETIRED LAST YEAR. HE'S GETTING ON IN YEARS.
WHAT?!
THAT'S TOO BAD.
I GUESS THERE'S NO POINT IN GOING...
THANKS FOR EVERYTHING. BYE.
WHAT WAS THAT ALL ABOUT?

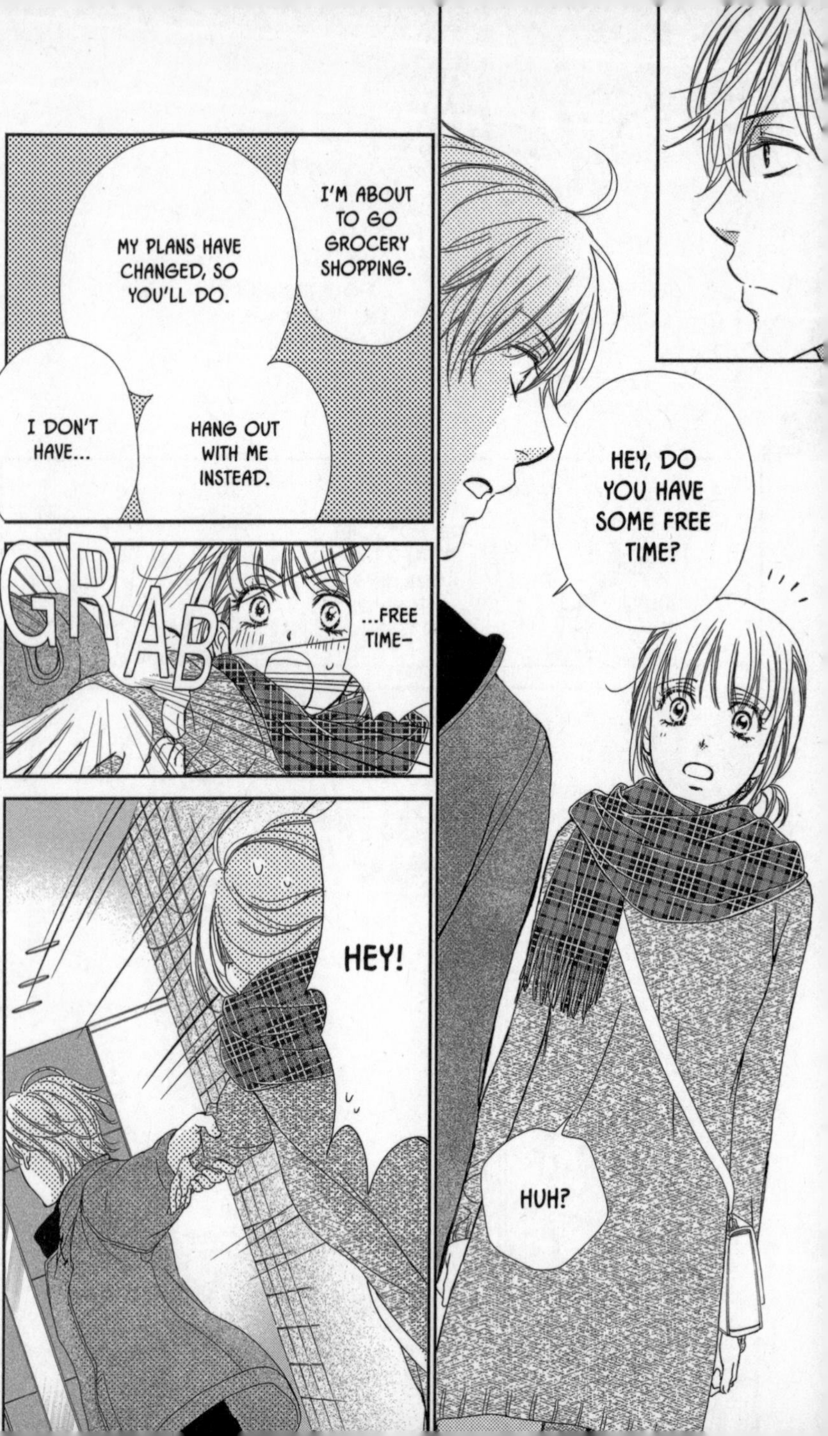
HEY, DO YOU HAVE SOME FREE TIME?
HUH?
I'M ABOUT TO GO GROCERY SHOPPING.
MY PLANS HAVE CHANGED, SO YOU'LL DO.
HANG OUT WITH ME INSTEAD.
I DON'T HAVE...
...FREE TIME–
GRAB
HEY!

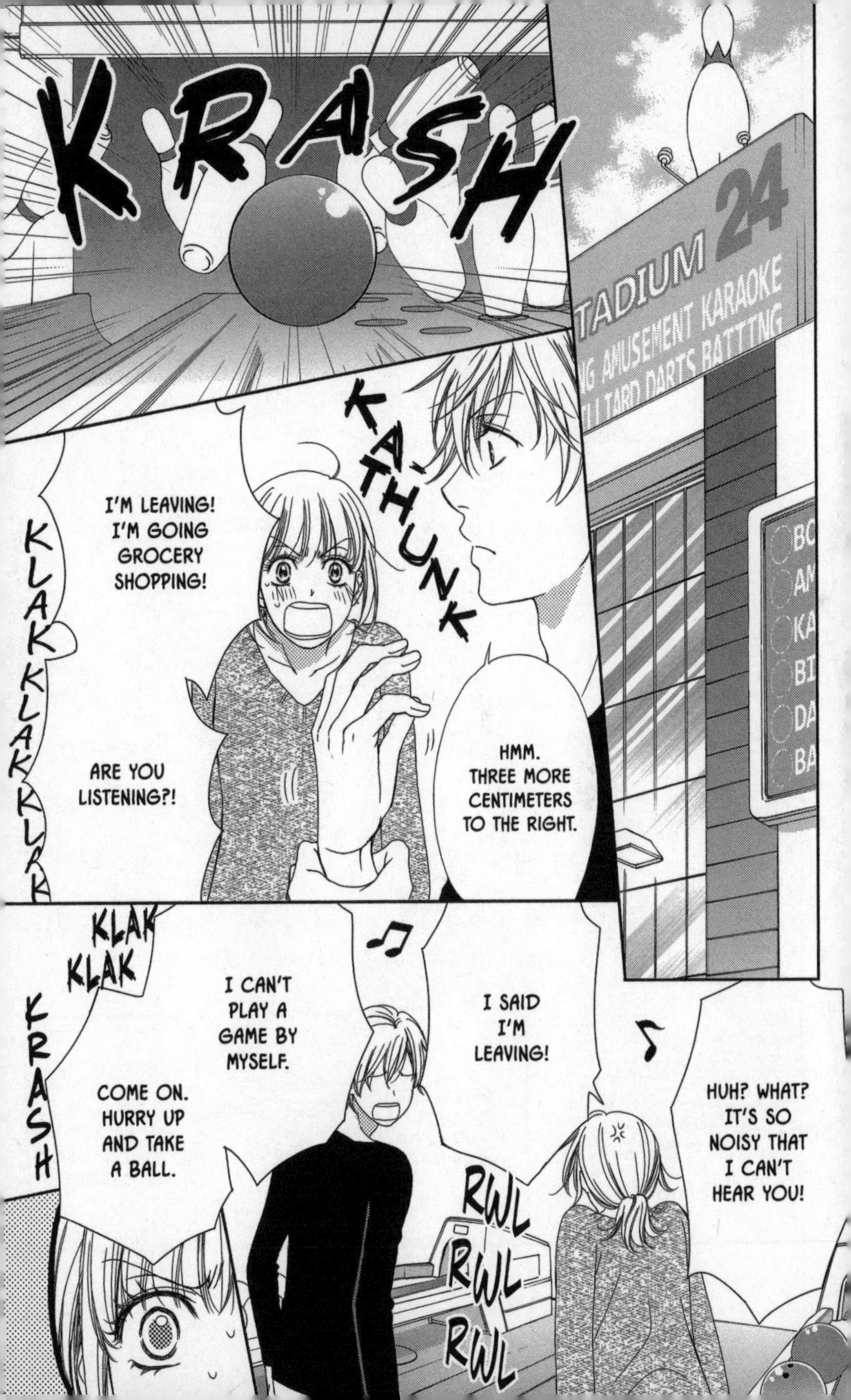
TADIUM 24
AMUSEMENT KARAOKE
DARTS BATTTNG
KRASH
KA-THUNK
HMM. THREE MORE CENTIMETERS TO THE RIGHT.
I'M LEAVING! I'M GOING GROCERY SHOPPING!
ARE YOU LISTENING?!
KLAKKLAKKLAKKLURK
HUH? WHAT? IT'S SO NOISY THAT I CAN'T HEAR YOU!
I SAID I'M LEAVING!
I CAN'T PLAY A GAME BY MYSELF.
COME ON. HURRY UP AND TAKE A BALL.
RWL RWL RWL RWL
KLAK KLAK
KRASH

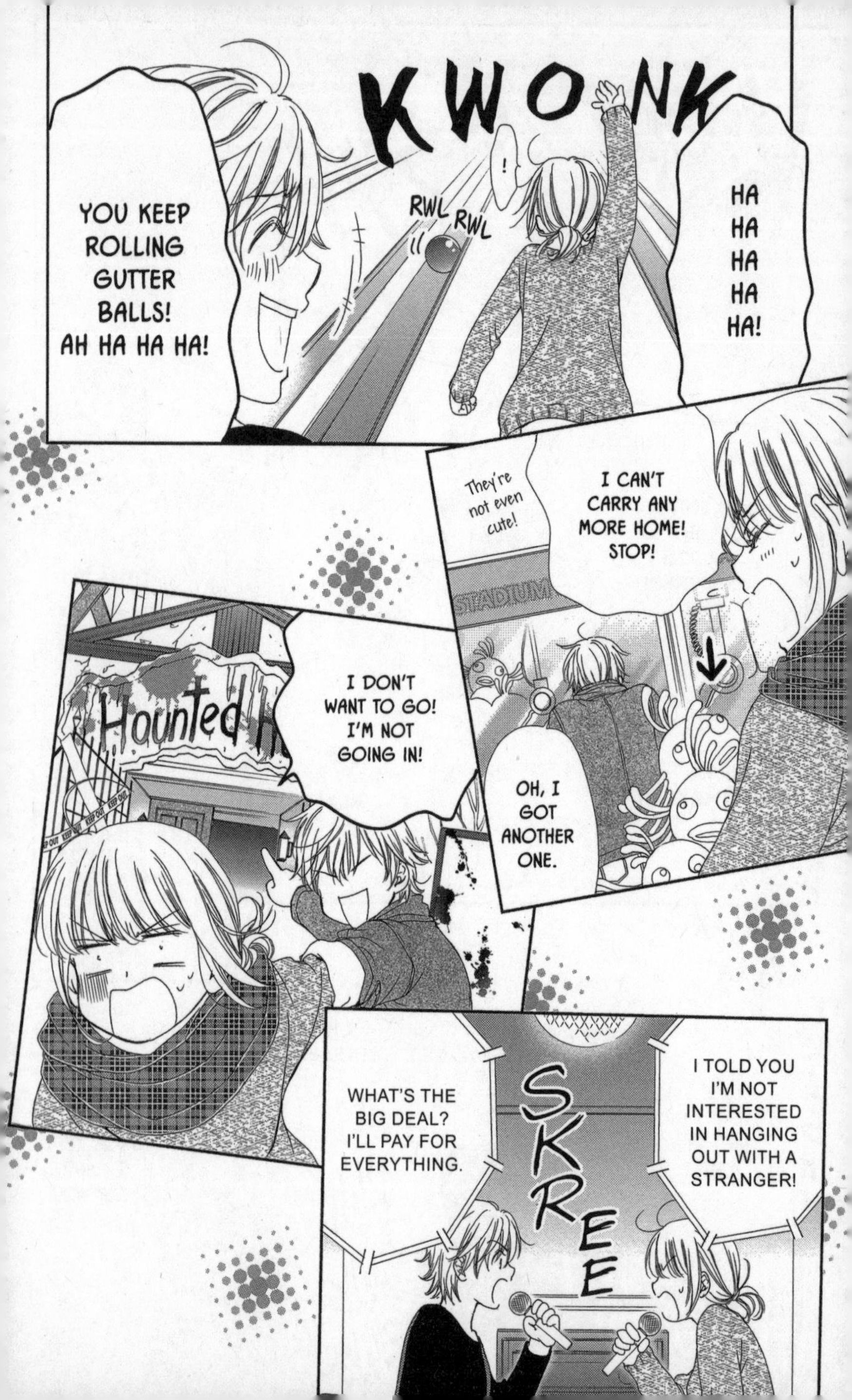
KWONK
HA HA HA HA HA!
!
RWL RWL
YOU KEEP ROLLING GUTTER BALLS! AH HA HA HA!
I CAN'T CARRY ANY MORE HOME! STOP!
They're not even cute!
STADIUM
OH, I GOT ANOTHER ONE.
Haunted H
I DON'T WANT TO GO! I'M NOT GOING IN!
KEEP OUT KEEP OUT KEEP OUT
I TOLD YOU I'M NOT INTERESTED IN HANGING OUT WITH A STRANGER!
SKREE
WHAT'S THE BIG DEAL? I'LL PAY FOR EVERYTHING.

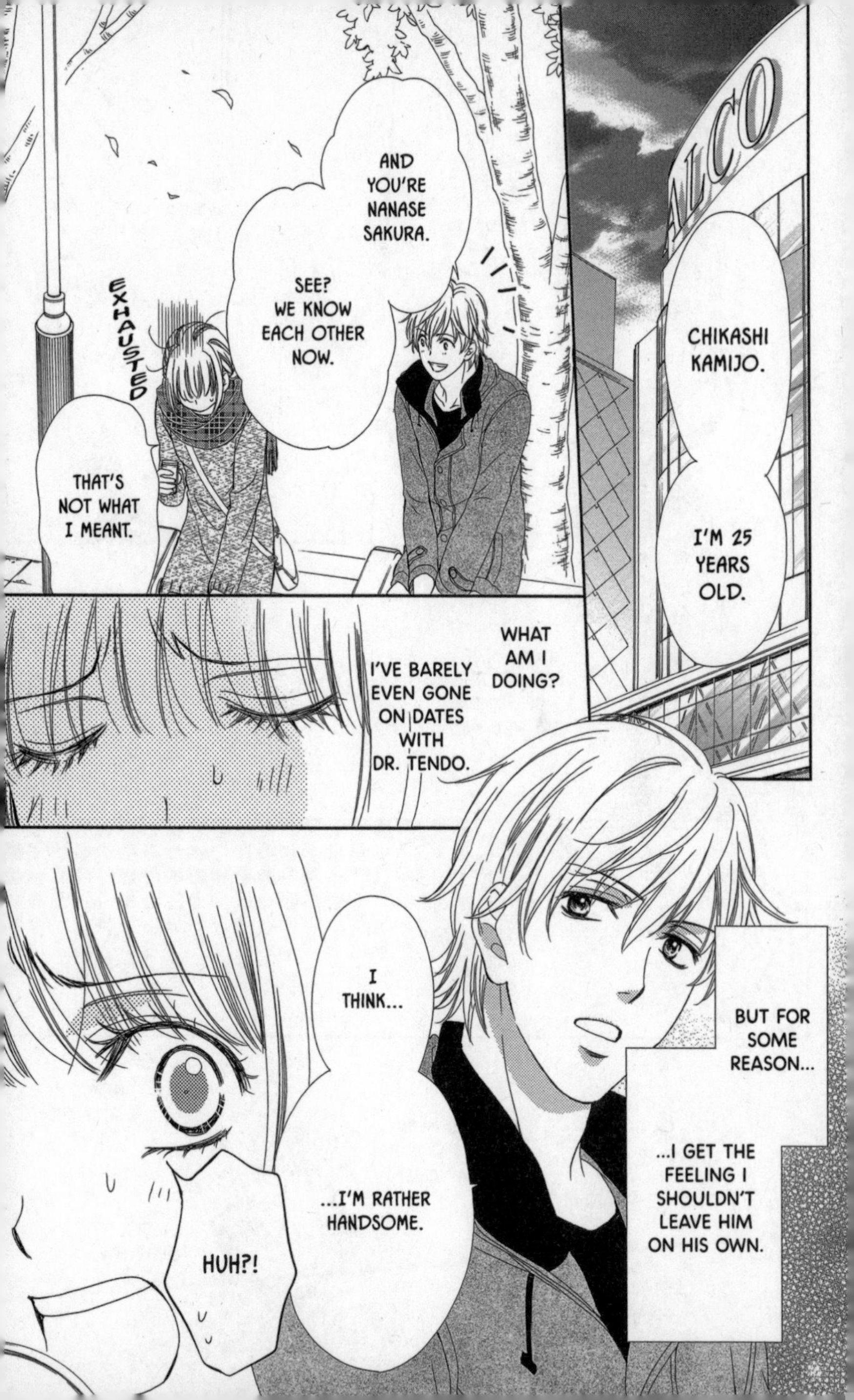
CHIKASHI KAMIJO.
I'M 25 YEARS OLD.
AND YOU'RE NANASE SAKURA.
SEE? WE KNOW EACH OTHER NOW.
EXHAUSTED
THAT'S NOT WHAT I MEANT.
WHAT AM I DOING?
I'VE BARELY EVEN GONE ON DATES WITH DR. TENDO.
BUT FOR SOME REASON...
...I GET THE FEELING I SHOULDN'T LEAVE HIM ON HIS OWN.
I THINK...
...I'M RATHER HANDSOME.
HUH?!

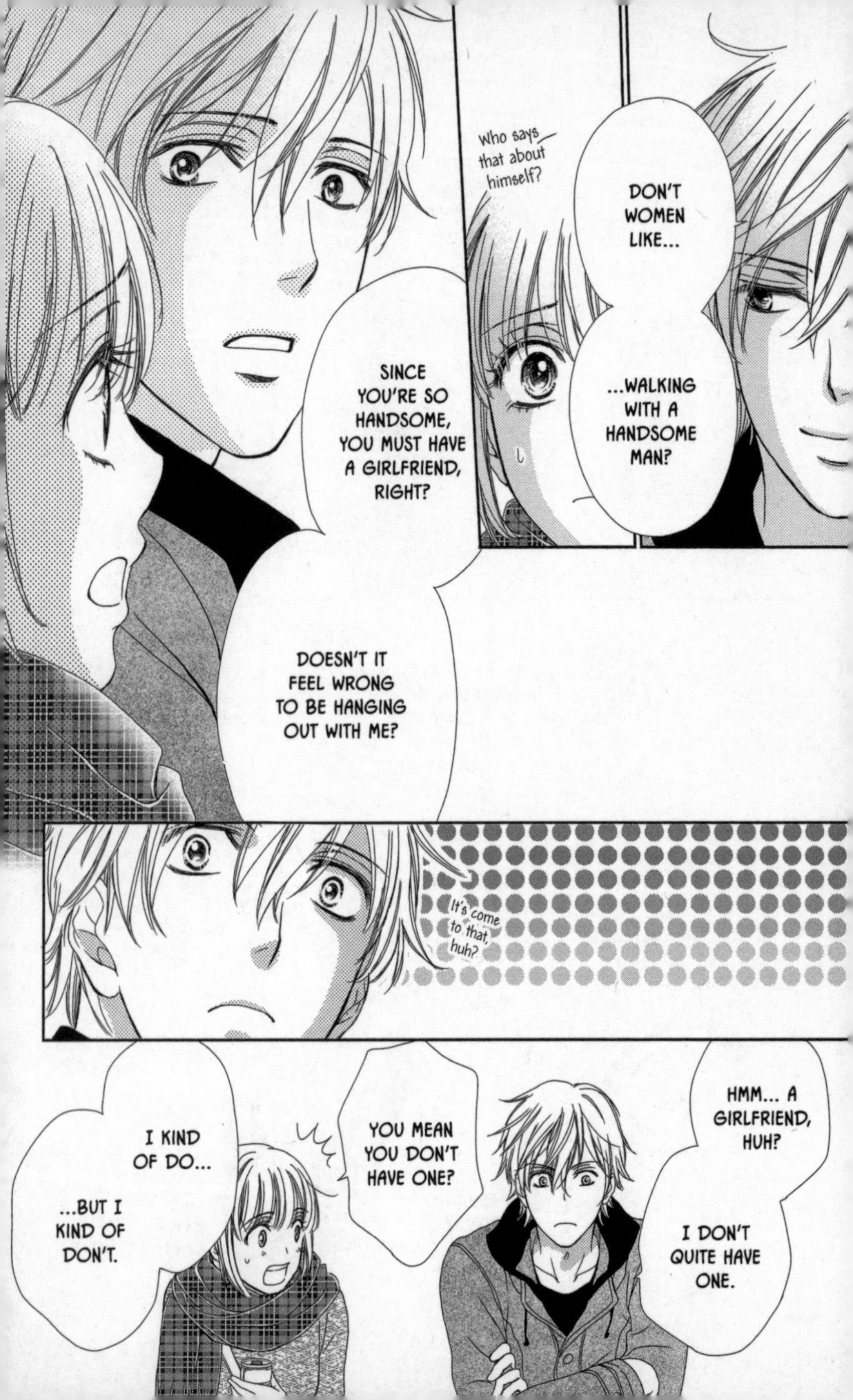
DON'T WOMEN LIKE...
...WALKING WITH A HANDSOME MAN?
Who says that about himself?
SINCE YOU'RE SO HANDSOME, YOU MUST HAVE A GIRLFRIEND, RIGHT?
DOESN'T IT FEEL WRONG TO BE HANGING OUT WITH ME?
It's come to that, huh?
HMM... A GIRLFRIEND, HUH?
I DON'T QUITE HAVE ONE.
YOU MEAN YOU DON'T HAVE ONE?
I KIND OF DO...
...BUT I KIND OF DON'T.

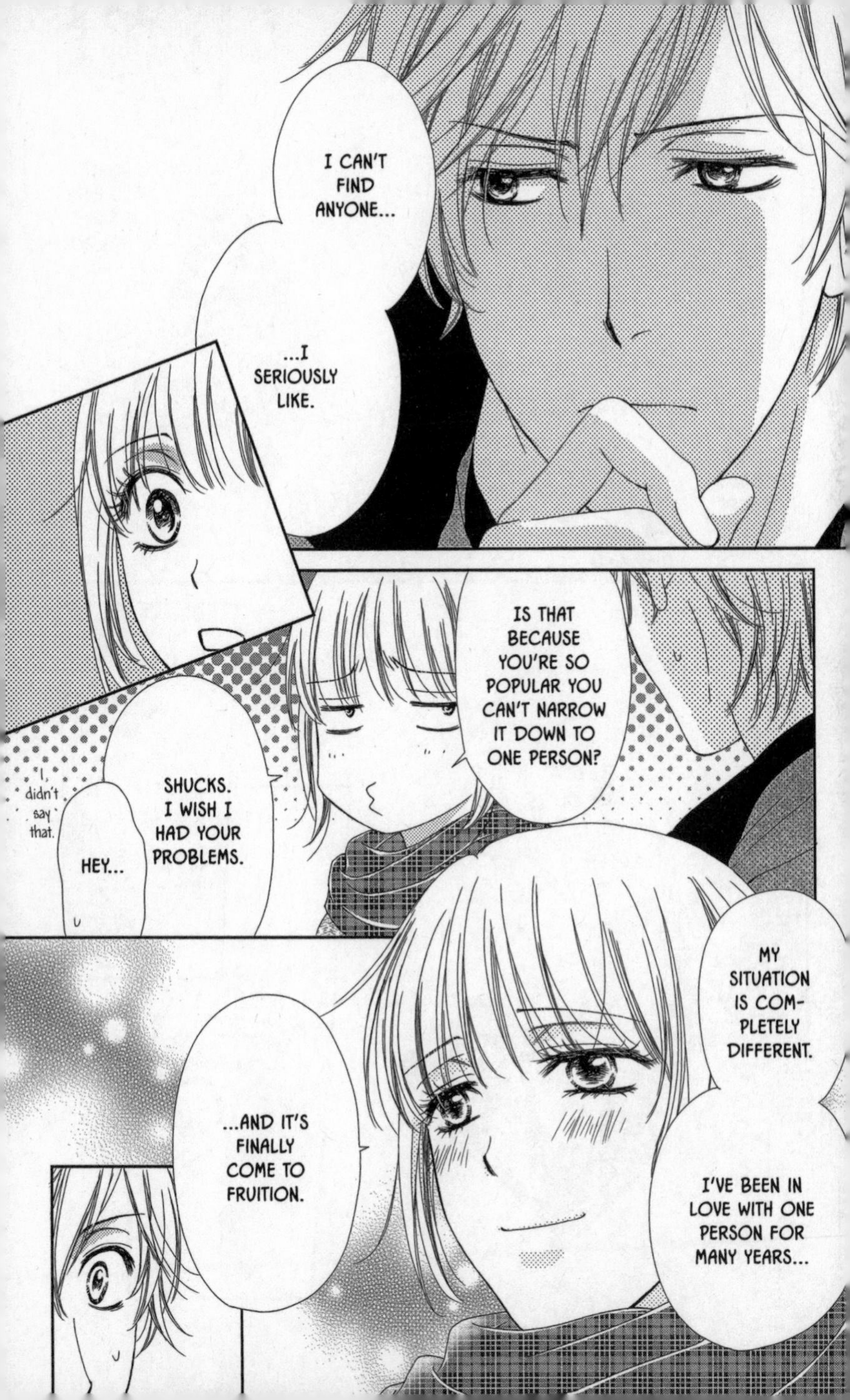
I CAN'T FIND ANYONE...
...I SERIOUSLY LIKE.
IS THAT BECAUSE YOU'RE SO POPULAR YOU CAN'T NARROW IT DOWN TO ONE PERSON?
SHUCKS. I WISH I HAD YOUR PROBLEMS.
HEY...
I didn't say that.
MY SITUATION IS COM-PLETELY DIFFERENT.
I'VE BEEN IN LOVE WITH ONE PERSON FOR MANY YEARS...
...AND IT'S FINALLY COME TO FRUITION.

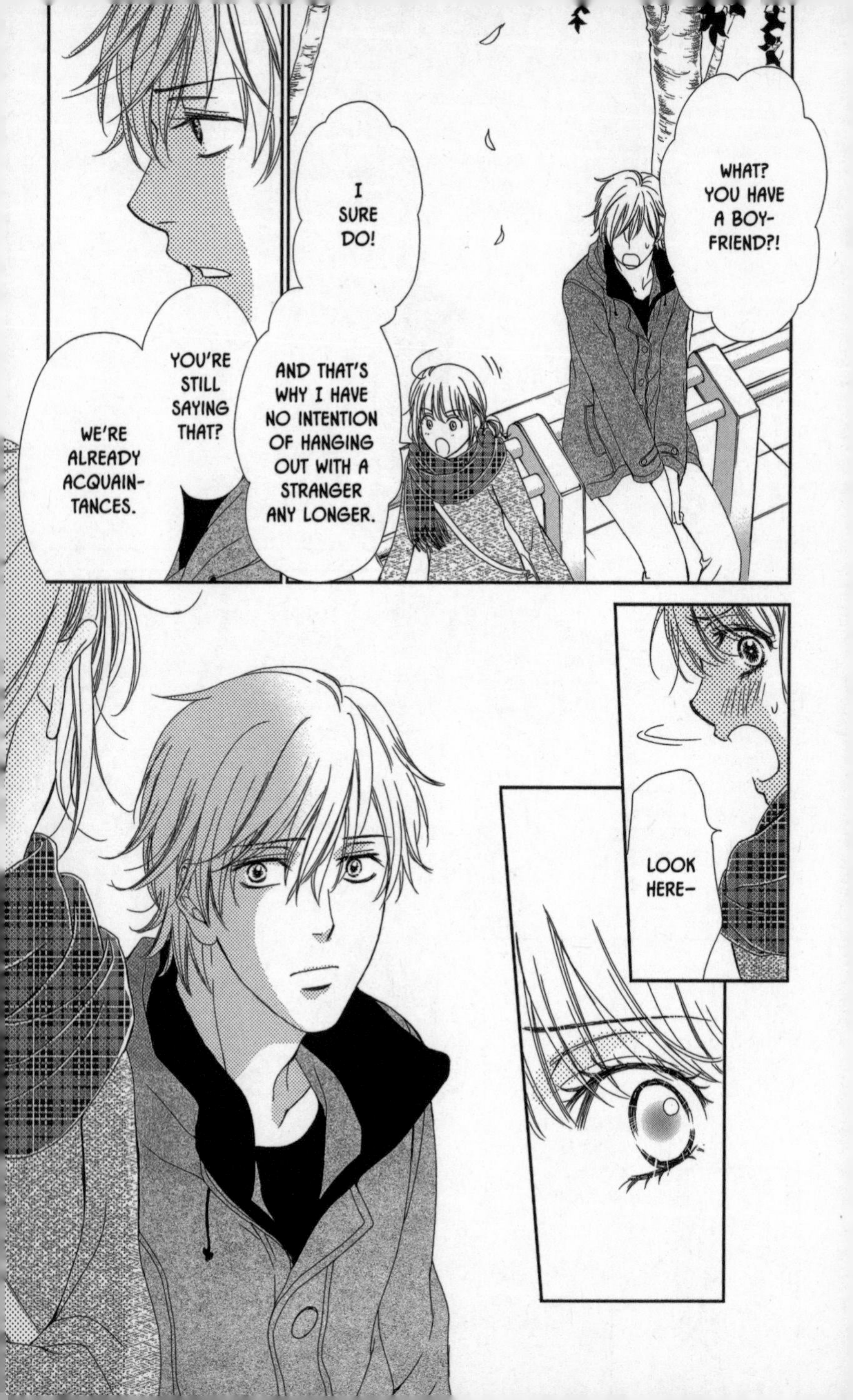
WHAT? YOU HAVE A BOY-FRIEND?!
I SURE DO!
AND THAT'S WHY I HAVE NO INTENTION OF HANGING OUT WITH A STRANGER ANY LONGER.
YOU'RE STILL SAYING THAT?
WE'RE ALREADY ACQUAINTANCES.
LOOK HERE—

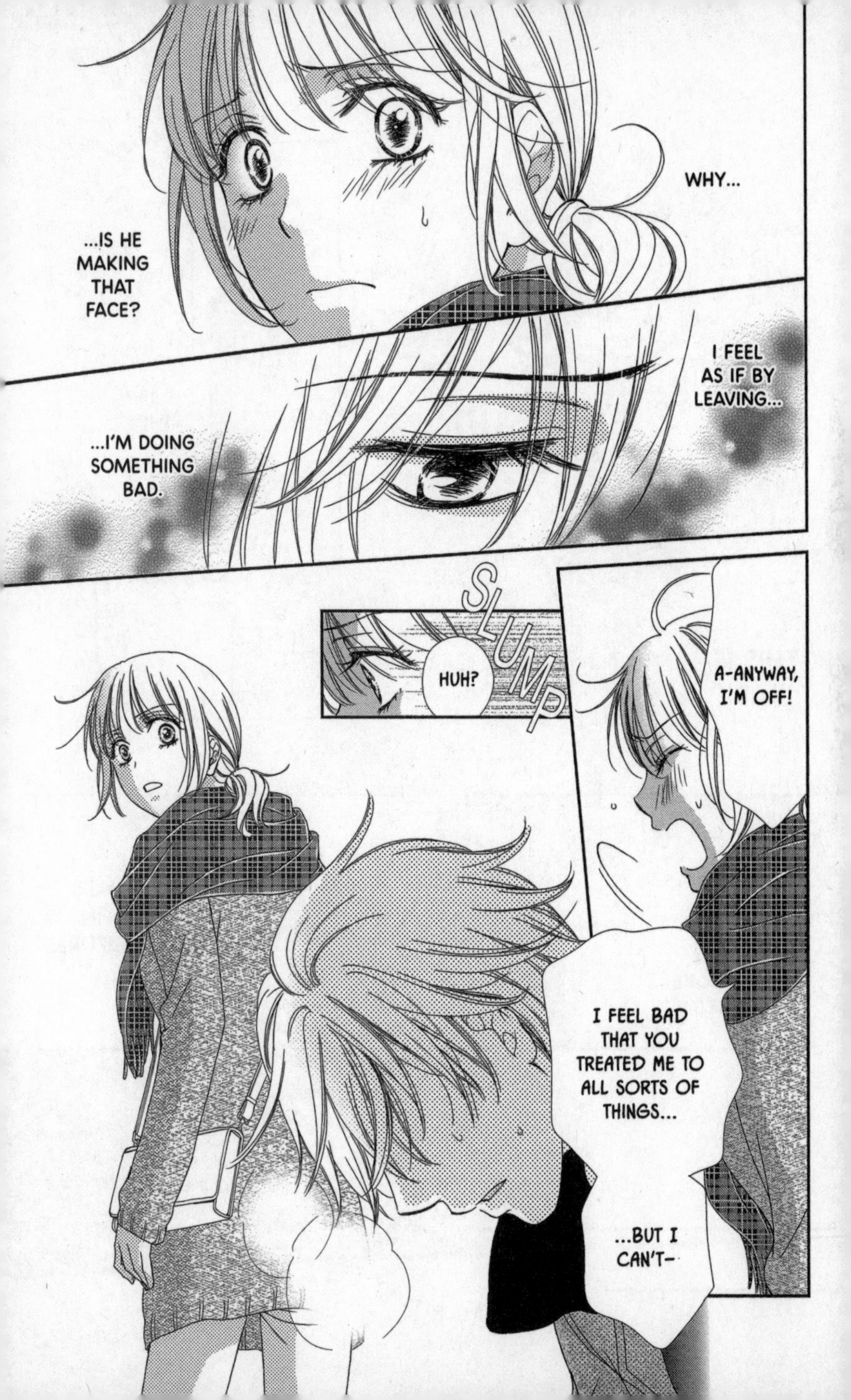
WHY...
...IS HE MAKING THAT FACE?
I FEEL AS IF BY LEAVING...
...I'M DOING SOMETHING BAD.
A-ANYWAY, I'M OFF!
SLUMP
HUH?
I FEEL BAD THAT YOU TREATED ME TO ALL SORTS OF THINGS...
...BUT I CAN'T-

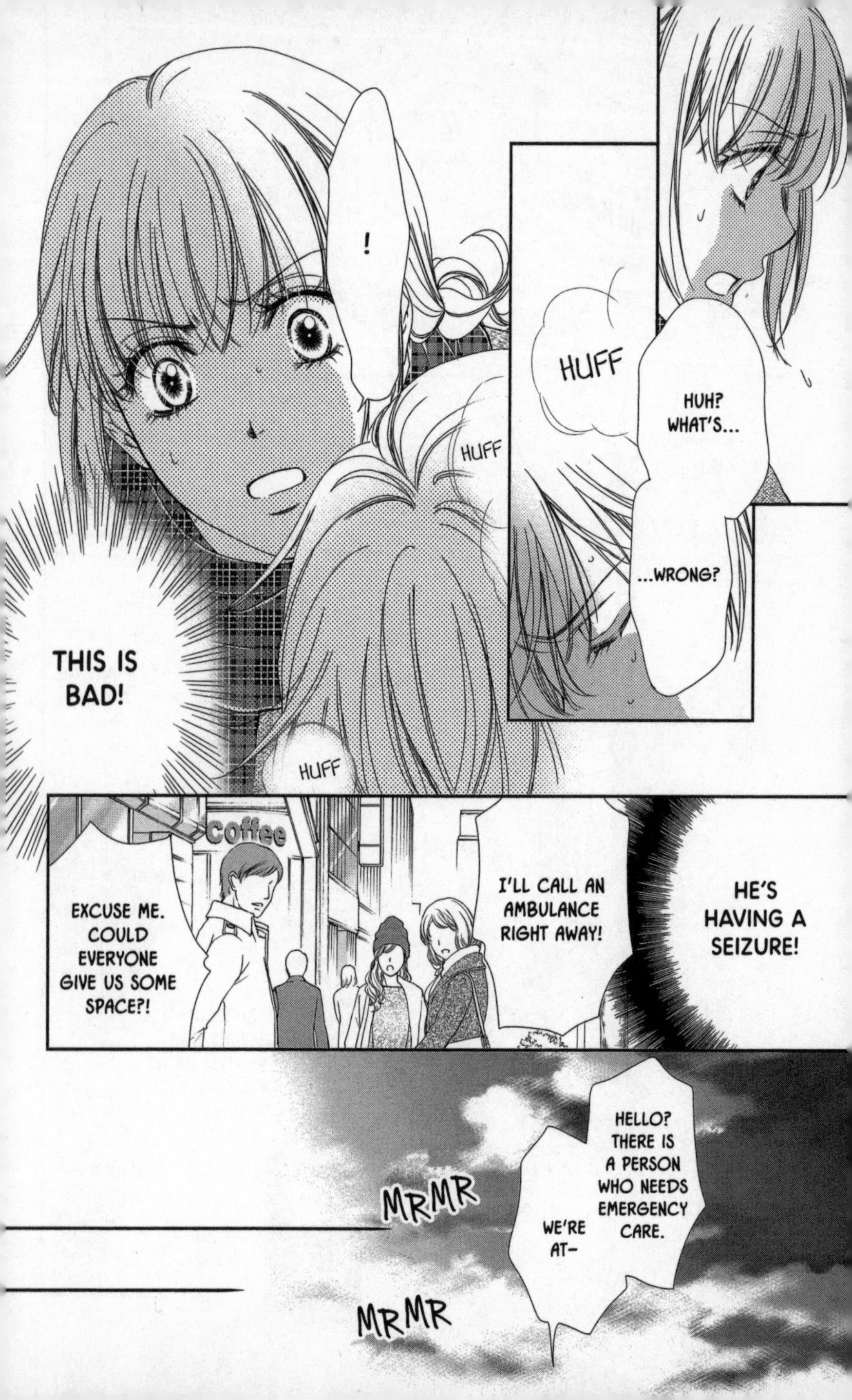
HUFF
HUH? WHAT'S...
...WRONG?
!
HUFF
THIS IS BAD!
HUFF
HE'S HAVING A SEIZURE!
I'LL CALL AN AMBULANCE RIGHT AWAY!
EXCUSE ME. COULD EVERYONE GIVE US SOME SPACE?!
Coffee
HELLO? THERE IS A PERSON WHO NEEDS EMERGENCY CARE.
WE'RE AT–
MRMR
MRMR

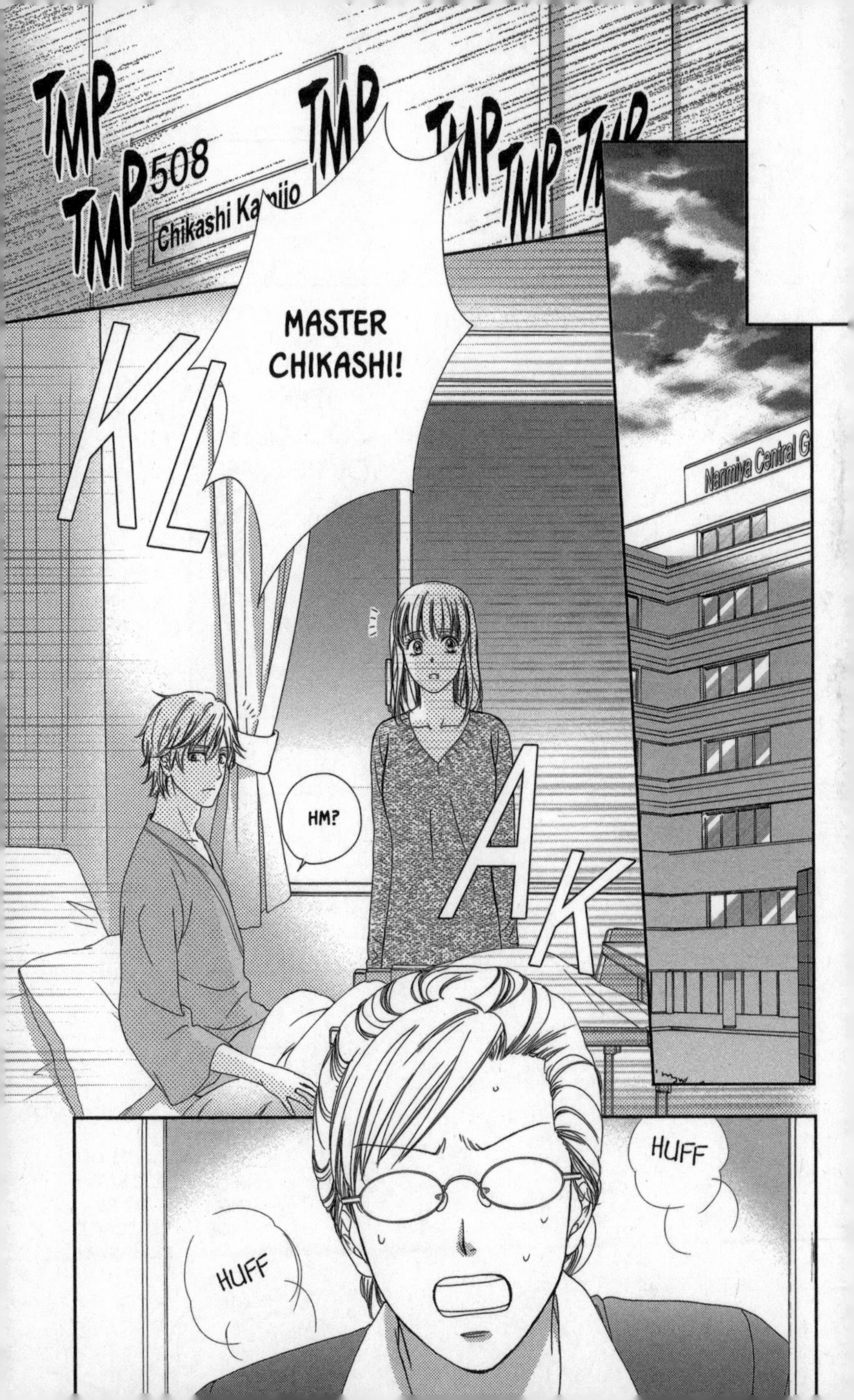
Narimiya Central
TMP TMP TMP TMP TMP
508
Chikashi Ka
MASTER CHIKASHI!
KL
AK
HM?
HUFF
HUFF

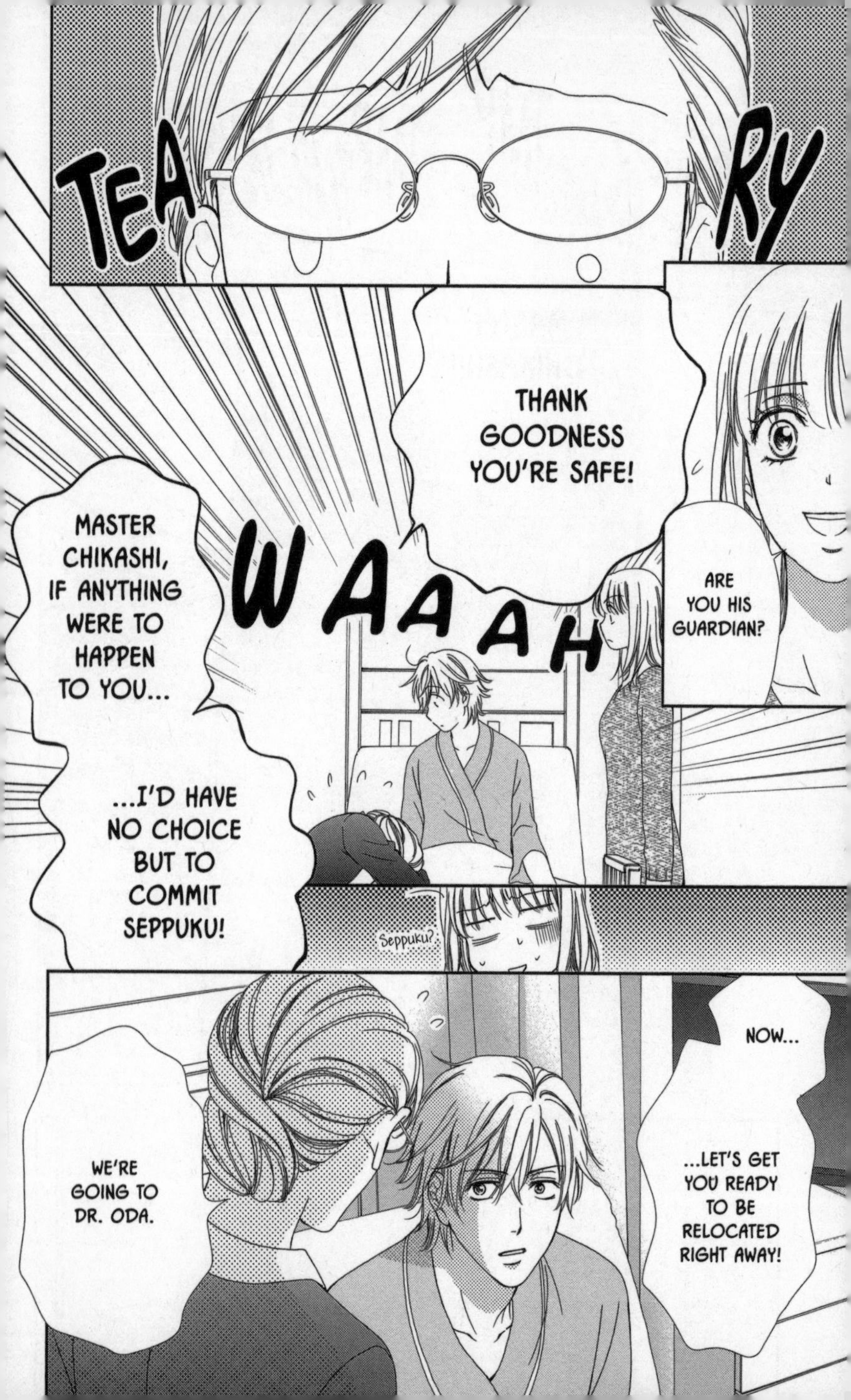
TEA
RY
ARE YOU HIS GUARDIAN?
THANK GOODNESS YOU'RE SAFE!
WAAAH
MASTER CHIKASHI, IF ANYTHING WERE TO HAPPEN TO YOU...
...I'D HAVE NO CHOICE BUT TO COMMIT SEPPUKU!
Seppuku?
NOW...
...LET'S GET YOU READY TO BE RELOCATED RIGHT AWAY!
WE'RE GOING TO DR. ODA.

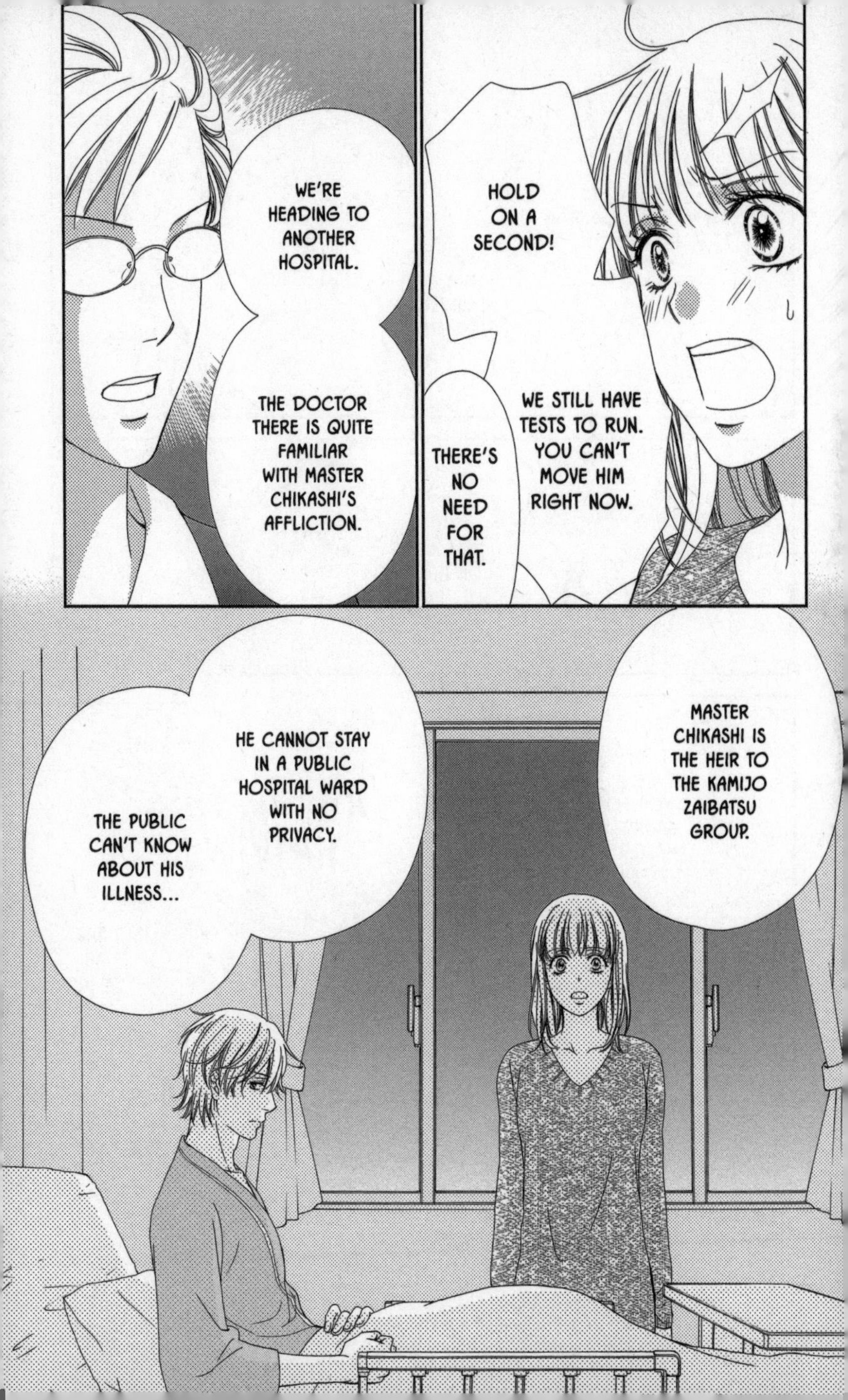
HOLD ON A SECOND!
WE STILL HAVE TESTS TO RUN. YOU CAN'T MOVE HIM RIGHT NOW.
THERE'S NO NEED FOR THAT.
WE'RE HEADING TO ANOTHER HOSPITAL.
THE DOCTOR THERE IS QUITE FAMILIAR WITH MASTER CHIKASHI'S AFFLICTION.
MASTER CHIKASHI IS THE HEIR TO THE KAMIJO ZAIBATSU GROUP.
HE CANNOT STAY IN A PUBLIC HOSPITAL WARD WITH NO PRIVACY.
THE PUBLIC CAN'T KNOW ABOUT HIS ILLNESS...

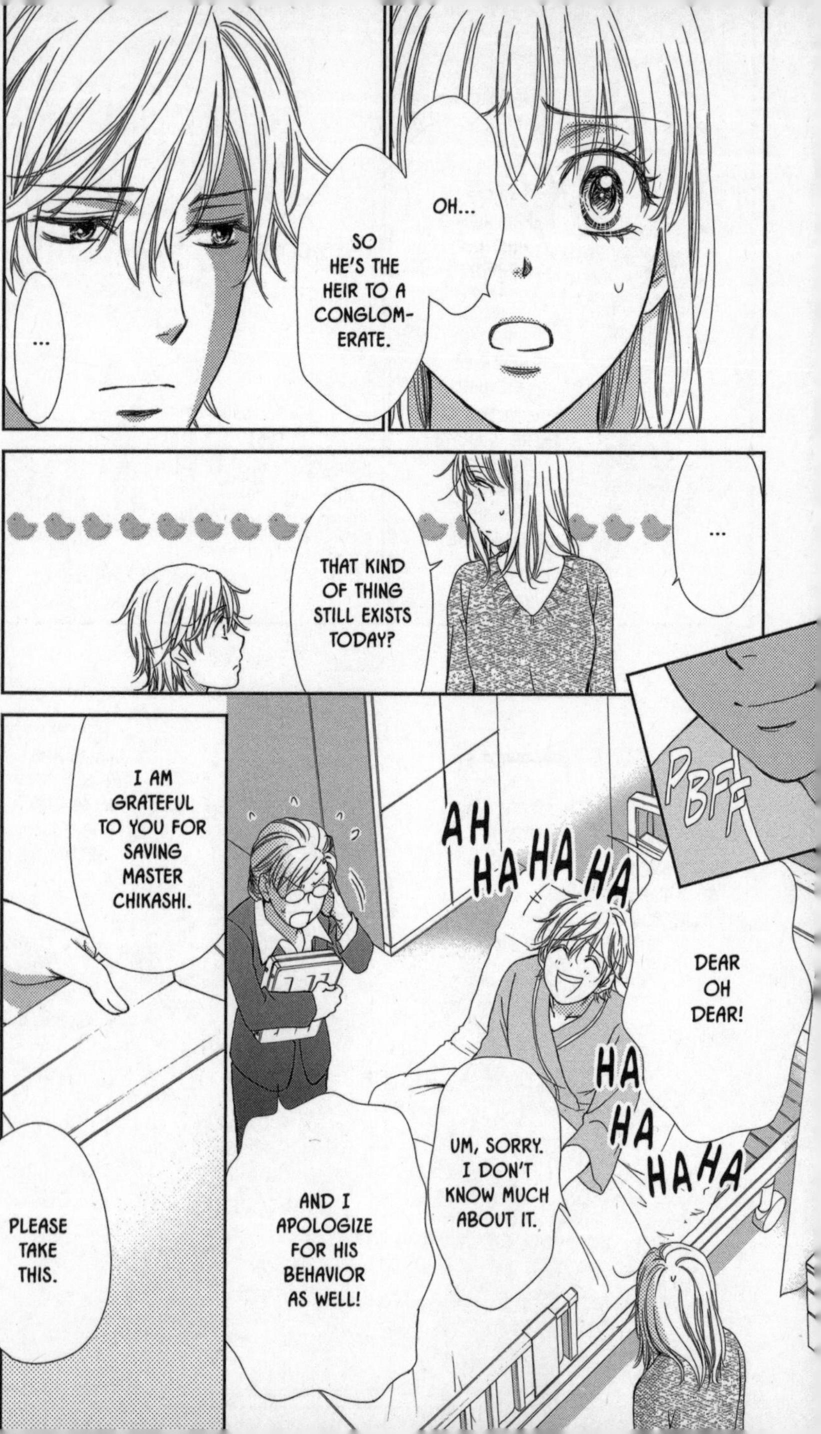
OH...
SO HE'S THE HEIR TO A CONGLOM-ERATE.
...
...
THAT KIND OF THING STILL EXISTS TODAY?
PBFF
DEAR OH DEAR!
AH HA HA HA
HA HA HAHA
UM, SORRY. I DON'T KNOW MUCH ABOUT IT.
AND I APOLOGIZE FOR HIS BEHAVIOR AS WELL!
I AM GRATEFUL TO YOU FOR SAVING MASTER CHIKASHI.
PLEASE TAKE THIS.

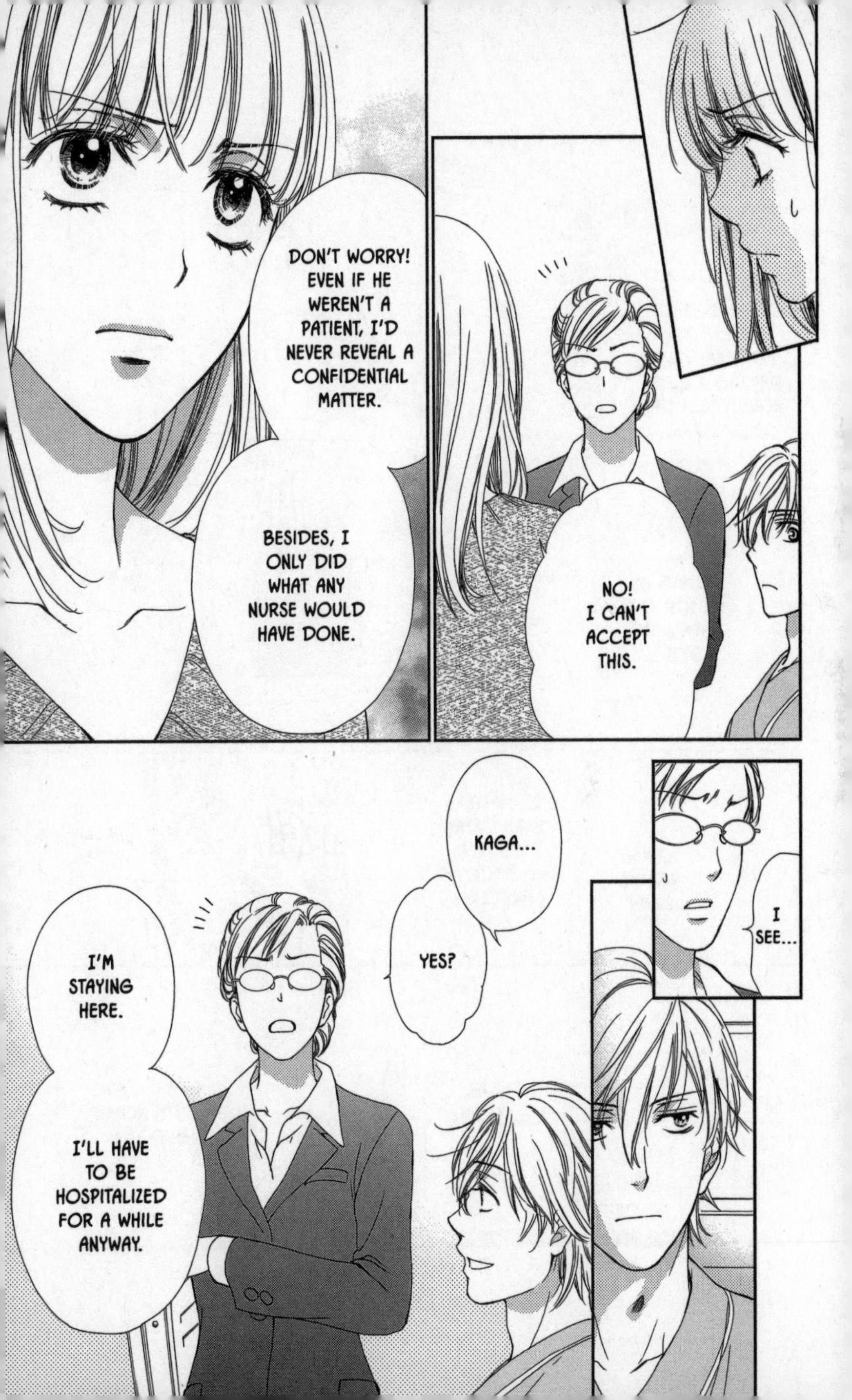
NO! I CAN'T ACCEPT THIS.
DON'T WORRY! EVEN IF HE WEREN'T A PATIENT, I'D NEVER REVEAL A CONFIDENTIAL MATTER.
BESIDES, I ONLY DID WHAT ANY NURSE WOULD HAVE DONE.
I SEE...
KAGA...
YES?
I'M STAYING HERE.
I'LL HAVE TO BE HOSPITALIZED FOR A WHILE ANYWAY.

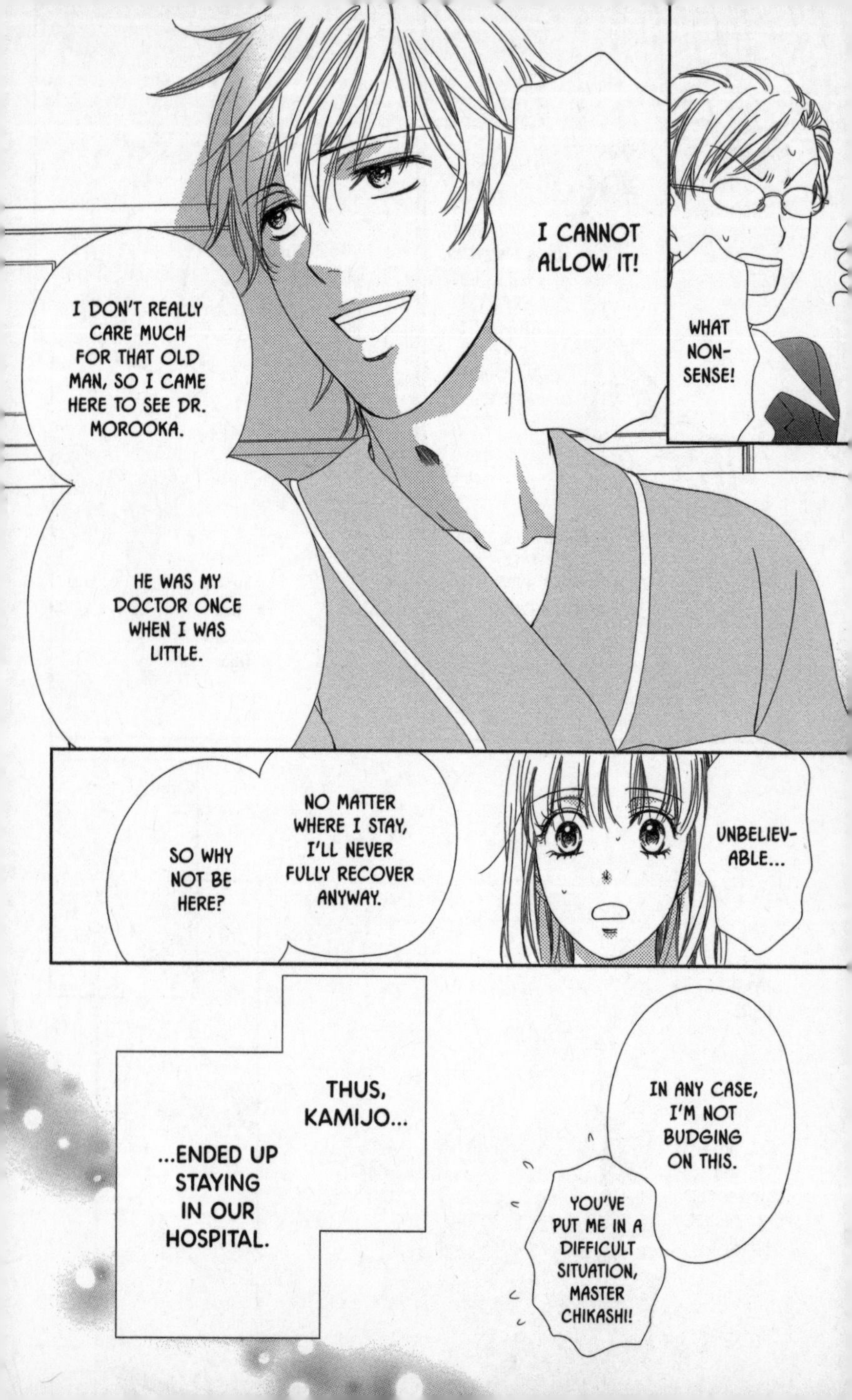
WHAT NON-SENSE!
I CANNOT ALLOW IT!
I DON'T REALLY CARE MUCH FOR THAT OLD MAN, SO I CAME HERE TO SEE DR. MOROOKA.
HE WAS MY DOCTOR ONCE WHEN I WAS LITTLE.
UNBELIEV-ABLE...
NO MATTER WHERE I STAY, I'LL NEVER FULLY RECOVER ANYWAY.
SO WHY NOT BE HERE?
IN ANY CASE, I'M NOT BUDGING ON THIS.
YOU'VE PUT ME IN A DIFFICULT SITUATION, MASTER CHIKASHI!
THUS, KAMIJO...
...ENDED UP STAYING IN OUR HOSPITAL.

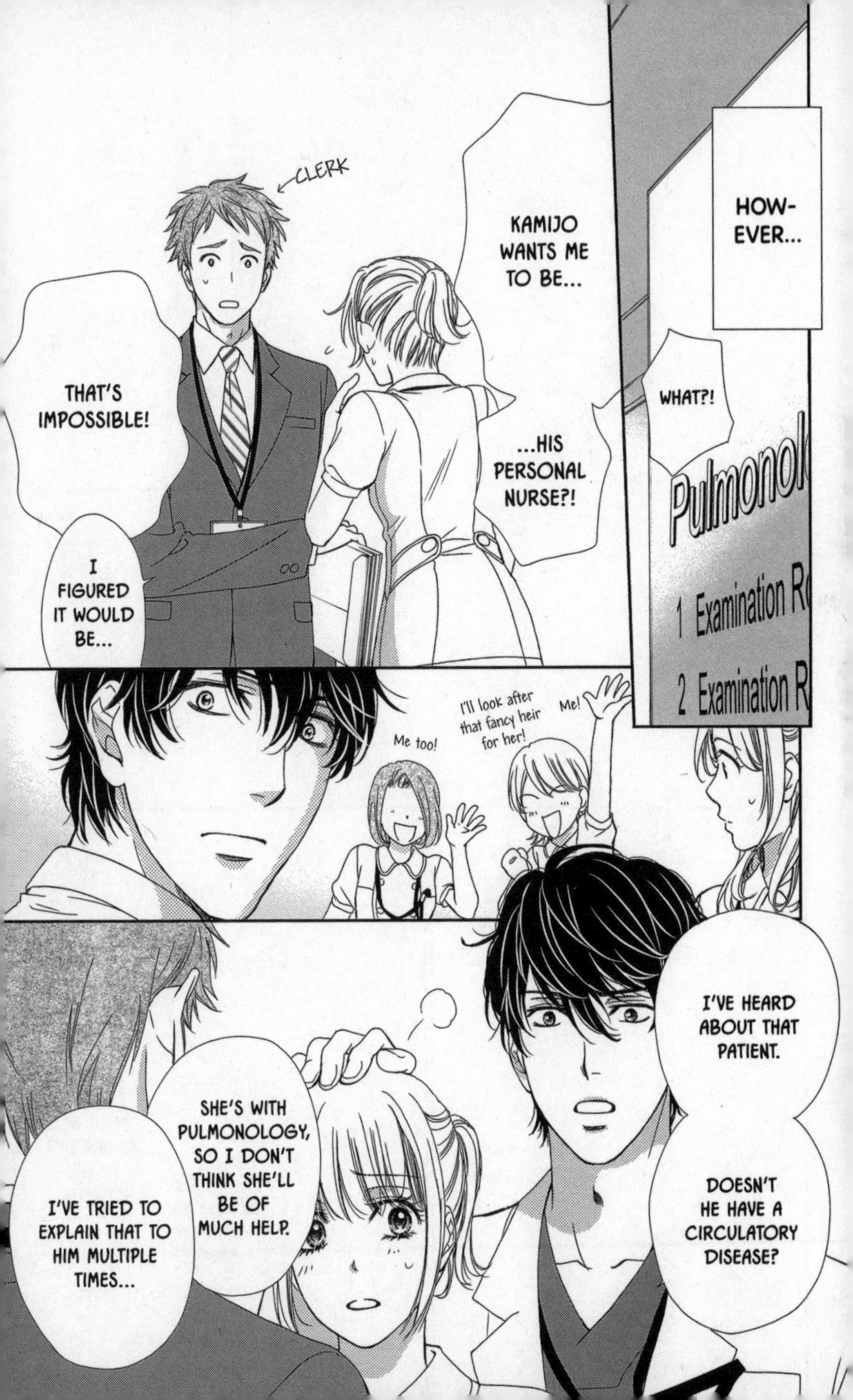
HOW-EVER...
WHAT?!
Pulmonol
1 Examination R
2 Examination R
KAMIJO WANTS ME TO BE...
...HIS PERSONAL NURSE?!
CLERK
THAT'S IMPOSSIBLE!
I FIGURED IT WOULD BE...
Me!
I'll look after that fancy heir for her!
Me too!
I'VE HEARD ABOUT THAT PATIENT.
DOESN'T HE HAVE A CIRCULATORY DISEASE?
SHE'S WITH PULMONOLOGY, SO I DON'T THINK SHE'LL BE OF MUCH HELP.
I'VE TRIED TO EXPLAIN THAT TO HIM MULTIPLE TIMES...

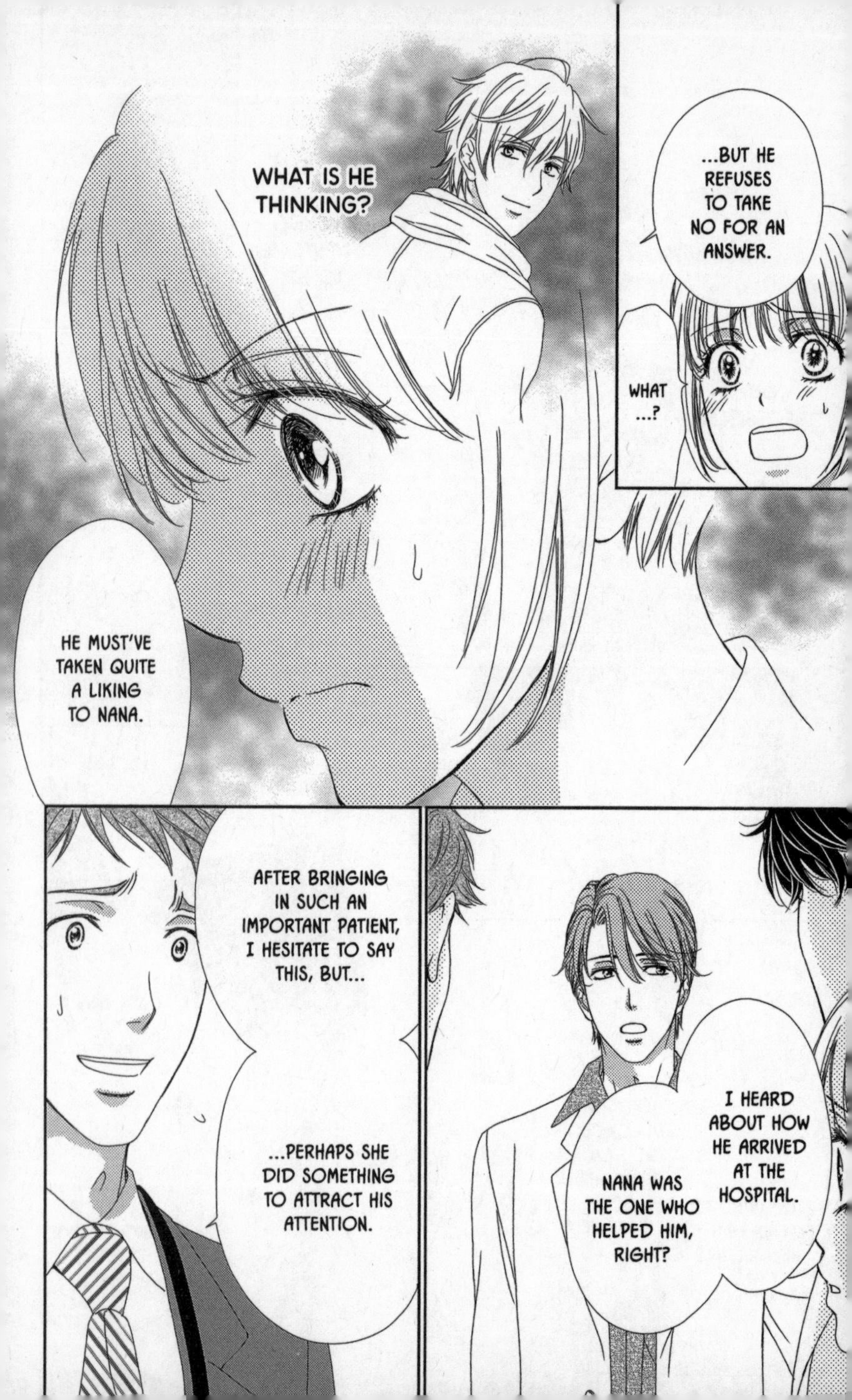
...BUT HE REFUSES TO TAKE NO FOR AN ANSWER.
WHAT ...?
WHAT IS HE THINKING?
HE MUST'VE TAKEN QUITE A LIKING TO NANA.
I HEARD ABOUT HOW HE ARRIVED AT THE HOSPITAL.
NANA WAS THE ONE WHO HELPED HIM, RIGHT?
AFTER BRINGING IN SUCH AN IMPORTANT PATIENT, I HESITATE TO SAY THIS, BUT...
...PERHAPS SHE DID SOMETHING TO ATTRACT HIS ATTENTION.

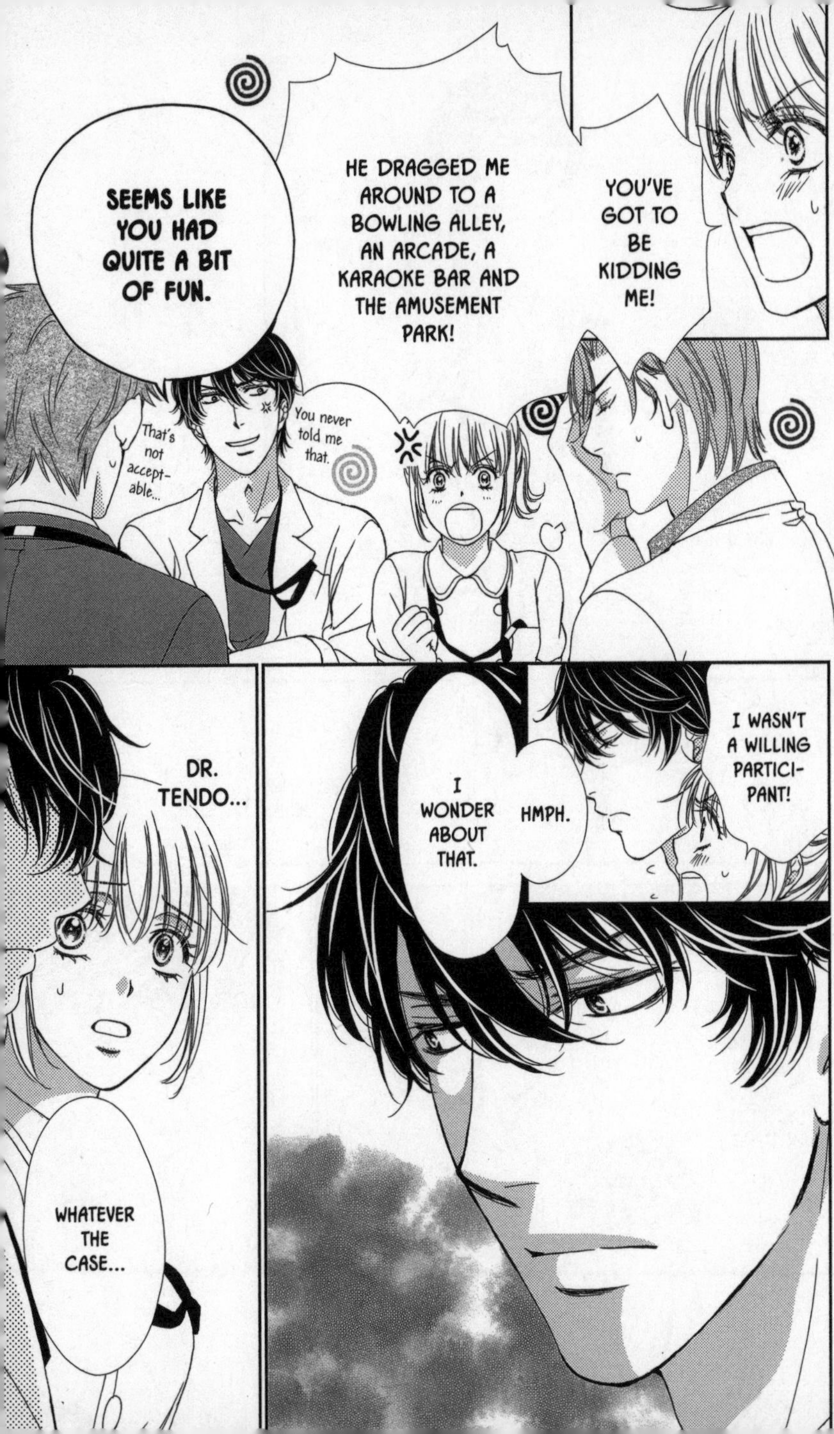
YOU'VE GOT TO BE KIDDING ME!
HE DRAGGED ME AROUND TO A BOWLING ALLEY, AN ARCADE, A KARAOKE BAR AND THE AMUSEMENT PARK!
SEEMS LIKE YOU HAD QUITE A BIT OF FUN.
You never told me that.
That's not accept-able...
I WASN'T A WILLING PARTICI-PANT!
HMPH.
I WONDER ABOUT THAT.
DR. TENDO...
WHATEVER THE CASE...

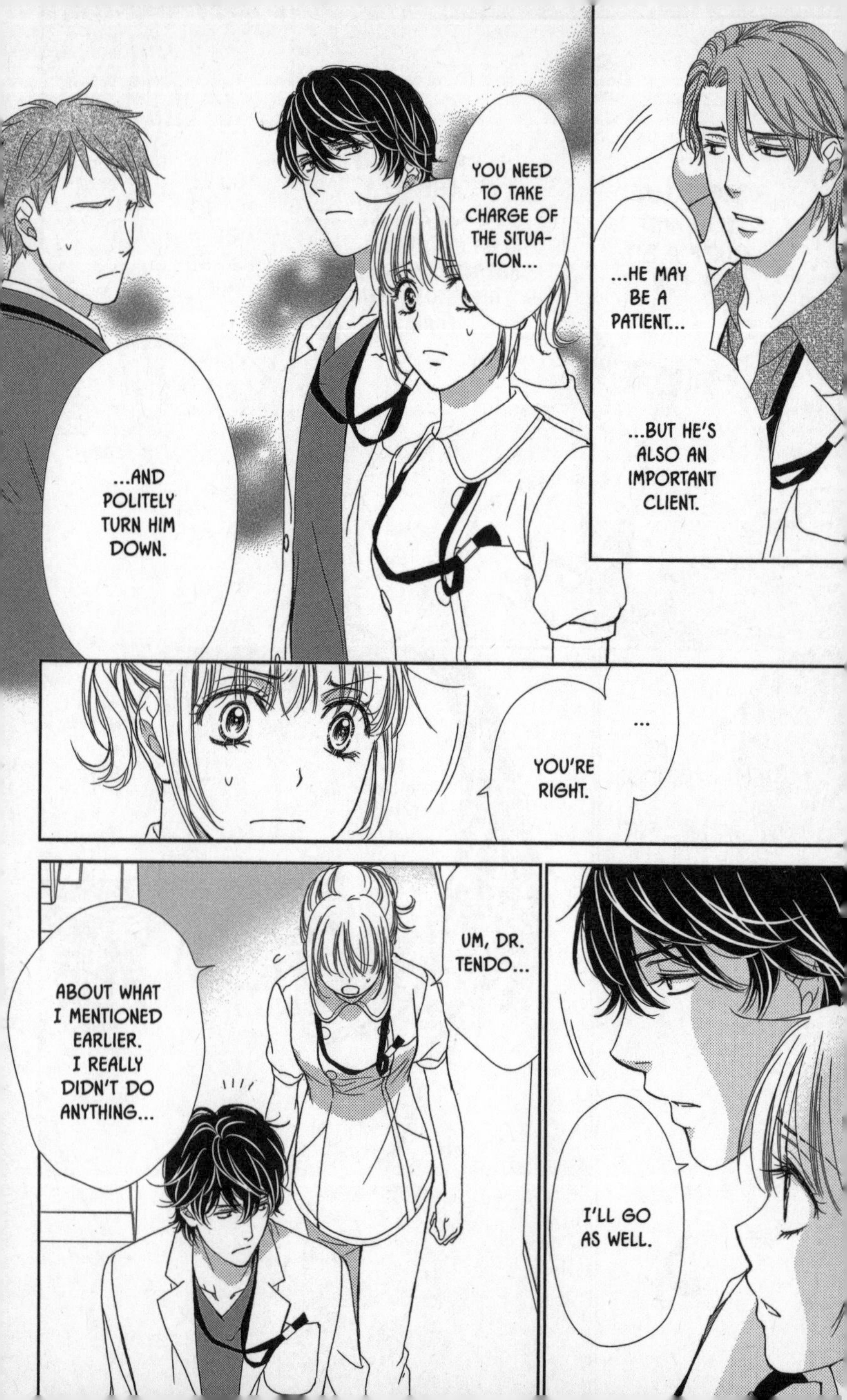
...HE MAY BE A PATIENT...
...BUT HE'S ALSO AN IMPORTANT CLIENT.
YOU NEED TO TAKE CHARGE OF THE SITUATION...
...AND POLITELY TURN HIM DOWN.
... YOU'RE RIGHT.
I'LL GO AS WELL.
UM, DR. TENDO...
ABOUT WHAT I MENTIONED EARLIER. I REALLY DIDN'T DO ANYTHING...

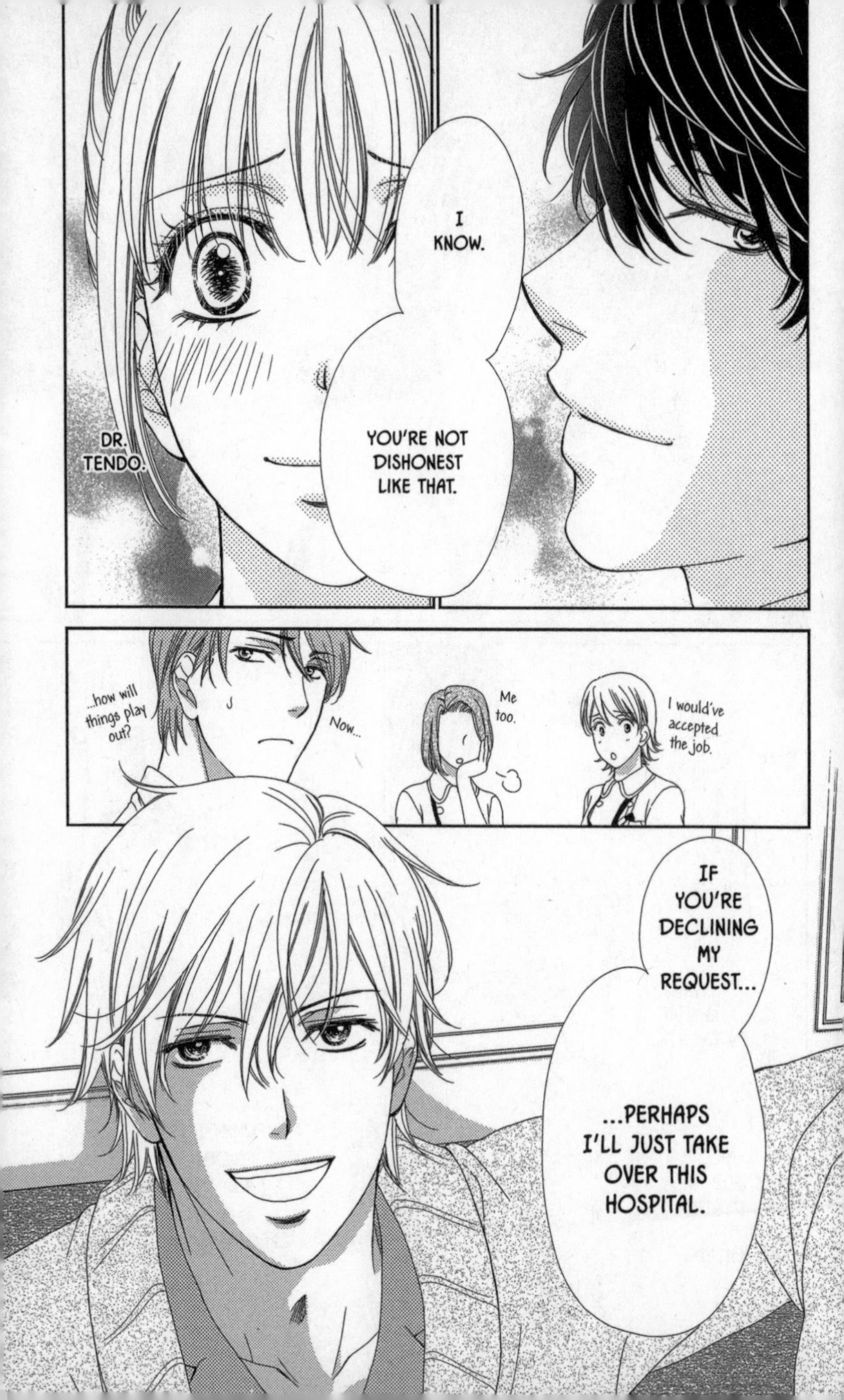
I KNOW.
YOU'RE NOT DISHONEST LIKE THAT.
DR. TENDO.
I would've accepted the job.
Me too.
Now...
...how will things play out?
IF YOU'RE DECLINING MY REQUEST...
...PERHAPS I'LL JUST TAKE OVER THIS HOSPITAL.

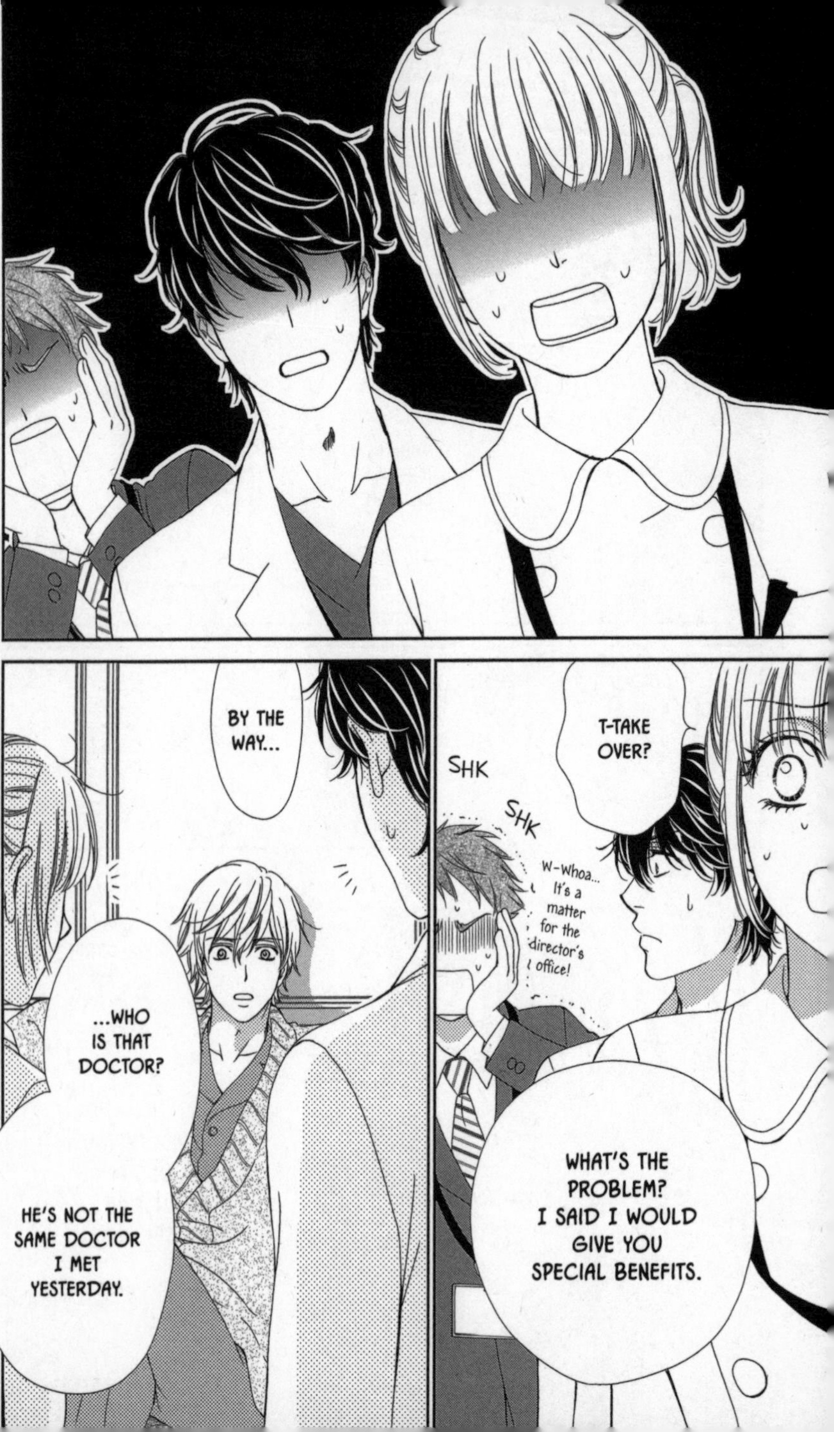
T-TAKE OVER?
SHK
SHK
W-Whoa... It's a matter for the director's office!
WHAT'S THE PROBLEM? I SAID I WOULD GIVE YOU SPECIAL BENEFITS.
BY THE WAY...
...WHO IS THAT DOCTOR?
HE'S NOT THE SAME DOCTOR I MET YESTERDAY.

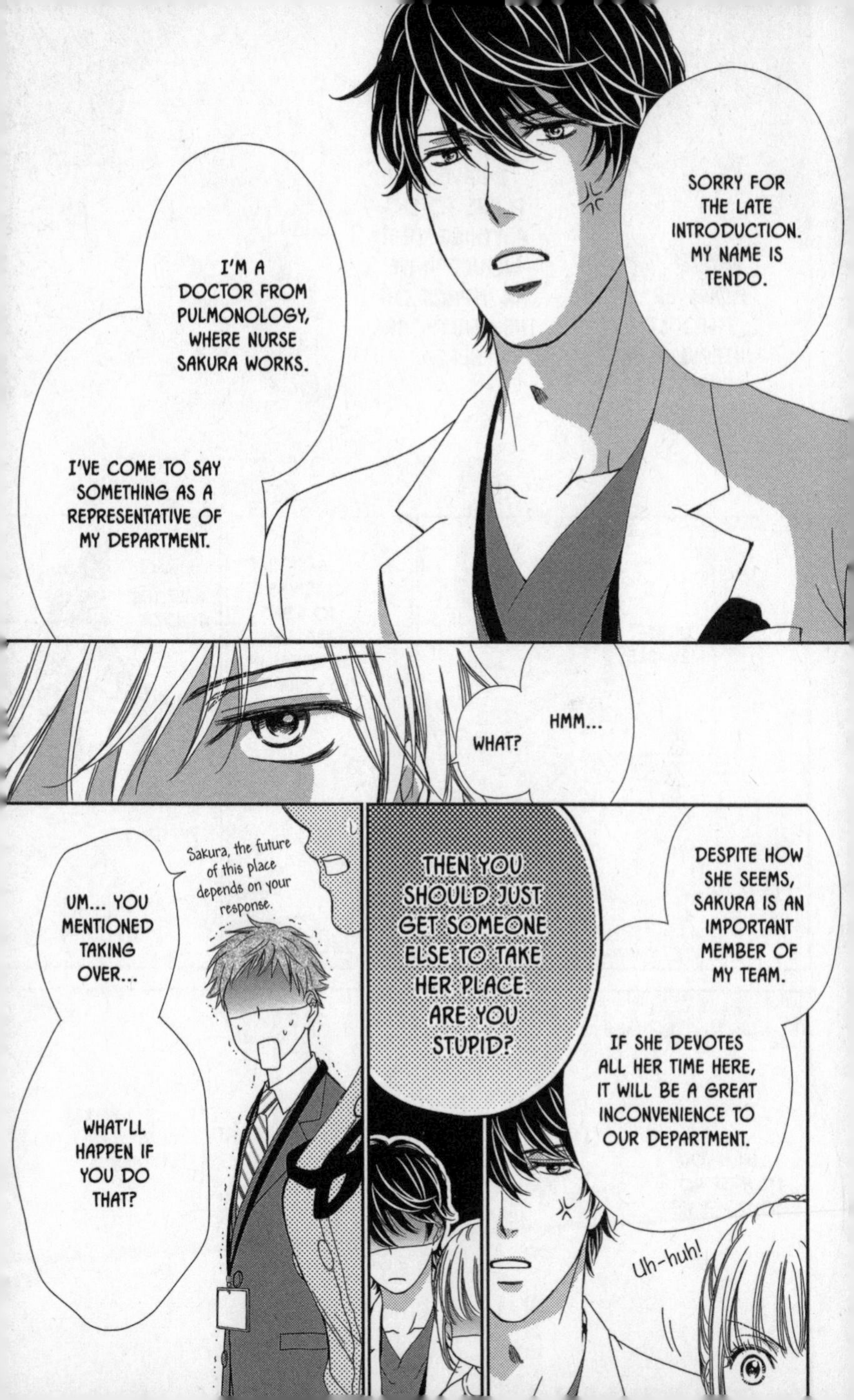
SORRY FOR THE LATE INTRODUCTION. MY NAME IS TENDO.
I'M A DOCTOR FROM PULMONOLOGY, WHERE NURSE SAKURA WORKS.
I'VE COME TO SAY SOMETHING AS A REPRESENTATIVE OF MY DEPARTMENT.
HMM...
WHAT?
DESPITE HOW SHE SEEMS, SAKURA IS AN IMPORTANT MEMBER OF MY TEAM.
IF SHE DEVOTES ALL HER TIME HERE, IT WILL BE A GREAT INCONVENIENCE TO OUR DEPARTMENT.
Uh-huh!
THEN YOU SHOULD JUST GET SOMEONE ELSE TO TAKE HER PLACE. ARE YOU STUPID?
Sakura, the future of this place depends on your response.
UM... YOU MENTIONED TAKING OVER...
WHAT'LL HAPPEN IF YOU DO THAT?

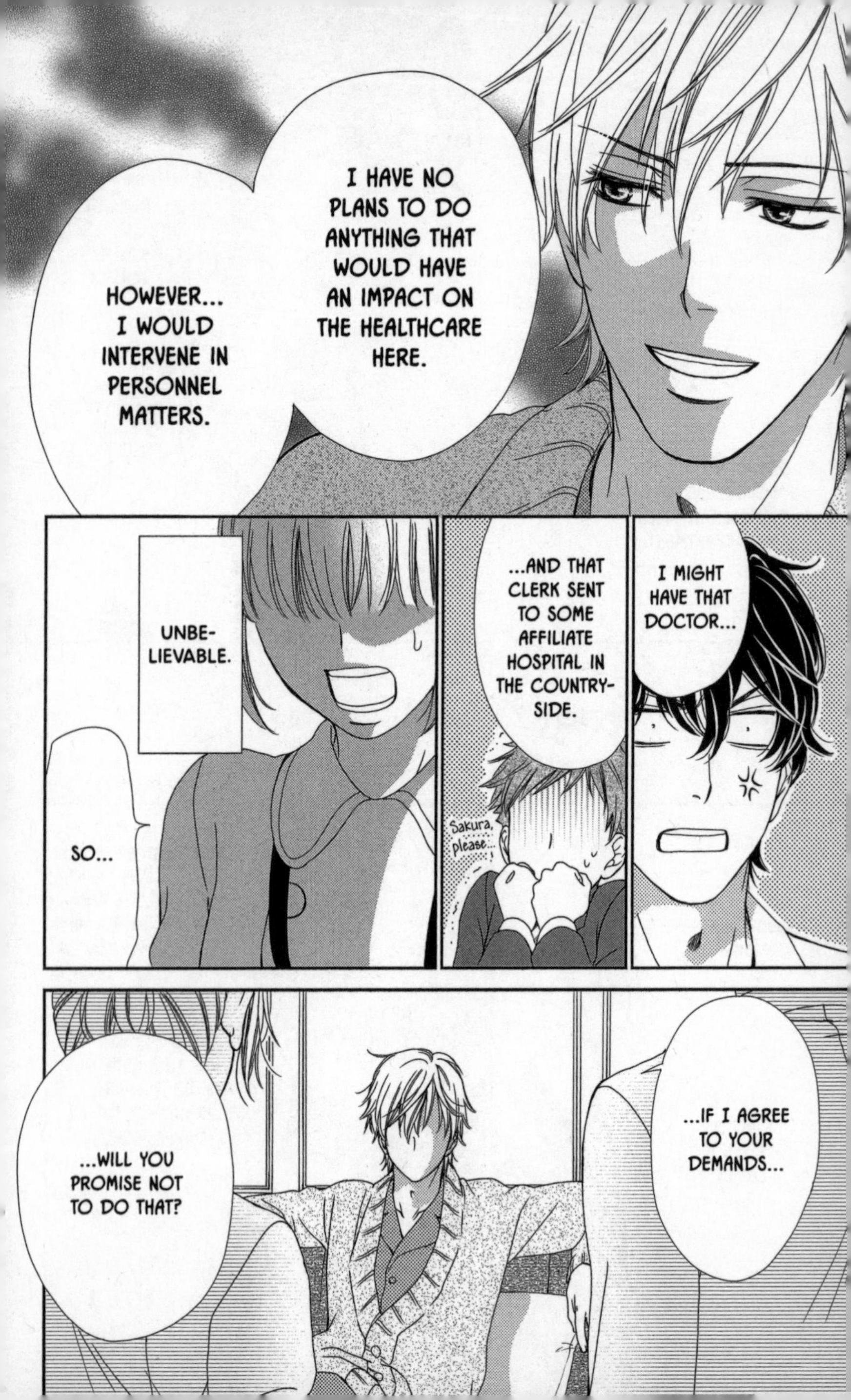
I HAVE NO PLANS TO DO ANYTHING THAT WOULD HAVE AN IMPACT ON THE HEALTHCARE HERE.
HOWEVER... I WOULD INTERVENE IN PERSONNEL MATTERS.
I MIGHT HAVE THAT DOCTOR...
...AND THAT CLERK SENT TO SOME AFFILIATE HOSPITAL IN THE COUNTRY-SIDE.
Sakura, please...
UNBE-LIEVABLE.
SO...
...IF I AGREE TO YOUR DEMANDS...
...WILL YOU PROMISE NOT TO DO THAT?

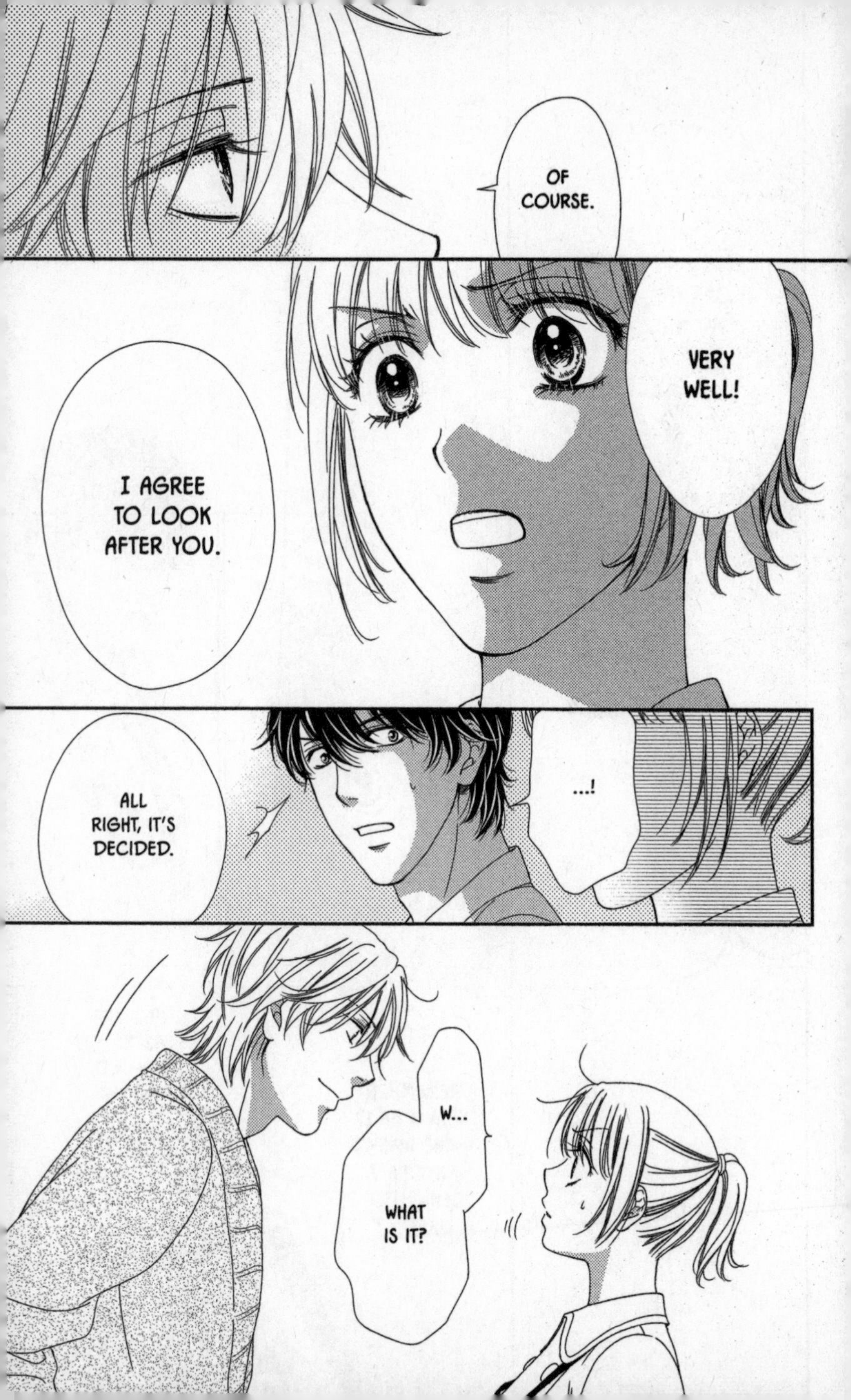
OF COURSE.
VERY WELL!
I AGREE TO LOOK AFTER YOU.
...!
ALL RIGHT, IT'S DECIDED.
W...
WHAT IS IT?

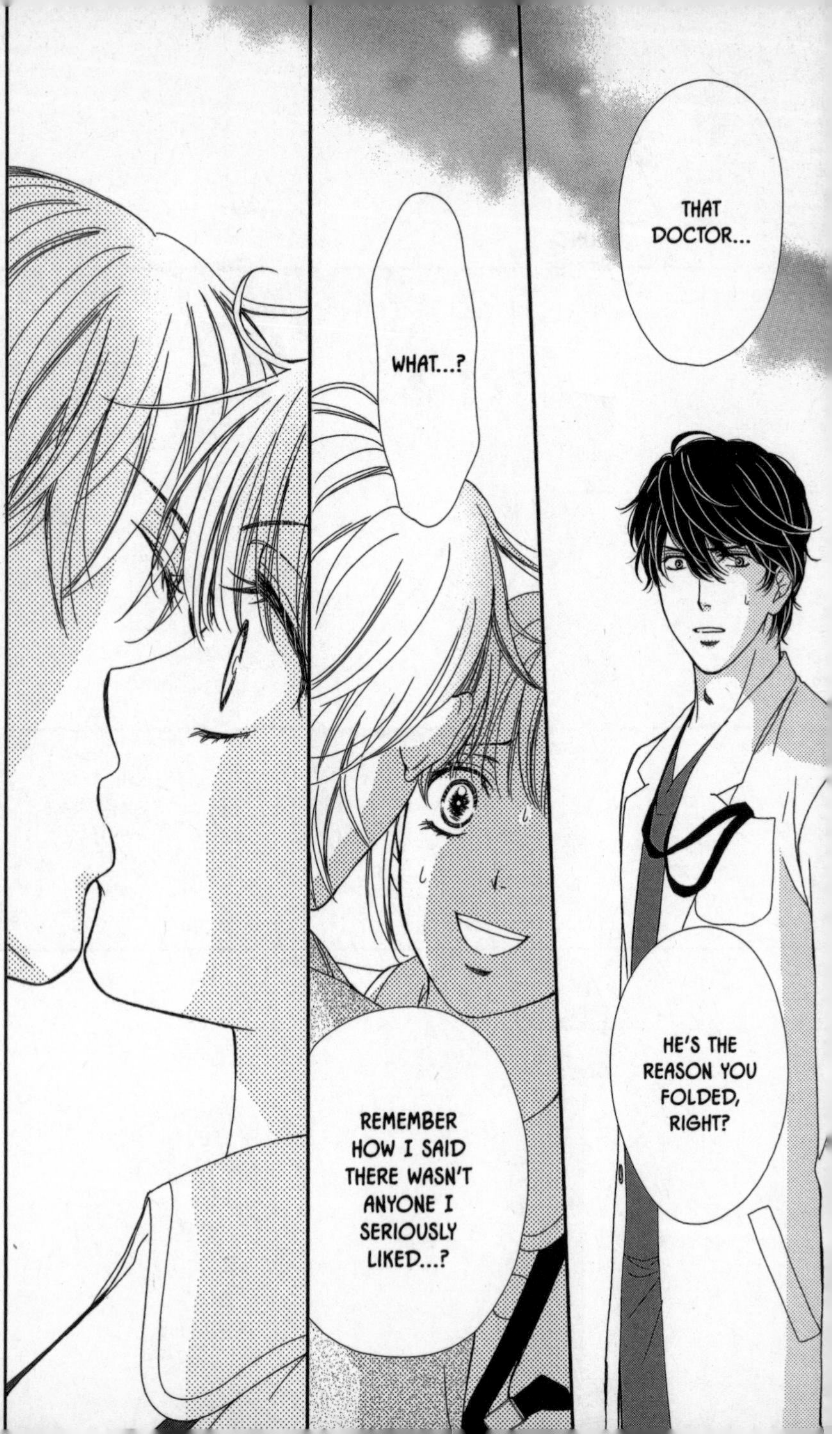
THAT DOCTOR...
HE'S THE REASON YOU FOLDED, RIGHT?
WHAT...?
REMEMBER HOW I SAID THERE WASN'T ANYONE I SERIOUSLY LIKED...?

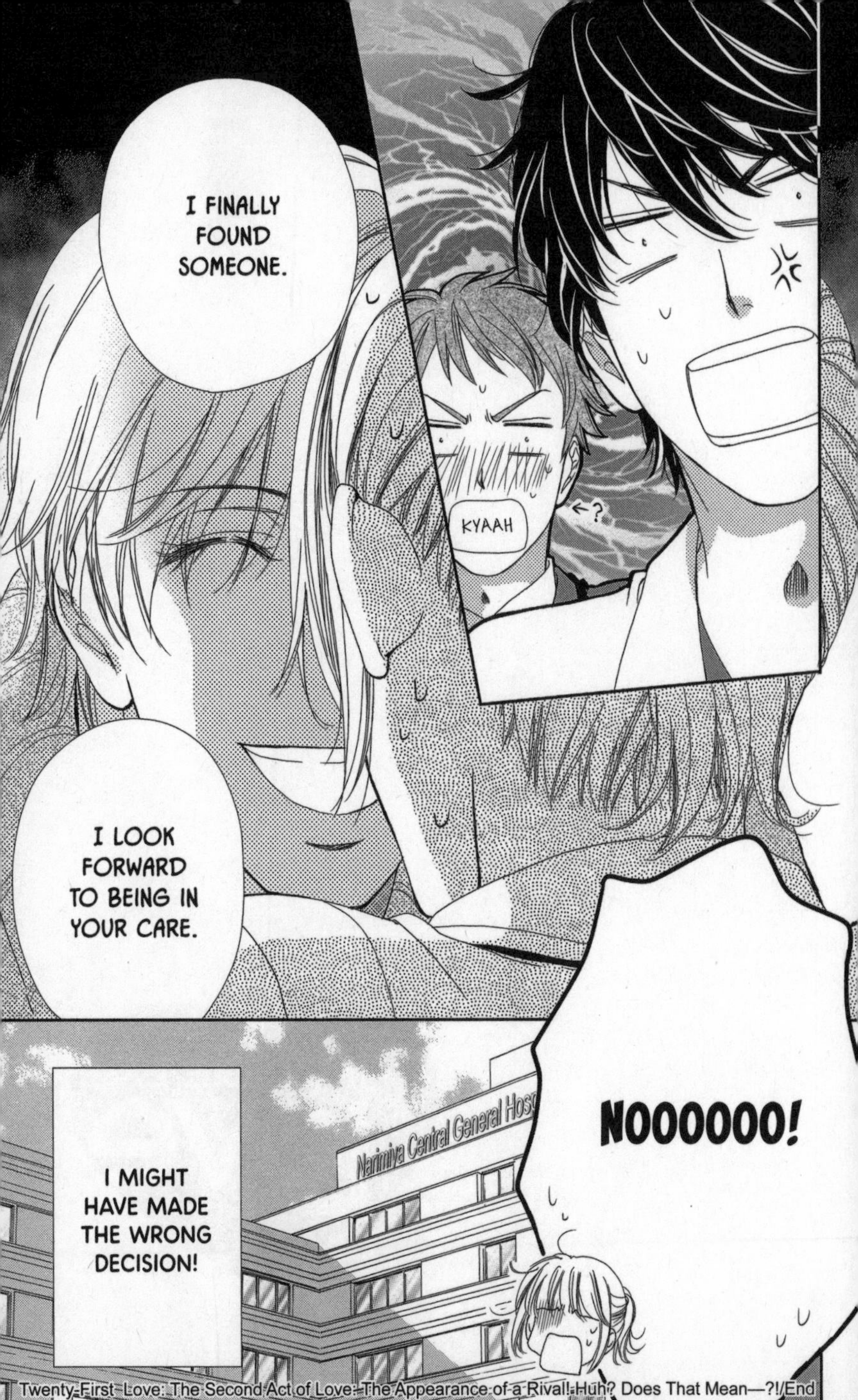
KYAAH
←?
I FINALLY FOUND SOMEONE.
I LOOK FORWARD TO BEING IN YOUR CARE.
NOOOOOO!
I MIGHT HAVE MADE THE WRONG DECISION!

Twenty-First Love: The Second Act of Love: The Appearance of a Rival! Huh? Does That Mean—?!/End

AN INCURABLE CASE OF LOVE

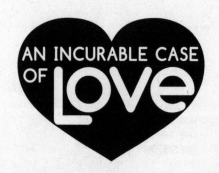

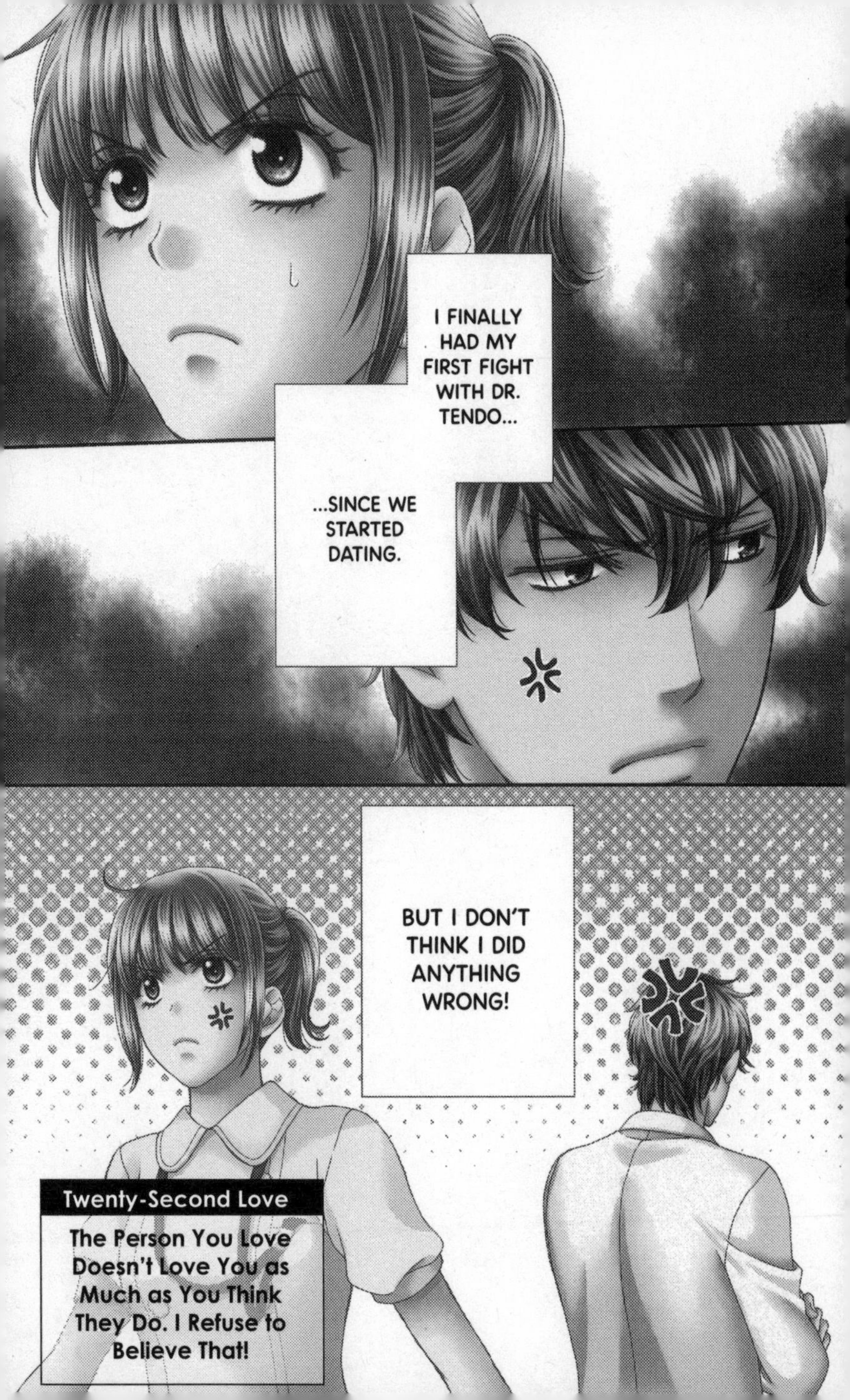
I FINALLY HAD MY FIRST FIGHT WITH DR. TENDO...
...SINCE WE STARTED DATING.
BUT I DON'T THINK I DID ANYTHING WRONG!
Twenty-Second Love
The Person You Love Doesn't Love You as Much as You Think They Do. I Refuse to Believe That!

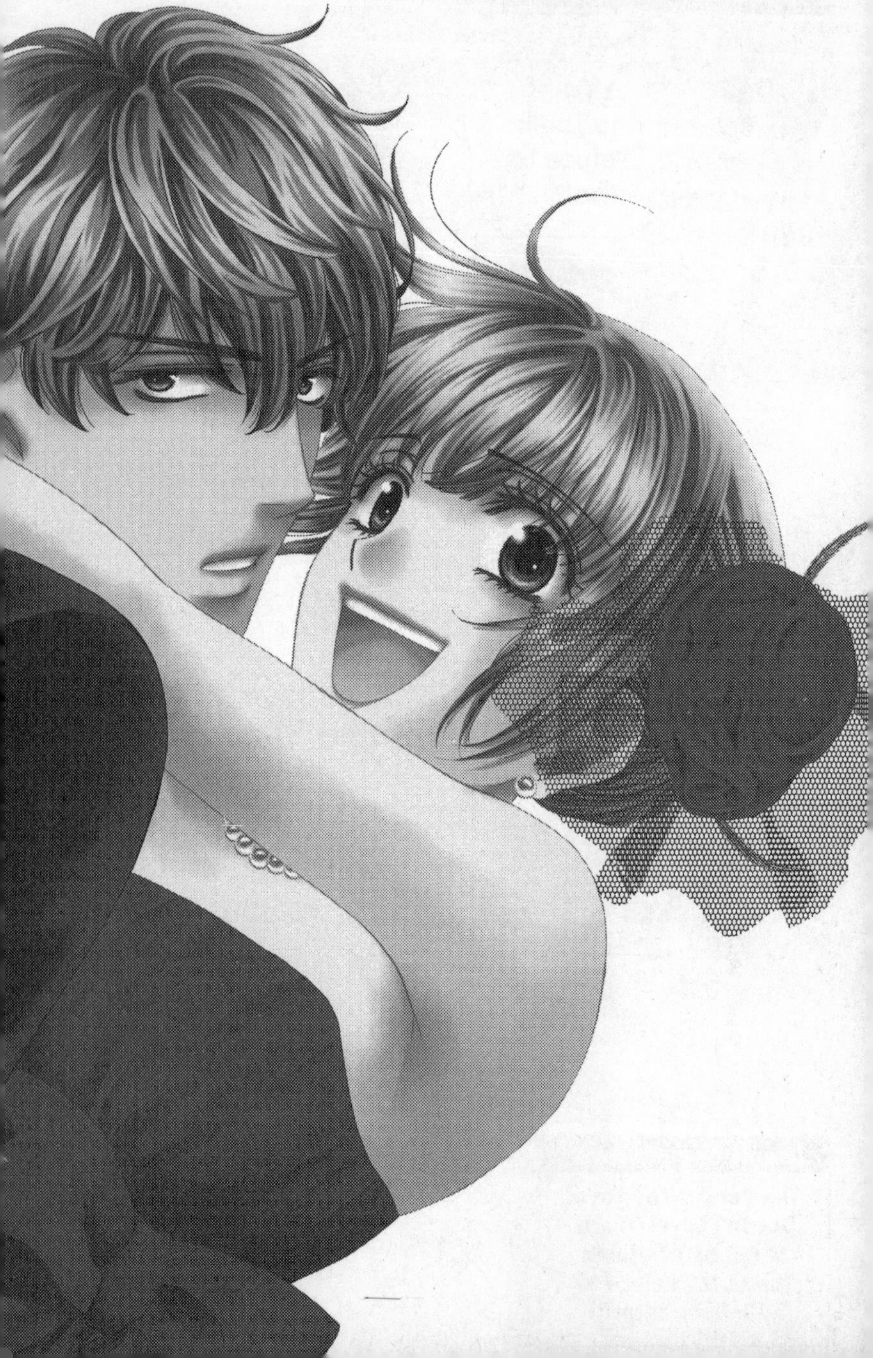

## Twenty-Second Love

# The Person You Love Doesn't Love You as Much as You Think They Do. I Refuse to Believe That!

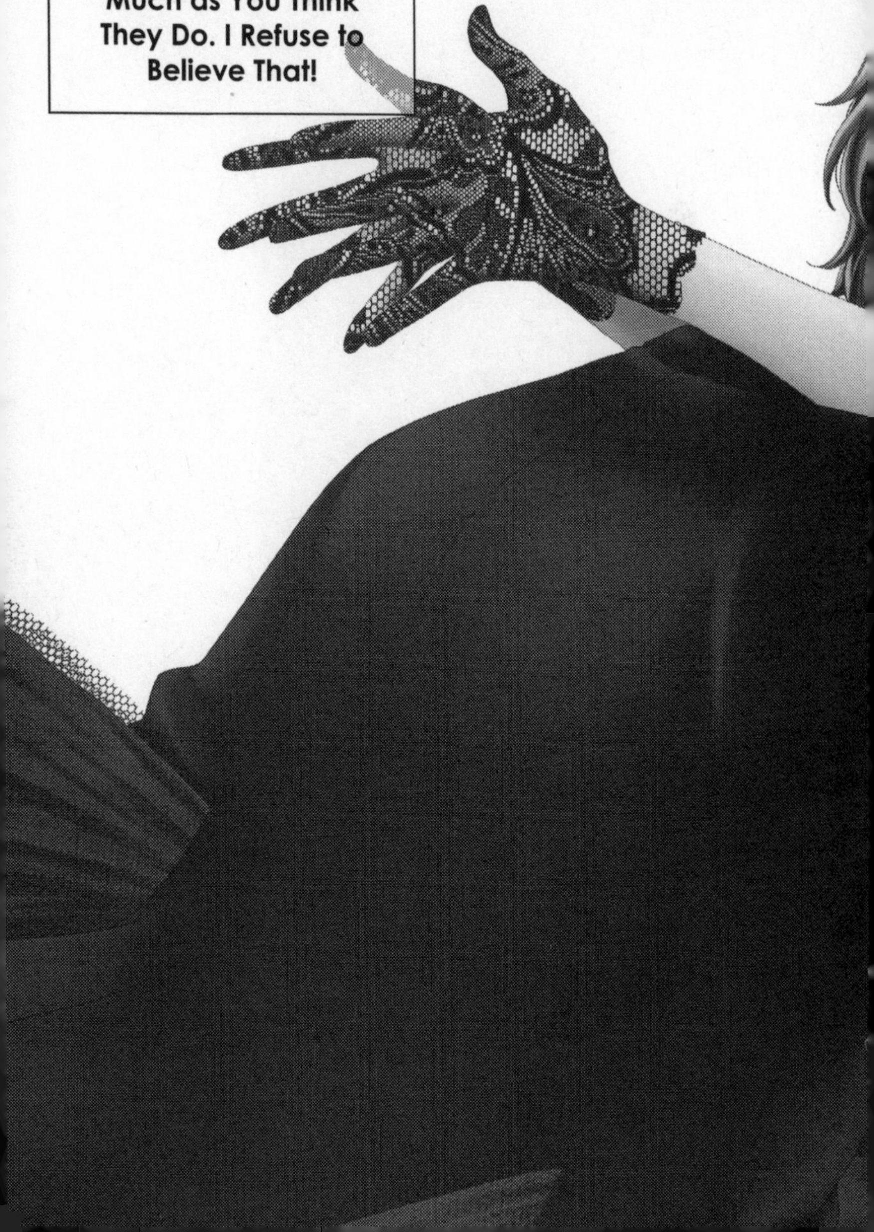

AN INCURABLE CASE OF LOVE

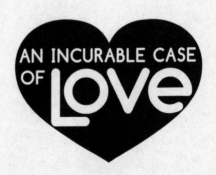

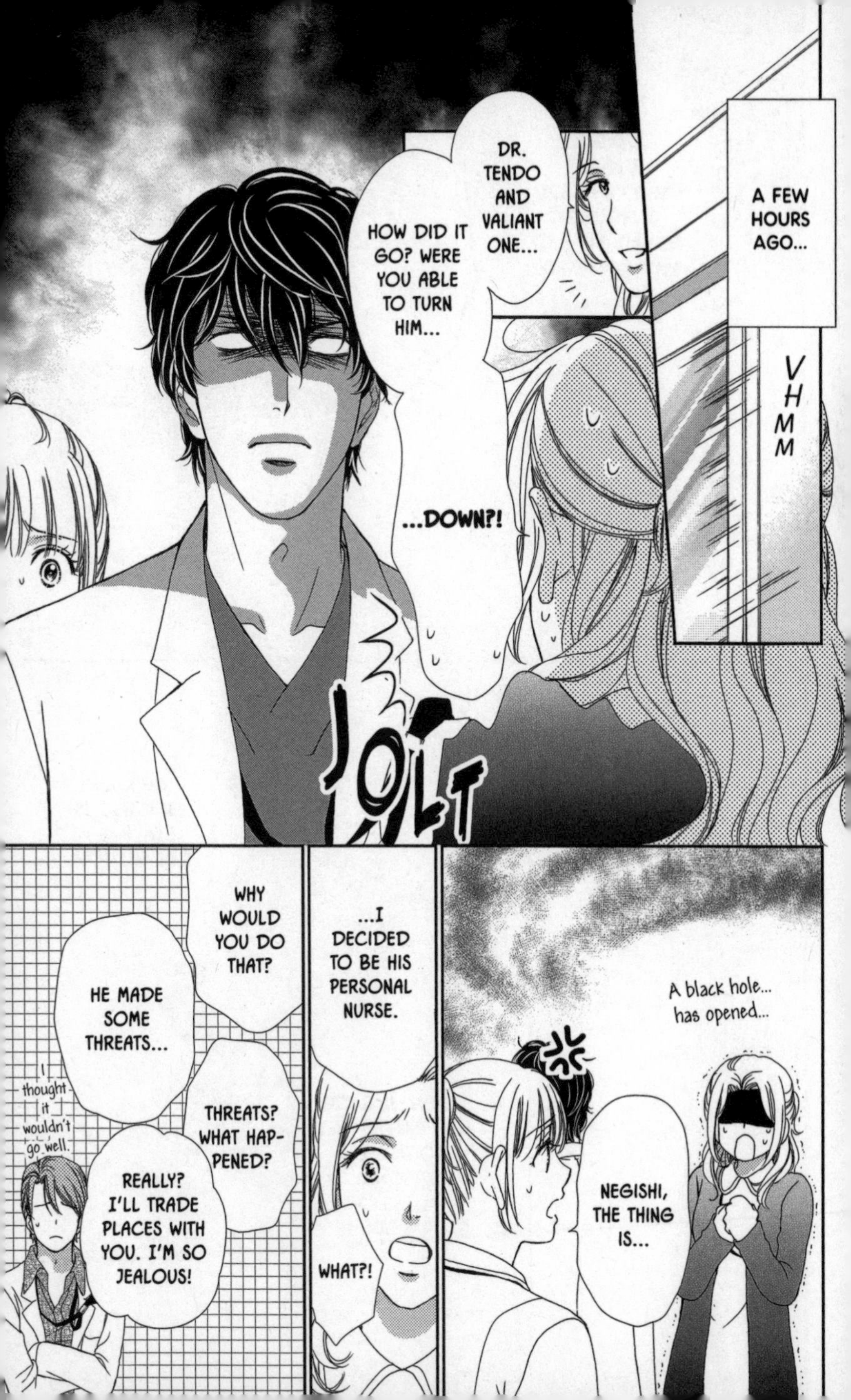
A FEW HOURS AGO...
VHMM
DR. TENDO AND VALIANT ONE...
HOW DID IT GO? WERE YOU ABLE TO TURN HIM...
...DOWN?!
JOLT
A black hole... has opened...
NEGISHI, THE THING IS...
...I DECIDED TO BE HIS PERSONAL NURSE.
WHAT?!
WHY WOULD YOU DO THAT?
HE MADE SOME THREATS...
THREATS? WHAT HAPPENED?
REALLY? I'LL TRADE PLACES WITH YOU. I'M SO JEALOUS!
I thought it wouldn't go well.

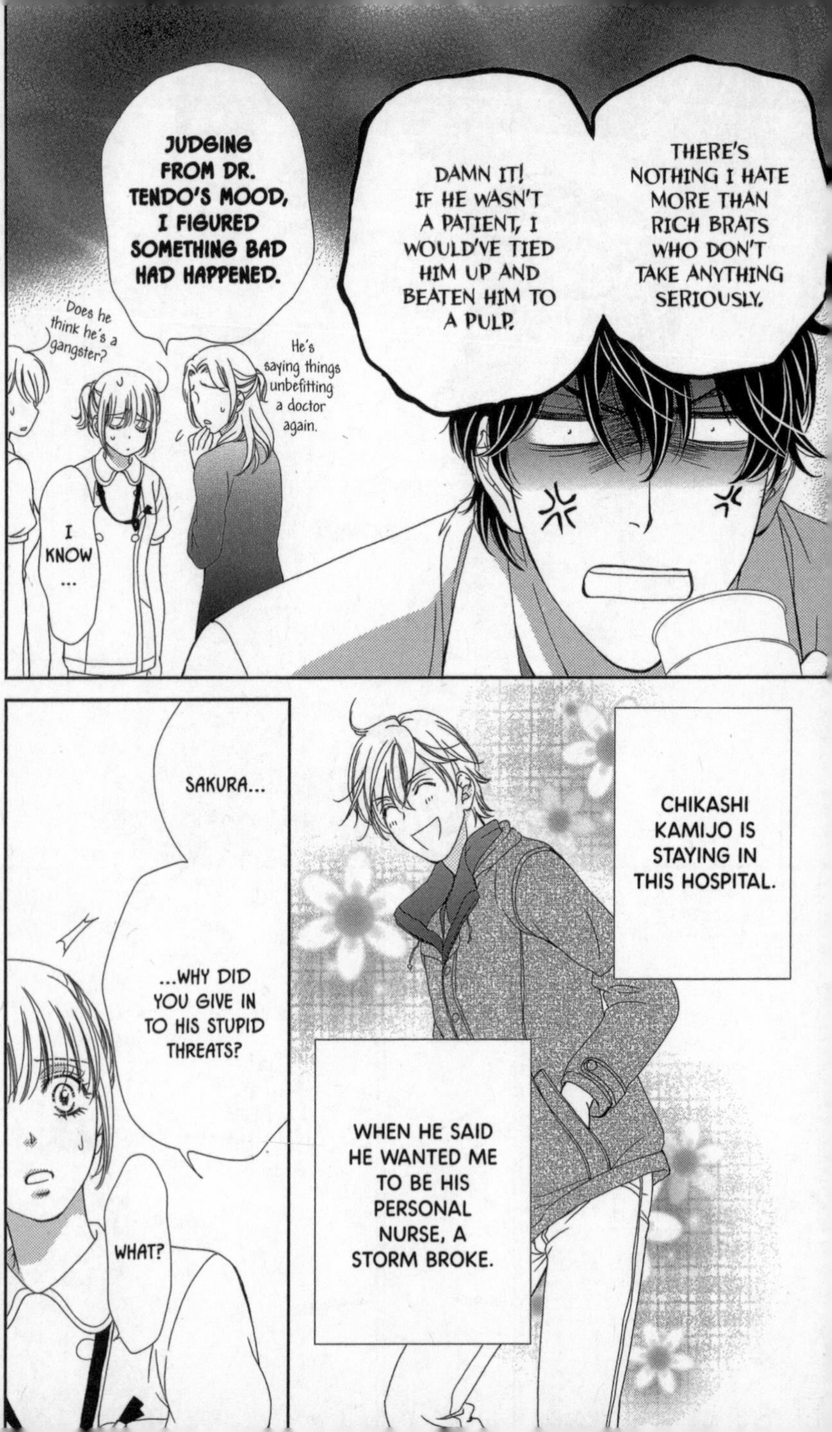
THERE'S NOTHING I HATE MORE THAN RICH BRATS WHO DON'T TAKE ANYTHING SERIOUSLY.
DAMN IT! IF HE WASN'T A PATIENT, I WOULD'VE TIED HIM UP AND BEATEN HIM TO A PULP.
JUDGING FROM DR. TENDO'S MOOD, I FIGURED SOMETHING BAD HAD HAPPENED.
He's saying things unbefitting a doctor again.
Does he think he's a gangster?
I KNOW ...
CHIKASHI KAMIJO IS STAYING IN THIS HOSPITAL.
WHEN HE SAID HE WANTED ME TO BE HIS PERSONAL NURSE, A STORM BROKE.
SAKURA...
...WHY DID YOU GIVE IN TO HIS STUPID THREATS?
WHAT?

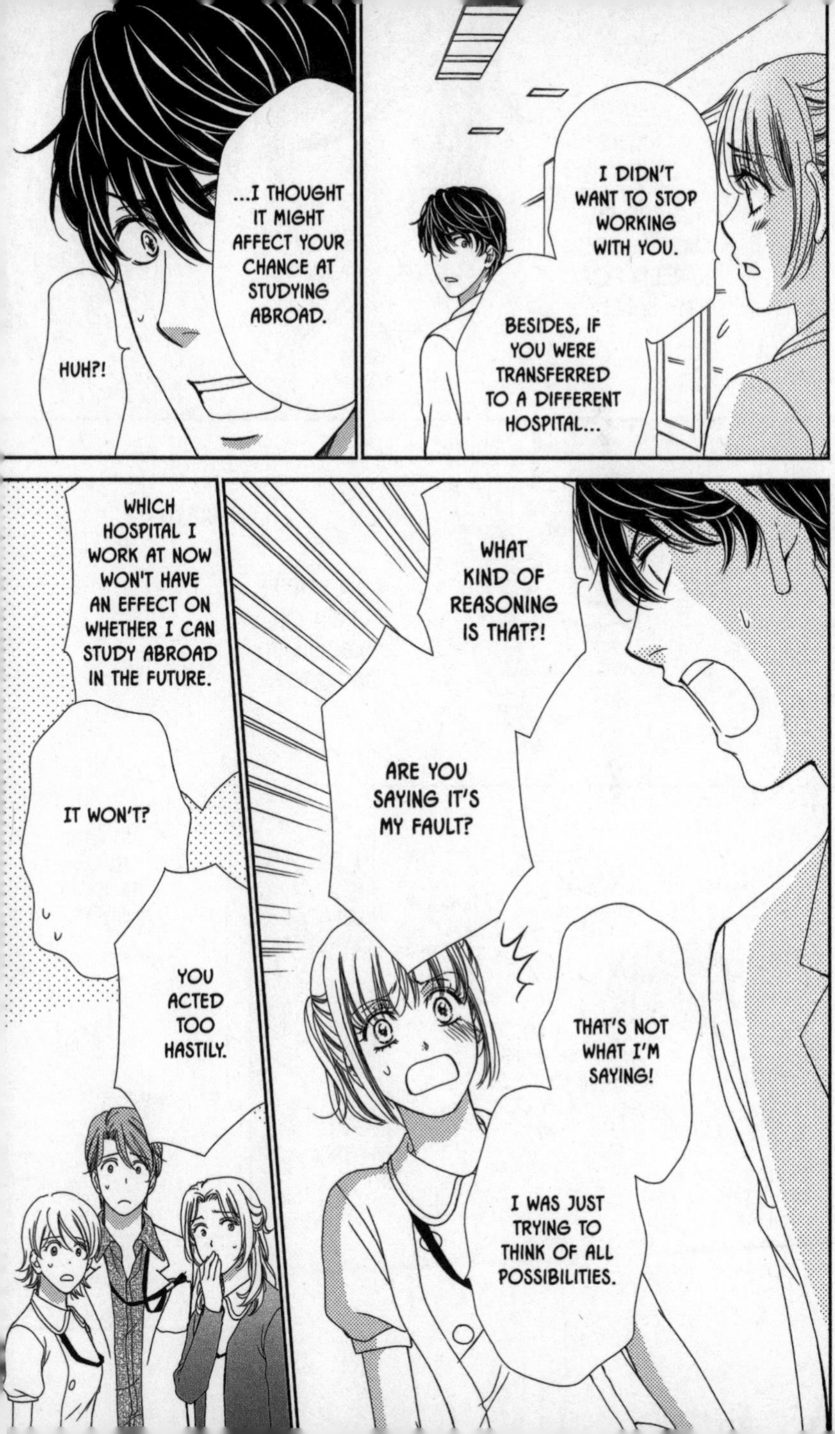
I DIDN'T WANT TO STOP WORKING WITH YOU.
BESIDES, IF YOU WERE TRANSFERRED TO A DIFFERENT HOSPITAL...
...I THOUGHT IT MIGHT AFFECT YOUR CHANCE AT STUDYING ABROAD.
HUH?!
WHAT KIND OF REASONING IS THAT?!
ARE YOU SAYING IT'S MY FAULT?
THAT'S NOT WHAT I'M SAYING!
I WAS JUST TRYING TO THINK OF ALL POSSIBILITIES.
WHICH HOSPITAL I WORK AT NOW WON'T HAVE AN EFFECT ON WHETHER I CAN STUDY ABROAD IN THE FUTURE.
IT WON'T?
YOU ACTED TOO HASTILY.

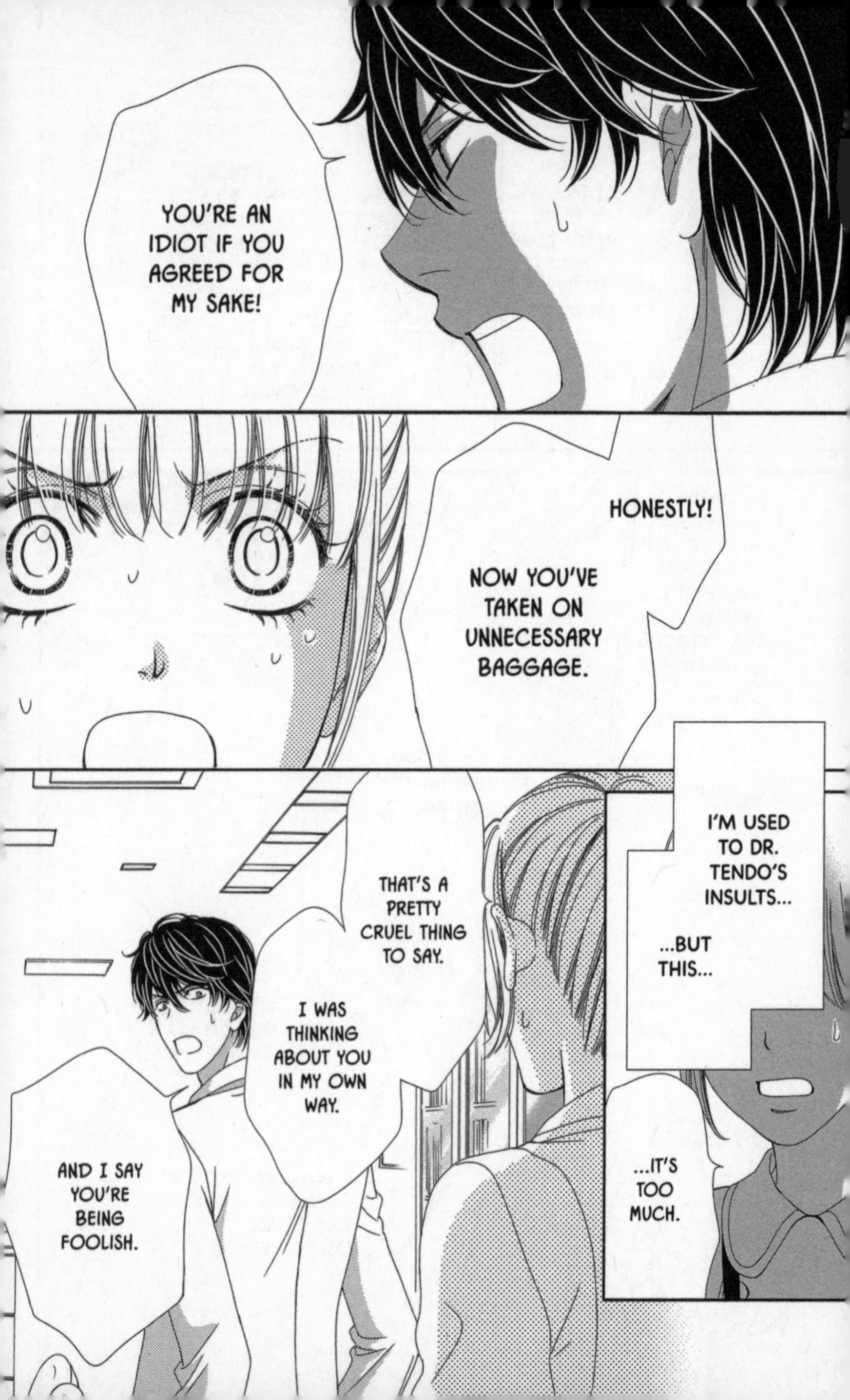
YOU'RE AN IDIOT IF YOU AGREED FOR MY SAKE!
HONESTLY!
NOW YOU'VE TAKEN ON UNNECESSARY BAGGAGE.
I'M USED TO DR. TENDO'S INSULTS...
...BUT THIS...
...IT'S TOO MUCH.
THAT'S A PRETTY CRUEL THING TO SAY.
I WAS THINKING ABOUT YOU IN MY OWN WAY.
AND I SAY YOU'RE BEING FOOLISH.

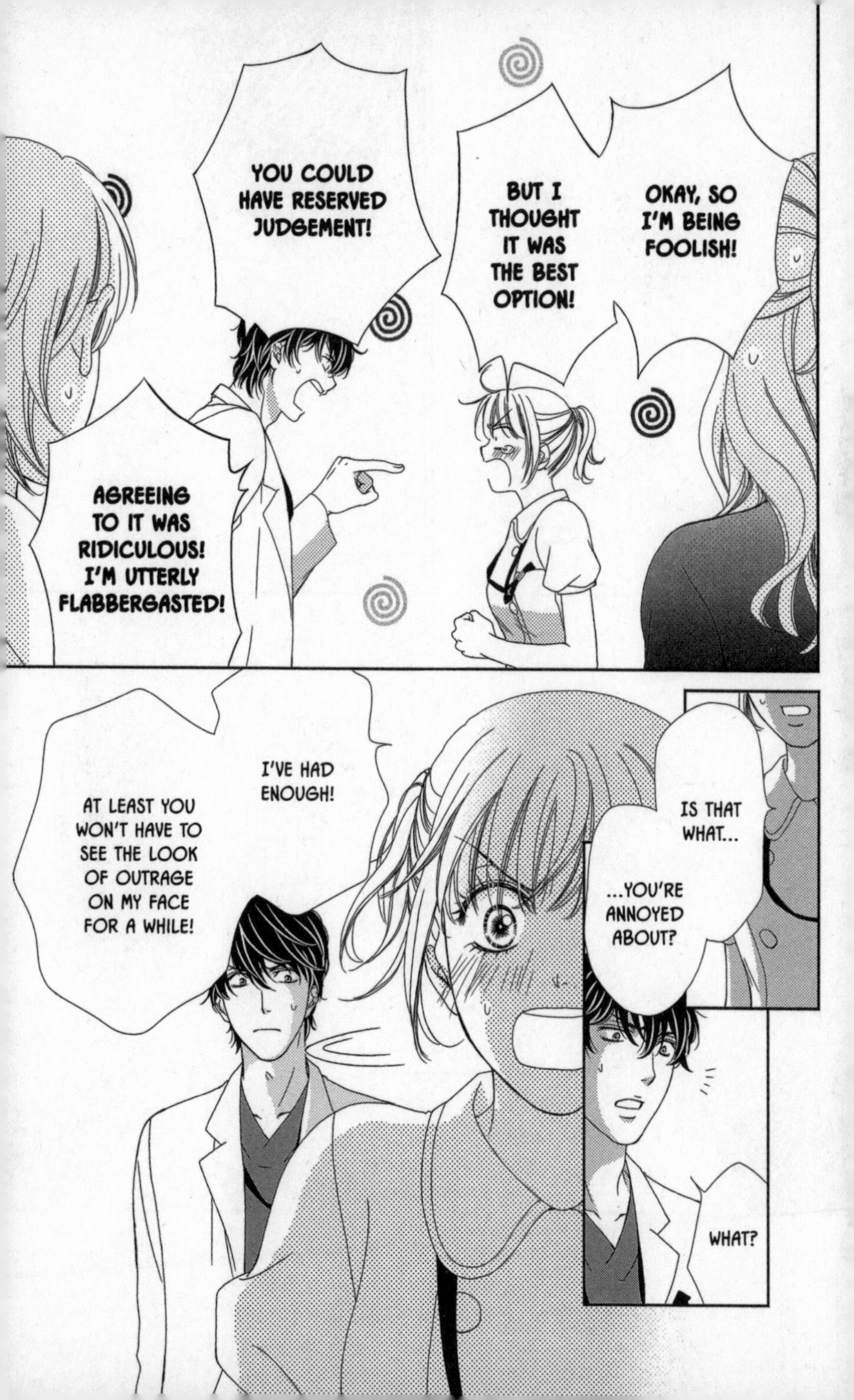
OKAY, SO I'M BEING FOOLISH!
BUT I THOUGHT IT WAS THE BEST OPTION!
YOU COULD HAVE RESERVED JUDGEMENT!
AGREEING TO IT WAS RIDICULOUS! I'M UTTERLY FLABBERGASTED!
IS THAT WHAT...
...YOU'RE ANNOYED ABOUT?
WHAT?
I'VE HAD ENOUGH!
AT LEAST YOU WON'T HAVE TO SEE THE LOOK OF OUTRAGE ON MY FACE FOR A WHILE!

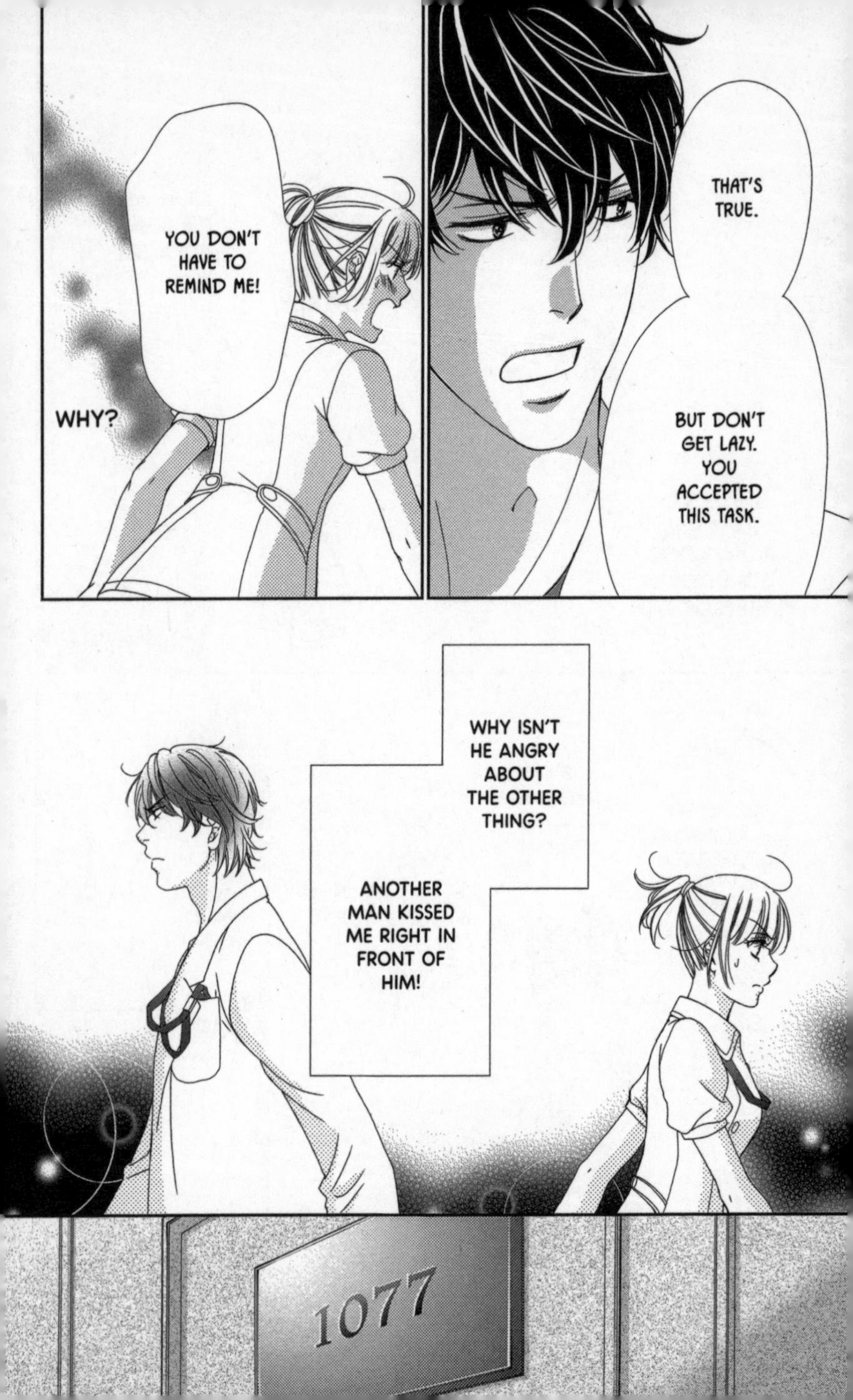
THAT'S TRUE.
BUT DON'T GET LAZY. YOU ACCEPTED THIS TASK.
YOU DON'T HAVE TO REMIND ME!
WHY?
WHY ISN'T HE ANGRY ABOUT THE OTHER THING?
ANOTHER MAN KISSED ME RIGHT IN FRONT OF HIM!
1077

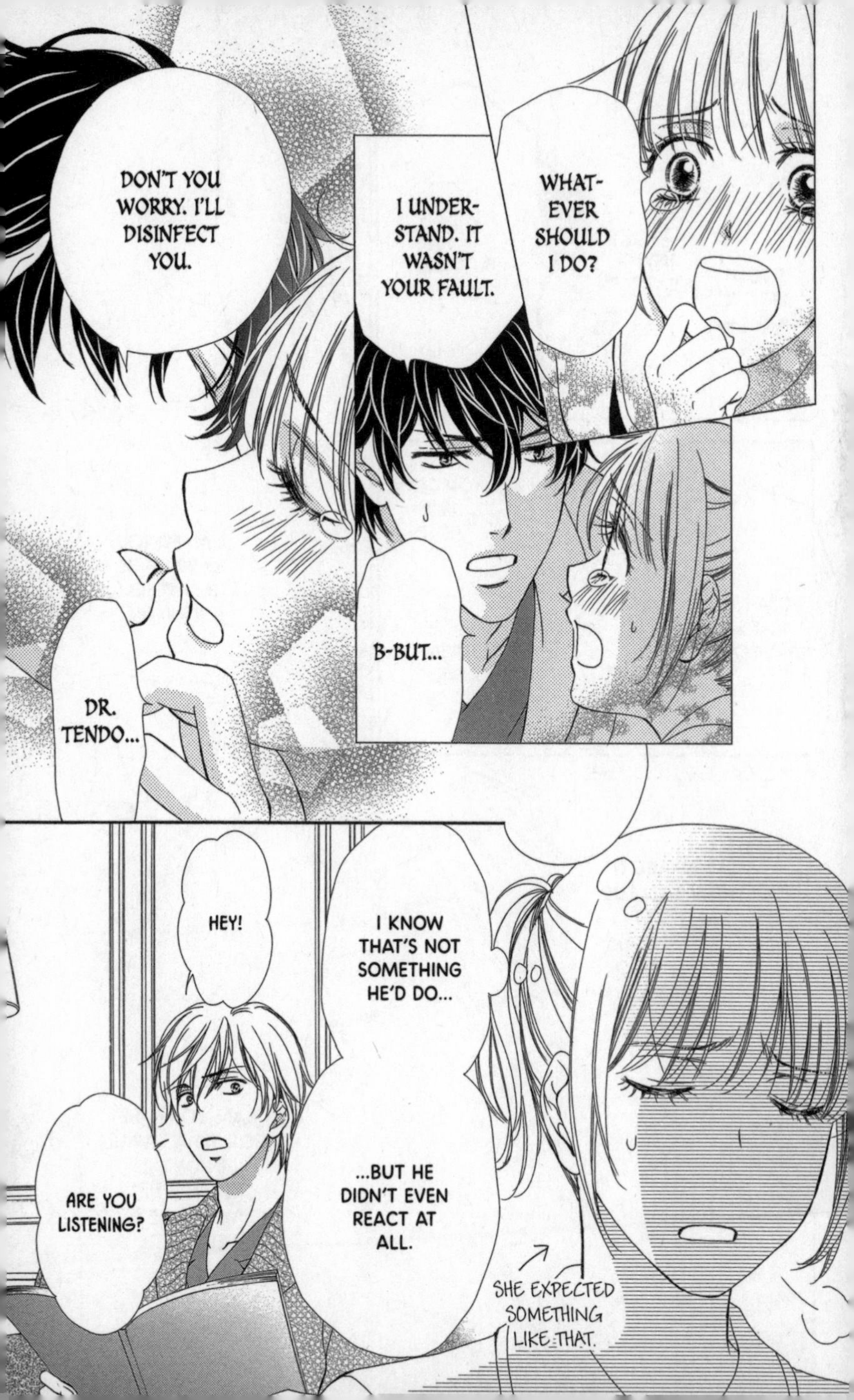
WHAT-EVER SHOULD I DO?
I UNDER-STAND. IT WASN'T YOUR FAULT.
B-BUT...
DON'T YOU WORRY. I'LL DISINFECT YOU.
DR. TENDO...
I KNOW THAT'S NOT SOMETHING HE'D DO...
...BUT HE DIDN'T EVEN REACT AT ALL.
SHE EXPECTED SOMETHING LIKE THAT.
HEY!
ARE YOU LISTENING?

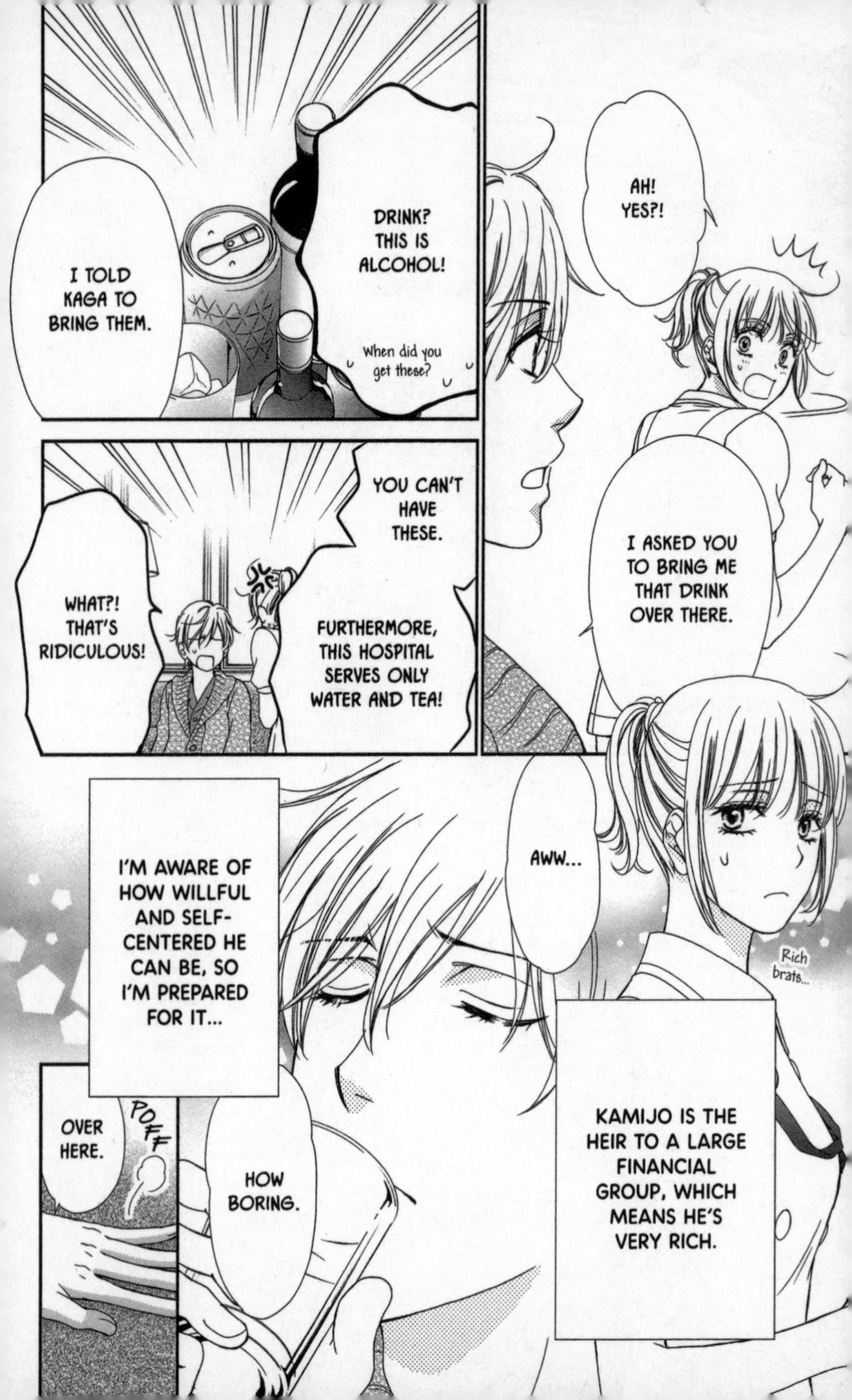
AH! YES?!
I ASKED YOU TO BRING ME THAT DRINK OVER THERE.
DRINK? THIS IS ALCOHOL!
When did you get these?
I TOLD KAGA TO BRING THEM.
YOU CAN'T HAVE THESE.
FURTHERMORE, THIS HOSPITAL SERVES ONLY WATER AND TEA!
WHAT?! THAT'S RIDICULOUS!
AWW...
Rich brats...
KAMIJO IS THE HEIR TO A LARGE FINANCIAL GROUP, WHICH MEANS HE'S VERY RICH.
I'M AWARE OF HOW WILLFUL AND SELF-CENTERED HE CAN BE, SO I'M PREPARED FOR IT...
HOW BORING.
OVER HERE.
POFF

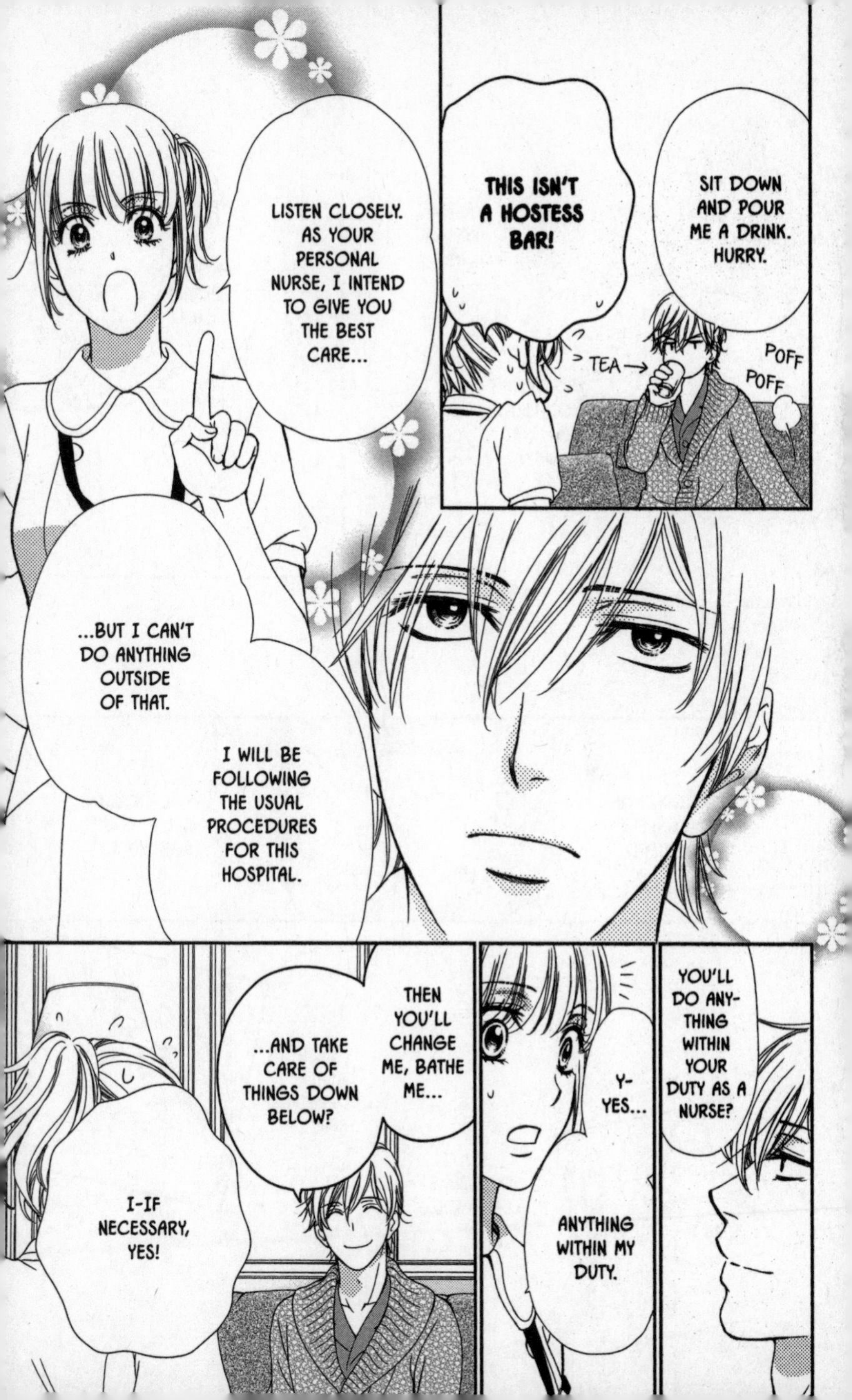
SIT DOWN AND POUR ME A DRINK. HURRY.
THIS ISN'T A HOSTESS BAR!
TEA
POFF POFF
LISTEN CLOSELY. AS YOUR PERSONAL NURSE, I INTEND TO GIVE YOU THE BEST CARE...
...BUT I CAN'T DO ANYTHING OUTSIDE OF THAT.
I WILL BE FOLLOWING THE USUAL PROCEDURES FOR THIS HOSPITAL.
YOU'LL DO ANYTHING WITHIN YOUR DUTY AS A NURSE?
Y-YES...
ANYTHING WITHIN MY DUTY.
THEN YOU'LL CHANGE ME, BATHE ME...
...AND TAKE CARE OF THINGS DOWN BELOW?
I-IF NECESSARY, YES!

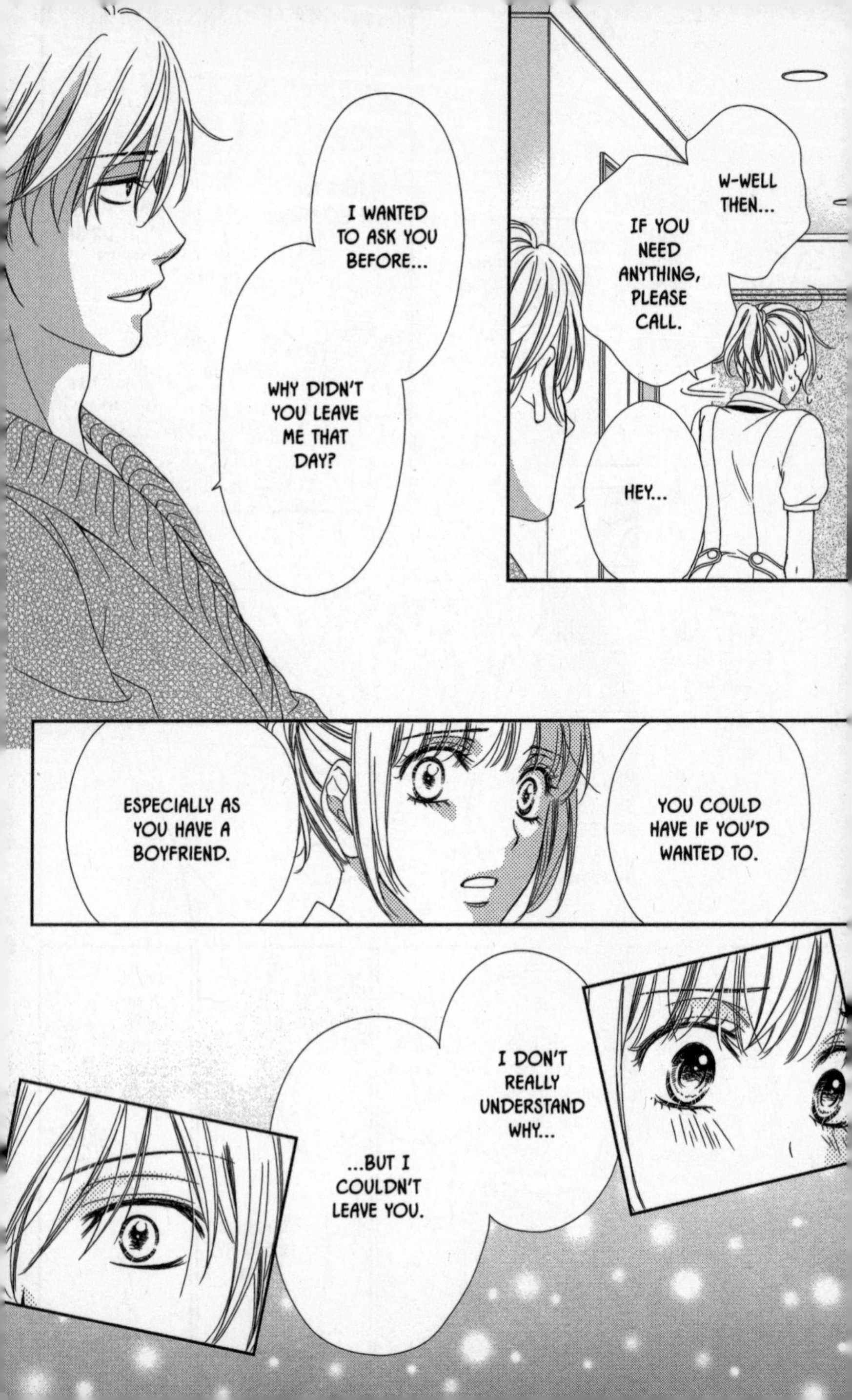
W-WELL THEN...
IF YOU NEED ANYTHING, PLEASE CALL.
HEY...
I WANTED TO ASK YOU BEFORE...
WHY DIDN'T YOU LEAVE ME THAT DAY?
YOU COULD HAVE IF YOU'D WANTED TO.
ESPECIALLY AS YOU HAVE A BOYFRIEND.
I DON'T REALLY UNDERSTAND WHY...
...BUT I COULDN'T LEAVE YOU.

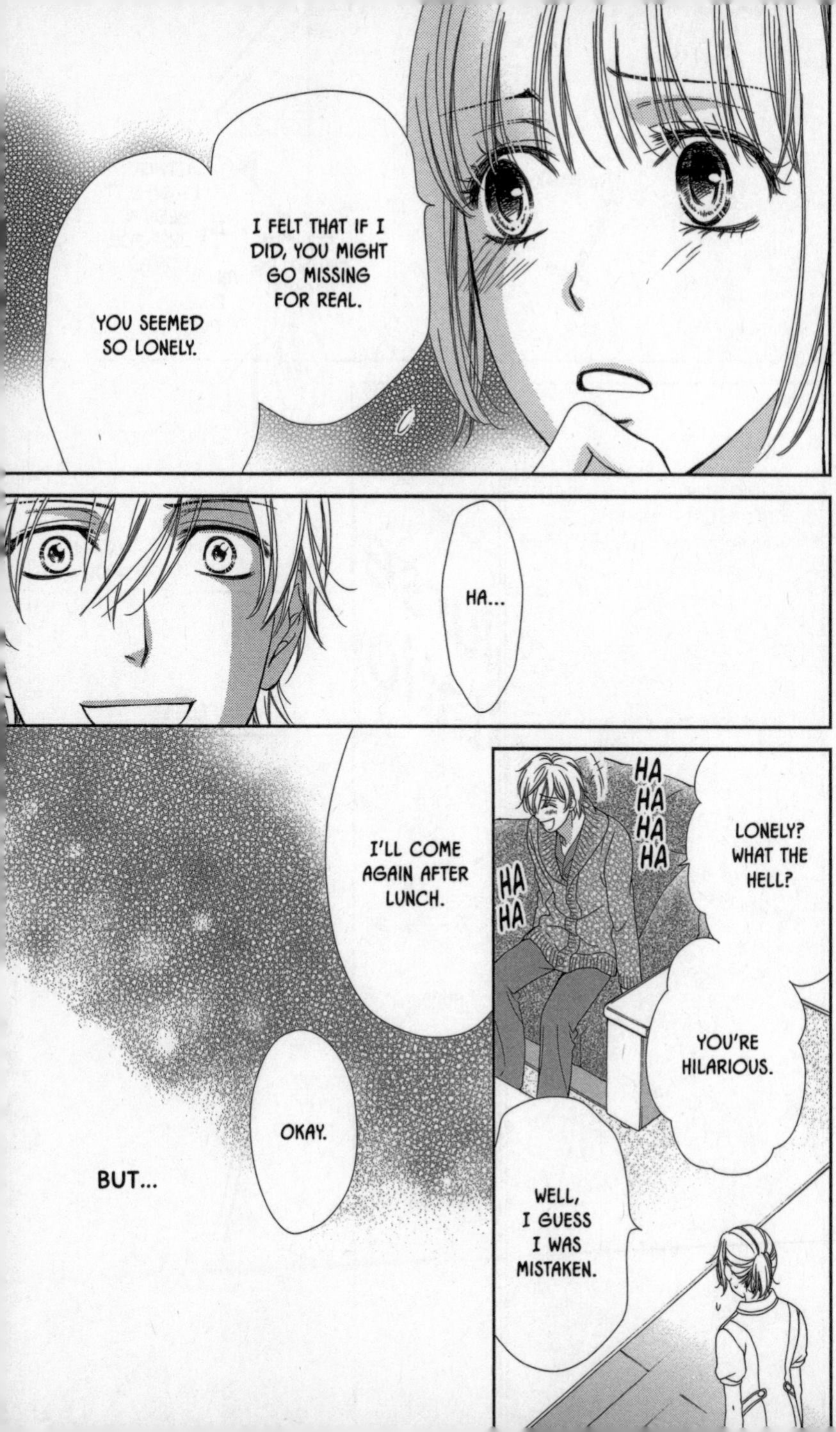
I FELT THAT IF I DID, YOU MIGHT GO MISSING FOR REAL.
YOU SEEMED SO LONELY.
HA...
LONELY? WHAT THE HELL?
HA HA HA HA
HA HA
YOU'RE HILARIOUS.
WELL, I GUESS I WAS MISTAKEN.
I'LL COME AGAIN AFTER LUNCH.
OKAY.
BUT...

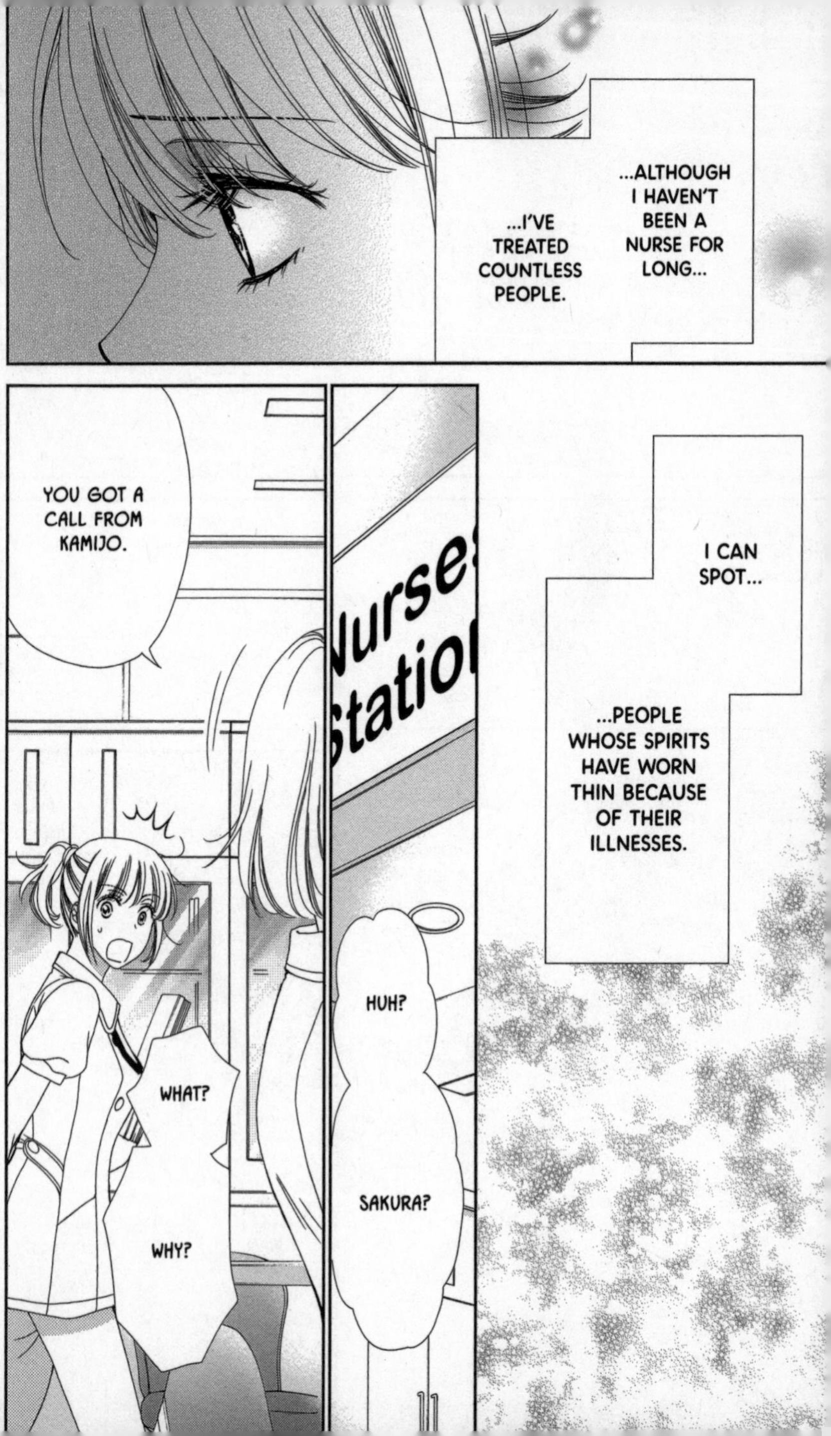
...ALTHOUGH I HAVEN'T BEEN A NURSE FOR LONG...
...I'VE TREATED COUNTLESS PEOPLE.
I CAN SPOT...
...PEOPLE WHOSE SPIRITS HAVE WORN THIN BECAUSE OF THEIR ILLNESSES.
HUH?
SAKURA?
YOU GOT A CALL FROM KAMIJO.
WHAT?
WHY?

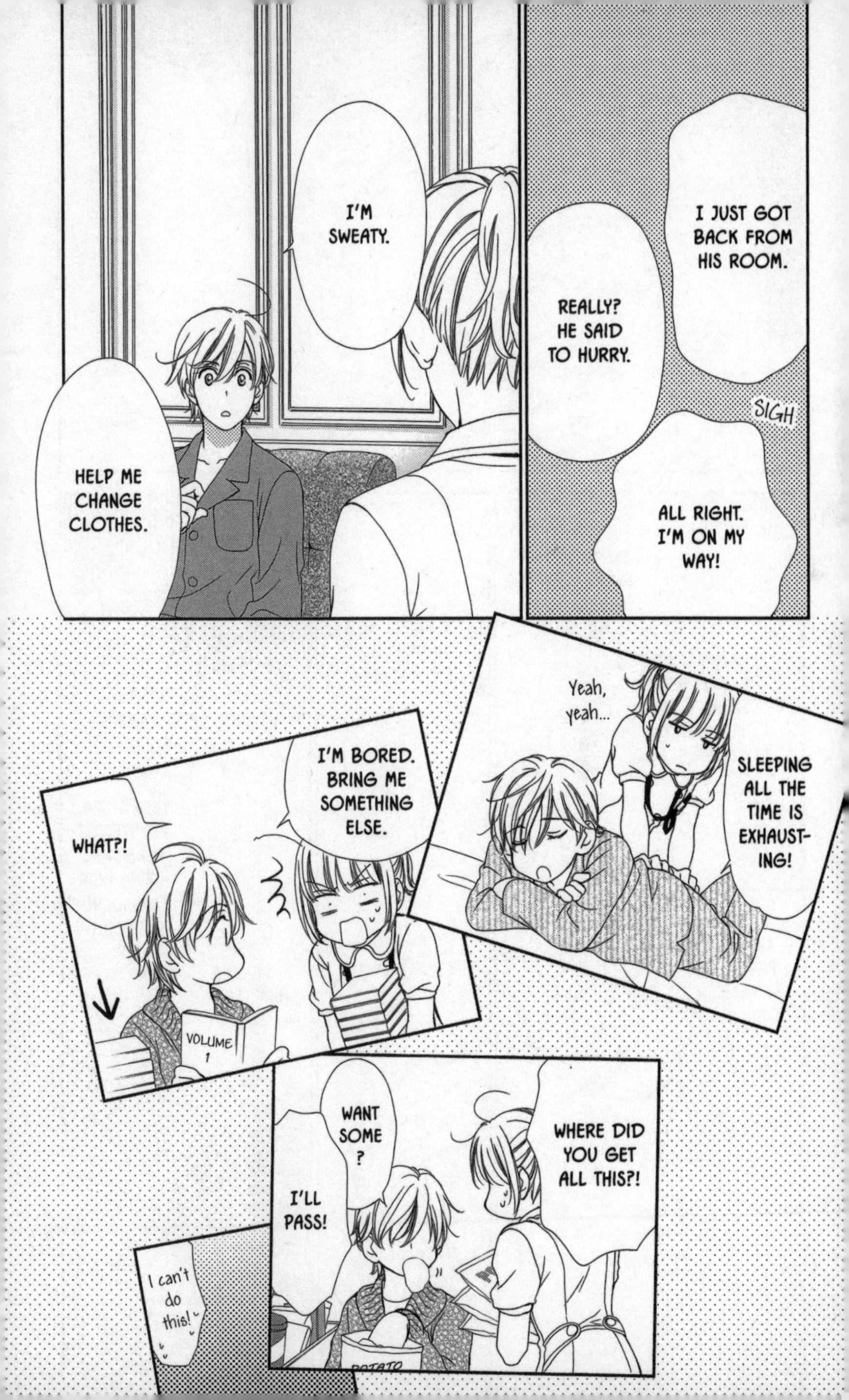

I JUST GOT BACK FROM HIS ROOM.
REALLY? HE SAID TO HURRY.
SIGH
ALL RIGHT. I'M ON MY WAY!
I'M SWEATY.
HELP ME CHANGE CLOTHES.
SLEEPING ALL THE TIME IS EXHAUSTING!
Yeah, yeah...
I'M BORED. BRING ME SOMETHING ELSE.
WHAT?!
VOLUME 1
WHERE DID YOU GET ALL THIS?!
WANT SOME?
I'LL PASS!
I can't do this!

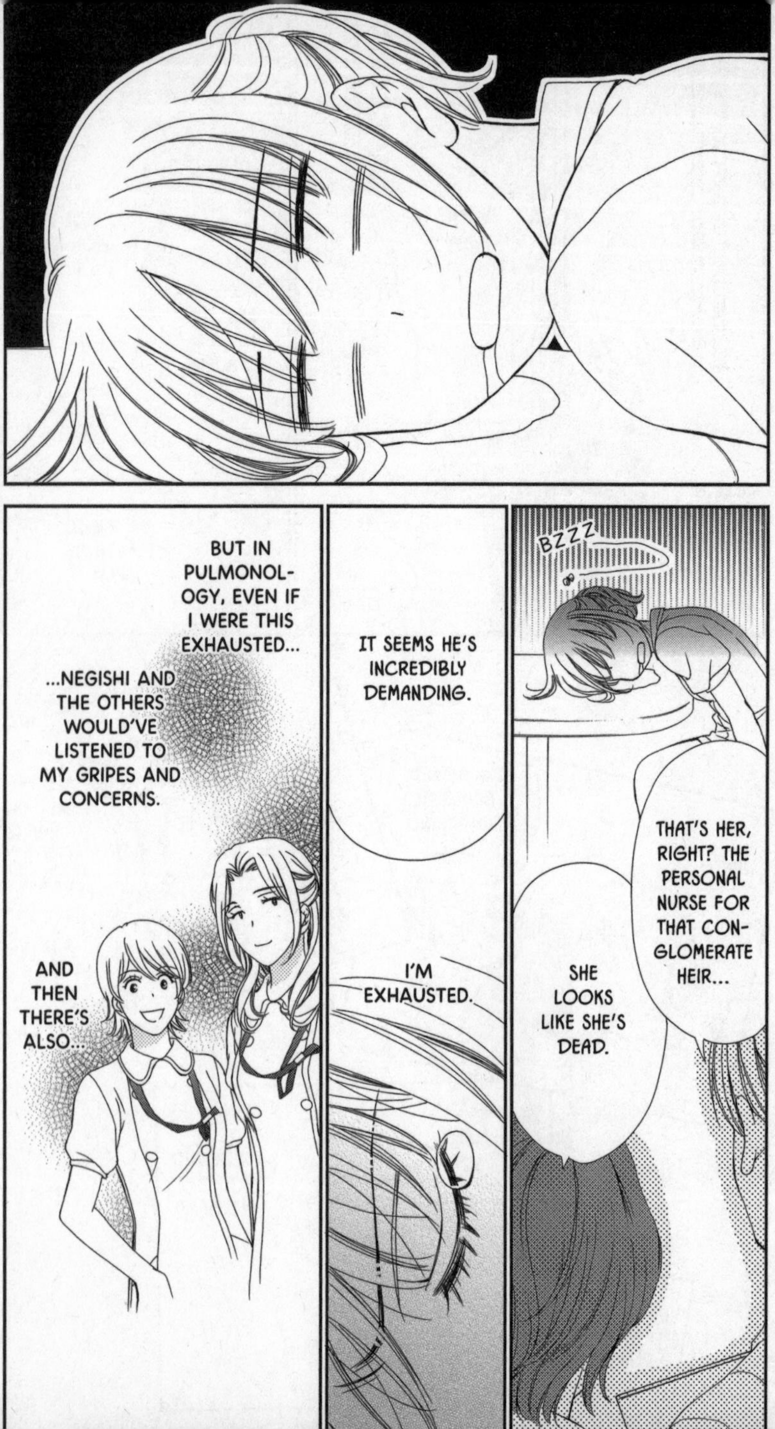
BZZZ
THAT'S HER, RIGHT? THE PERSONAL NURSE FOR THAT CONGLOMERATE HEIR...
SHE LOOKS LIKE SHE'S DEAD.
IT SEEMS HE'S INCREDIBLY DEMANDING.
I'M EXHAUSTED.
BUT IN PULMONOLOGY, EVEN IF I WERE THIS EXHAUSTED...
...NEGISHI AND THE OTHERS WOULD'VE LISTENED TO MY GRIPES AND CONCERNS.
AND THEN THERE'S ALSO...

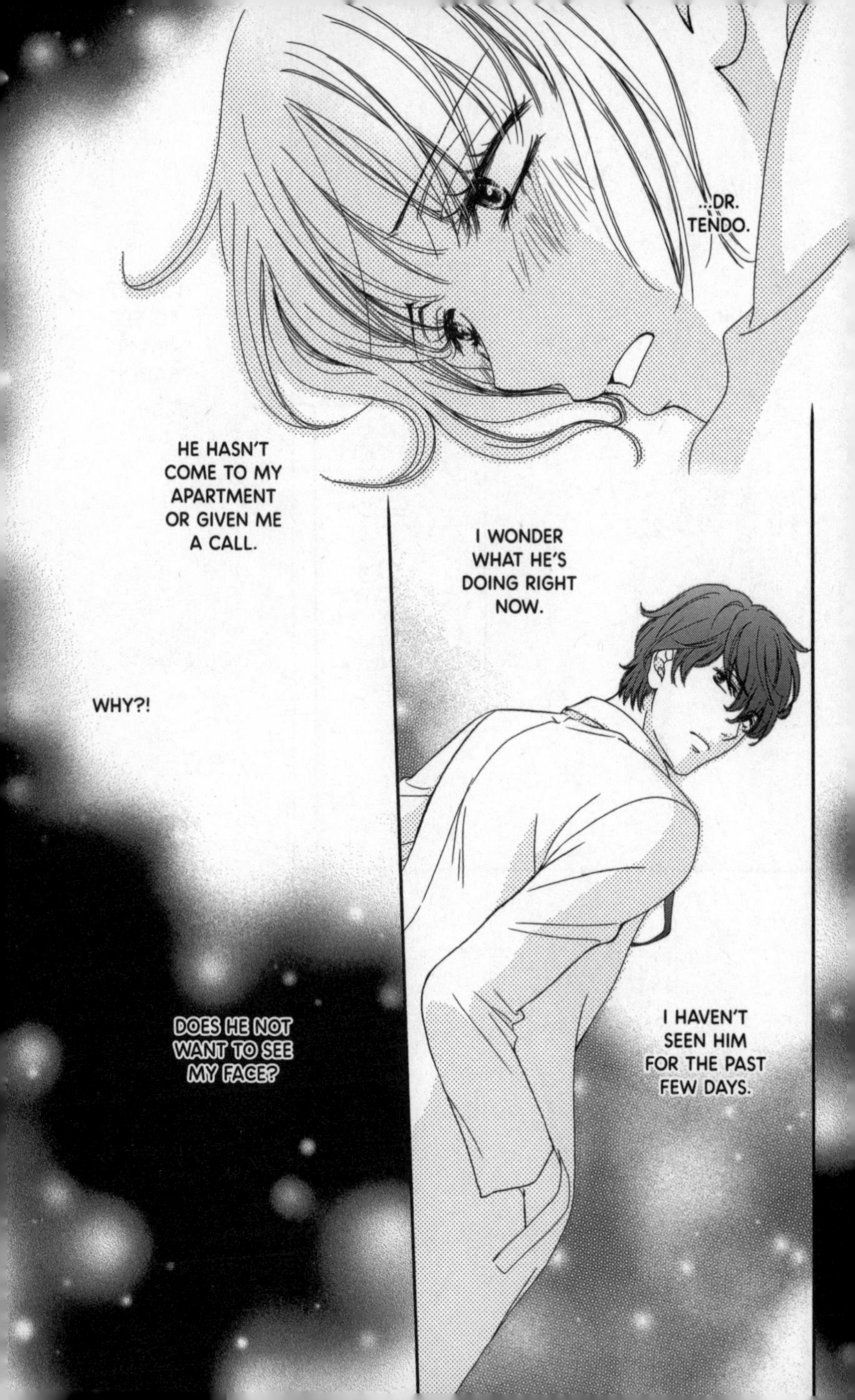
...DR. TENDO.
I WONDER WHAT HE'S DOING RIGHT NOW.
I HAVEN'T SEEN HIM FOR THE PAST FEW DAYS.
HE HASN'T COME TO MY APARTMENT OR GIVEN ME A CALL.
WHY?!
DOES HE NOT WANT TO SEE MY FACE?

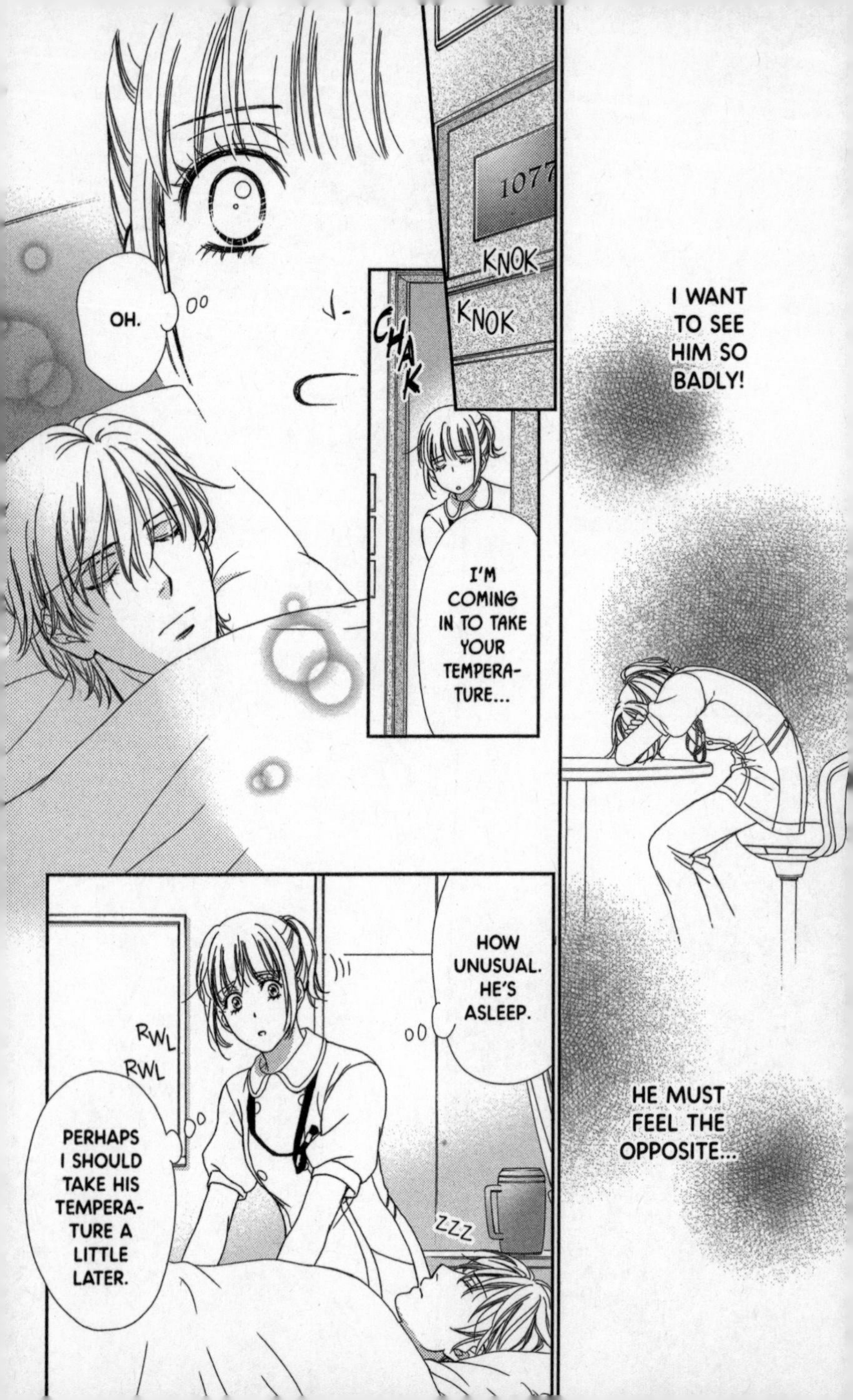
I WANT TO SEE HIM SO BADLY!
HE MUST FEEL THE OPPOSITE...
1077
KNOK
KNOK
CHAK
I'M COMING IN TO TAKE YOUR TEMPERATURE...
OH.
HOW UNUSUAL. HE'S ASLEEP.
RWL
RWL
PERHAPS I SHOULD TAKE HIS TEMPERATURE A LITTLE LATER.
ZZZ

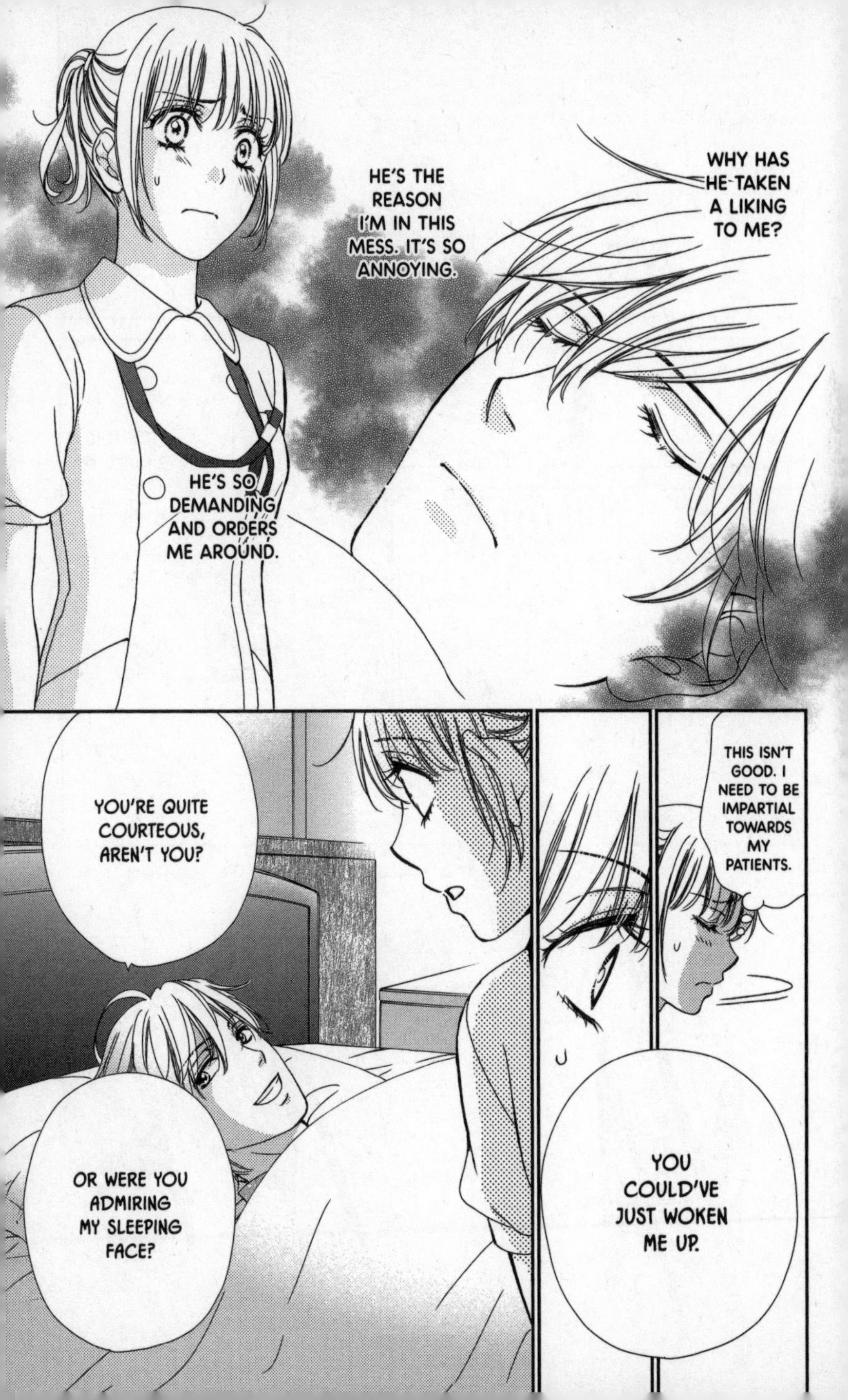
WHY HAS HE TAKEN A LIKING TO ME?
HE'S THE REASON I'M IN THIS MESS. IT'S SO ANNOYING.
HE'S SO DEMANDING AND ORDERS ME AROUND.
THIS ISN'T GOOD. I NEED TO BE IMPARTIAL TOWARDS MY PATIENTS.
YOU COULD'VE JUST WOKEN ME UP.
YOU'RE QUITE COURTEOUS, AREN'T YOU?
OR WERE YOU ADMIRING MY SLEEPING FACE?

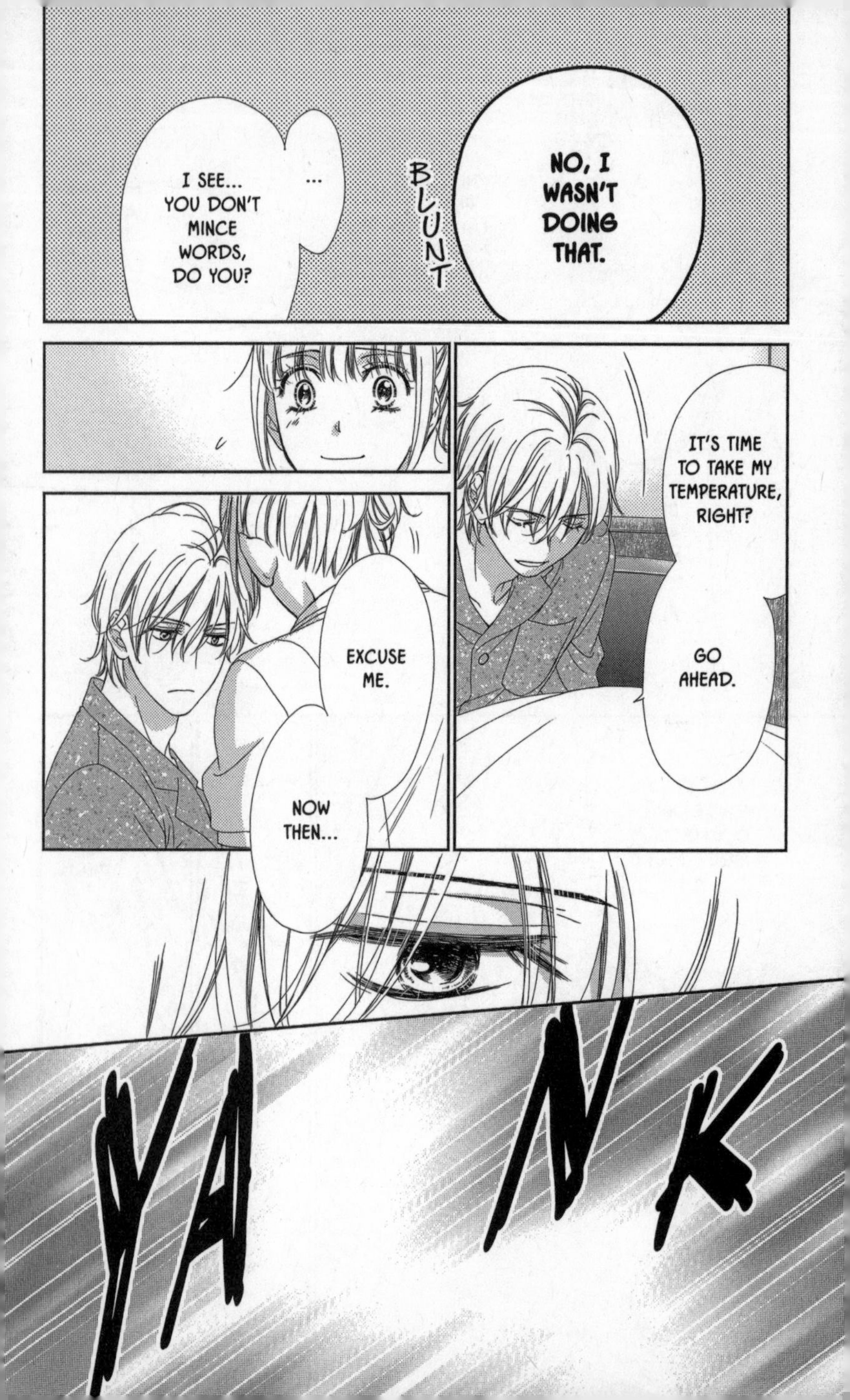
NO, I WASN'T DOING THAT.
BLUNT
...
I SEE... YOU DON'T MINCE WORDS, DO YOU?
IT'S TIME TO TAKE MY TEMPERATURE, RIGHT?
GO AHEAD.
EXCUSE ME.
NOW THEN...
YANK

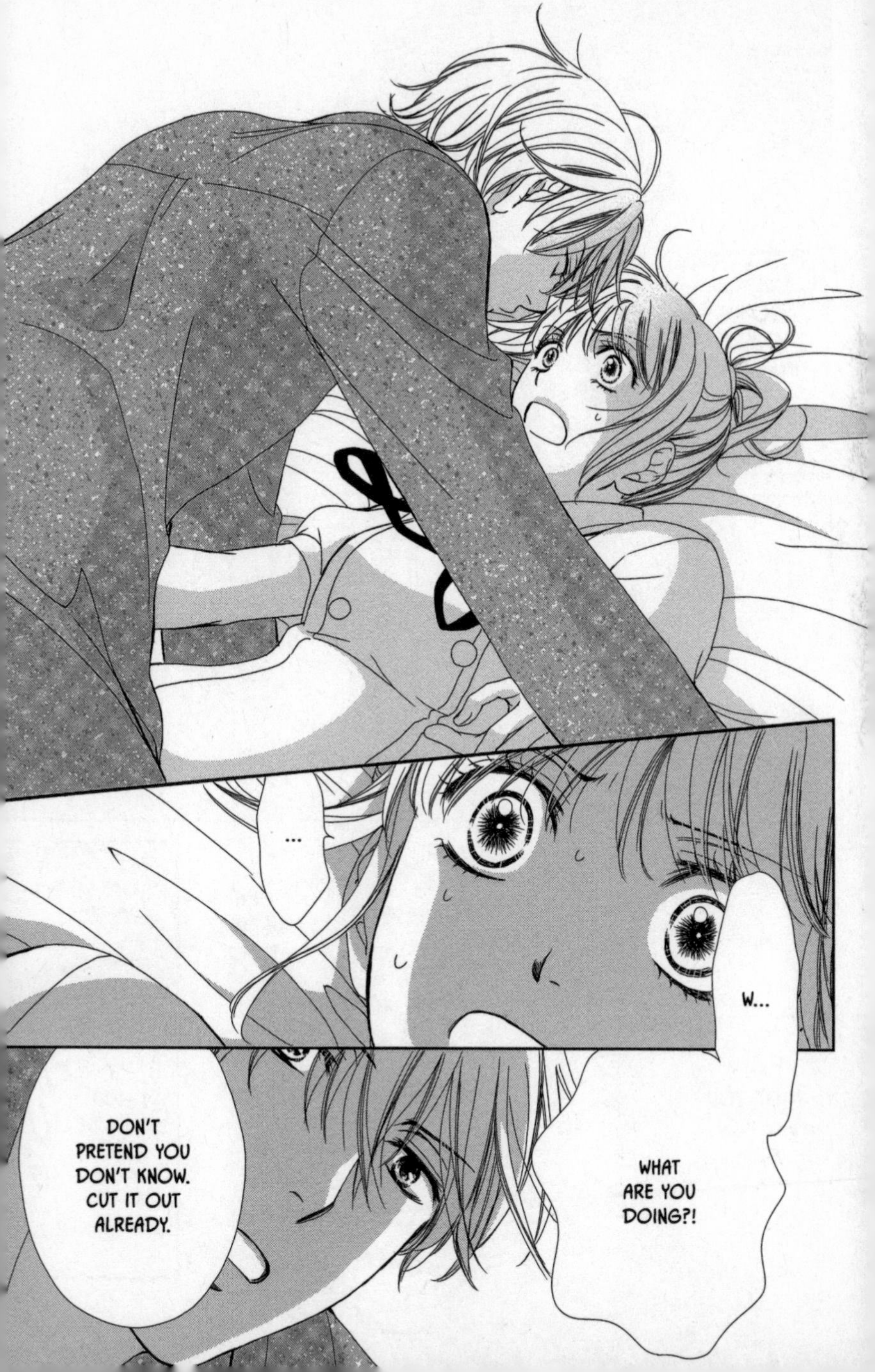
W...
...
WHAT ARE YOU DOING?!
DON'T PRETEND YOU DON'T KNOW. CUT IT OUT ALREADY.

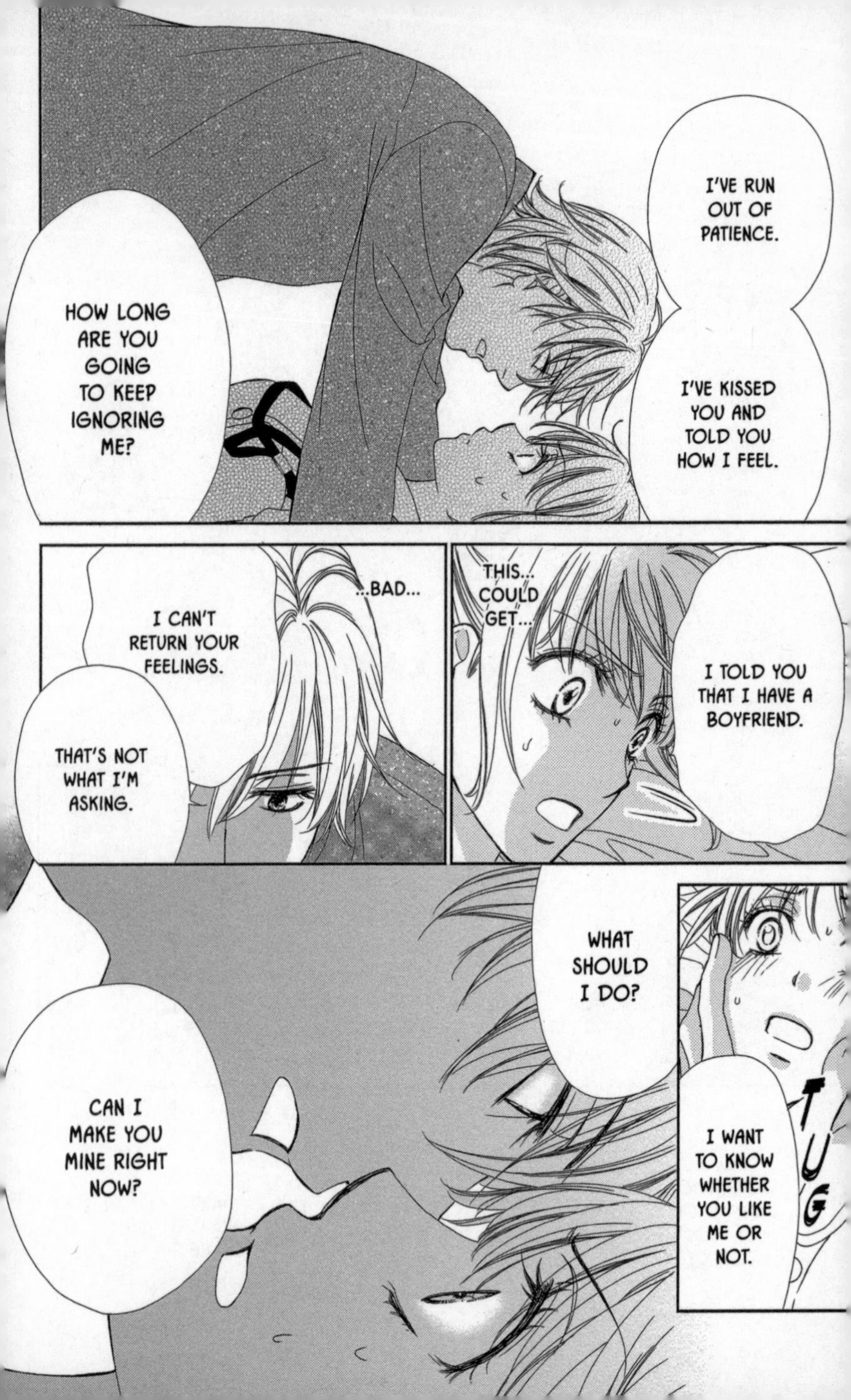
I'VE RUN OUT OF PATIENCE.
I'VE KISSED YOU AND TOLD YOU HOW I FEEL.
HOW LONG ARE YOU GOING TO KEEP IGNORING ME?
I TOLD YOU THAT I HAVE A BOYFRIEND.
THIS... COULD GET...
...BAD...
I CAN'T RETURN YOUR FEELINGS.
THAT'S NOT WHAT I'M ASKING.
TUG
I WANT TO KNOW WHETHER YOU LIKE ME OR NOT.
WHAT SHOULD I DO?
CAN I MAKE YOU MINE RIGHT NOW?

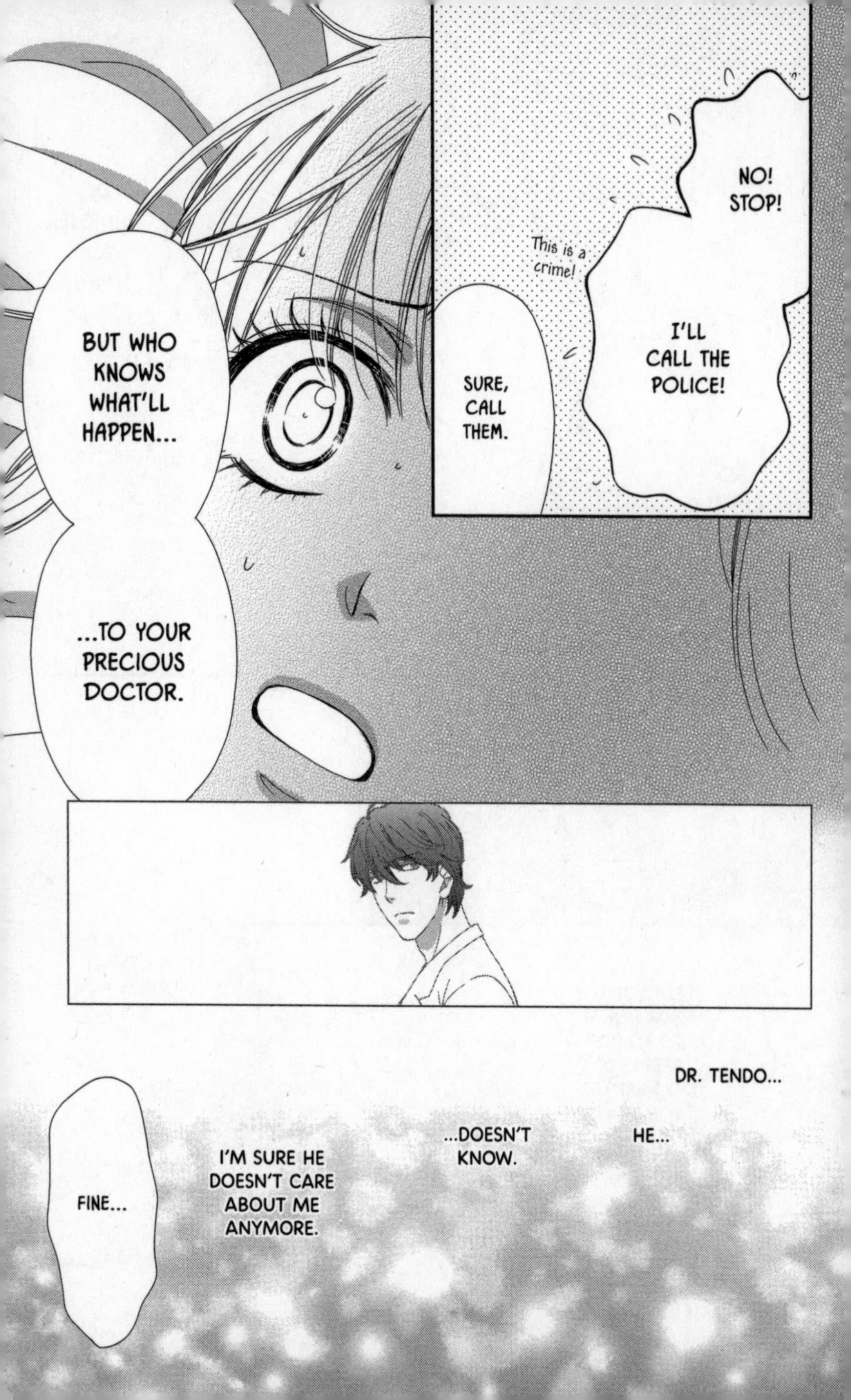
NO! STOP!
This is a crime!
I'LL CALL THE POLICE!
SURE, CALL THEM.
BUT WHO KNOWS WHAT'LL HAPPEN...
...TO YOUR PRECIOUS DOCTOR.
DR. TENDO...
HE...
...DOESN'T KNOW.
I'M SURE HE DOESN'T CARE ABOUT ME ANYMORE.
FINE...

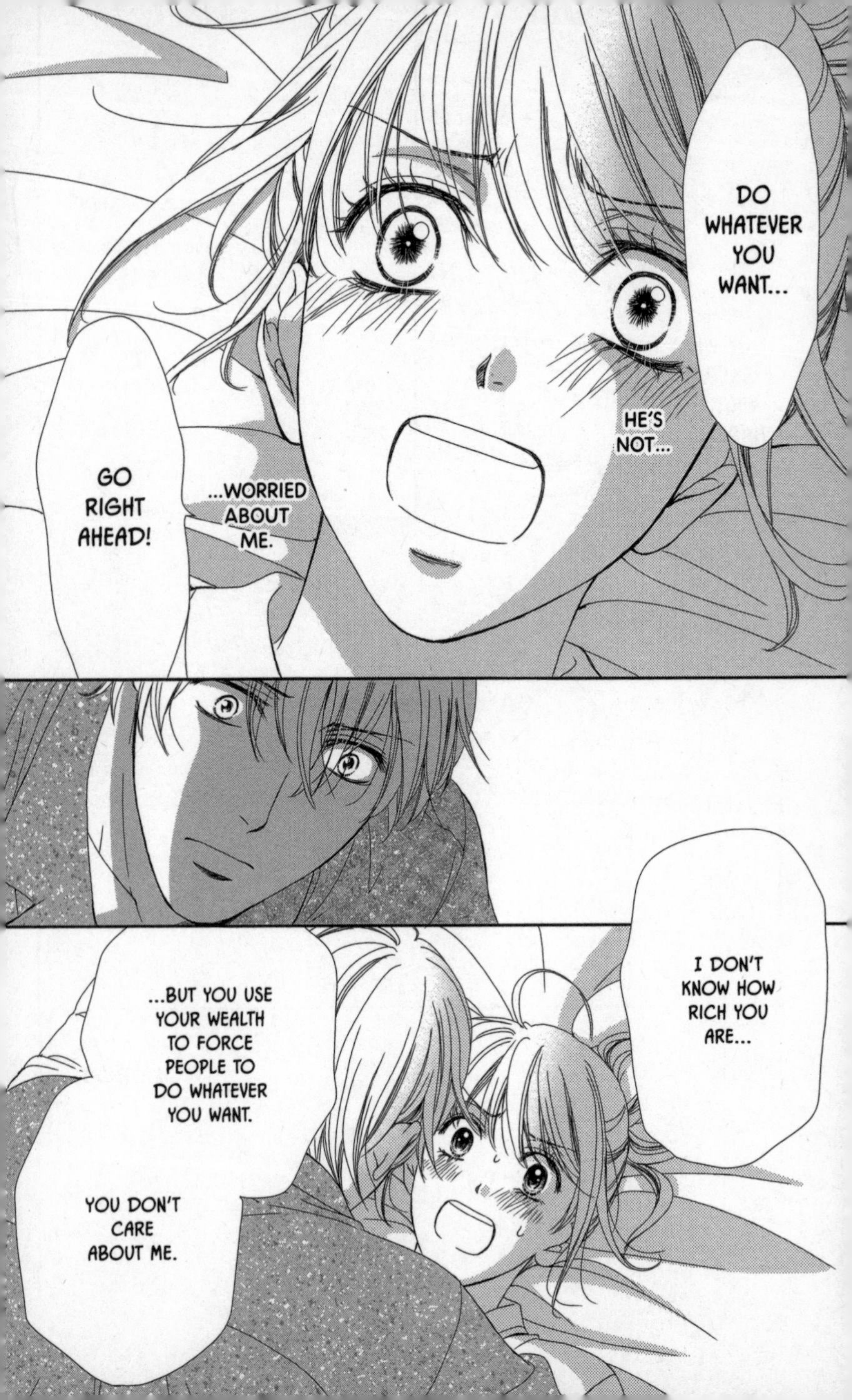
DO WHATEVER YOU WANT...
HE'S NOT...
...WORRIED ABOUT ME.
GO RIGHT AHEAD!
I DON'T KNOW HOW RICH YOU ARE...
...BUT YOU USE YOUR WEALTH TO FORCE PEOPLE TO DO WHATEVER YOU WANT.
YOU DON'T CARE ABOUT ME.

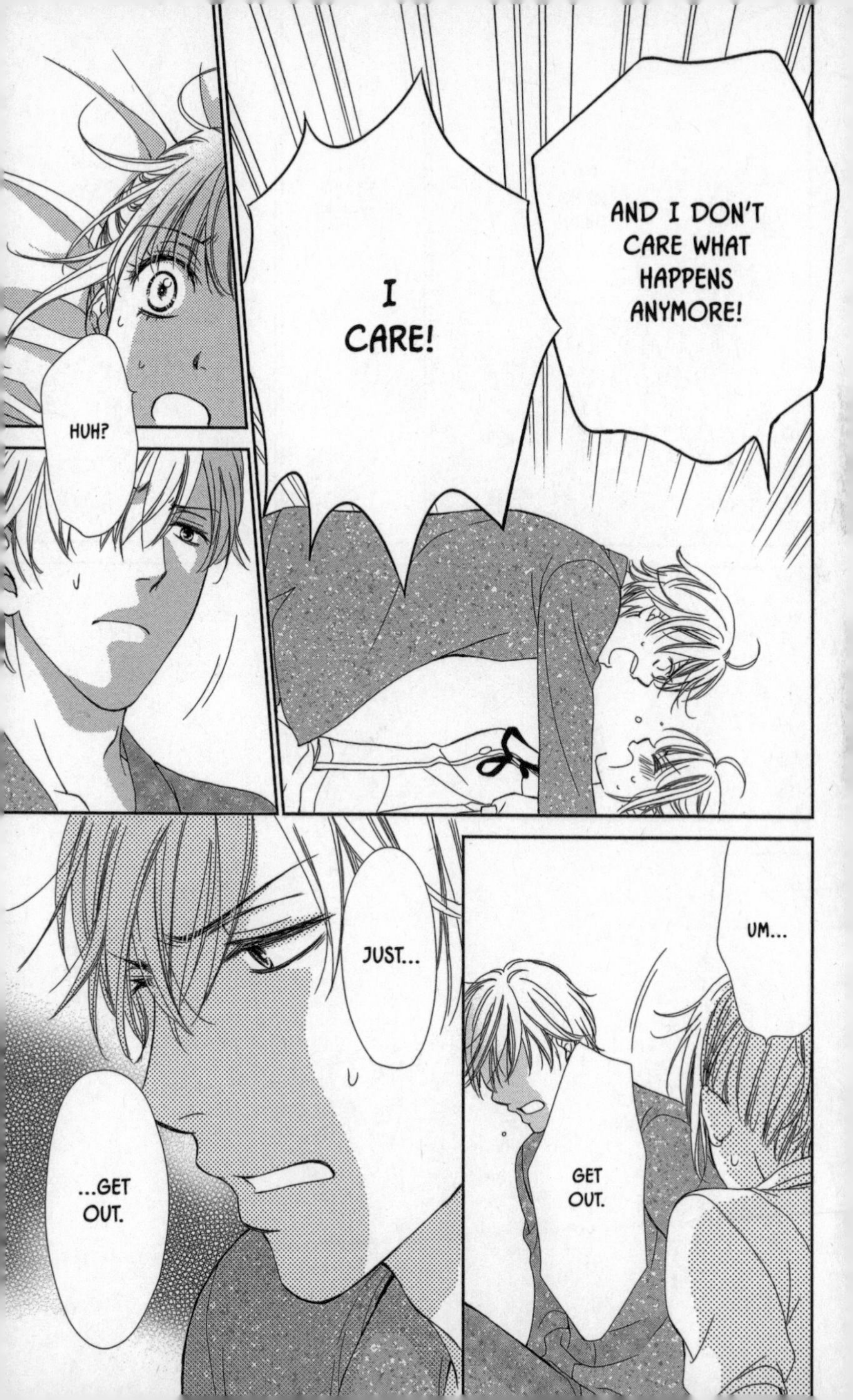
AND I DON'T CARE WHAT HAPPENS ANYMORE!
I CARE!
HUH?
UM...
GET OUT.
JUST...
...GET OUT.

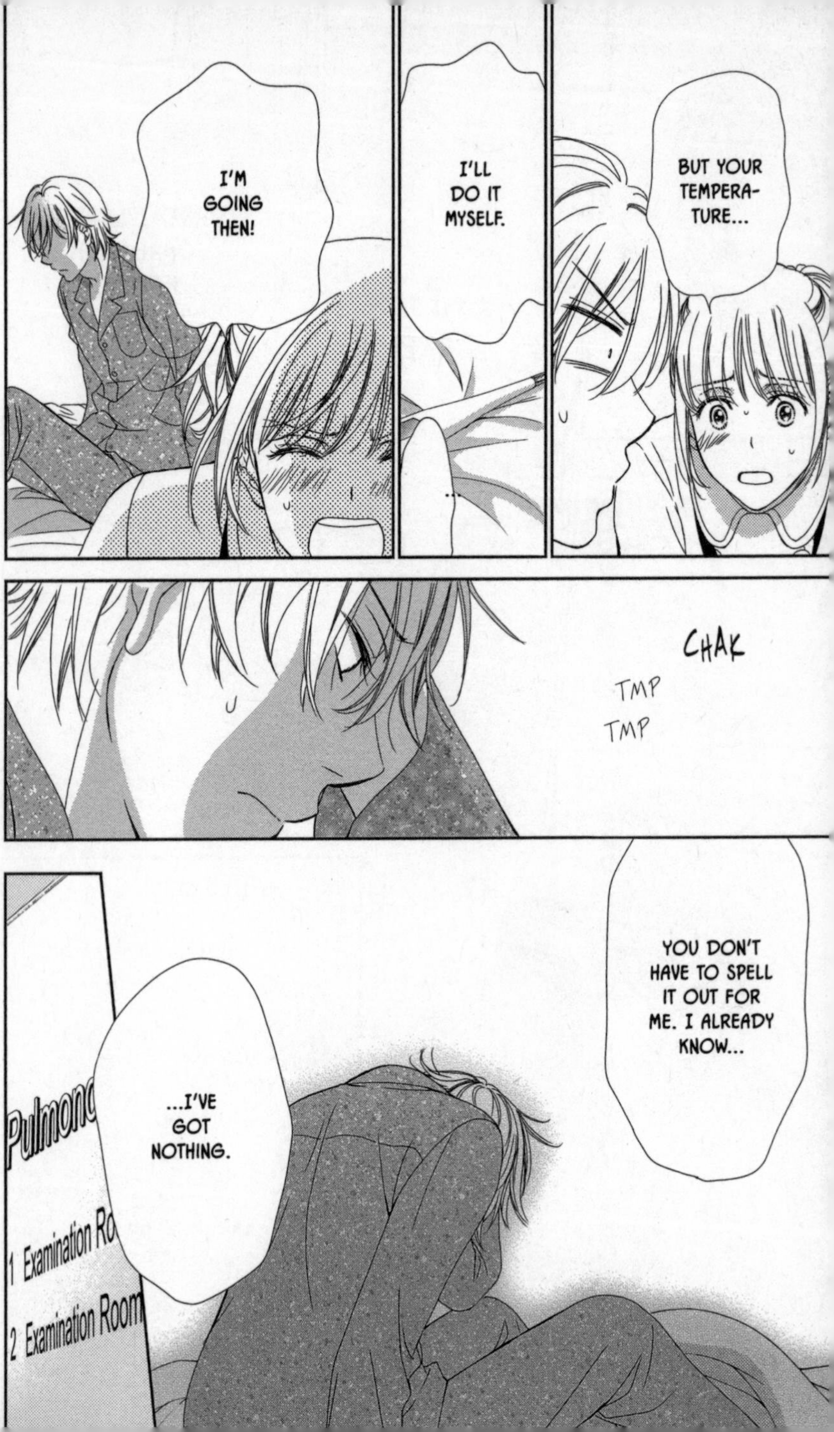
BUT YOUR TEMPERA-TURE...
I'LL DO IT MYSELF.
...
I'M GOING THEN!
CHAK
TMP TMP
YOU DON'T HAVE TO SPELL IT OUT FOR ME. I ALREADY KNOW...
...I'VE GOT NOTHING.
Pulmona
1 Examination Ro
2 Examination Room

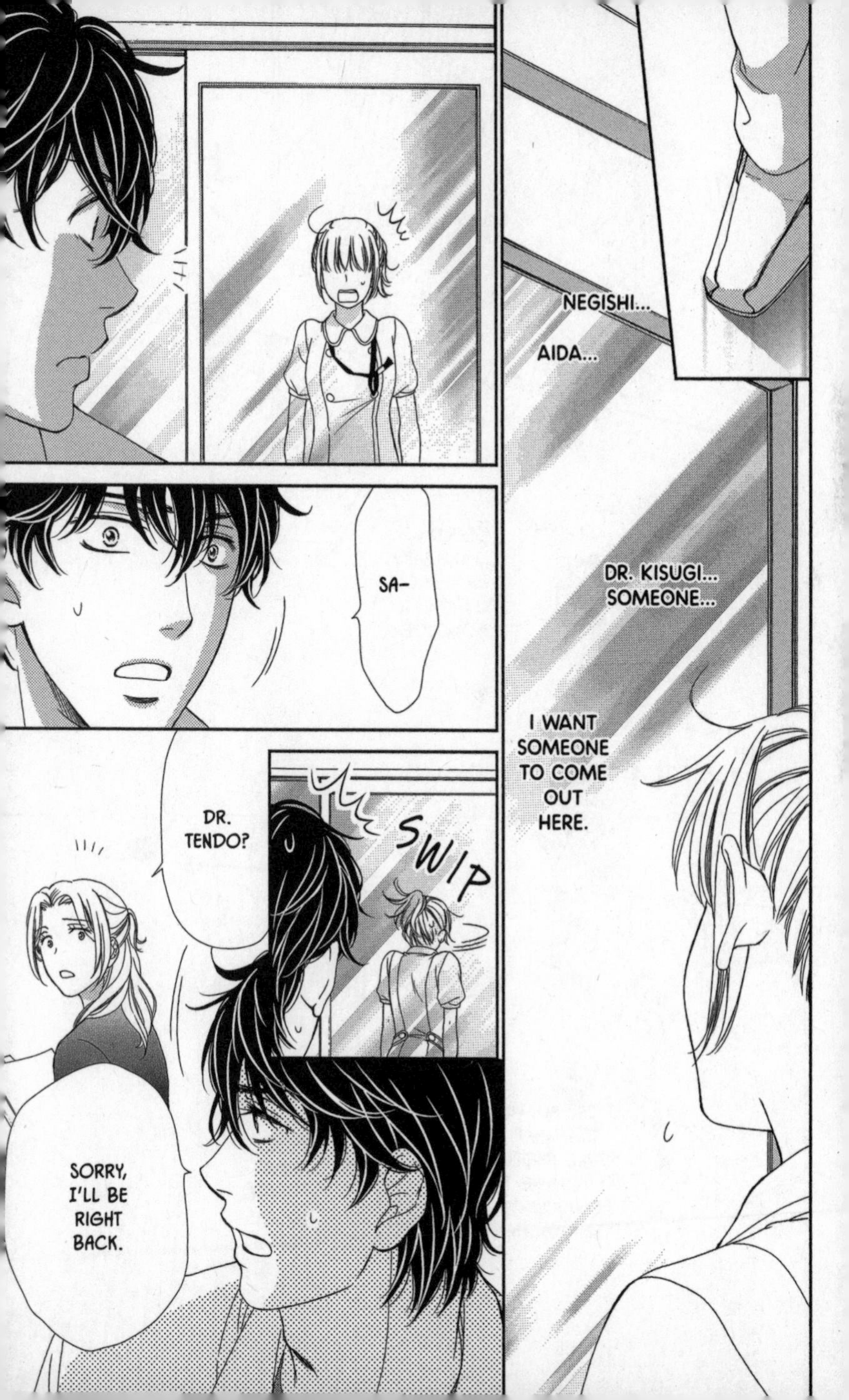
NEGISHI...
AIDA...
DR. KISUGI... SOMEONE...
I WANT SOMEONE TO COME OUT HERE.
SA-
SWIP
DR. TENDO?
SORRY, I'LL BE RIGHT BACK.

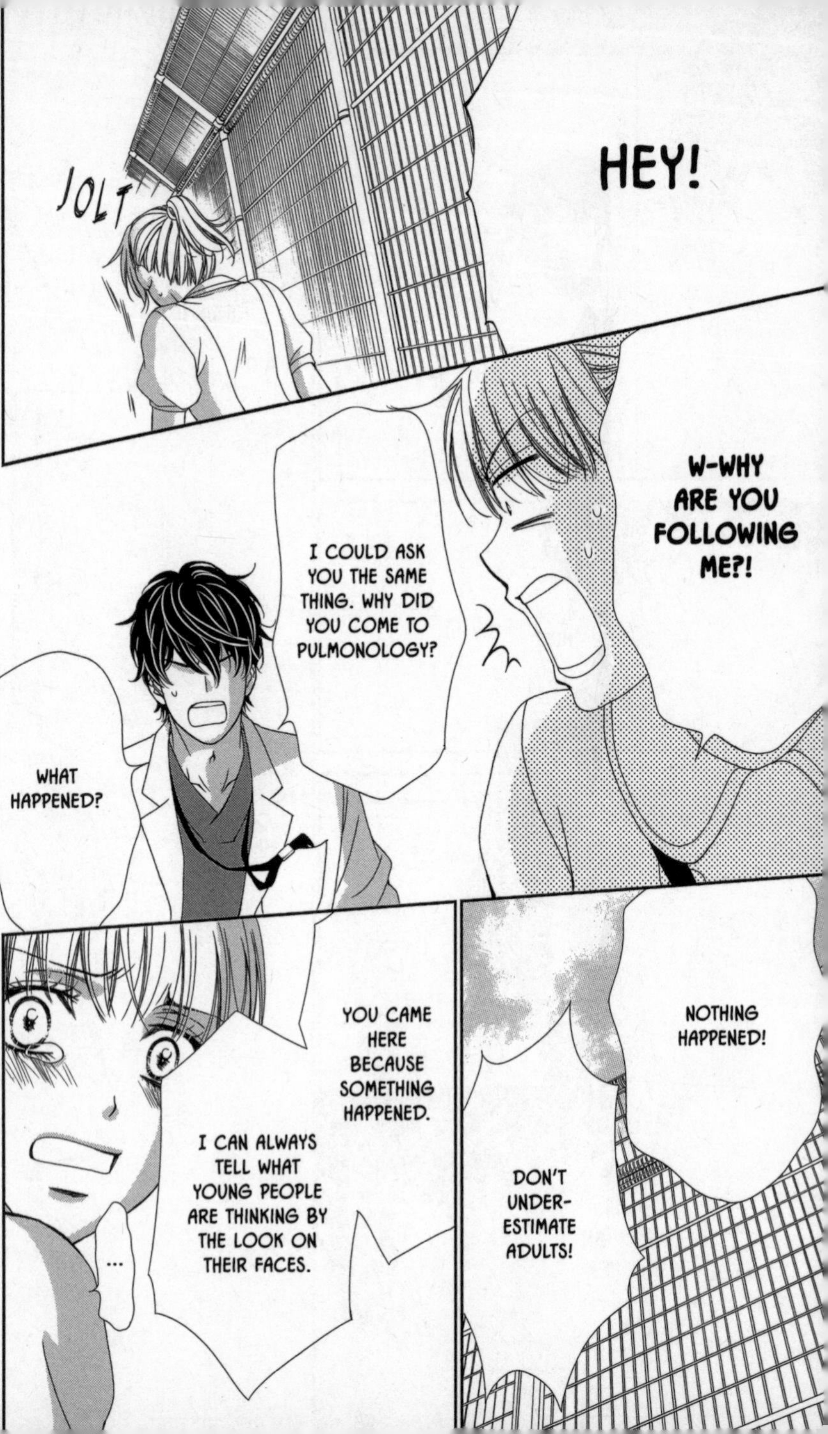
HEY!
JOLT
W-WHY ARE YOU FOLLOWING ME?!
I COULD ASK YOU THE SAME THING. WHY DID YOU COME TO PULMONOLOGY?
WHAT HAPPENED?
NOTHING HAPPENED!
DON'T UNDER-ESTIMATE ADULTS!
YOU CAME HERE BECAUSE SOMETHING HAPPENED.
I CAN ALWAYS TELL WHAT YOUNG PEOPLE ARE THINKING BY THE LOOK ON THEIR FACES.
...

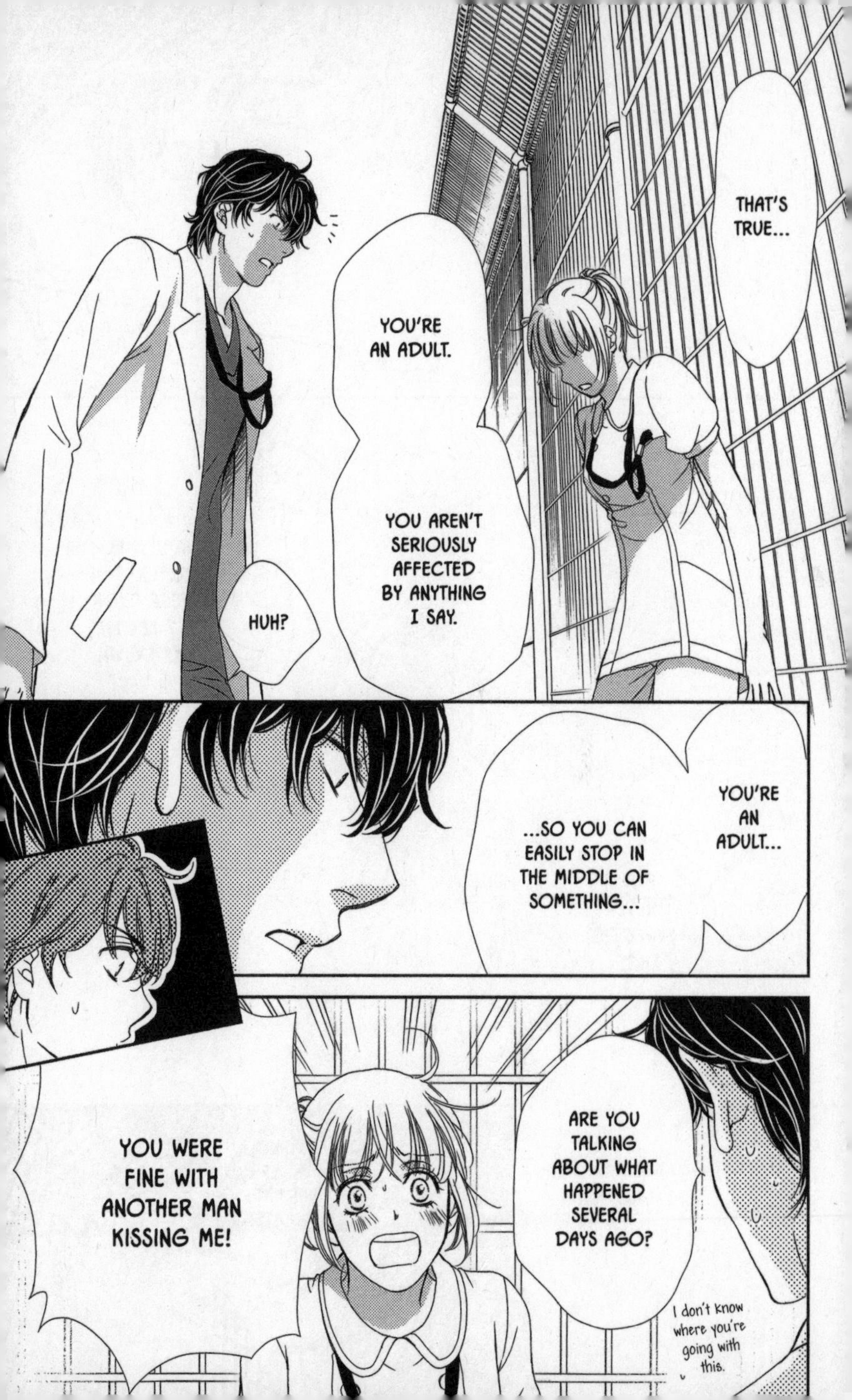
THAT'S TRUE...
YOU'RE AN ADULT.
YOU AREN'T SERIOUSLY AFFECTED BY ANYTHING I SAY.
HUH?
YOU'RE AN ADULT...
...SO YOU CAN EASILY STOP IN THE MIDDLE OF SOMETHING...
ARE YOU TALKING ABOUT WHAT HAPPENED SEVERAL DAYS AGO?
I don't know where you're going with this.
YOU WERE FINE WITH ANOTHER MAN KISSING ME!

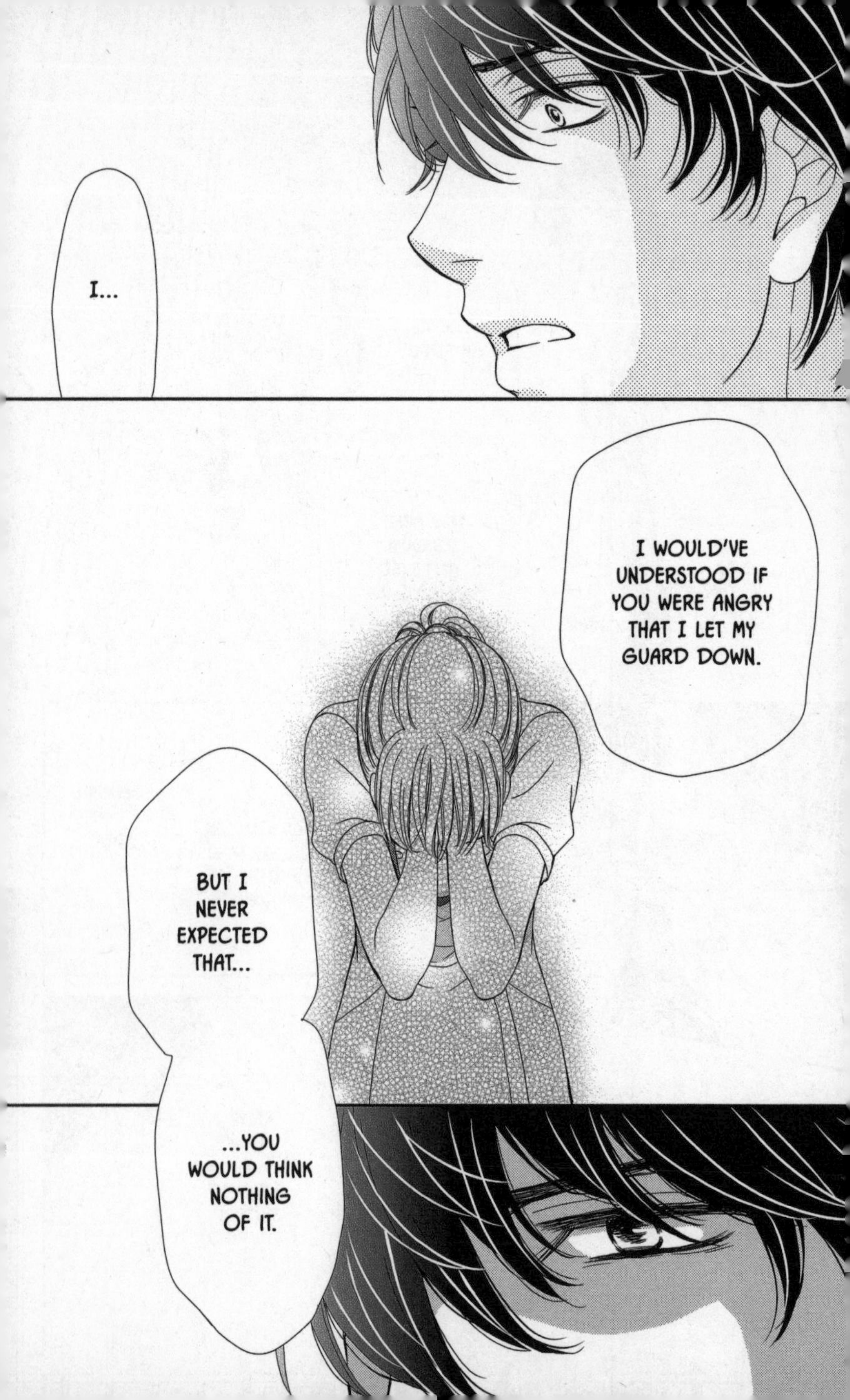
I...
I WOULD'VE UNDERSTOOD IF YOU WERE ANGRY THAT I LET MY GUARD DOWN.
BUT I NEVER EXPECTED THAT...
...YOU WOULD THINK NOTHING OF IT.

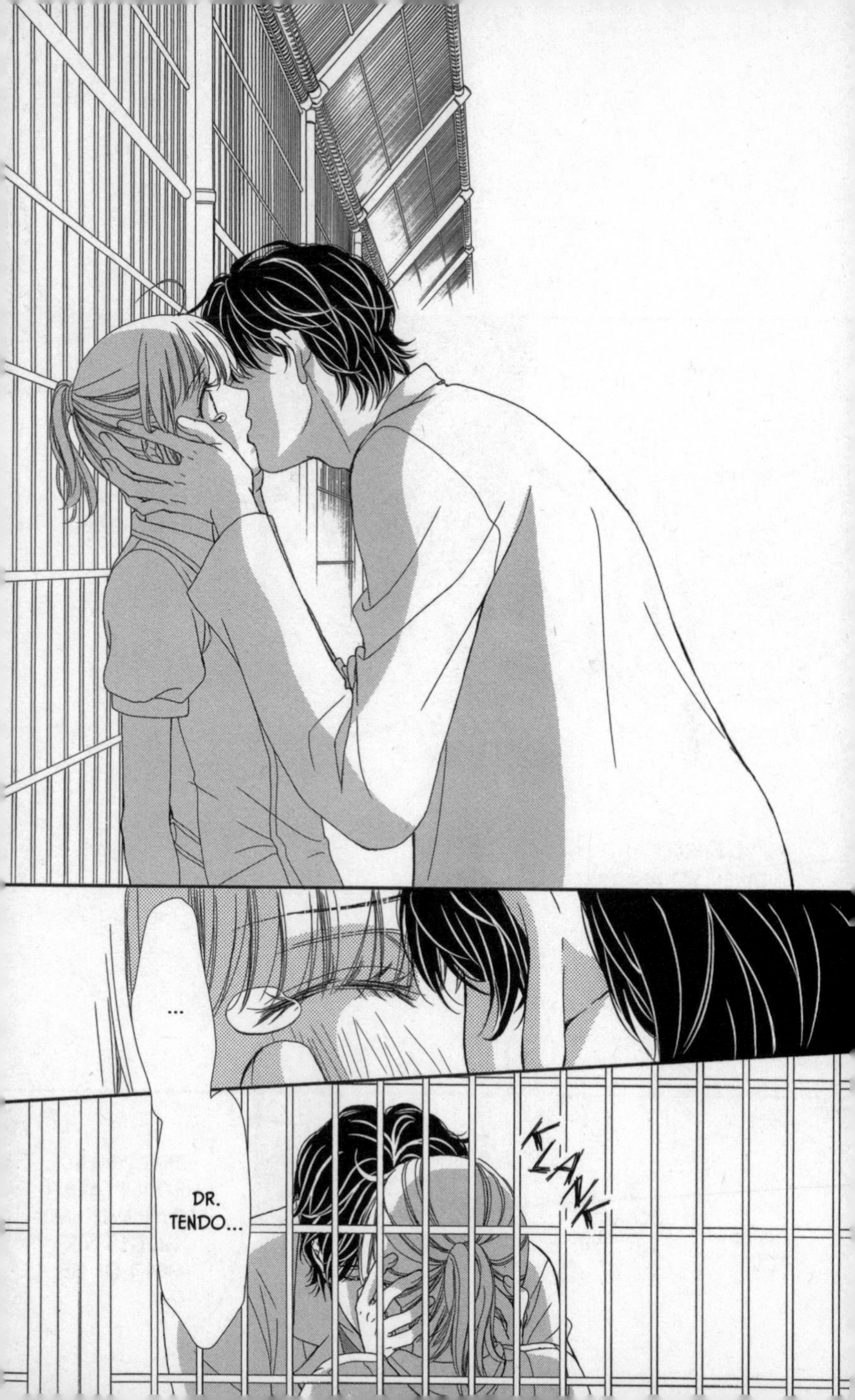
...
DR. TENDO...
KLANK

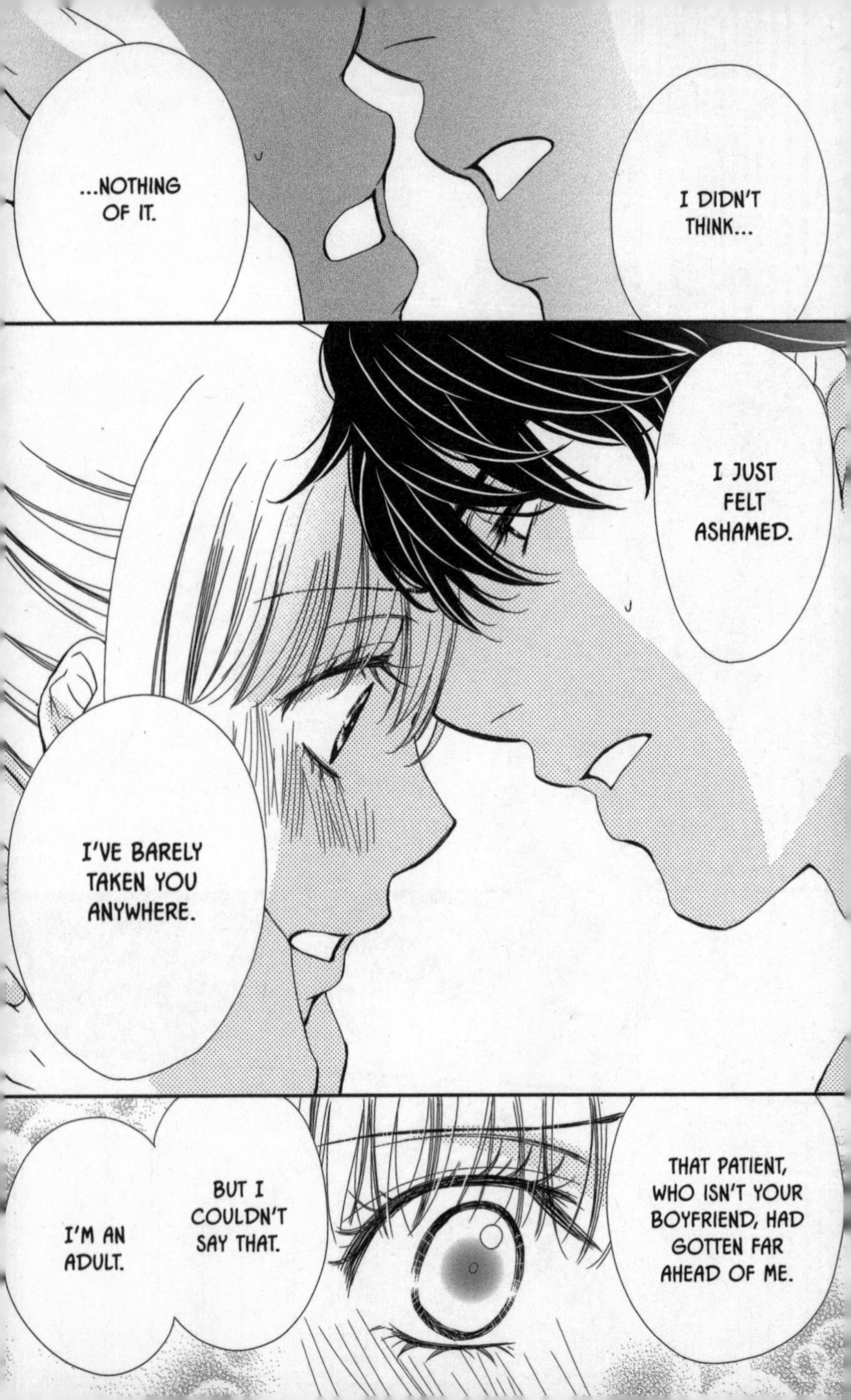
I DIDN'T THINK...
...NOTHING OF IT.
I JUST FELT ASHAMED.
I'VE BARELY TAKEN YOU ANYWHERE.
THAT PATIENT, WHO ISN'T YOUR BOYFRIEND, HAD GOTTEN FAR AHEAD OF ME.
BUT I COULDN'T SAY THAT.
I'M AN ADULT.

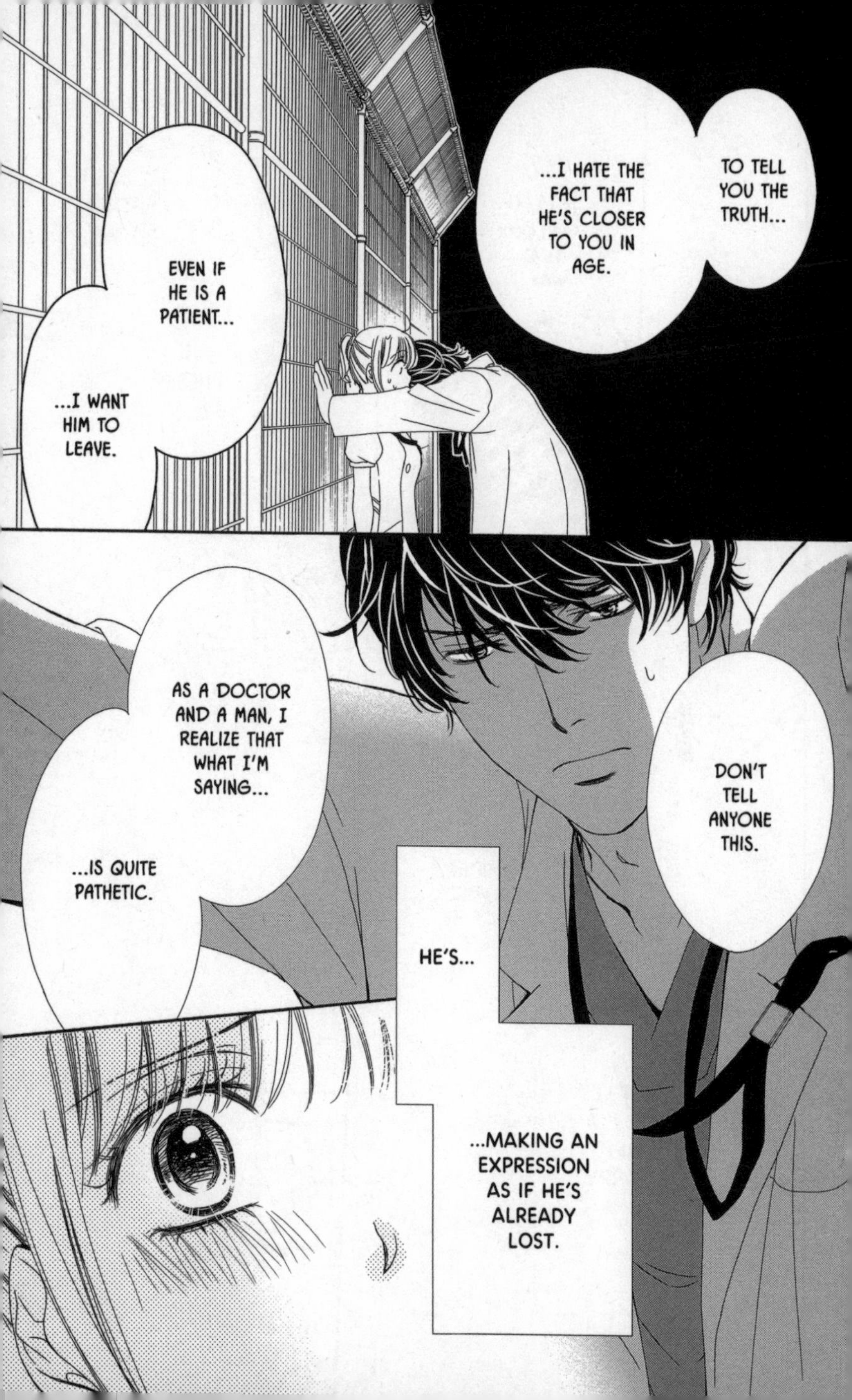
TO TELL YOU THE TRUTH...
...I HATE THE FACT THAT HE'S CLOSER TO YOU IN AGE.
EVEN IF HE IS A PATIENT...
...I WANT HIM TO LEAVE.
DON'T TELL ANYONE THIS.
AS A DOCTOR AND A MAN, I REALIZE THAT WHAT I'M SAYING...
...IS QUITE PATHETIC.
HE'S...
...MAKING AN EXPRESSION AS IF HE'S ALREADY LOST.

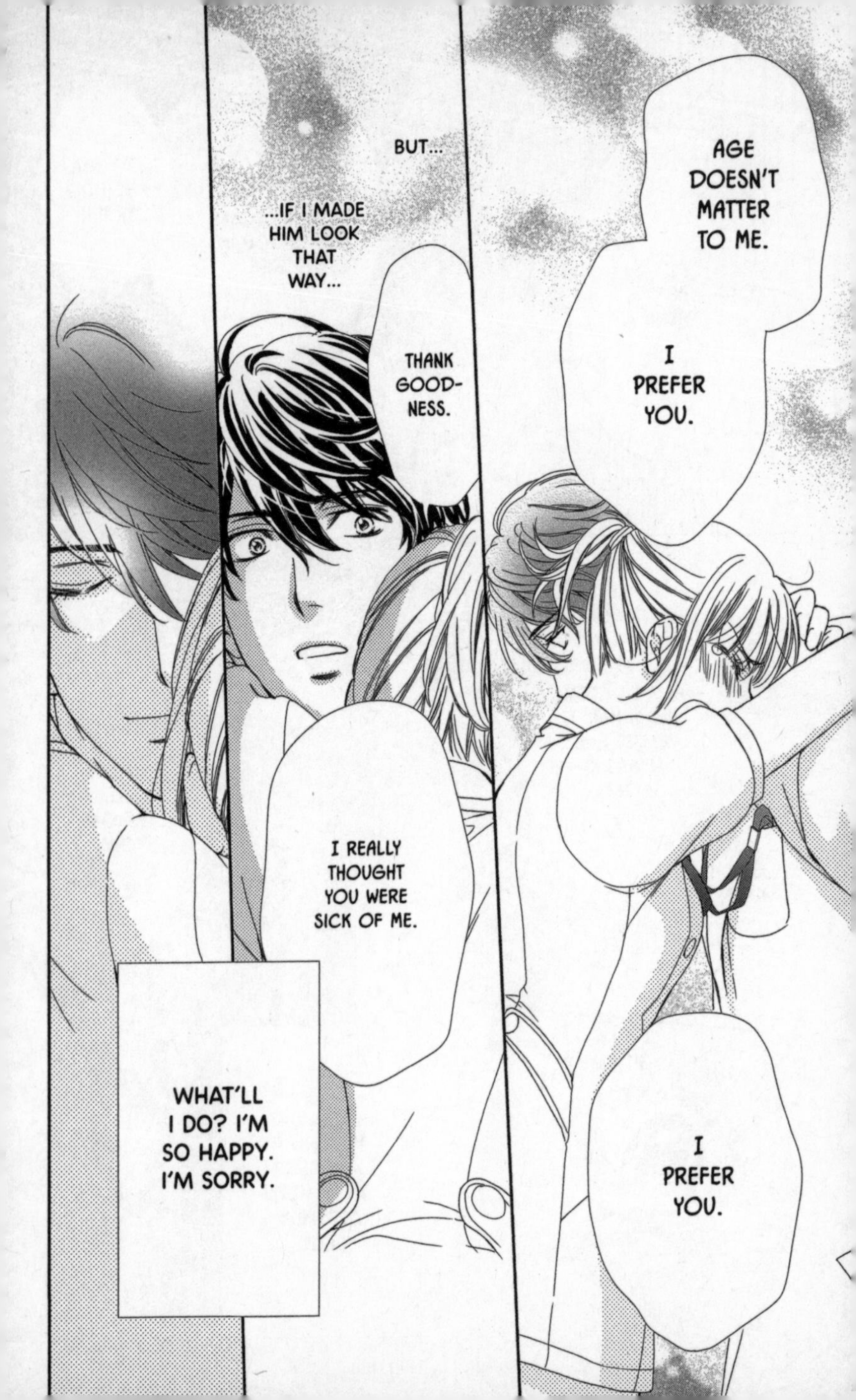
AGE DOESN'T MATTER TO ME.
I PREFER YOU.
I PREFER YOU.
BUT...
...IF I MADE HIM LOOK THAT WAY...
THANK GOODNESS.
I REALLY THOUGHT YOU WERE SICK OF ME.
WHAT'LL I DO? I'M SO HAPPY. I'M SORRY.

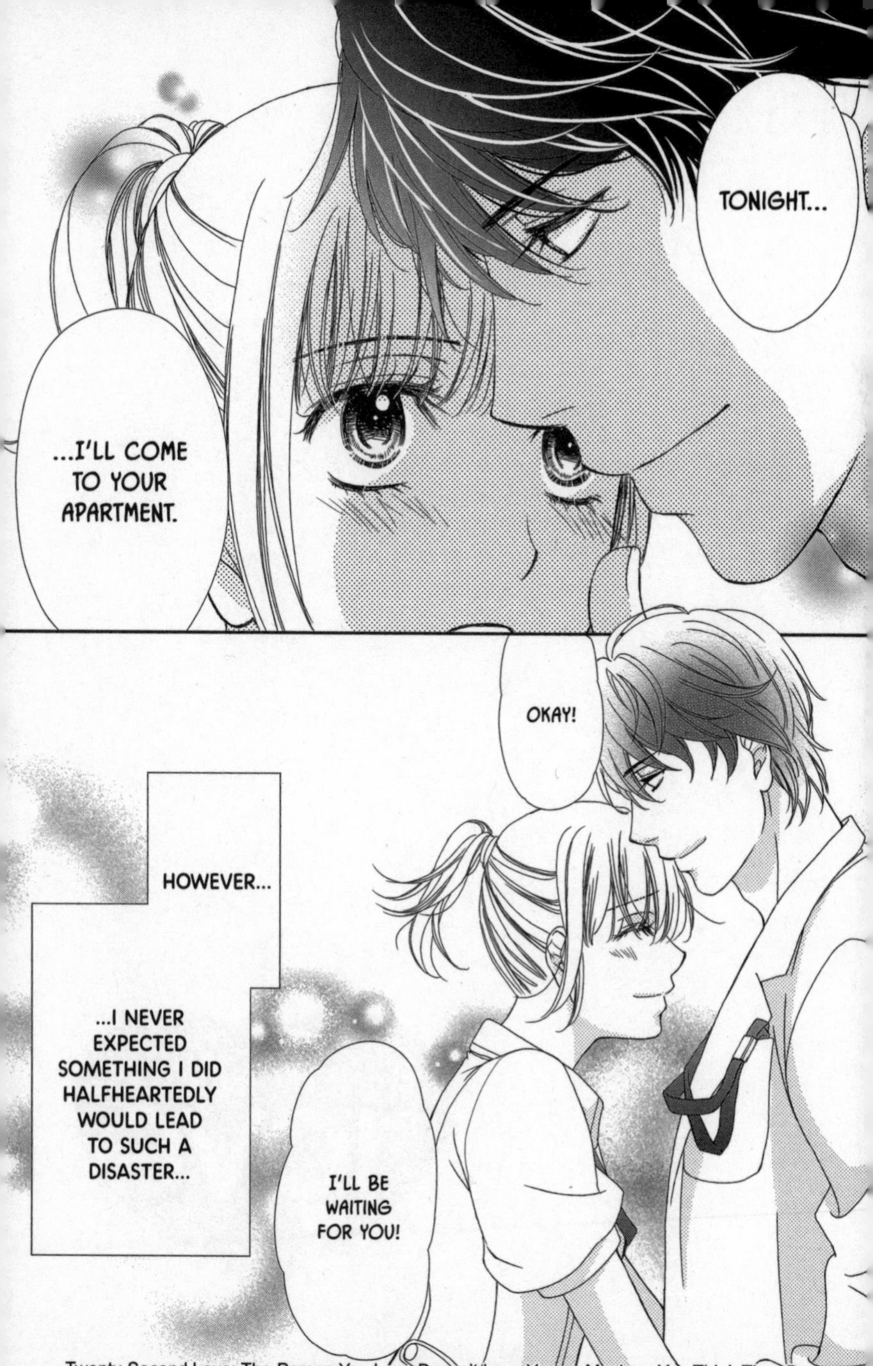
TONIGHT...
...I'LL COME TO YOUR APARTMENT.
OKAY!
I'LL BE WAITING FOR YOU!
HOWEVER...
...I NEVER EXPECTED SOMETHING I DID HALFHEARTEDLY WOULD LEAD TO SUCH A DISASTER...

Twenty-Second Love: The Person You Love Doesn't Love You as Much as You Think They Do. I Refuse to Believe That!/End

AN INCURABLE CASE
OF LoVe

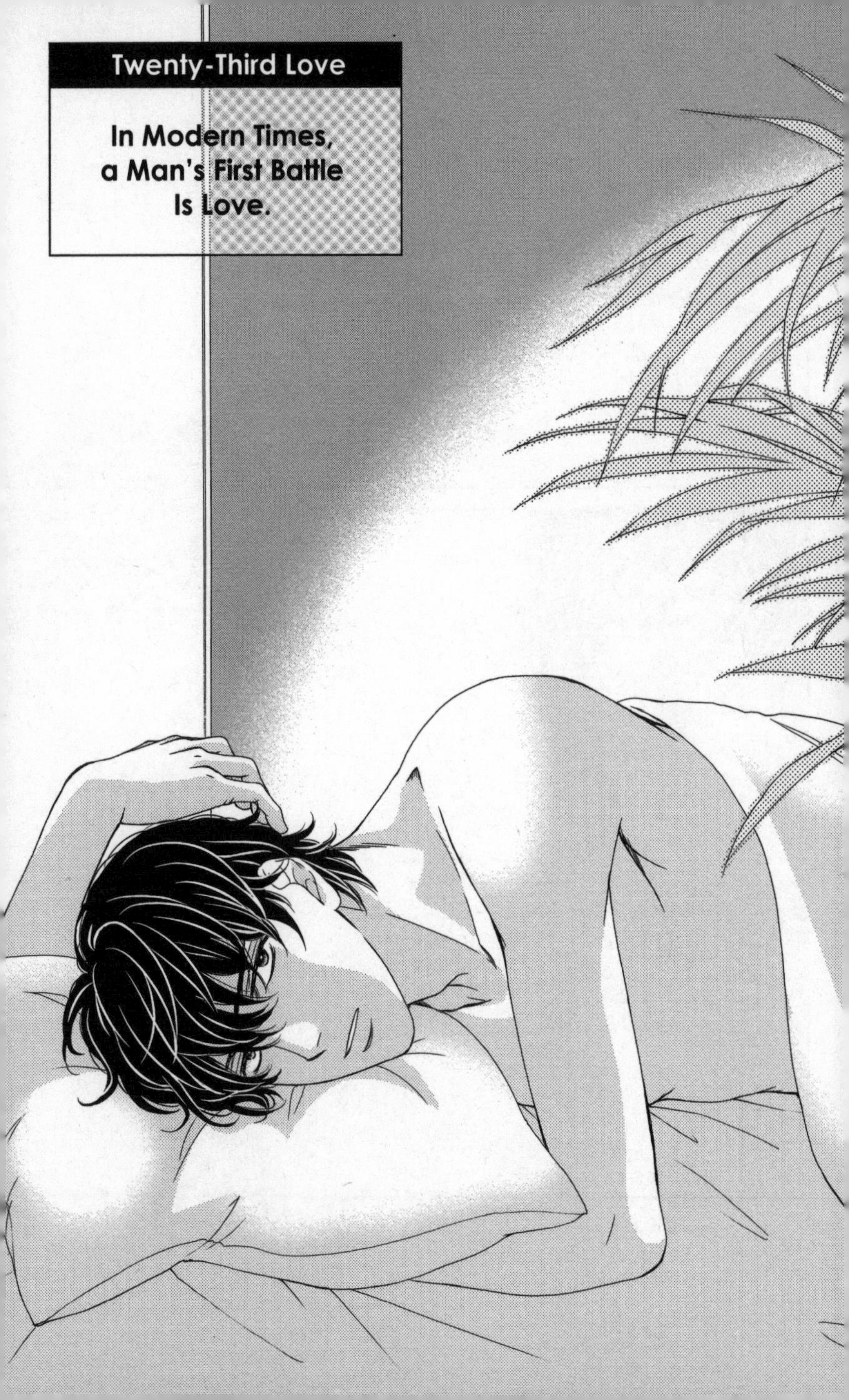
Twenty-Third Love
In Modern Times, a Man's First Battle Is Love.

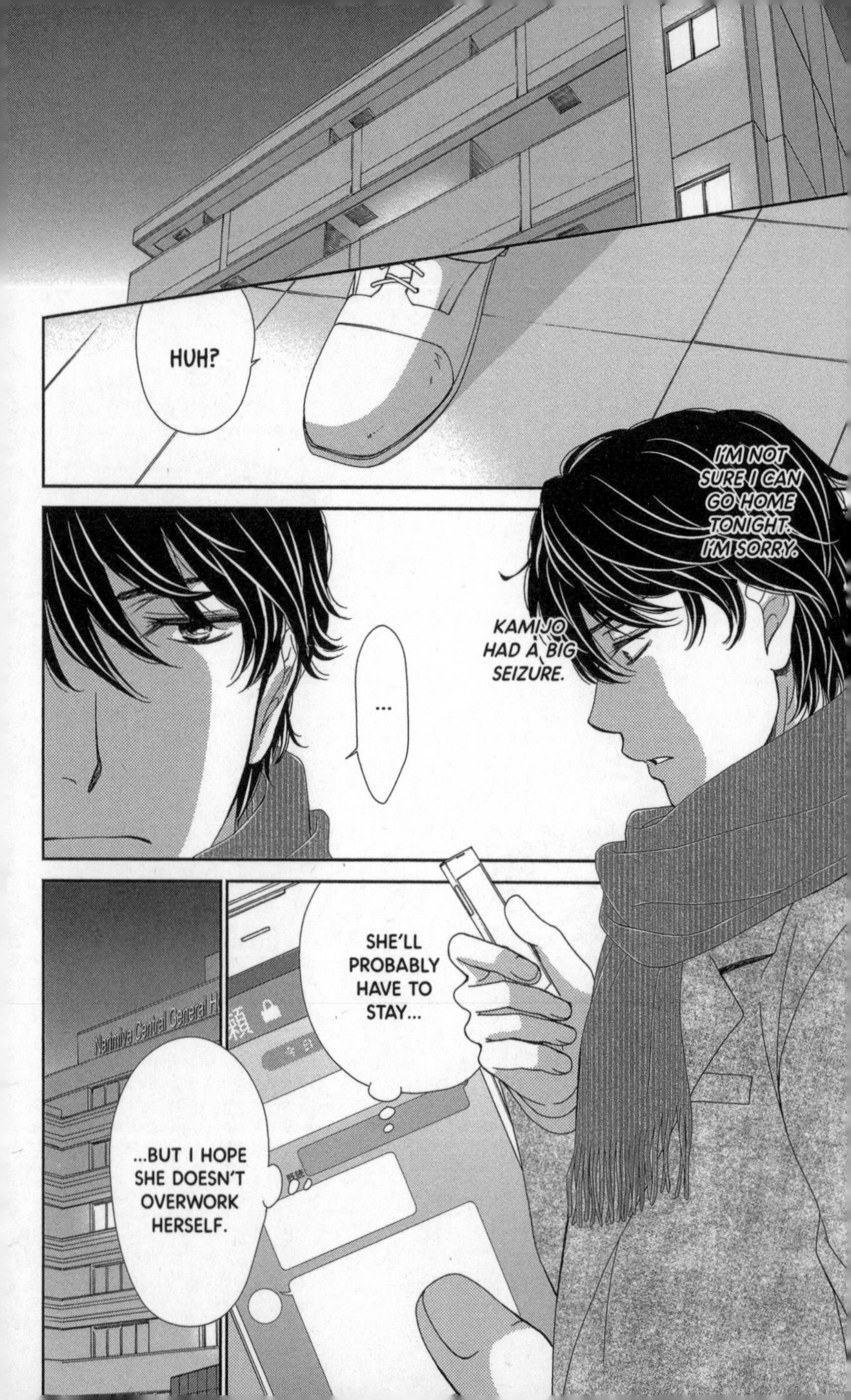
HUH?
I'M NOT SURE I CAN GO HOME TONIGHT. I'M SORRY.
KAMIJO HAD A BIG SEIZURE.
...
SHE'LL PROBABLY HAVE TO STAY...
...BUT I HOPE SHE DOESN'T OVERWORK HERSELF.
Narimiya Central General H

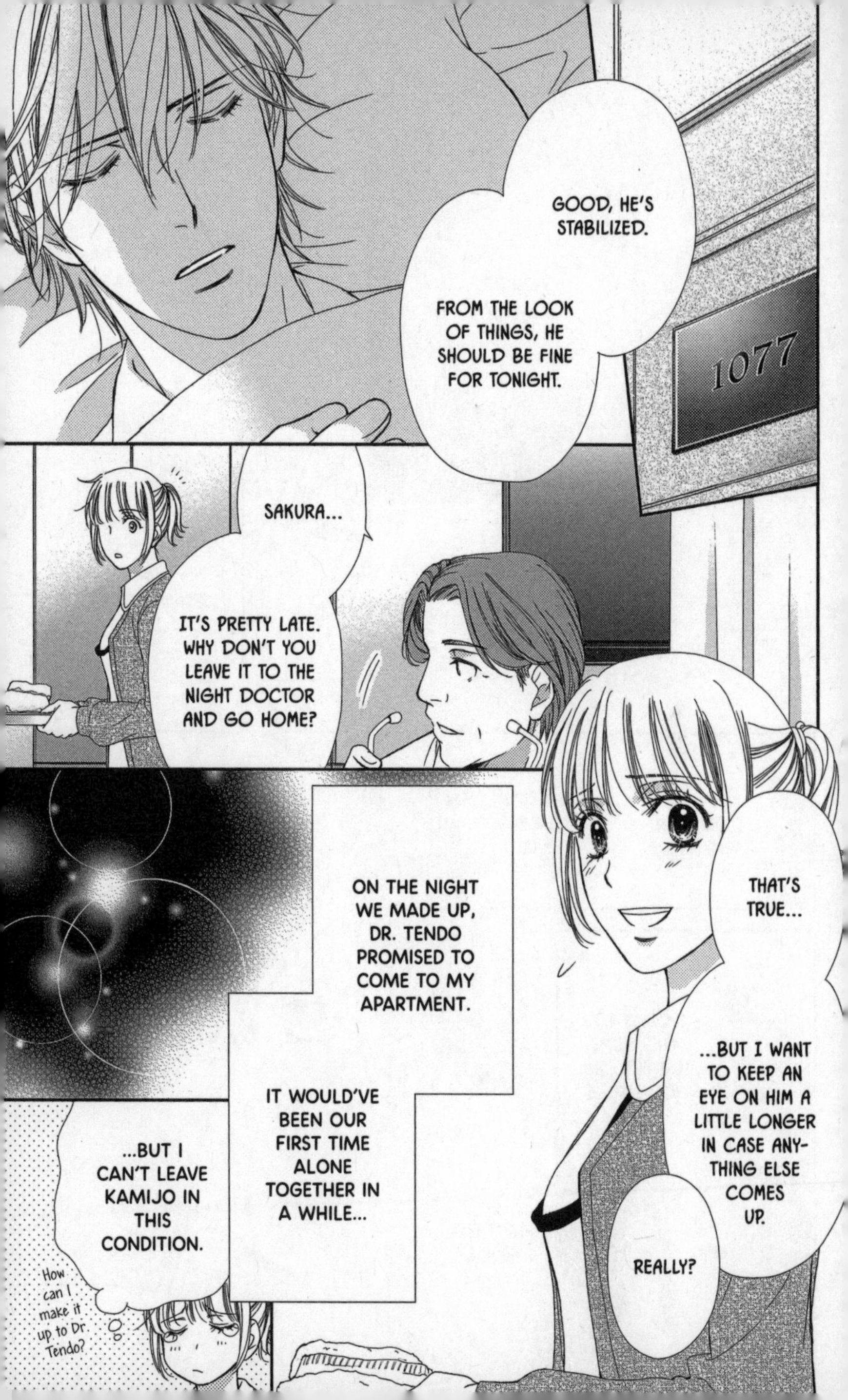
GOOD, HE'S STABILIZED.
FROM THE LOOK OF THINGS, HE SHOULD BE FINE FOR TONIGHT.
1077
SAKURA...
IT'S PRETTY LATE. WHY DON'T YOU LEAVE IT TO THE NIGHT DOCTOR AND GO HOME?
THAT'S TRUE...
...BUT I WANT TO KEEP AN EYE ON HIM A LITTLE LONGER IN CASE ANY-THING ELSE COMES UP.
REALLY?
ON THE NIGHT WE MADE UP, DR. TENDO PROMISED TO COME TO MY APARTMENT.
IT WOULD'VE BEEN OUR FIRST TIME ALONE TOGETHER IN A WHILE...
...BUT I CAN'T LEAVE KAMIJO IN THIS CONDITION.
How can I make it up to Dr. Tendo?

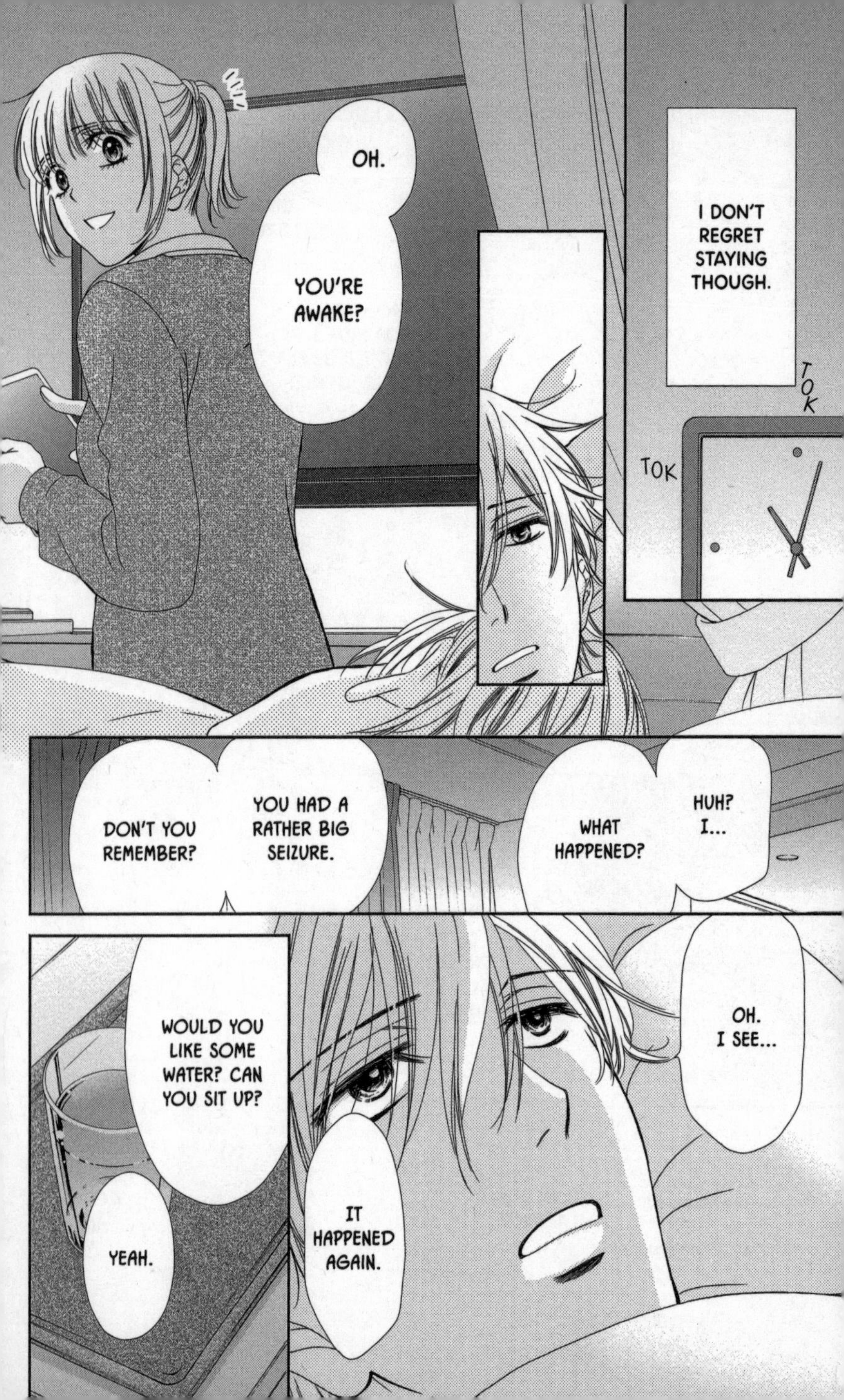
I DON'T REGRET STAYING THOUGH.
TOK
TOK
OH.
YOU'RE AWAKE?
HUH? I...
WHAT HAPPENED?
YOU HAD A RATHER BIG SEIZURE.
DON'T YOU REMEMBER?
OH. I SEE...
IT HAPPENED AGAIN.
WOULD YOU LIKE SOME WATER? CAN YOU SIT UP?
YEAH.

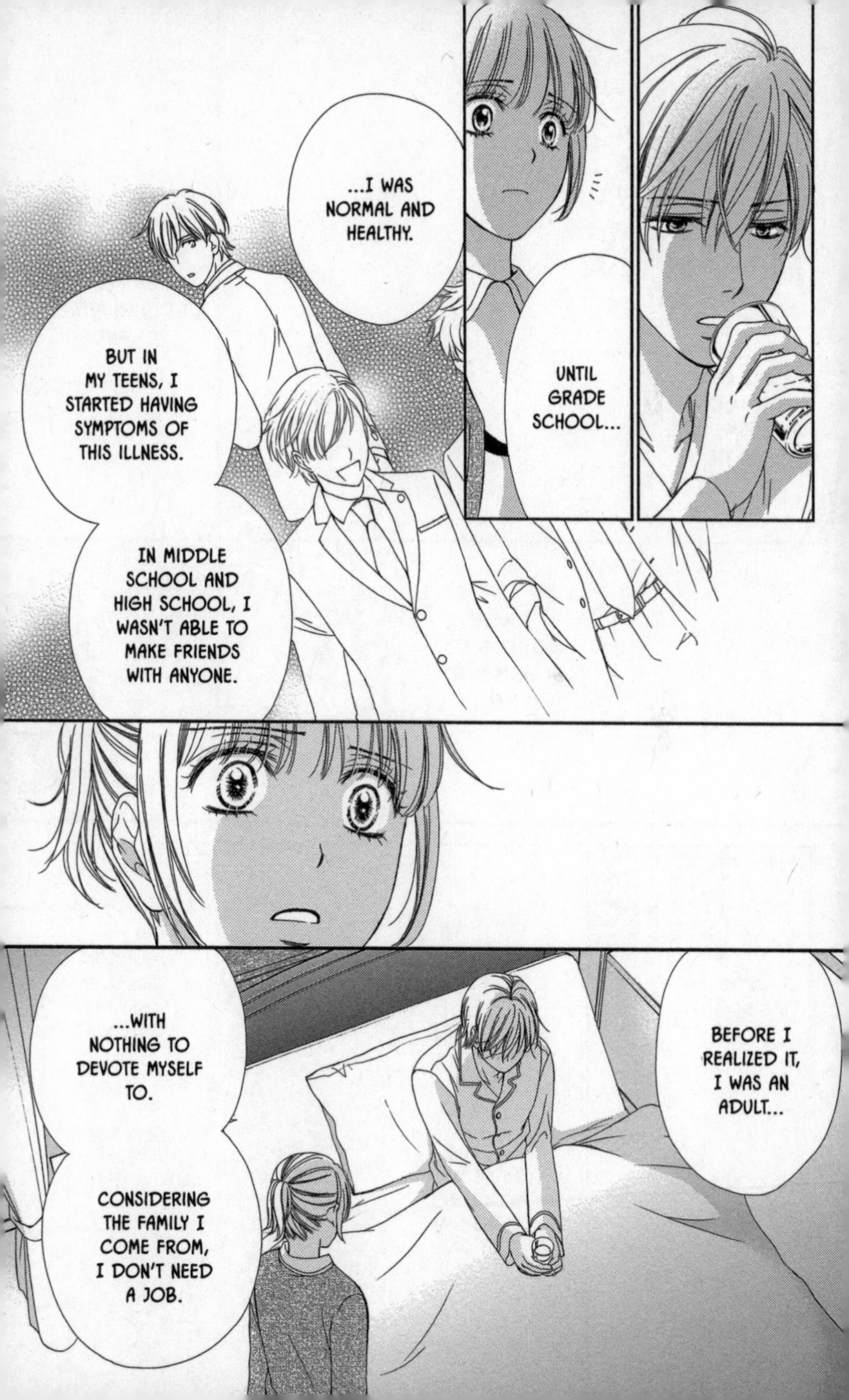
UNTIL GRADE SCHOOL...
...I WAS NORMAL AND HEALTHY.
BUT IN MY TEENS, I STARTED HAVING SYMPTOMS OF THIS ILLNESS.
IN MIDDLE SCHOOL AND HIGH SCHOOL, I WASN'T ABLE TO MAKE FRIENDS WITH ANYONE.
BEFORE I REALIZED IT, I WAS AN ADULT...
...WITH NOTHING TO DEVOTE MYSELF TO.
CONSIDERING THE FAMILY I COME FROM, I DON'T NEED A JOB.

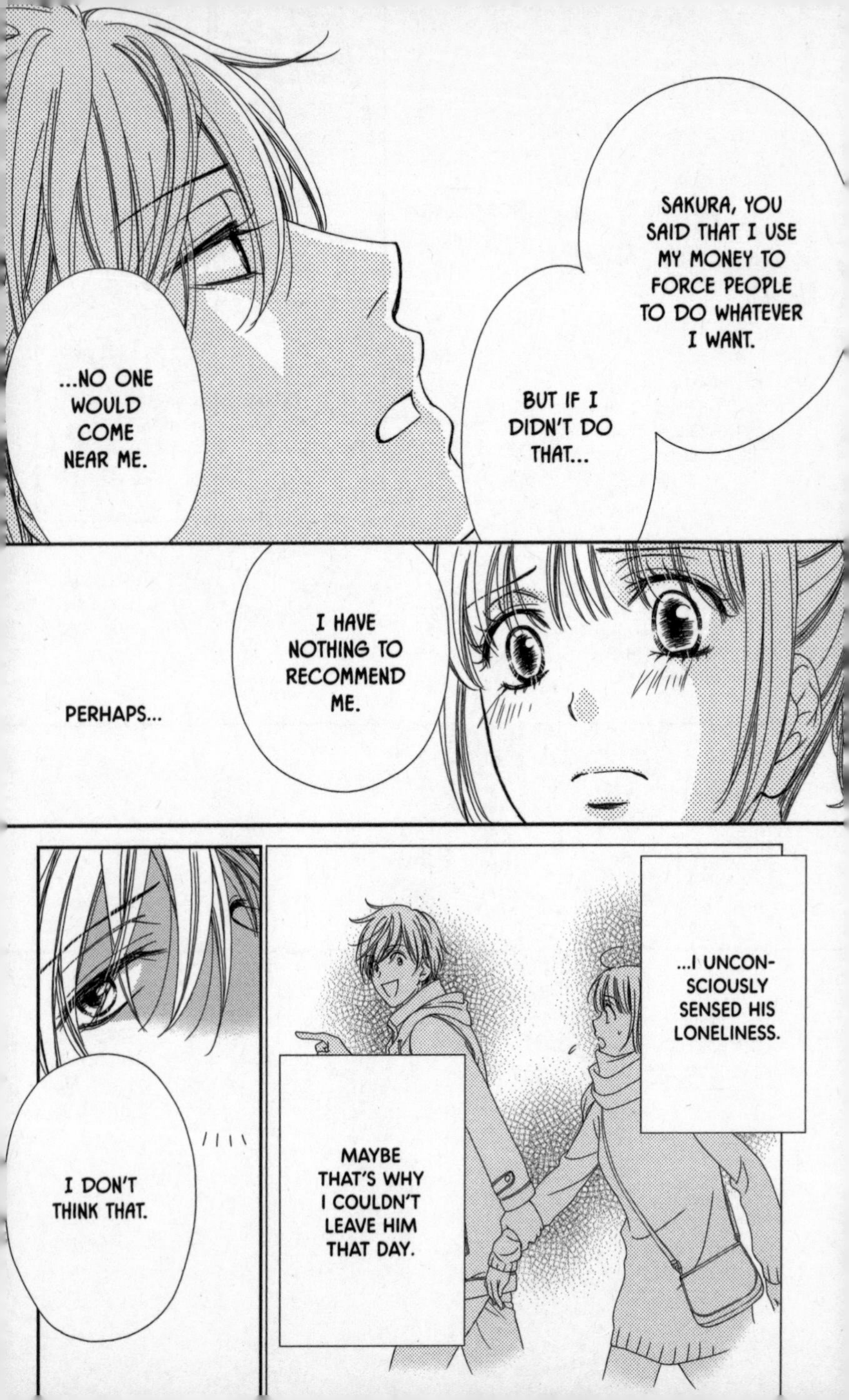
SAKURA, YOU SAID THAT I USE MY MONEY TO FORCE PEOPLE TO DO WHATEVER I WANT.
BUT IF I DIDN'T DO THAT...
...NO ONE WOULD COME NEAR ME.
I HAVE NOTHING TO RECOMMEND ME.
PERHAPS...
...I UNCONSCIOUSLY SENSED HIS LONELINESS.
MAYBE THAT'S WHY I COULDN'T LEAVE HIM THAT DAY.
I DON'T THINK THAT.

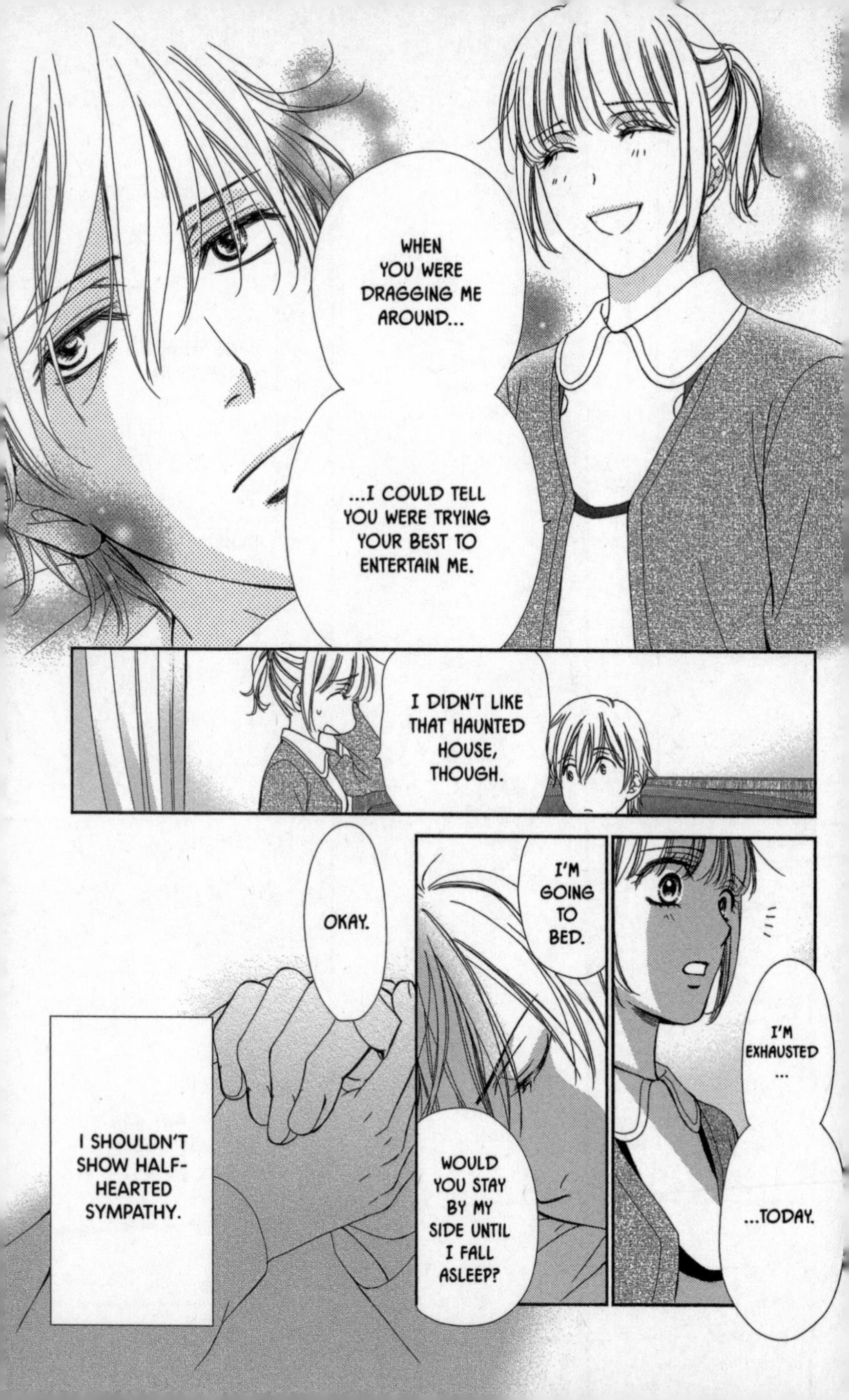
WHEN YOU WERE DRAGGING ME AROUND...
...I COULD TELL YOU WERE TRYING YOUR BEST TO ENTERTAIN ME.
I DIDN'T LIKE THAT HAUNTED HOUSE, THOUGH.
I'M EXHAUSTED...
...TODAY.
I'M GOING TO BED.
WOULD YOU STAY BY MY SIDE UNTIL I FALL ASLEEP?
OKAY.
I SHOULDN'T SHOW HALF-HEARTED SYMPATHY.

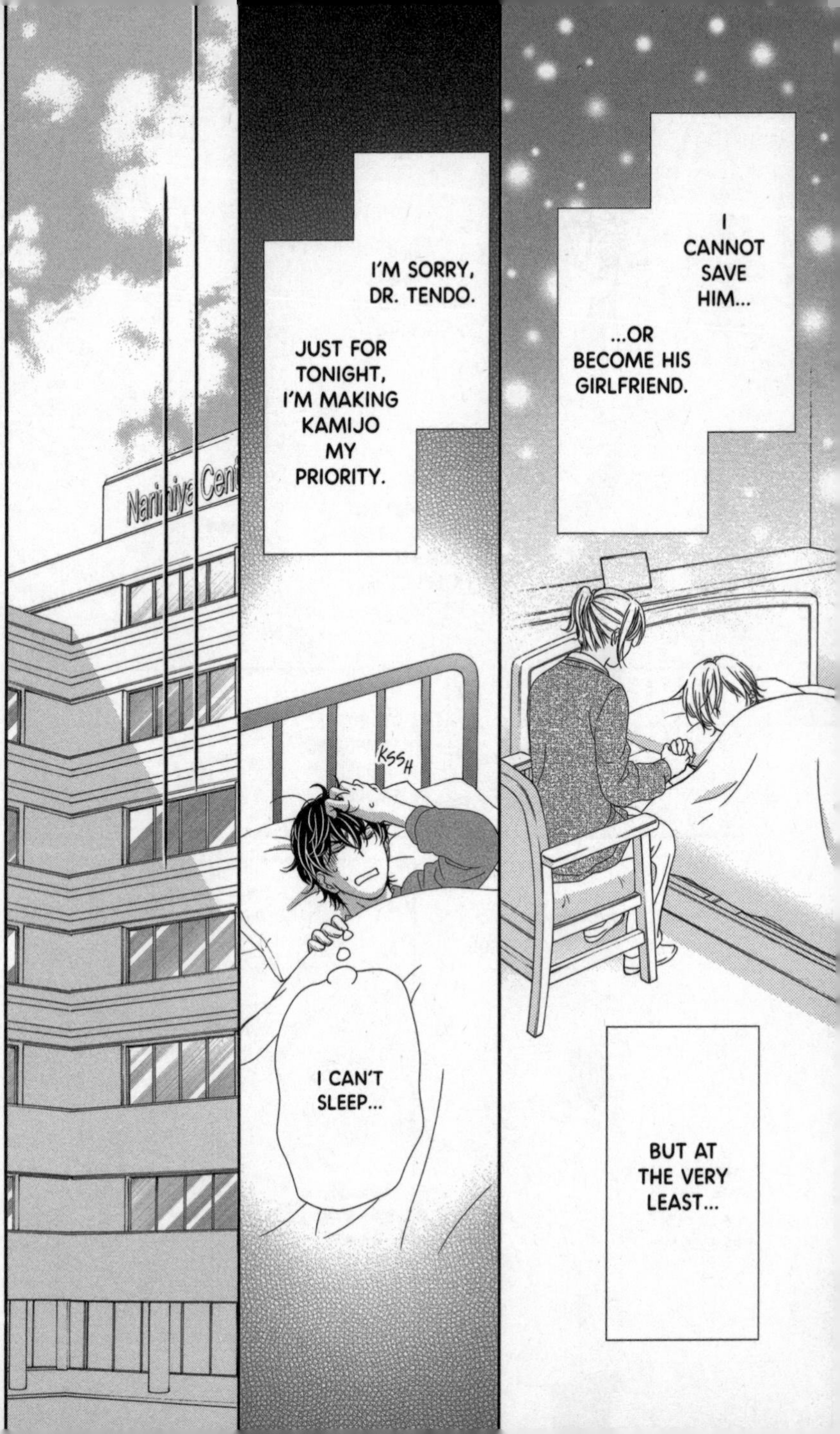
I CANNOT SAVE HIM...
...OR BECOME HIS GIRLFRIEND.
BUT AT THE VERY LEAST...
I'M SORRY, DR. TENDO.
JUST FOR TONIGHT, I'M MAKING KAMIJO MY PRIORITY.
KSSH
I CAN'T SLEEP...

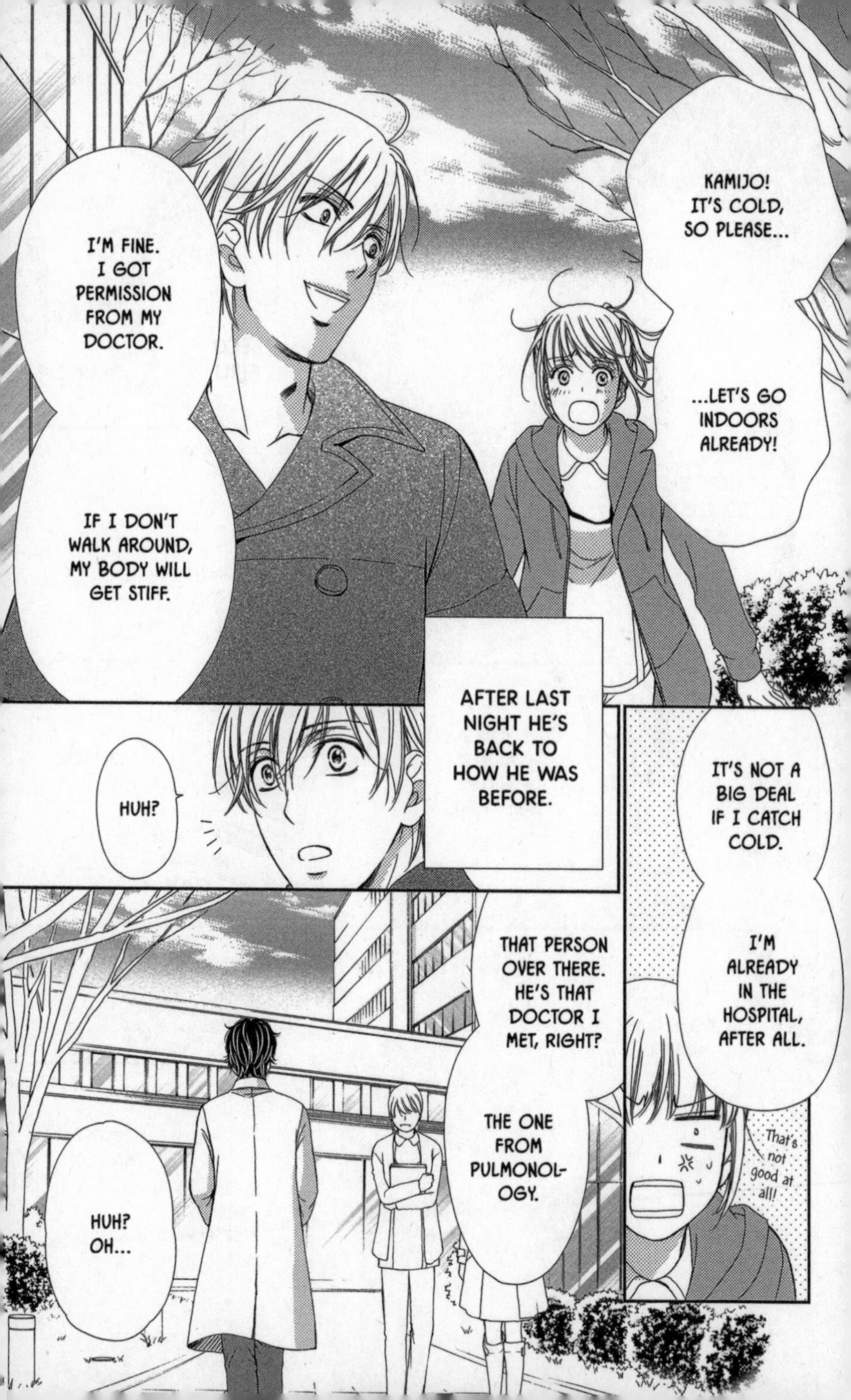
KAMIJO! IT'S COLD, SO PLEASE...
...LET'S GO INDOORS ALREADY!
I'M FINE. I GOT PERMISSION FROM MY DOCTOR.
IF I DON'T WALK AROUND, MY BODY WILL GET STIFF.
IT'S NOT A BIG DEAL IF I CATCH COLD.
I'M ALREADY IN THE HOSPITAL, AFTER ALL.
That's not good at all!
AFTER LAST NIGHT HE'S BACK TO HOW HE WAS BEFORE.
HUH?
THAT PERSON OVER THERE. HE'S THAT DOCTOR I MET, RIGHT?
THE ONE FROM PULMONOL-OGY.
HUH? OH...

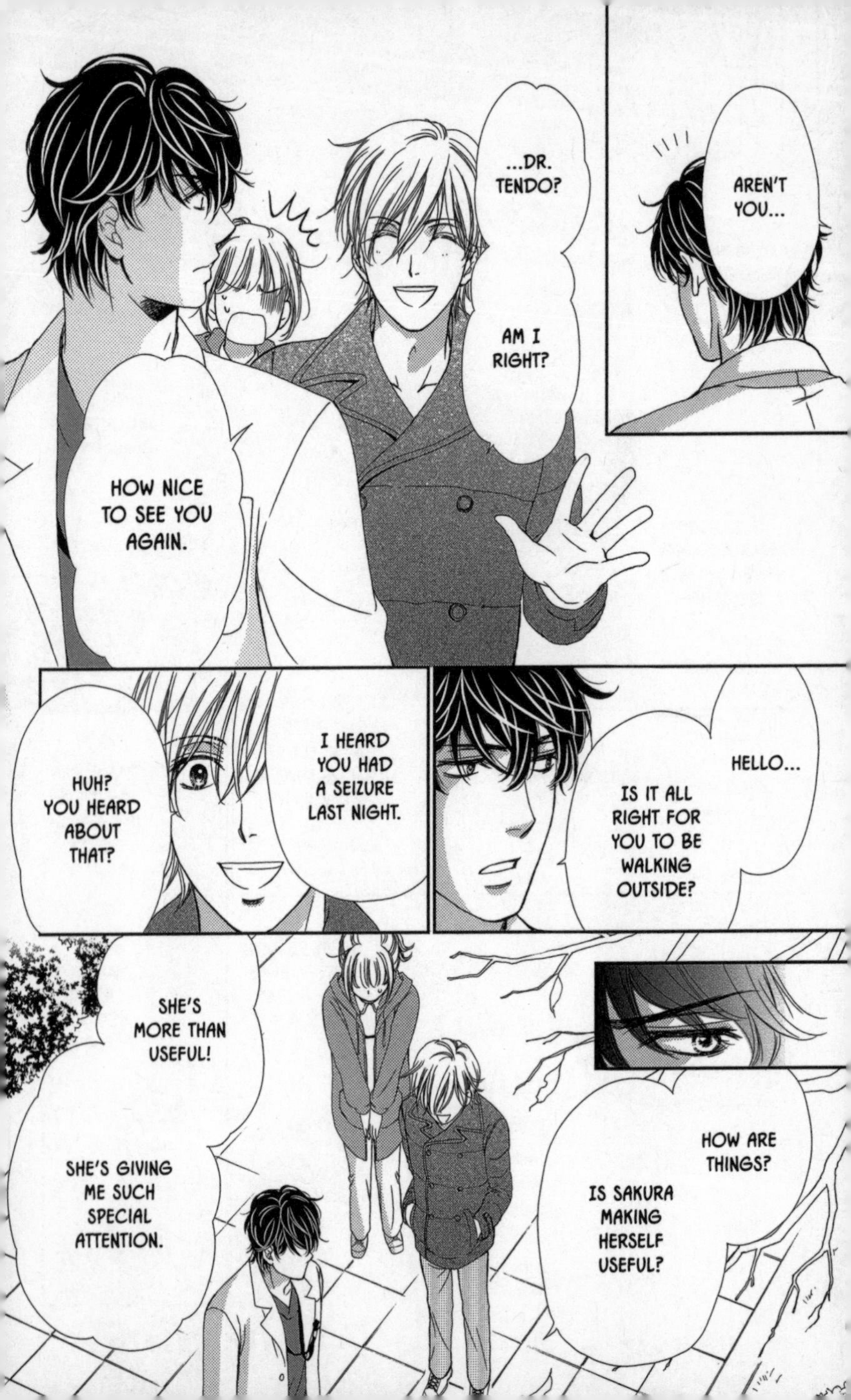
AREN'T YOU...
...DR. TENDO?
AM I RIGHT?
HOW NICE TO SEE YOU AGAIN.
HELLO...
IS IT ALL RIGHT FOR YOU TO BE WALKING OUTSIDE?
I HEARD YOU HAD A SEIZURE LAST NIGHT.
HUH? YOU HEARD ABOUT THAT?
HOW ARE THINGS?
IS SAKURA MAKING HERSELF USEFUL?
SHE'S MORE THAN USEFUL!
SHE'S GIVING ME SUCH SPECIAL ATTENTION.

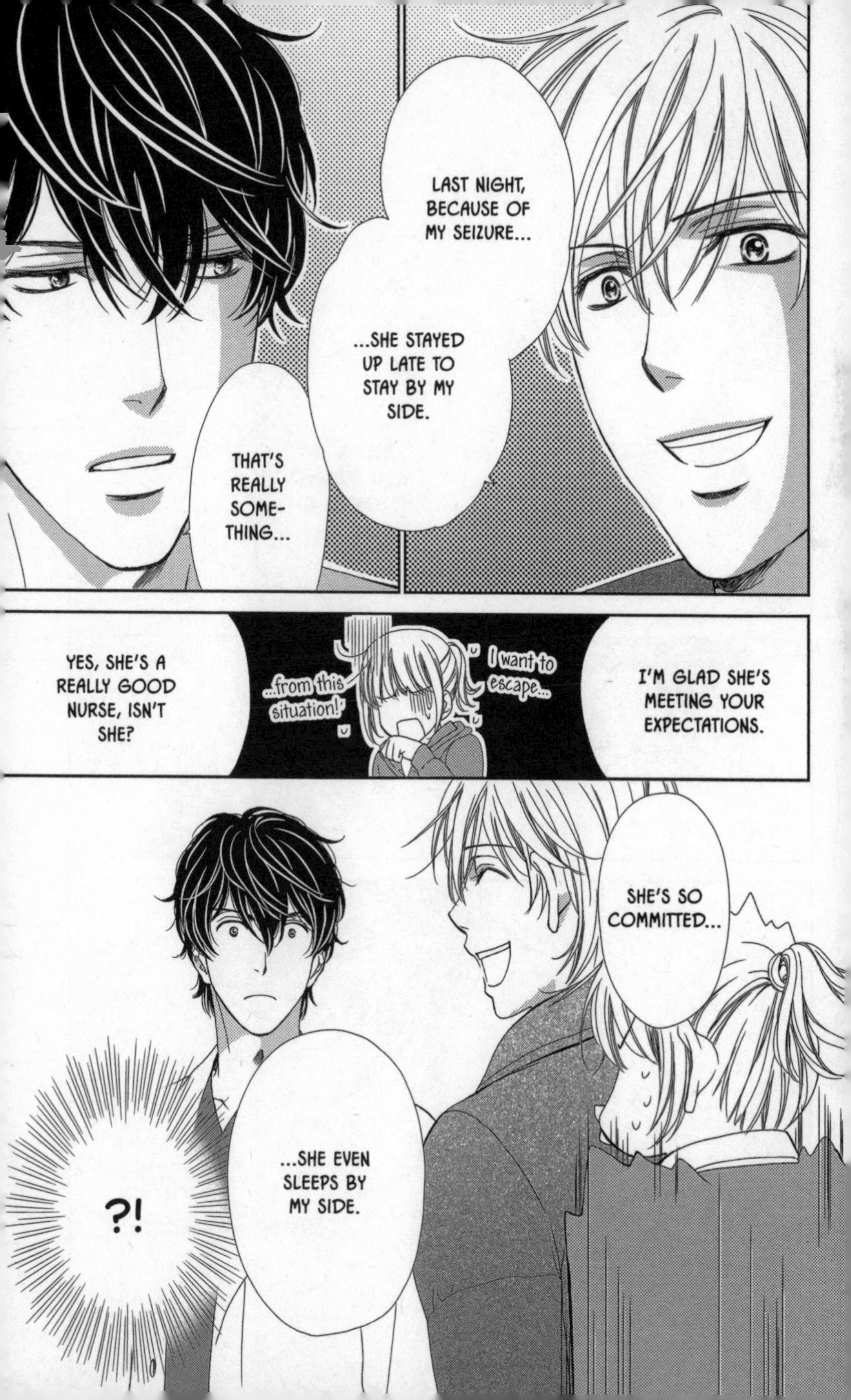
LAST NIGHT, BECAUSE OF MY SEIZURE...
...SHE STAYED UP LATE TO STAY BY MY SIDE.
THAT'S REALLY SOME-THING...
I'M GLAD SHE'S MEETING YOUR EXPECTATIONS.
I want to escape...
...from this situation!
YES, SHE'S A REALLY GOOD NURSE, ISN'T SHE?
SHE'S SO COMMITTED...
...SHE EVEN SLEEPS BY MY SIDE.
?!

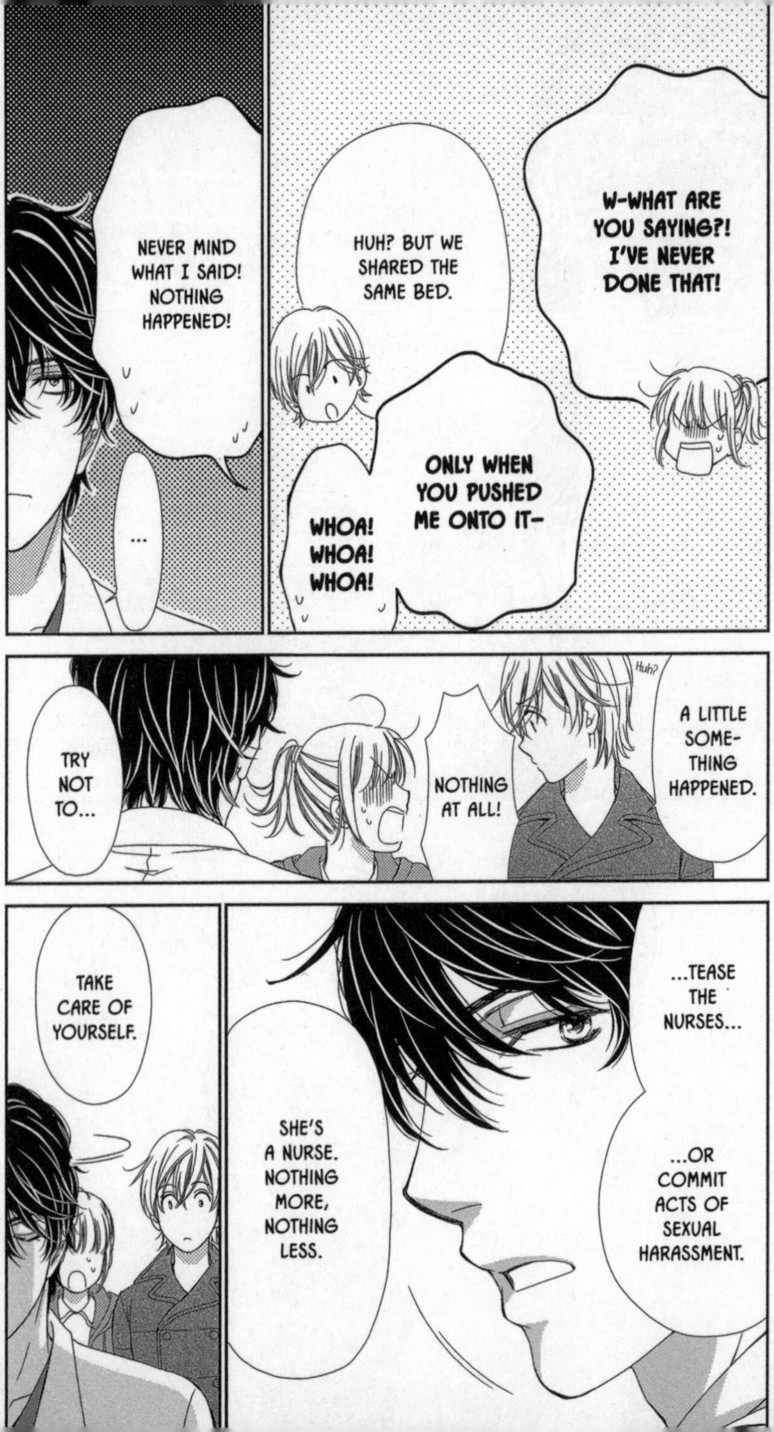
W-WHAT ARE YOU SAYING?! I'VE NEVER DONE THAT!
HUH? BUT WE SHARED THE SAME BED.
ONLY WHEN YOU PUSHED ME ONTO IT-
WHOA! WHOA! WHOA!
NEVER MIND WHAT I SAID! NOTHING HAPPENED!
...
Huh?
A LITTLE SOME-THING HAPPENED.
NOTHING AT ALL!
TRY NOT TO...
...TEASE THE NURSES...
...OR COMMIT ACTS OF SEXUAL HARASSMENT.
SHE'S A NURSE. NOTHING MORE, NOTHING LESS.
TAKE CARE OF YOURSELF.

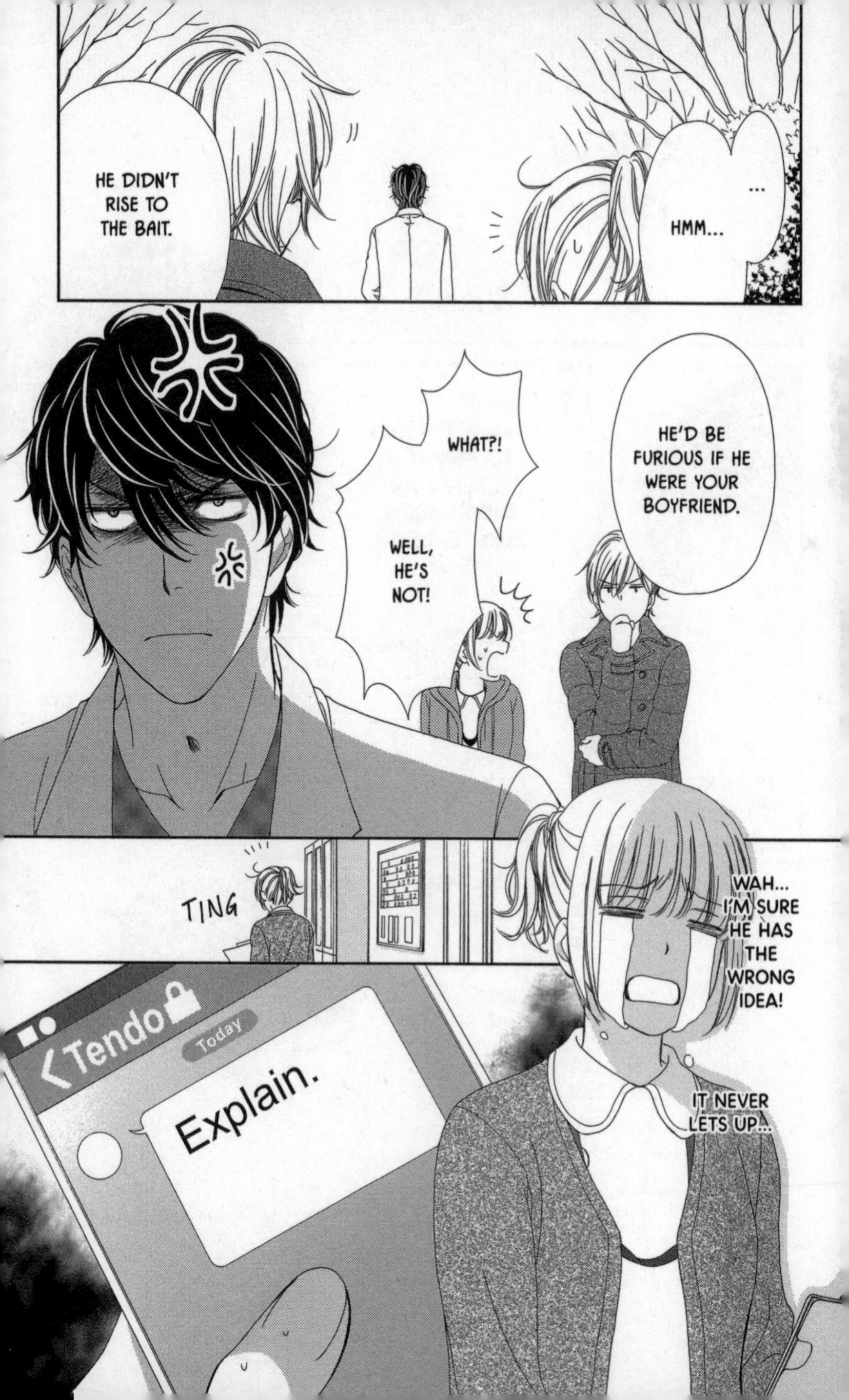
...
HMM...
HE DIDN'T RISE TO THE BAIT.
HE'D BE FURIOUS IF HE WERE YOUR BOYFRIEND.
WHAT?!
WELL, HE'S NOT!
WAH... I'M SURE HE HAS THE WRONG IDEA!
TING
Tendo
Today
Explain.
IT NEVER LETS UP...

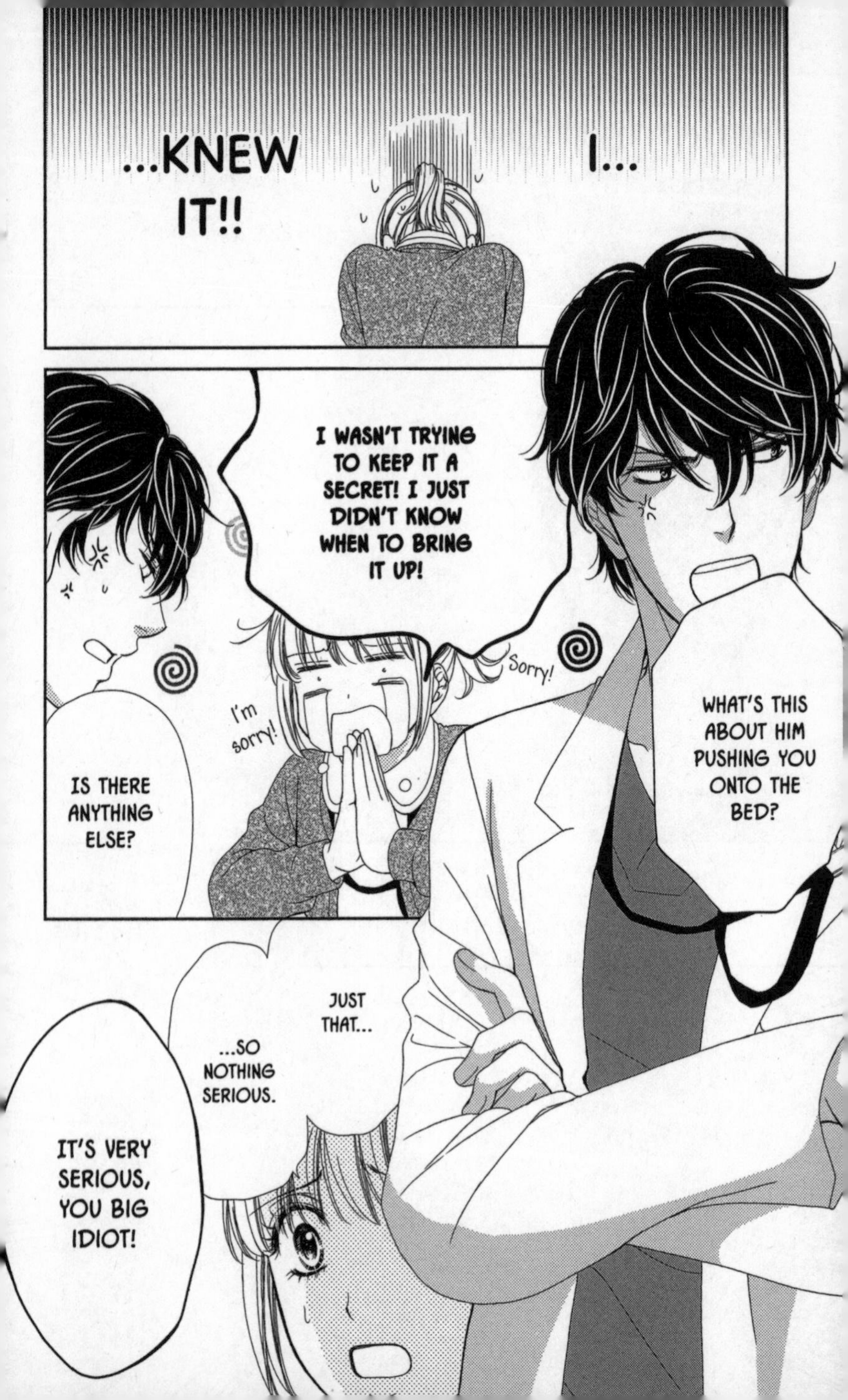
I...
...KNEW IT!!
WHAT'S THIS ABOUT HIM PUSHING YOU ONTO THE BED?
I WASN'T TRYING TO KEEP IT A SECRET! I JUST DIDN'T KNOW WHEN TO BRING IT UP!
Sorry!
I'm sorry!
IS THERE ANYTHING ELSE?
JUST THAT...
...SO NOTHING SERIOUS.
IT'S VERY SERIOUS, YOU BIG IDIOT!

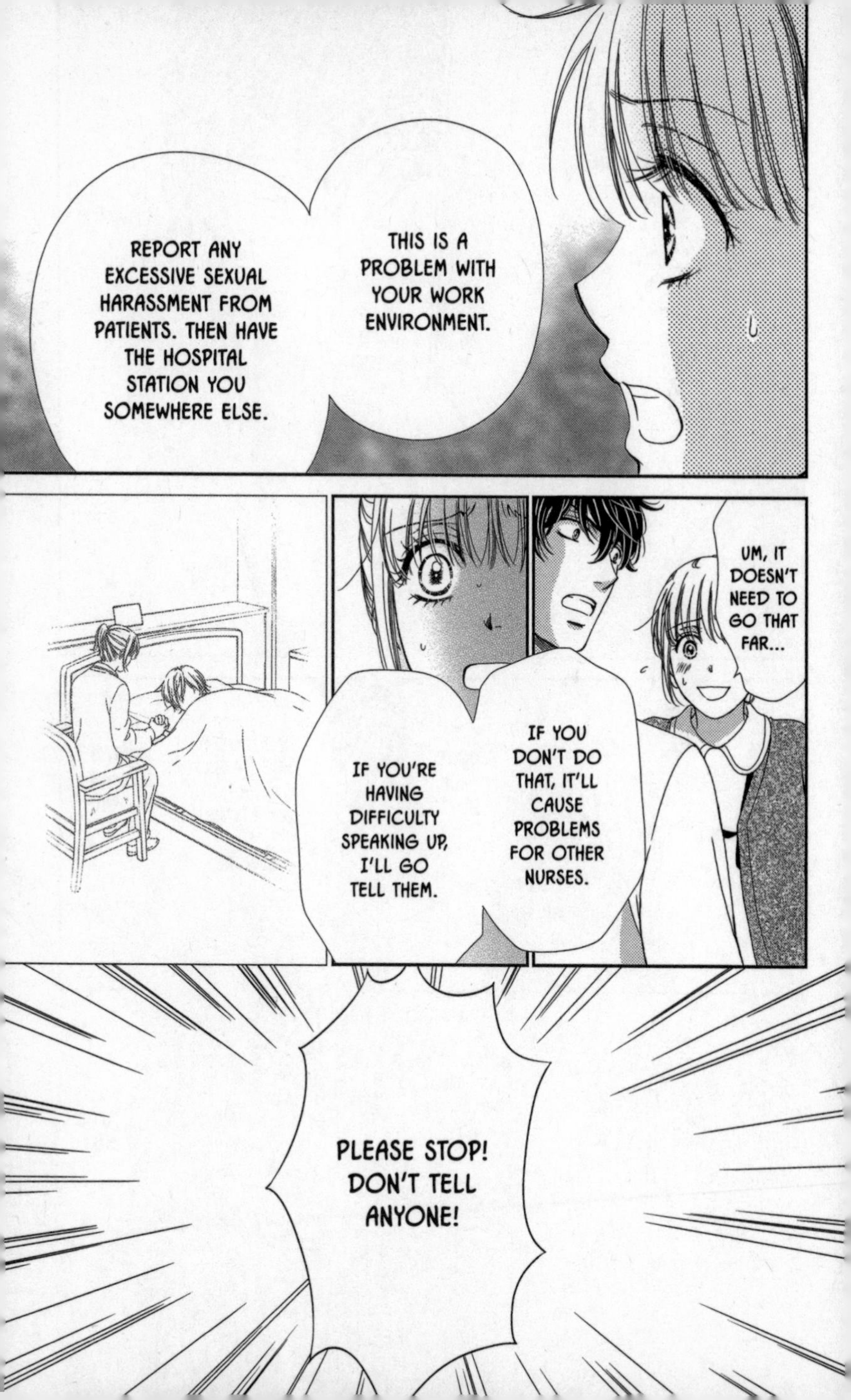
THIS IS A PROBLEM WITH YOUR WORK ENVIRONMENT.
REPORT ANY EXCESSIVE SEXUAL HARASSMENT FROM PATIENTS. THEN HAVE THE HOSPITAL STATION YOU SOMEWHERE ELSE.
UM, IT DOESN'T NEED TO GO THAT FAR...
IF YOU DON'T DO THAT, IT'LL CAUSE PROBLEMS FOR OTHER NURSES.
IF YOU'RE HAVING DIFFICULTY SPEAKING UP, I'LL GO TELL THEM.
PLEASE STOP! DON'T TELL ANYONE!

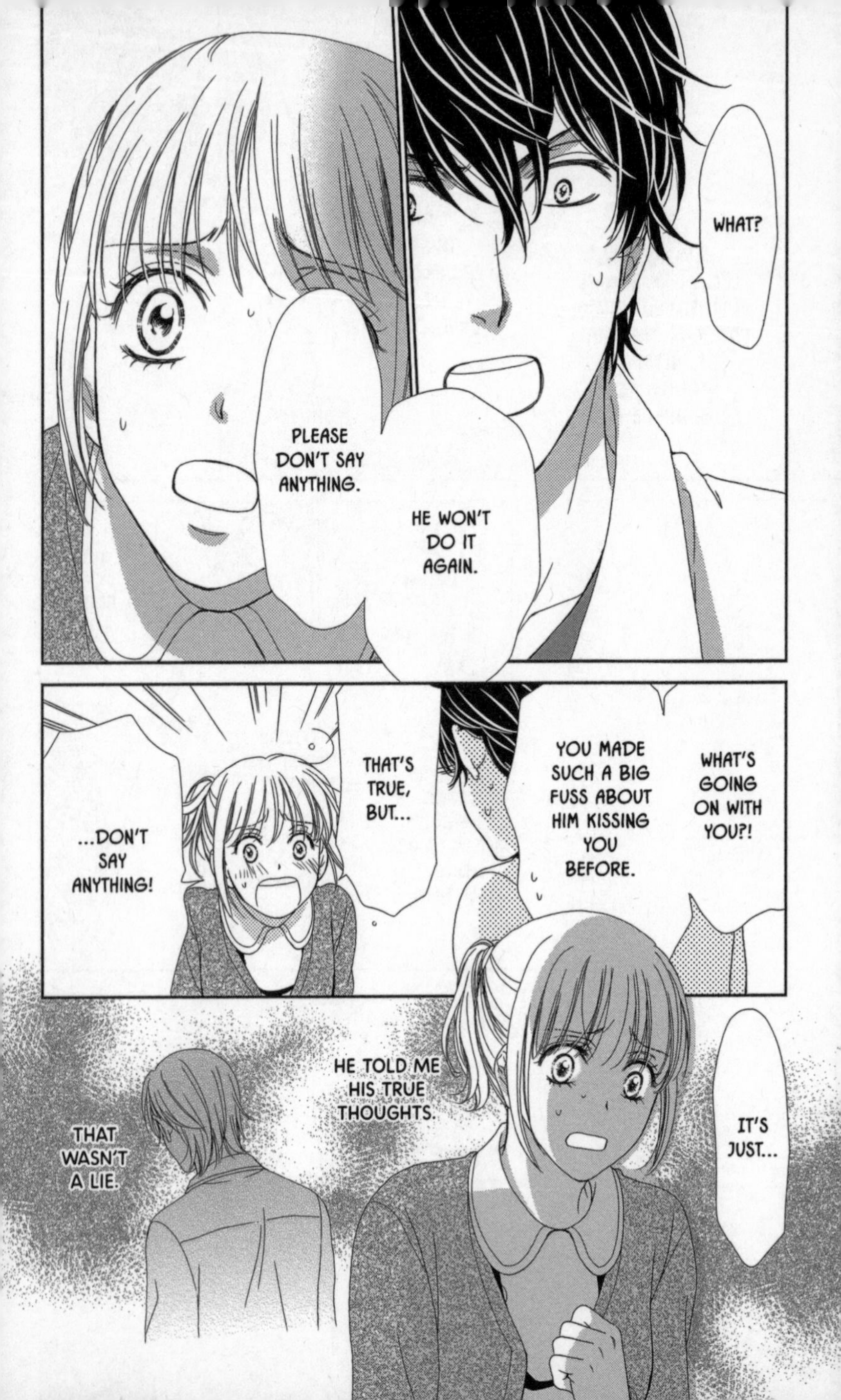
WHAT?
PLEASE DON'T SAY ANYTHING.
HE WON'T DO IT AGAIN.
WHAT'S GOING ON WITH YOU?!
YOU MADE SUCH A BIG FUSS ABOUT HIM KISSING YOU BEFORE.
THAT'S TRUE, BUT...
...DON'T SAY ANYTHING!
IT'S JUST...
HE TOLD ME HIS TRUE THOUGHTS.
THAT WASN'T A LIE.

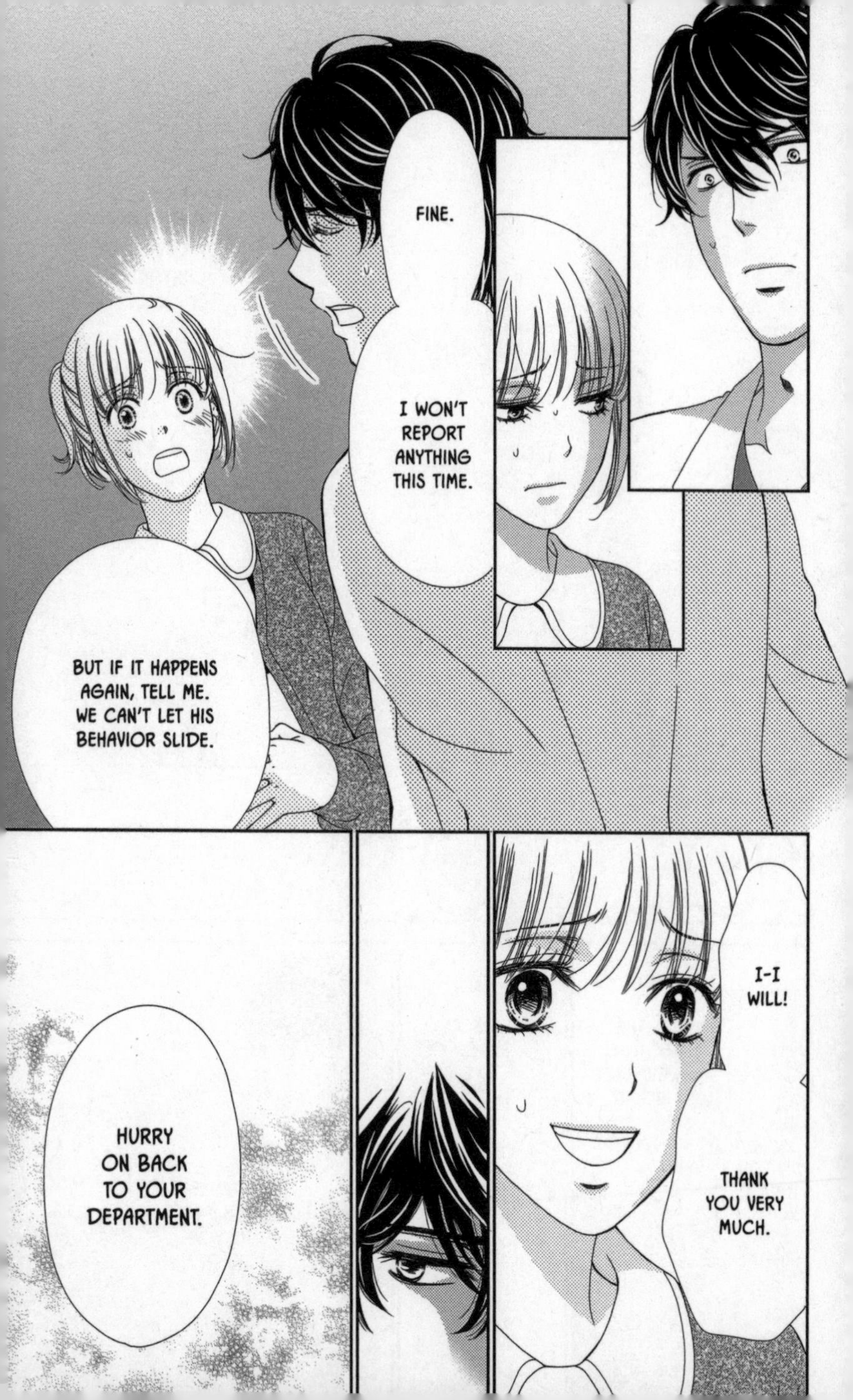
FINE.
I WON'T REPORT ANYTHING THIS TIME.
BUT IF IT HAPPENS AGAIN, TELL ME. WE CAN'T LET HIS BEHAVIOR SLIDE.
I-I WILL!
THANK YOU VERY MUCH.
HURRY ON BACK TO YOUR DEPARTMENT.

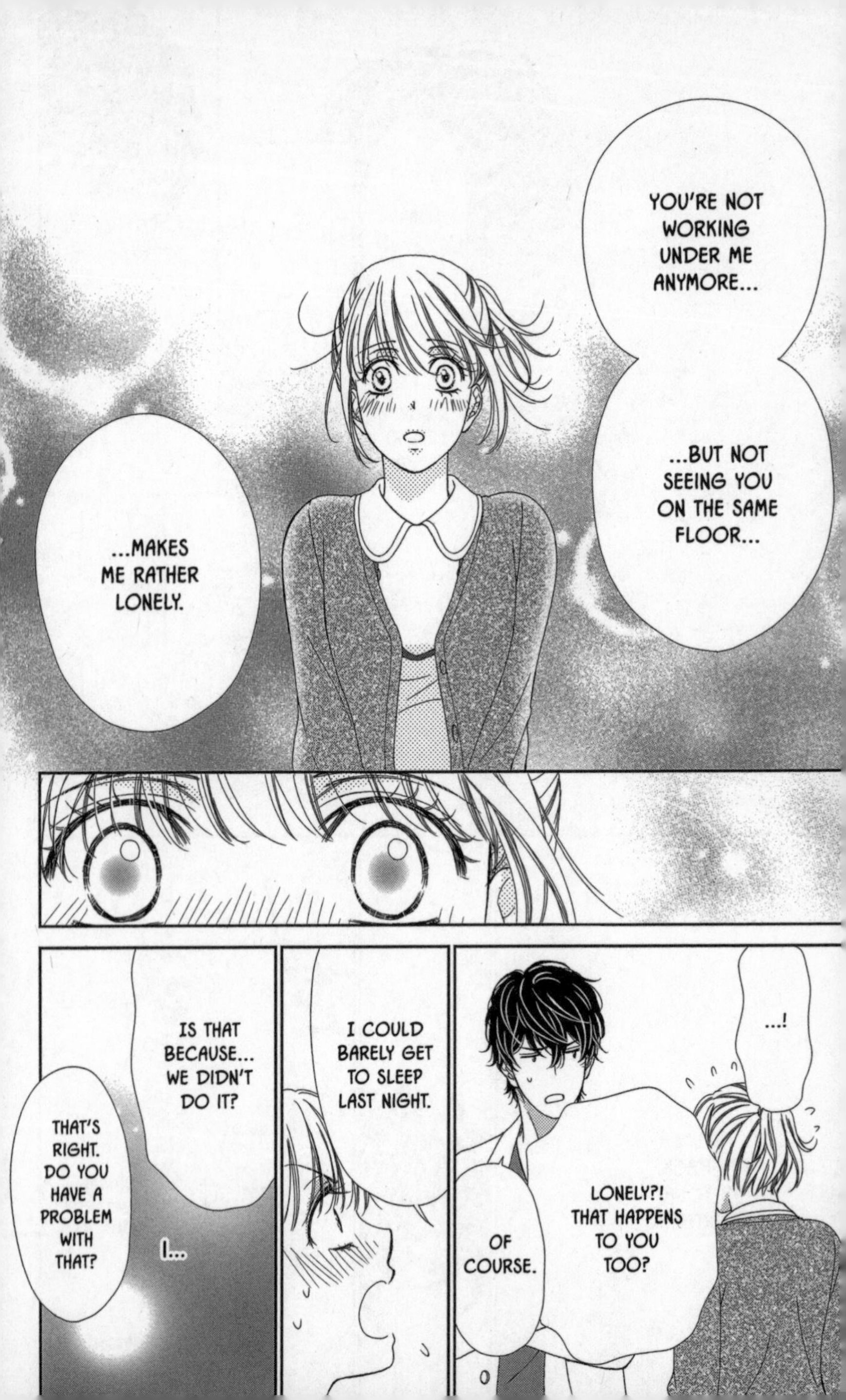
YOU'RE NOT WORKING UNDER ME ANYMORE...
...BUT NOT SEEING YOU ON THE SAME FLOOR...
...MAKES ME RATHER LONELY.
...!
LONELY?! THAT HAPPENS TO YOU TOO?
OF COURSE.
I COULD BARELY GET TO SLEEP LAST NIGHT.
IS THAT BECAUSE... WE DIDN'T DO IT?
THAT'S RIGHT. DO YOU HAVE A PROBLEM WITH THAT?
I...

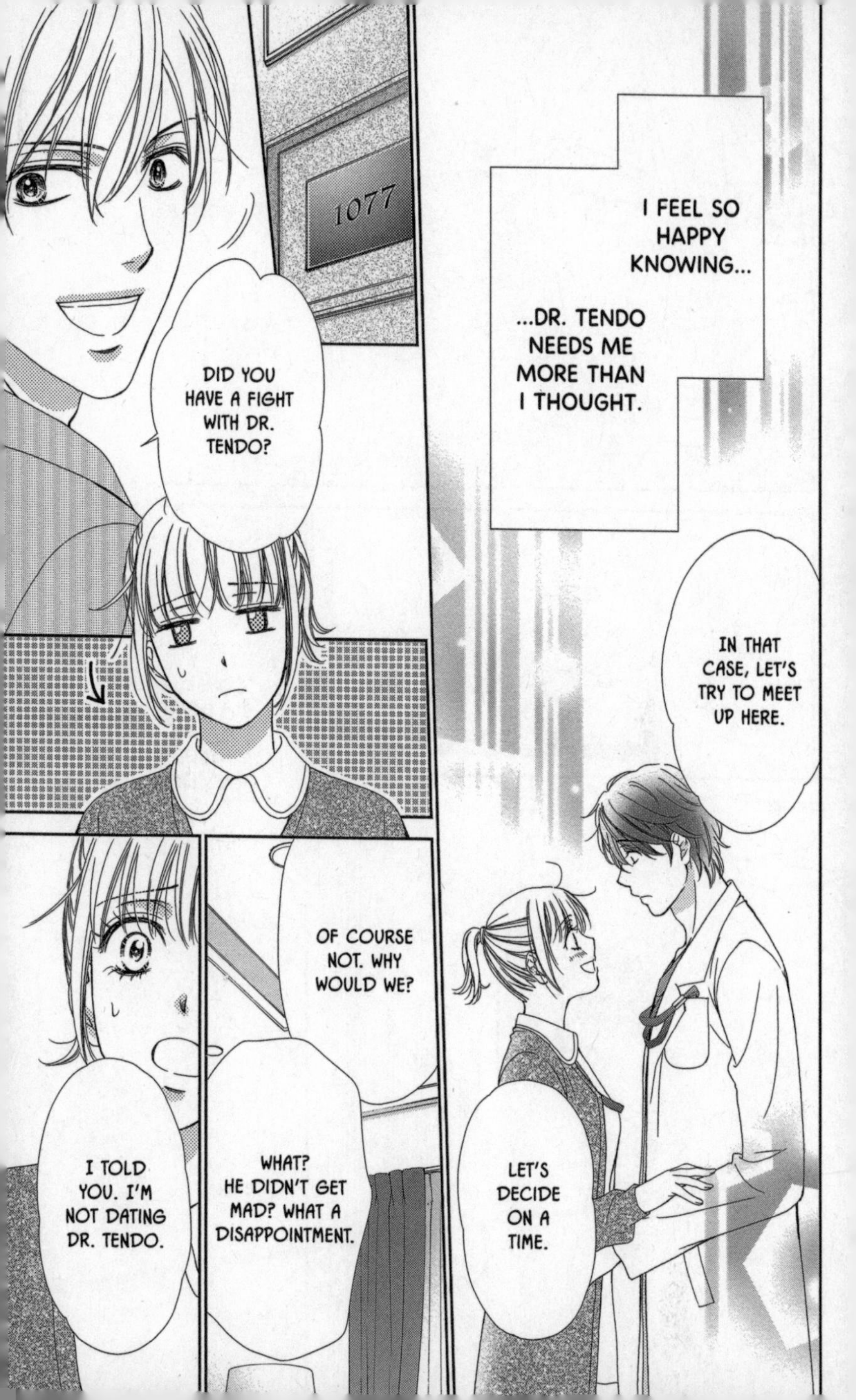
I FEEL SO HAPPY KNOWING...
...DR. TENDO NEEDS ME MORE THAN I THOUGHT.
IN THAT CASE, LET'S TRY TO MEET UP HERE.
LET'S DECIDE ON A TIME.
1077
DID YOU HAVE A FIGHT WITH DR. TENDO?
OF COURSE NOT. WHY WOULD WE?
WHAT? HE DIDN'T GET MAD? WHAT A DISAPPOINTMENT.
I TOLD YOU. I'M NOT DATING DR. TENDO.

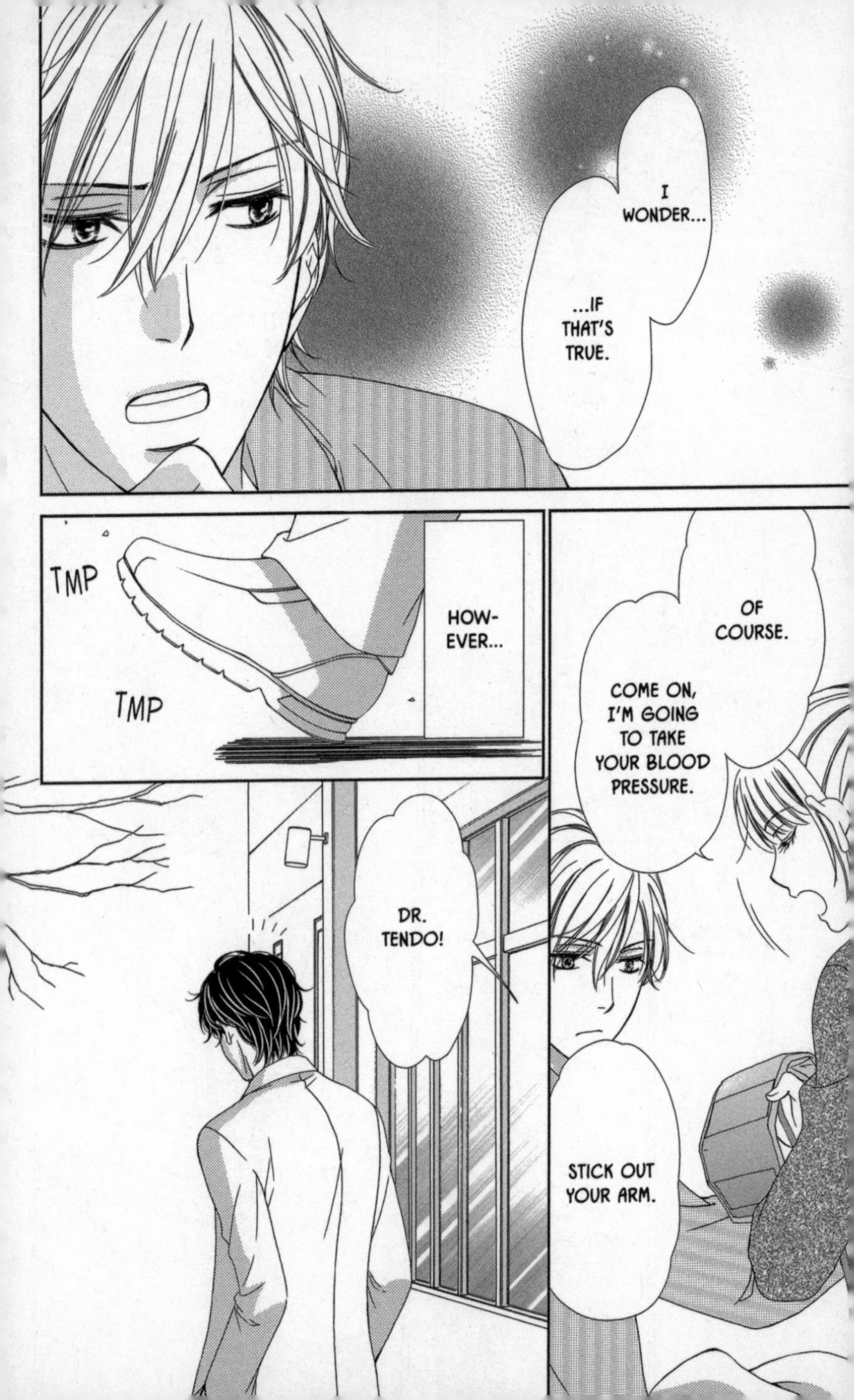
I WONDER...
...IF THAT'S TRUE.
OF COURSE.
COME ON, I'M GOING TO TAKE YOUR BLOOD PRESSURE.
STICK OUT YOUR ARM.
HOW-EVER...
TMP
TMP
DR. TENDO!

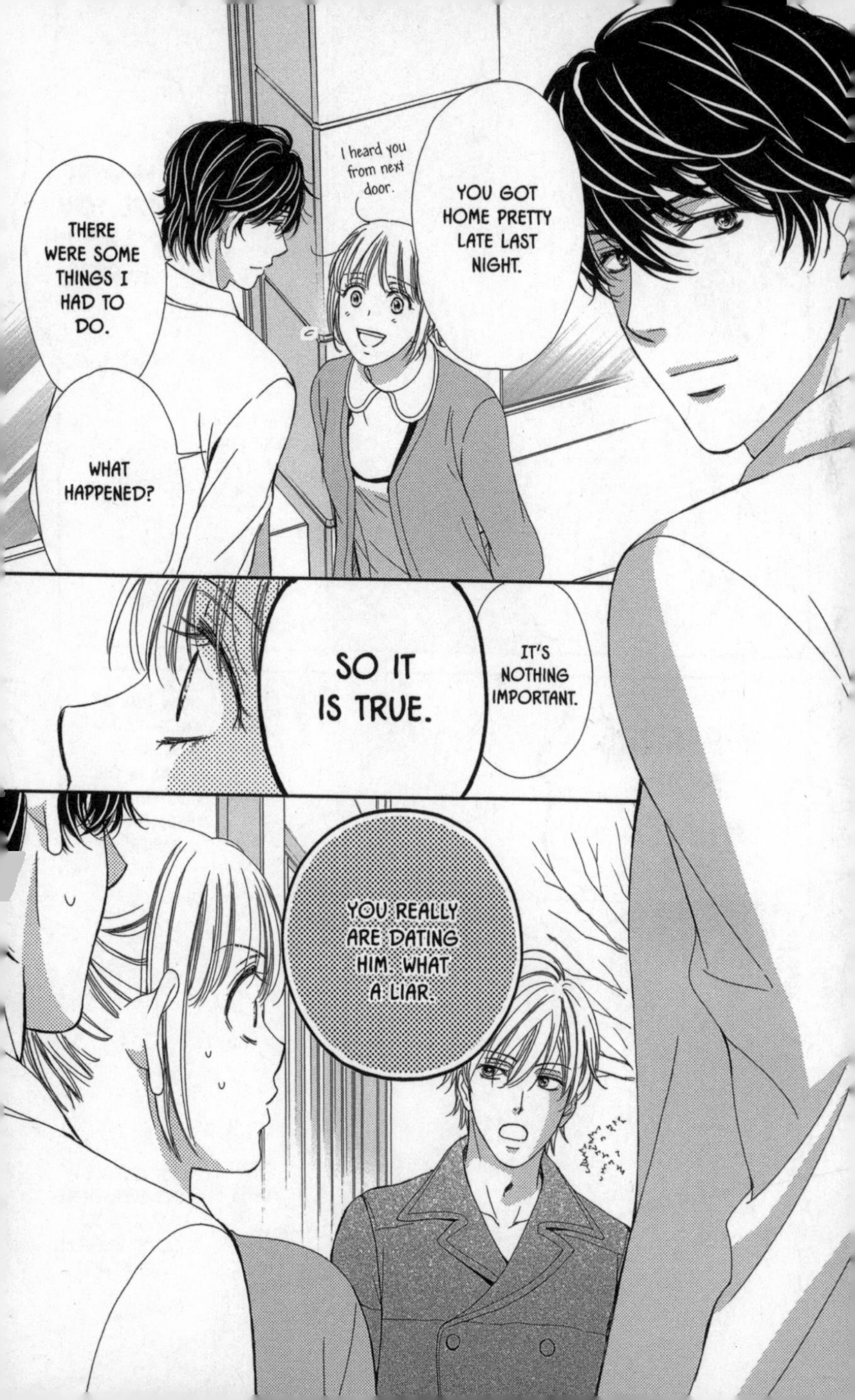
YOU GOT HOME PRETTY LATE LAST NIGHT.
I heard you from next door.
THERE WERE SOME THINGS I HAD TO DO.
WHAT HAPPENED?
IT'S NOTHING IMPORTANT.
SO IT IS TRUE.
YOU REALLY ARE DATING HIM. WHAT A LIAR.

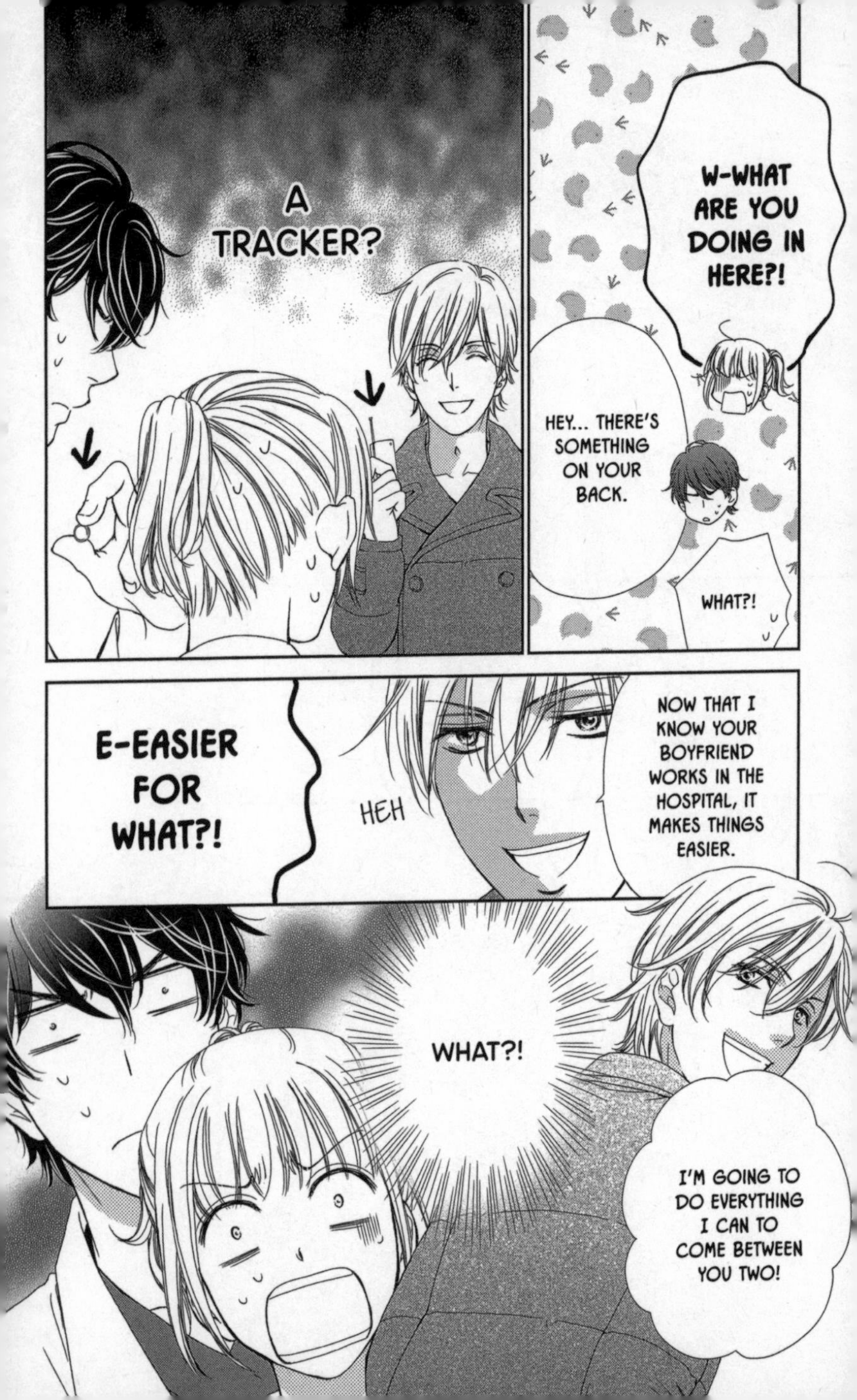
W-WHAT ARE YOU DOING IN HERE?!
HEY... THERE'S SOMETHING ON YOUR BACK.
WHAT?!
A TRACKER?
NOW THAT I KNOW YOUR BOYFRIEND WORKS IN THE HOSPITAL, IT MAKES THINGS EASIER.
HEH
E-EASIER FOR WHAT?!
I'M GOING TO DO EVERYTHING I CAN TO COME BETWEEN YOU TWO!
WHAT?!

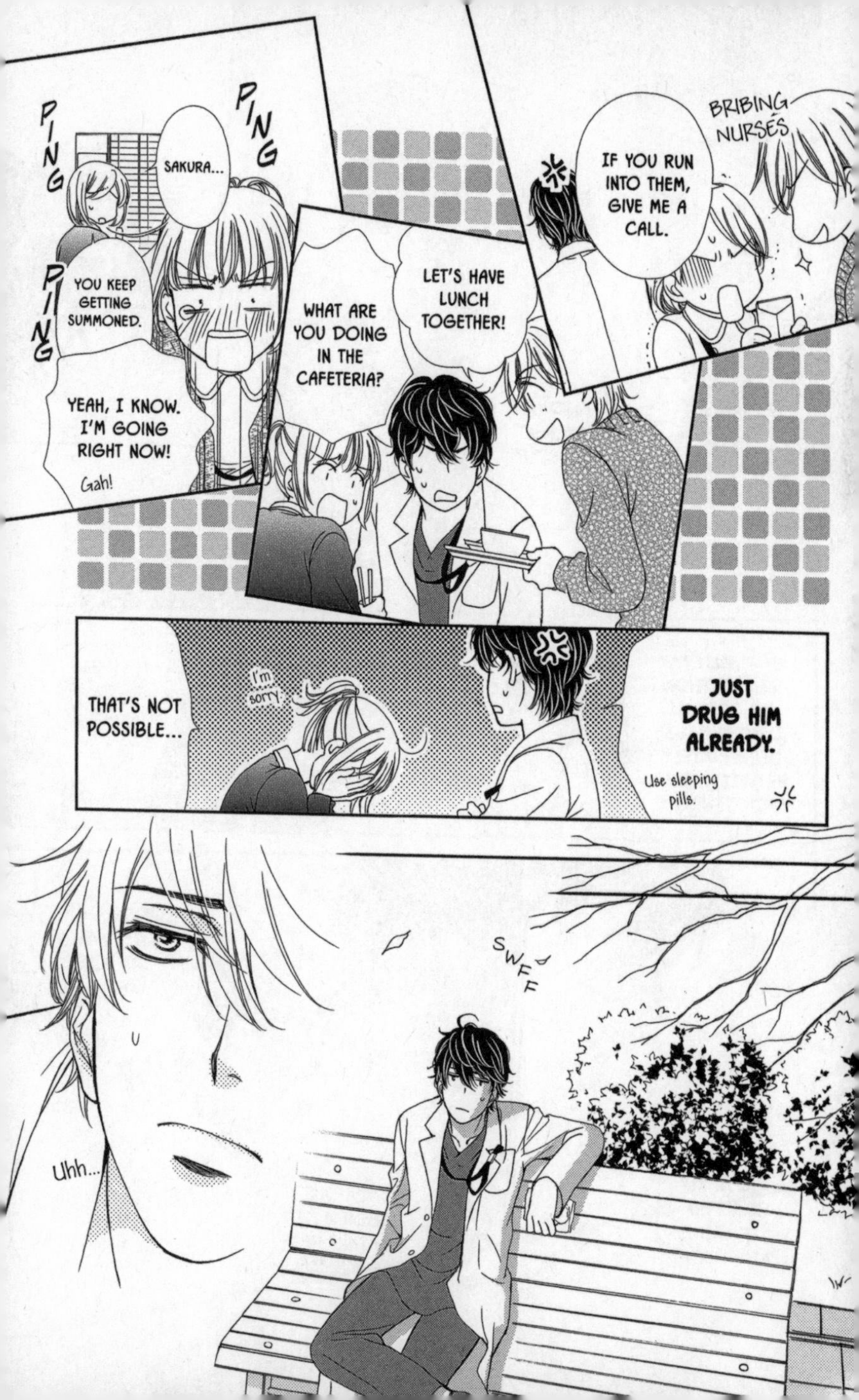
BRIBING NURSES
IF YOU RUN INTO THEM, GIVE ME A CALL.
PING PING
SAKURA...
PING
YOU KEEP GETTING SUMMONED.
PING
YEAH, I KNOW. I'M GOING RIGHT NOW!
Gah!
LET'S HAVE LUNCH TOGETHER!
WHAT ARE YOU DOING IN THE CAFETERIA?
JUST DRUG HIM ALREADY.
Use sleeping pills.
I'm sorry.
THAT'S NOT POSSIBLE...
SWFF
Uhh...

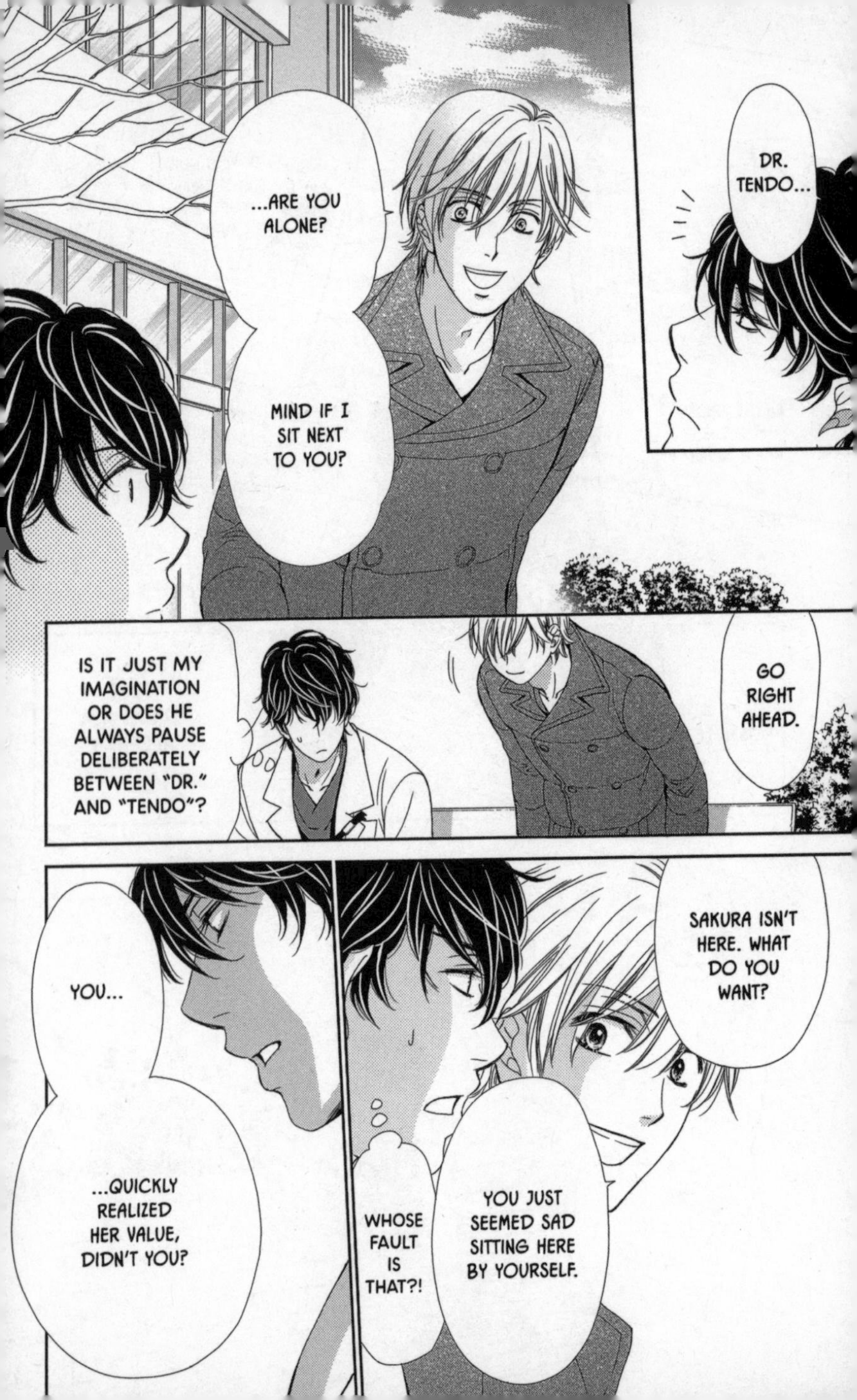
DR. TENDO...
...ARE YOU ALONE?
MIND IF I SIT NEXT TO YOU?
GO RIGHT AHEAD.
IS IT JUST MY IMAGINATION OR DOES HE ALWAYS PAUSE DELIBERATELY BETWEEN "DR." AND "TENDO"?
SAKURA ISN'T HERE. WHAT DO YOU WANT?
YOU JUST SEEMED SAD SITTING HERE BY YOURSELF.
WHOSE FAULT IS THAT?!
YOU...
...QUICKLY REALIZED HER VALUE, DIDN'T YOU?

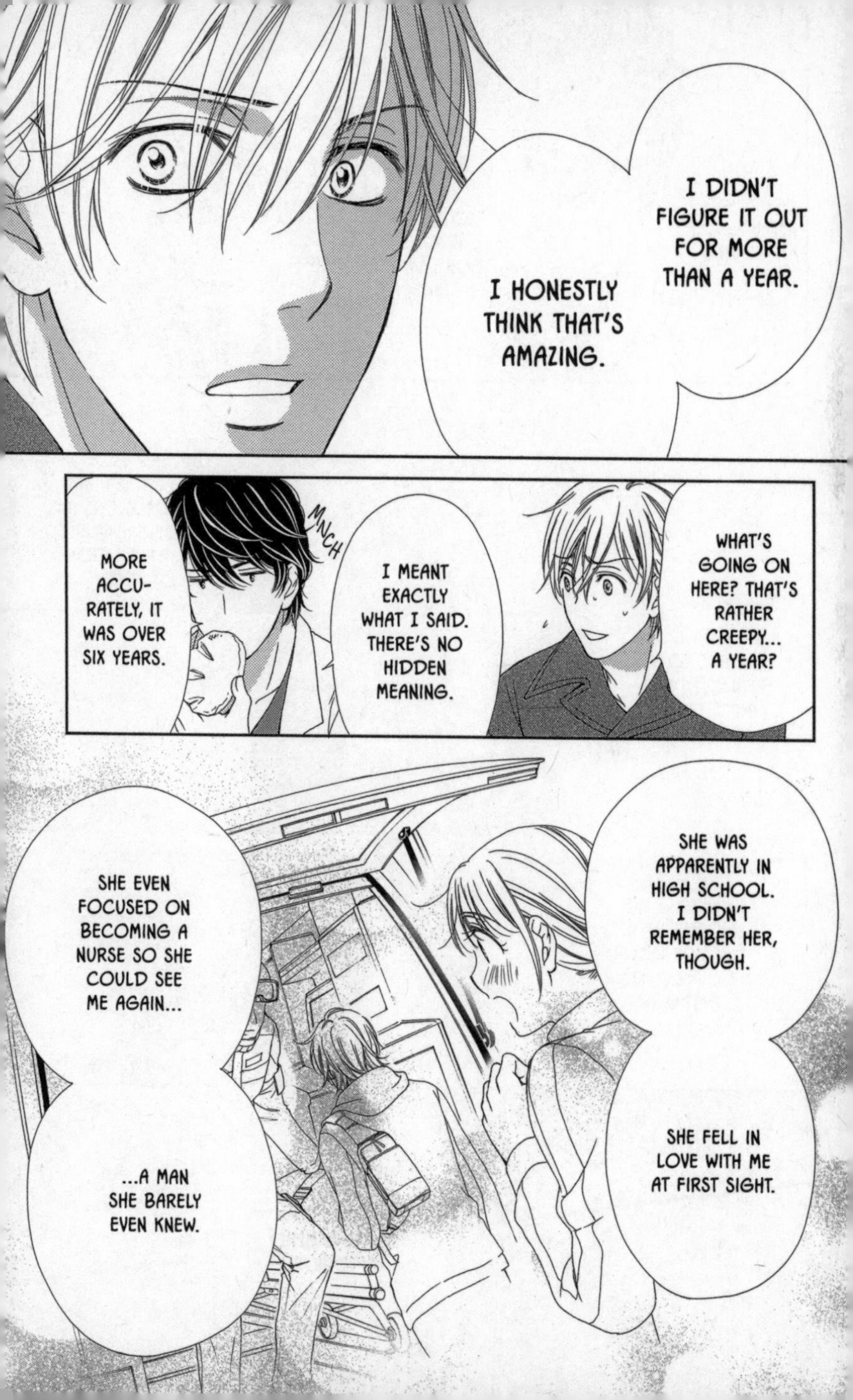
I DIDN'T FIGURE IT OUT FOR MORE THAN A YEAR.
I HONESTLY THINK THAT'S AMAZING.
WHAT'S GOING ON HERE? THAT'S RATHER CREEPY... A YEAR?
MNCH
I MEANT EXACTLY WHAT I SAID. THERE'S NO HIDDEN MEANING.
MORE ACCU-RATELY, IT WAS OVER SIX YEARS.
SHE WAS APPARENTLY IN HIGH SCHOOL. I DIDN'T REMEMBER HER, THOUGH.
SHE FELL IN LOVE WITH ME AT FIRST SIGHT.
SHE EVEN FOCUSED ON BECOMING A NURSE SO SHE COULD SEE ME AGAIN...
...A MAN SHE BARELY EVEN KNEW.

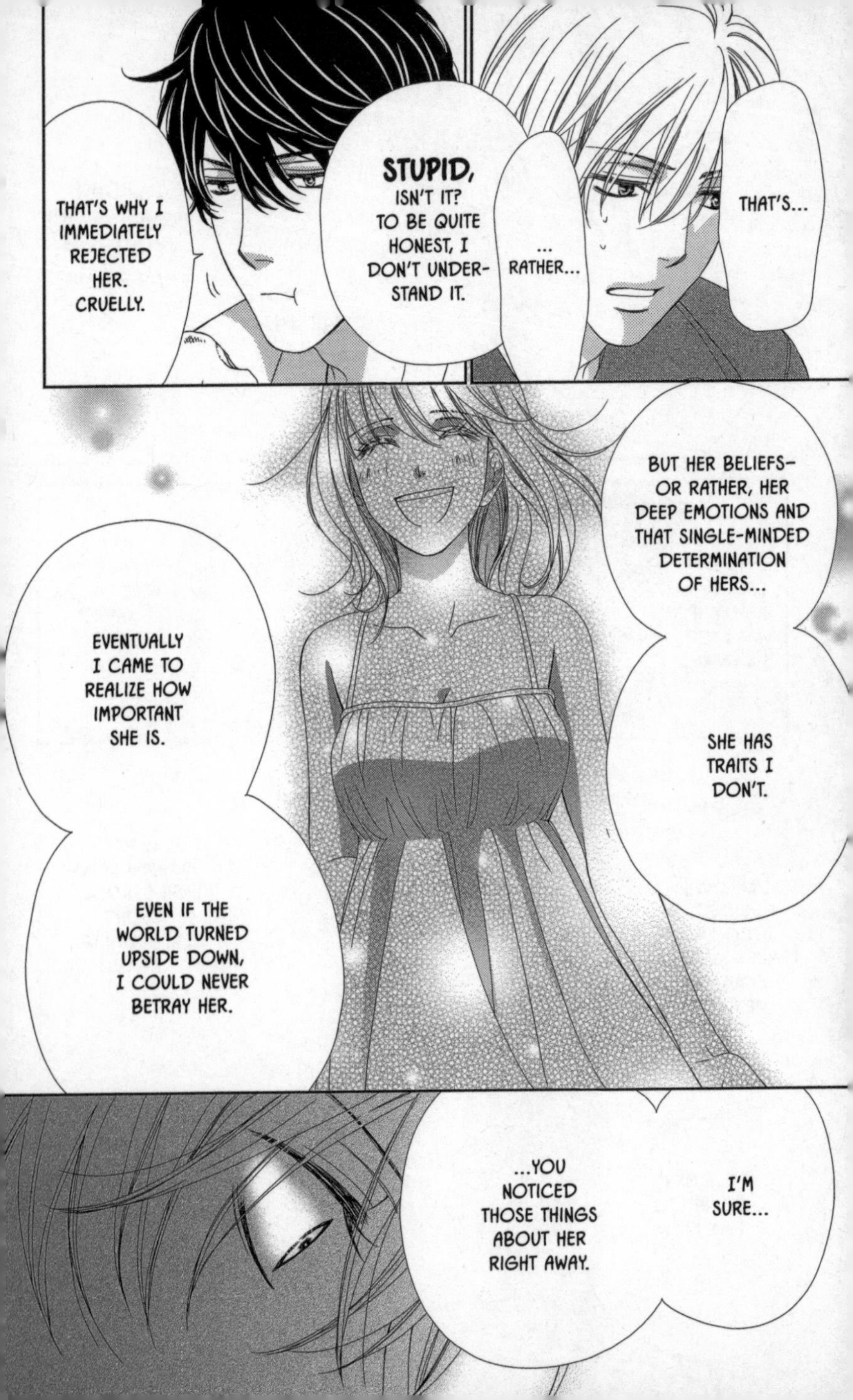
THAT'S...
... RATHER...
**STUPID,** ISN'T IT? TO BE QUITE HONEST, I DON'T UNDERSTAND IT.
THAT'S WHY I IMMEDIATELY REJECTED HER. CRUELLY.
BUT HER BELIEFS—OR RATHER, HER DEEP EMOTIONS AND THAT SINGLE-MINDED DETERMINATION OF HERS...
SHE HAS TRAITS I DON'T.
EVENTUALLY I CAME TO REALIZE HOW IMPORTANT SHE IS.
EVEN IF THE WORLD TURNED UPSIDE DOWN, I COULD NEVER BETRAY HER.
I'M SURE...
...YOU NOTICED THOSE THINGS ABOUT HER RIGHT AWAY.

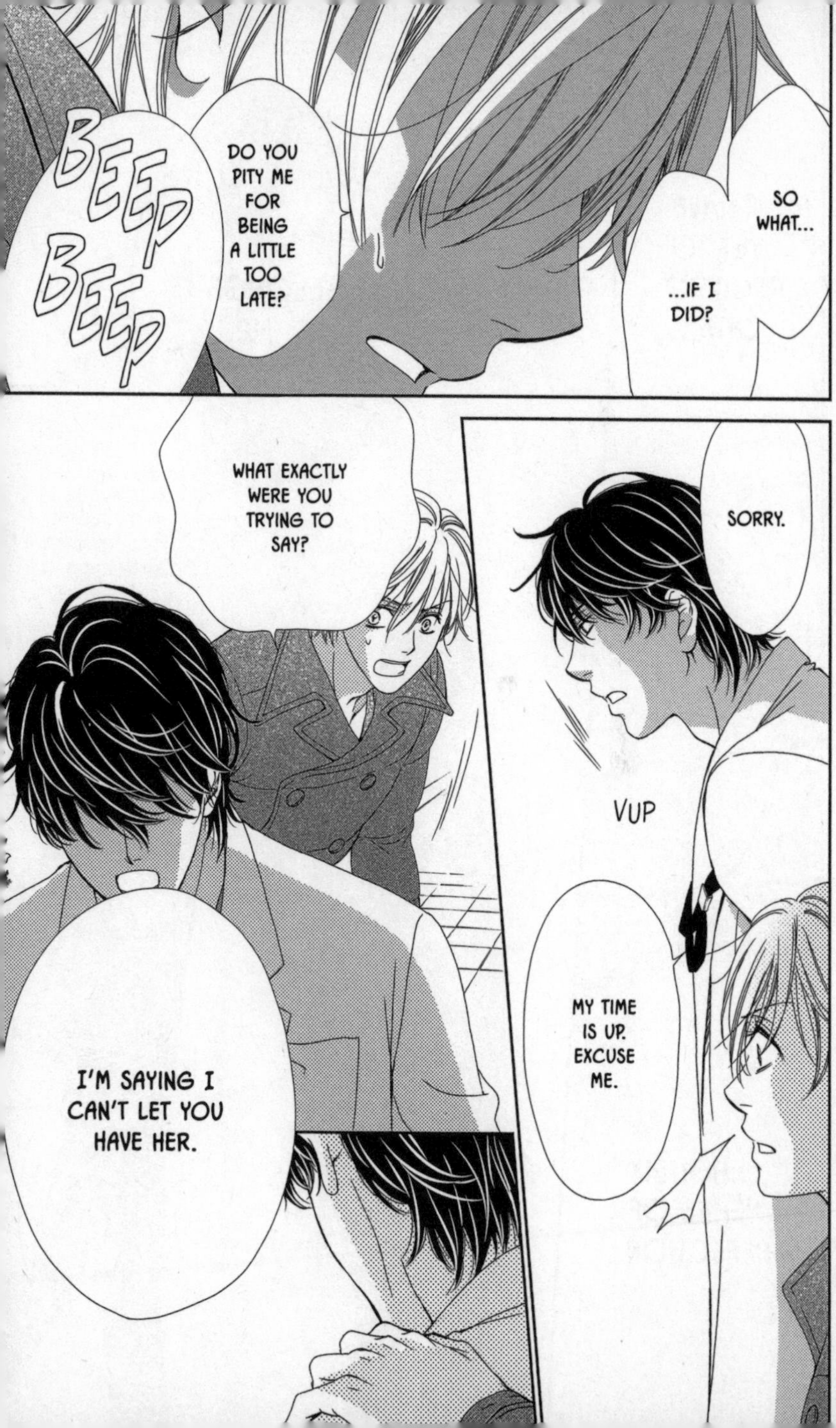
SO WHAT...
...IF I DID?
BEEP BEEP
DO YOU PITY ME FOR BEING A LITTLE TOO LATE?
SORRY.
VUP
MY TIME IS UP. EXCUSE ME.
WHAT EXACTLY WERE YOU TRYING TO SAY?
I'M SAYING I CAN'T LET YOU HAVE HER.

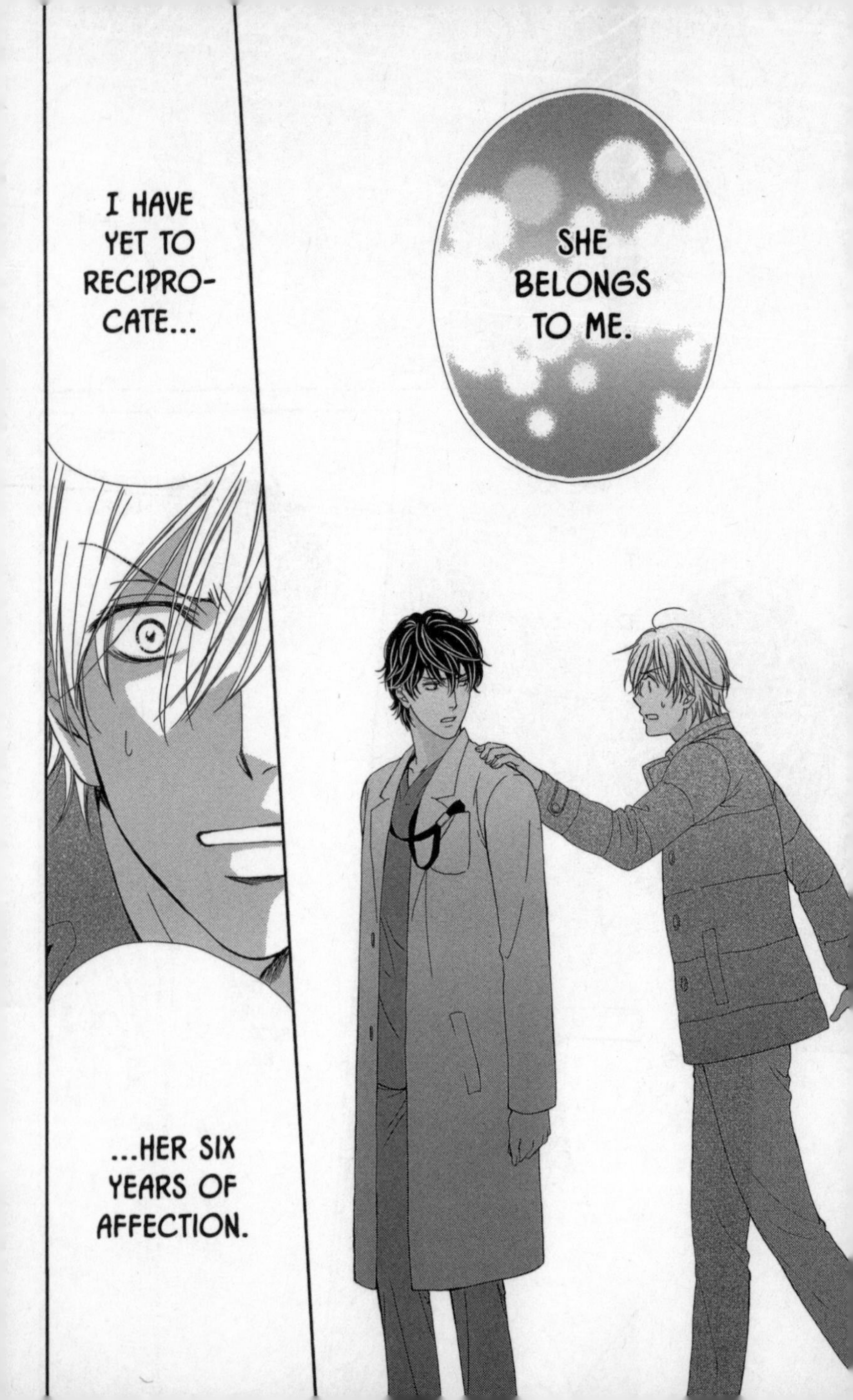
SHE BELONGS TO ME.
I HAVE YET TO RECIPROCATE...
...HER SIX YEARS OF AFFECTION.

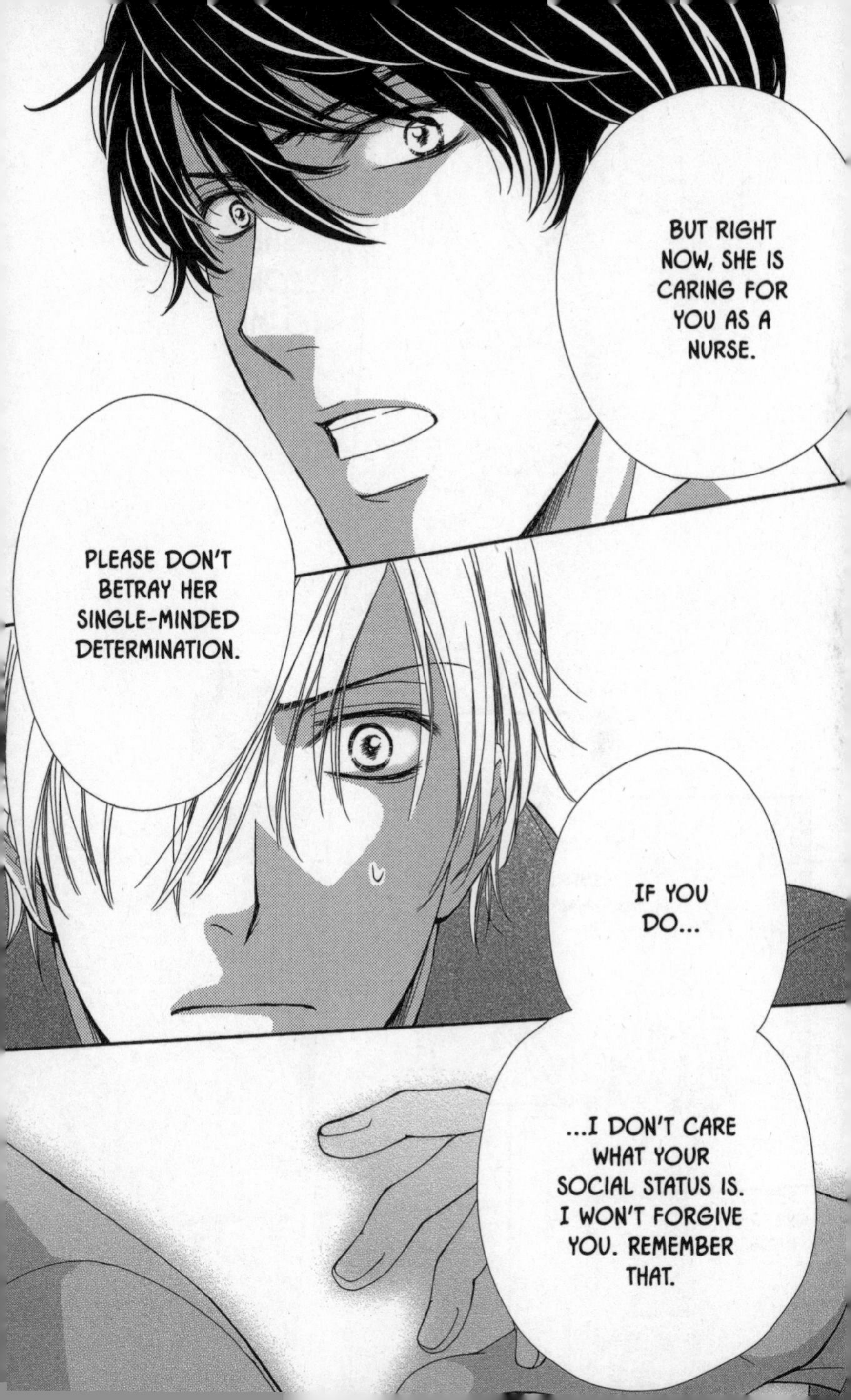
BUT RIGHT NOW, SHE IS CARING FOR YOU AS A NURSE.
PLEASE DON'T BETRAY HER SINGLE-MINDED DETERMINATION.
IF YOU DO...
...I DON'T CARE WHAT YOUR SOCIAL STATUS IS. I WON'T FORGIVE YOU. REMEMBER THAT.

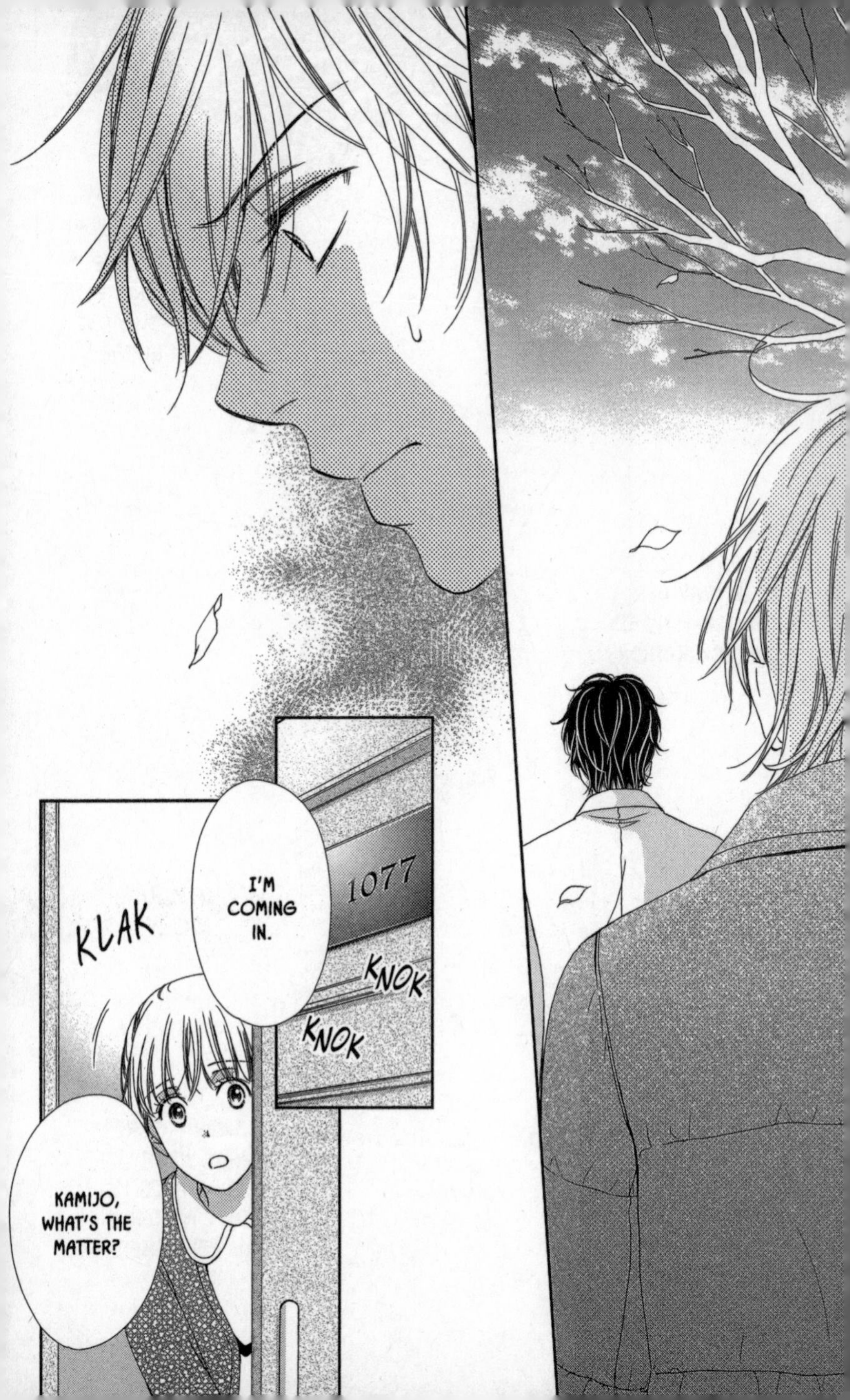
1077
KNOK
KNOK
I'M COMING IN.
KLAK
KAMIJO, WHAT'S THE MATTER?

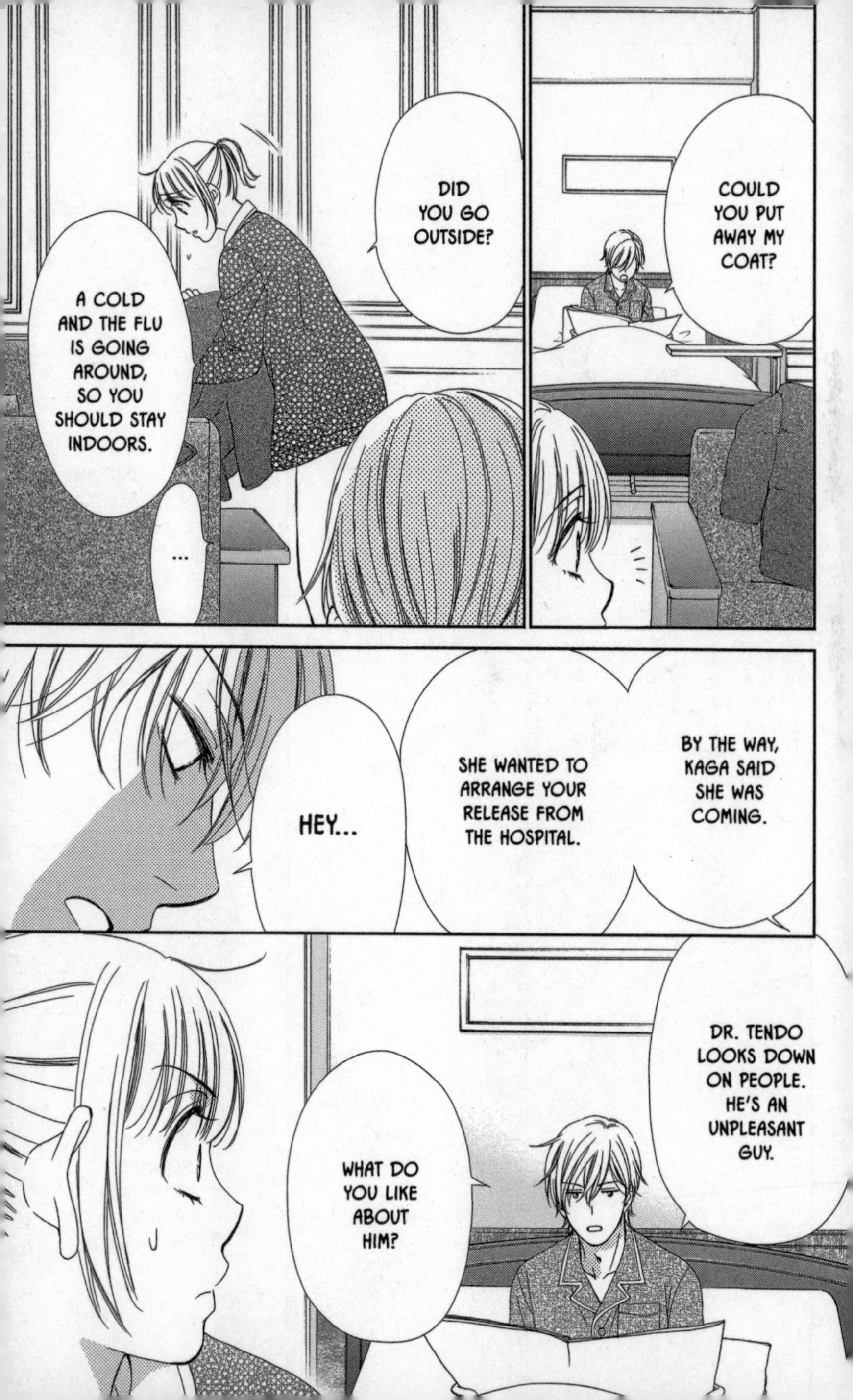
COULD YOU PUT AWAY MY COAT?
DID YOU GO OUTSIDE?
A COLD AND THE FLU IS GOING AROUND, SO YOU SHOULD STAY INDOORS.
...
BY THE WAY, KAGA SAID SHE WAS COMING.
SHE WANTED TO ARRANGE YOUR RELEASE FROM THE HOSPITAL.
HEY...
DR. TENDO LOOKS DOWN ON PEOPLE. HE'S AN UNPLEASANT GUY.
WHAT DO YOU LIKE ABOUT HIM?

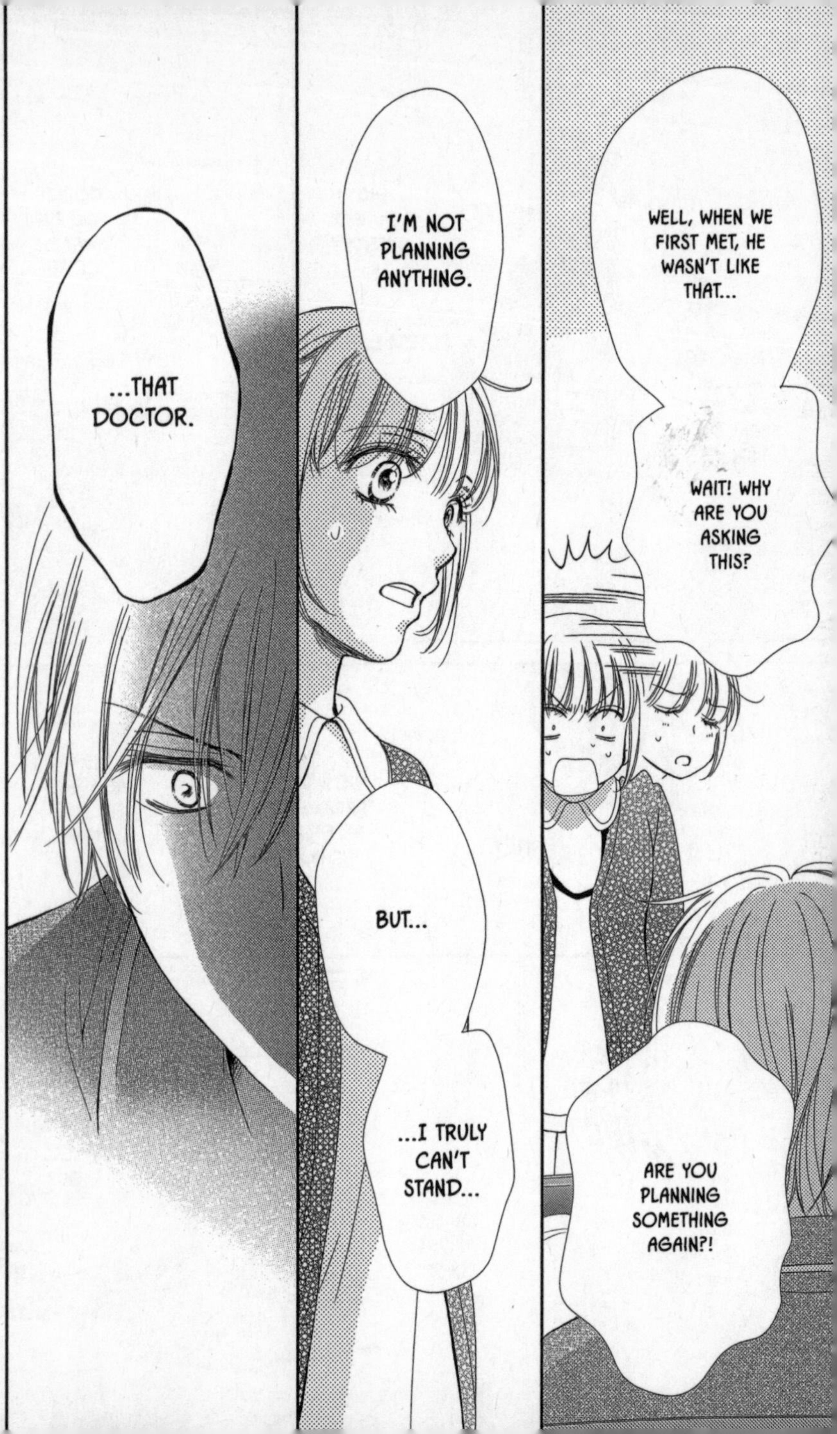
WELL, WHEN WE FIRST MET, HE WASN'T LIKE THAT...
WAIT! WHY ARE YOU ASKING THIS?
ARE YOU PLANNING SOMETHING AGAIN?!
I'M NOT PLANNING ANYTHING.
BUT...
...I TRULY CAN'T STAND...
...THAT DOCTOR.

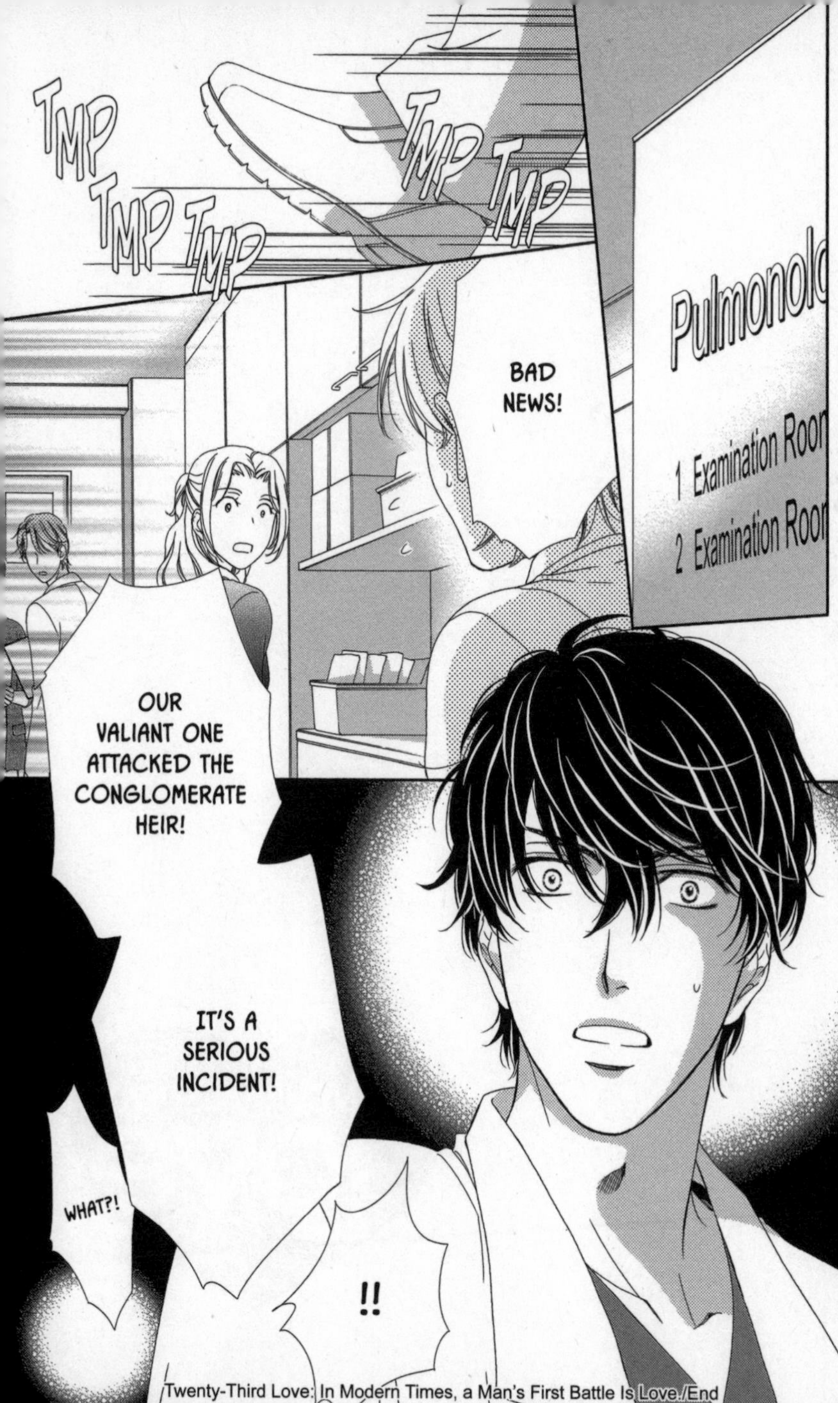
Pulmonolo
1 Examination Roo
2 Examination Roo
TMP TMP
TMP TMP TMP
BAD NEWS!
OUR VALIANT ONE ATTACKED THE CONGLOMERATE HEIR!
IT'S A SERIOUS INCIDENT!
!!
WHAT?!

Twenty-Third Love: In Modern Times, a Man's First Battle Is Love./End

AN INCURABLE CASE
OF LOVE

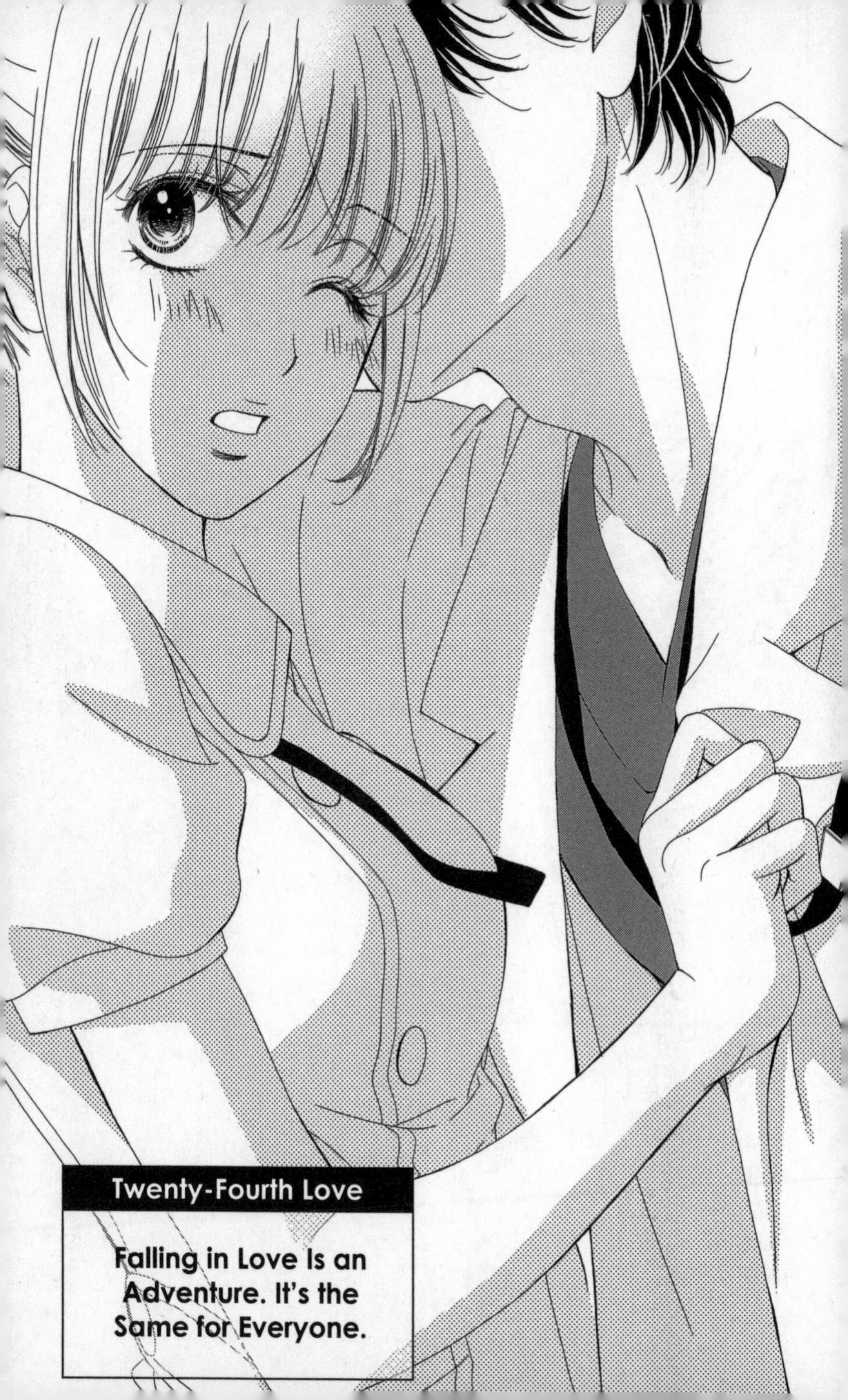
Twenty-Fourth Love
Falling in Love Is an Adventure. It's the Same for Everyone.

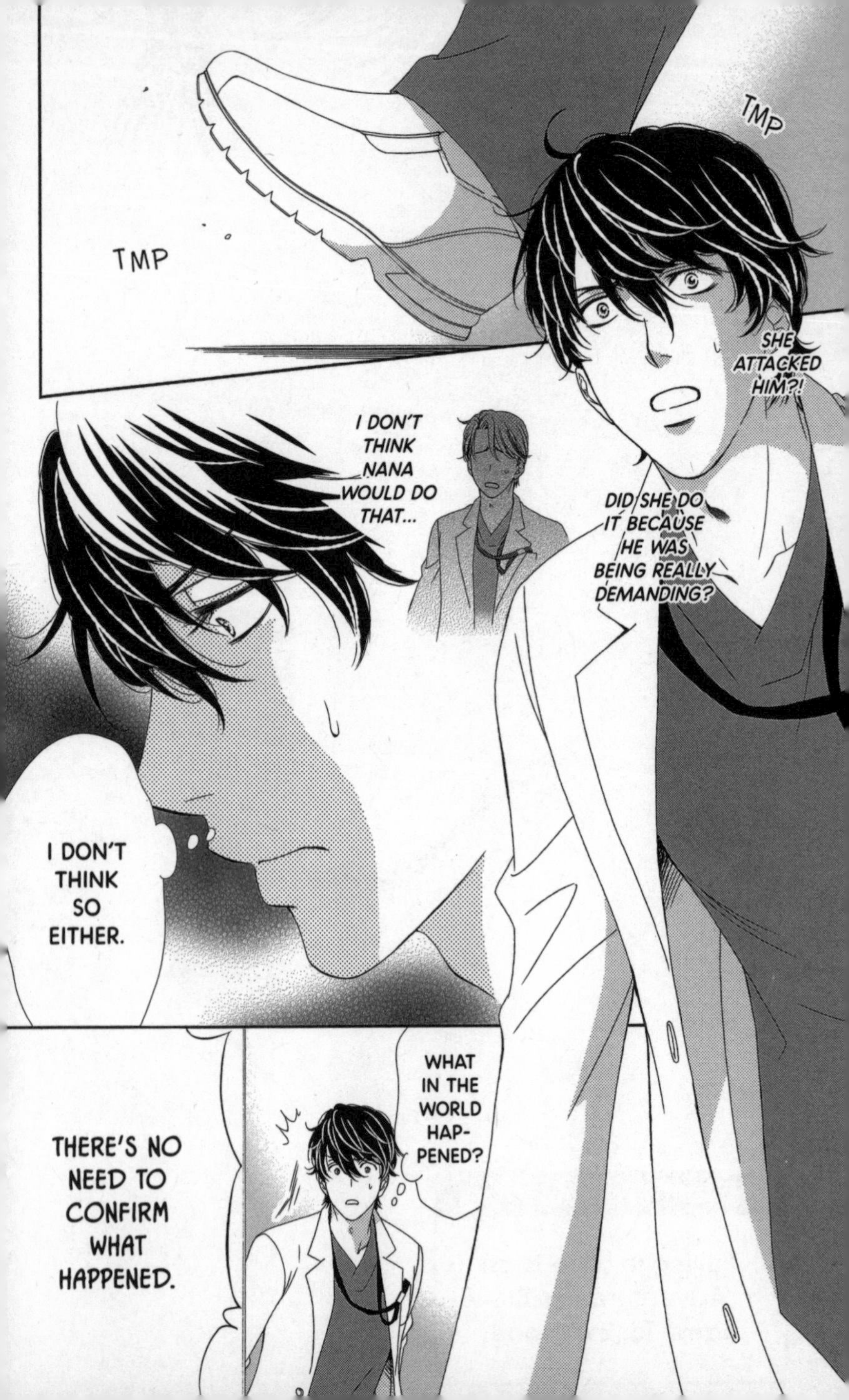
TMP
TMP
SHE ATTACKED HIM?!
DID SHE DO IT BECAUSE HE WAS BEING REALLY DEMANDING?
I DON'T THINK NANA WOULD DO THAT...
I DON'T THINK SO EITHER.
WHAT IN THE WORLD HAP-PENED?
THERE'S NO NEED TO CONFIRM WHAT HAPPENED.

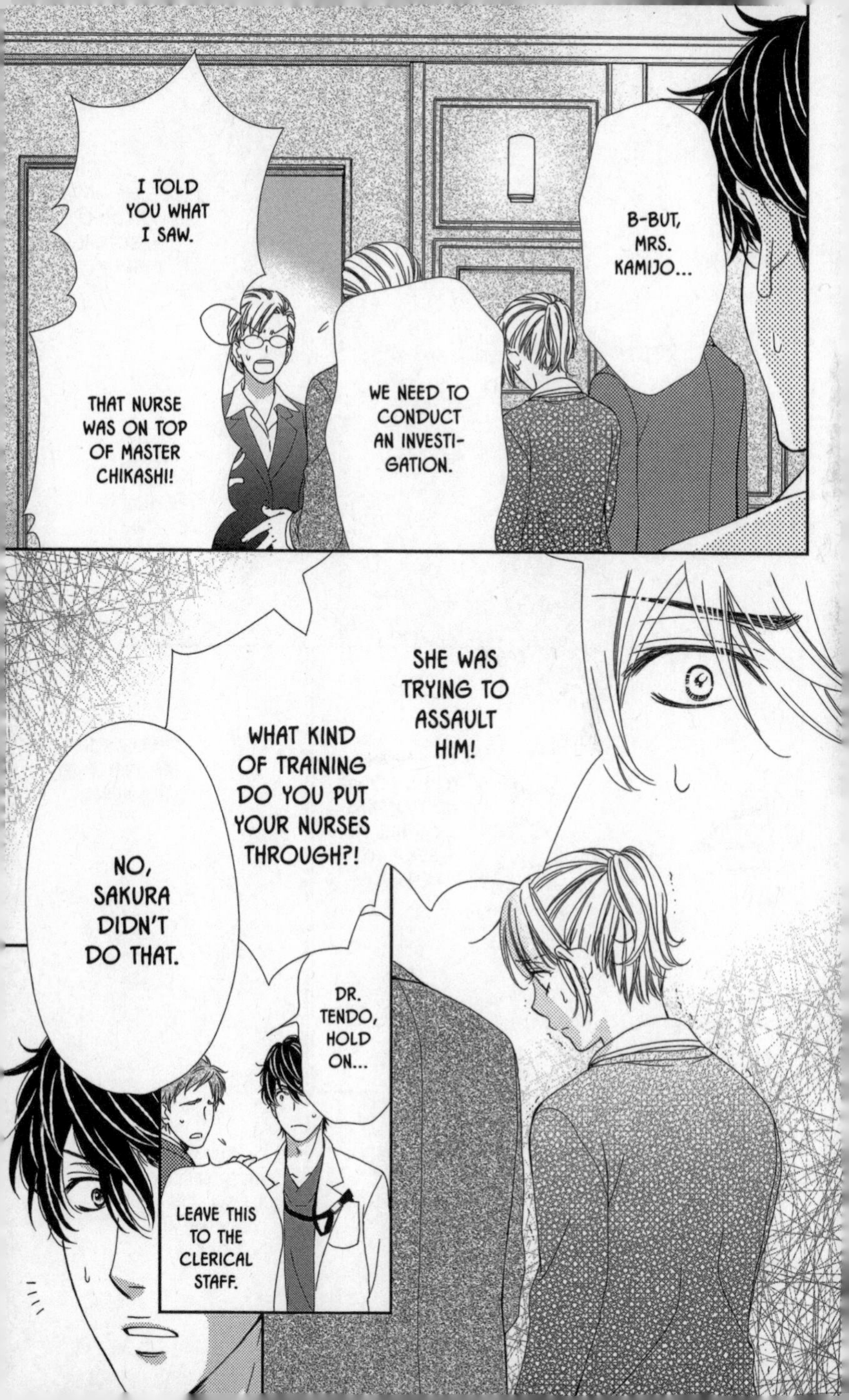
B-BUT, MRS. KAMIJO...
WE NEED TO CONDUCT AN INVESTIGATION.
I TOLD YOU WHAT I SAW.
THAT NURSE WAS ON TOP OF MASTER CHIKASHI!
SHE WAS TRYING TO ASSAULT HIM!
WHAT KIND OF TRAINING DO YOU PUT YOUR NURSES THROUGH?!
NO, SAKURA DIDN'T DO THAT.
DR. TENDO, HOLD ON...
LEAVE THIS TO THE CLERICAL STAFF.

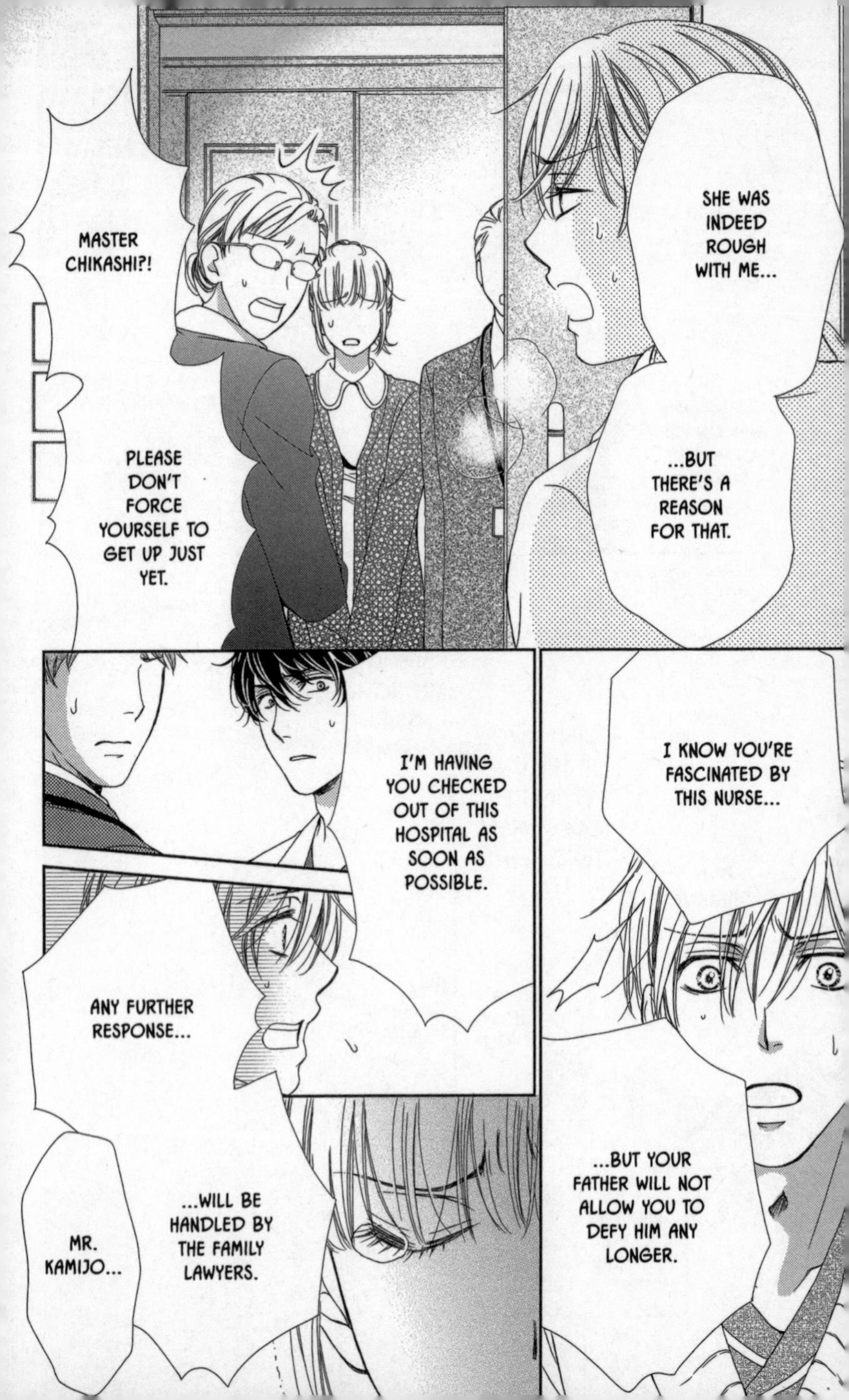
SHE WAS INDEED ROUGH WITH ME...
...BUT THERE'S A REASON FOR THAT.
MASTER CHIKASHI?!
PLEASE DON'T FORCE YOURSELF TO GET UP JUST YET.
I KNOW YOU'RE FASCINATED BY THIS NURSE...
...BUT YOUR FATHER WILL NOT ALLOW YOU TO DEFY HIM ANY LONGER.
I'M HAVING YOU CHECKED OUT OF THIS HOSPITAL AS SOON AS POSSIBLE.
ANY FURTHER RESPONSE...
...WILL BE HANDLED BY THE FAMILY LAWYERS.
MR. KAMIJO...

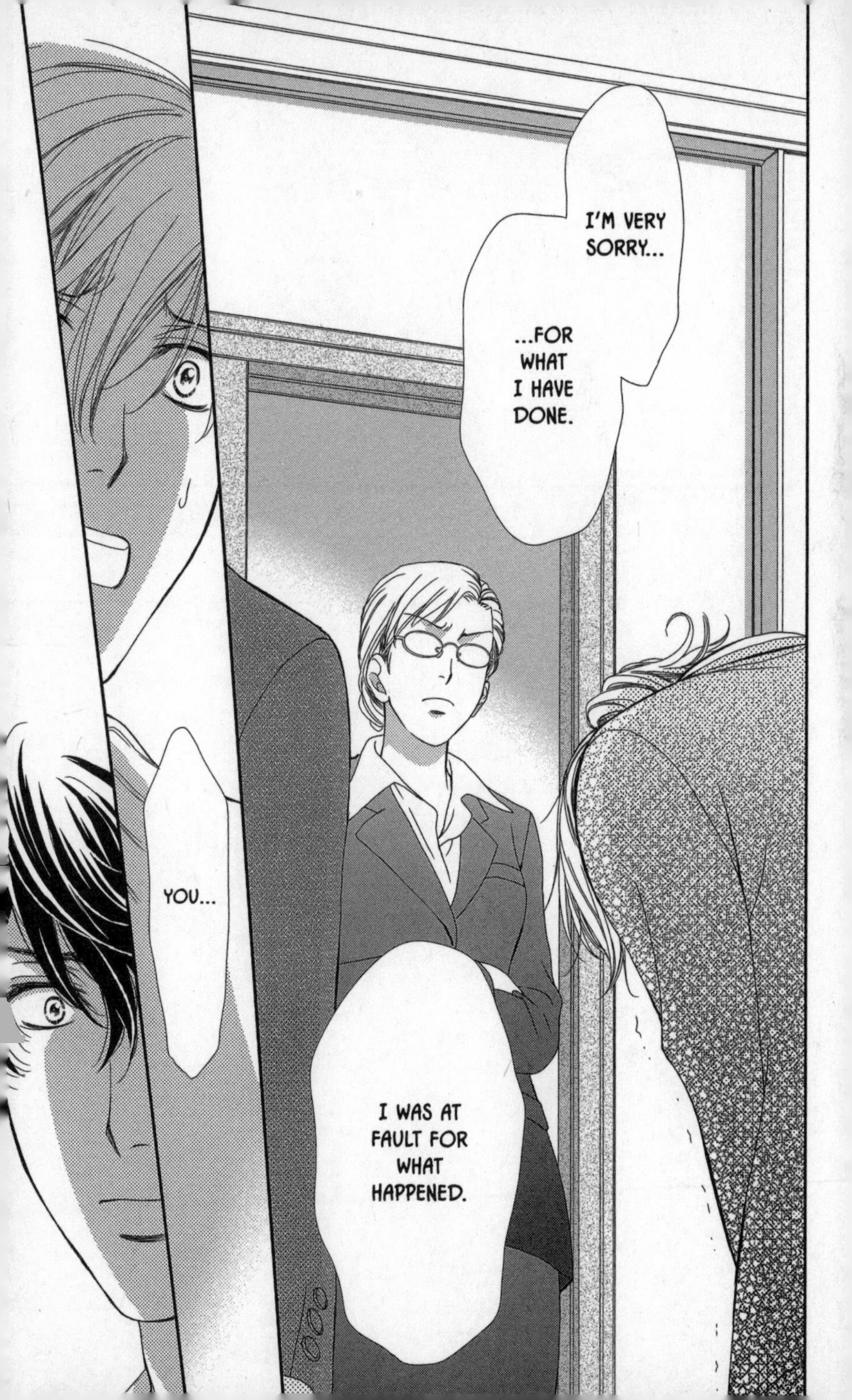
I'M VERY SORRY...
...FOR WHAT I HAVE DONE.
I WAS AT FAULT FOR WHAT HAPPENED.
YOU...

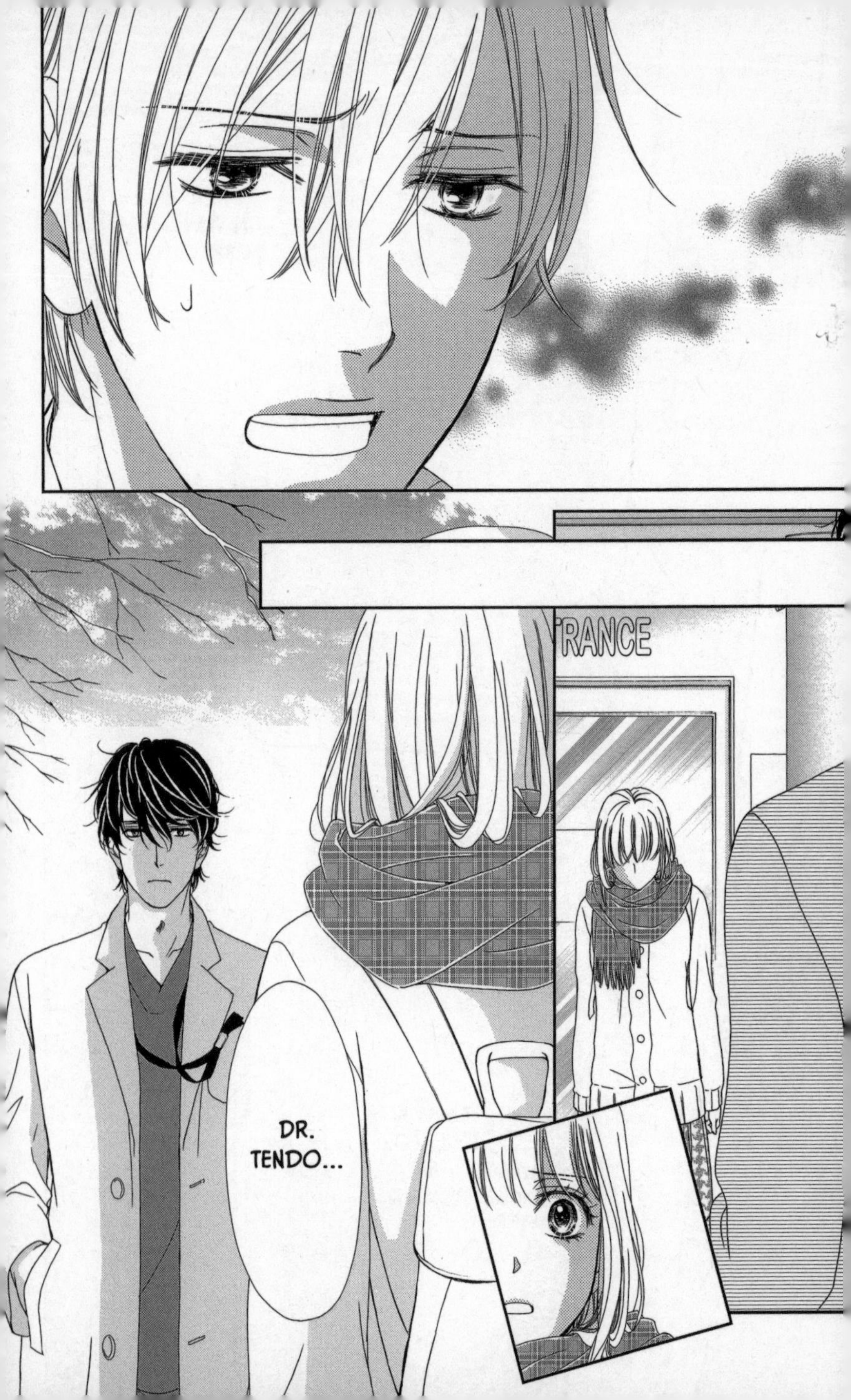
RANCE
DR. TENDO...

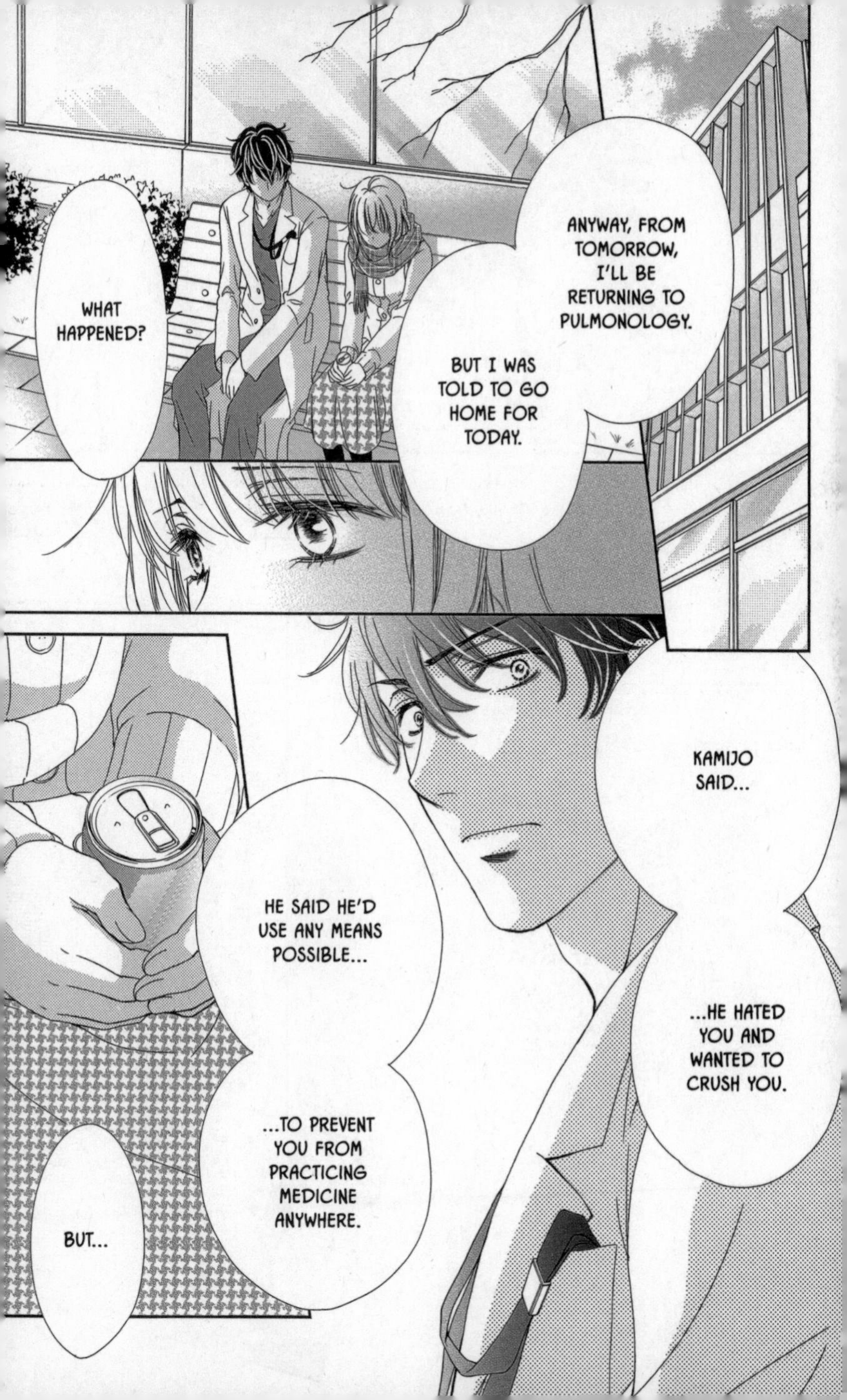
ANYWAY, FROM TOMORROW, I'LL BE RETURNING TO PULMONOLOGY.
BUT I WAS TOLD TO GO HOME FOR TODAY.
WHAT HAPPENED?
KAMIJO SAID...
...HE HATED YOU AND WANTED TO CRUSH YOU.
HE SAID HE'D USE ANY MEANS POSSIBLE...
...TO PREVENT YOU FROM PRACTICING MEDICINE ANYWHERE.
BUT...

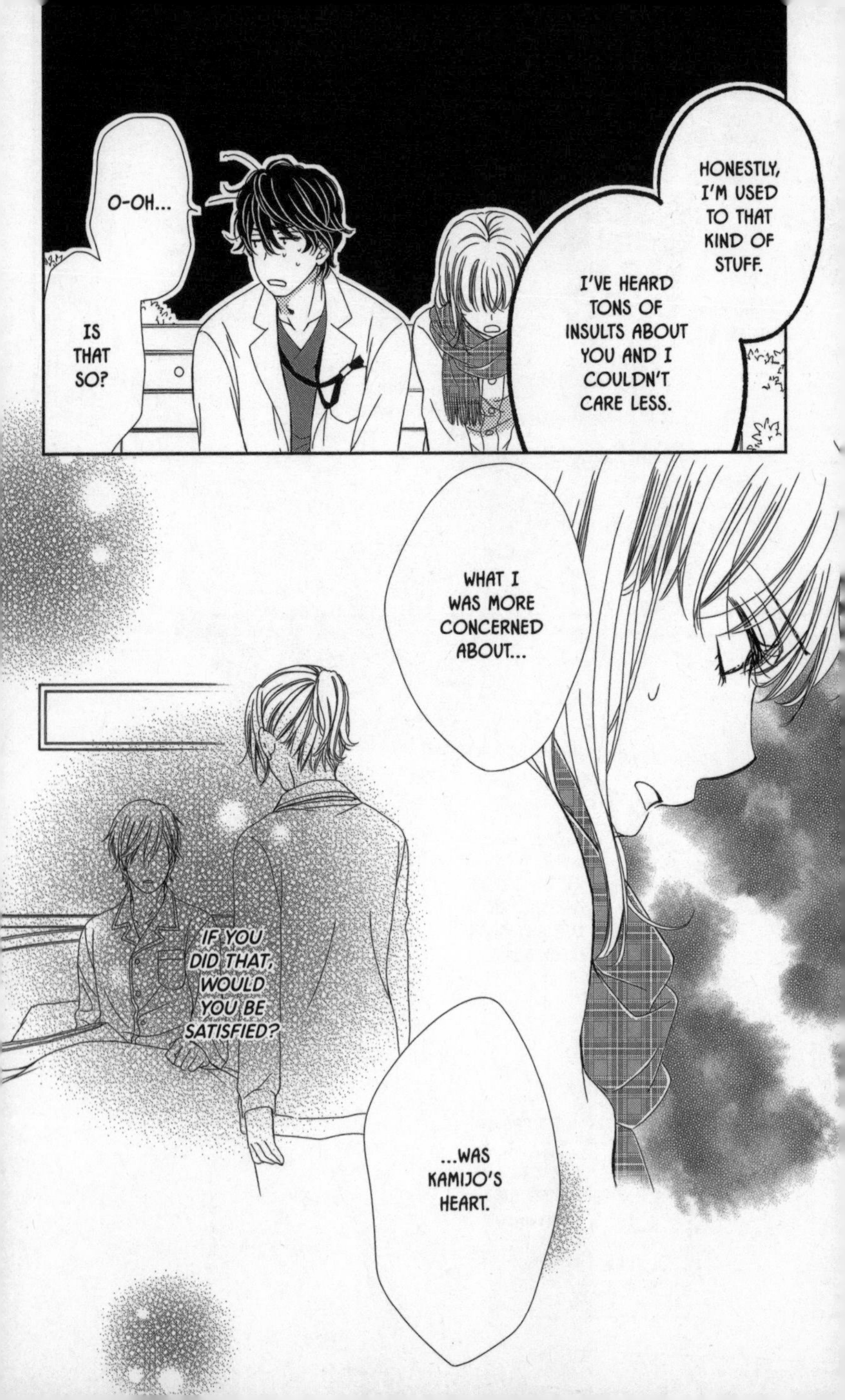
HONESTLY, I'M USED TO THAT KIND OF STUFF.
I'VE HEARD TONS OF INSULTS ABOUT YOU AND I COULDN'T CARE LESS.
O-OH...
IS THAT SO?
WHAT I WAS MORE CONCERNED ABOUT...
IF YOU DID THAT, WOULD YOU BE SATISFIED?
...WAS KAMIJO'S HEART.

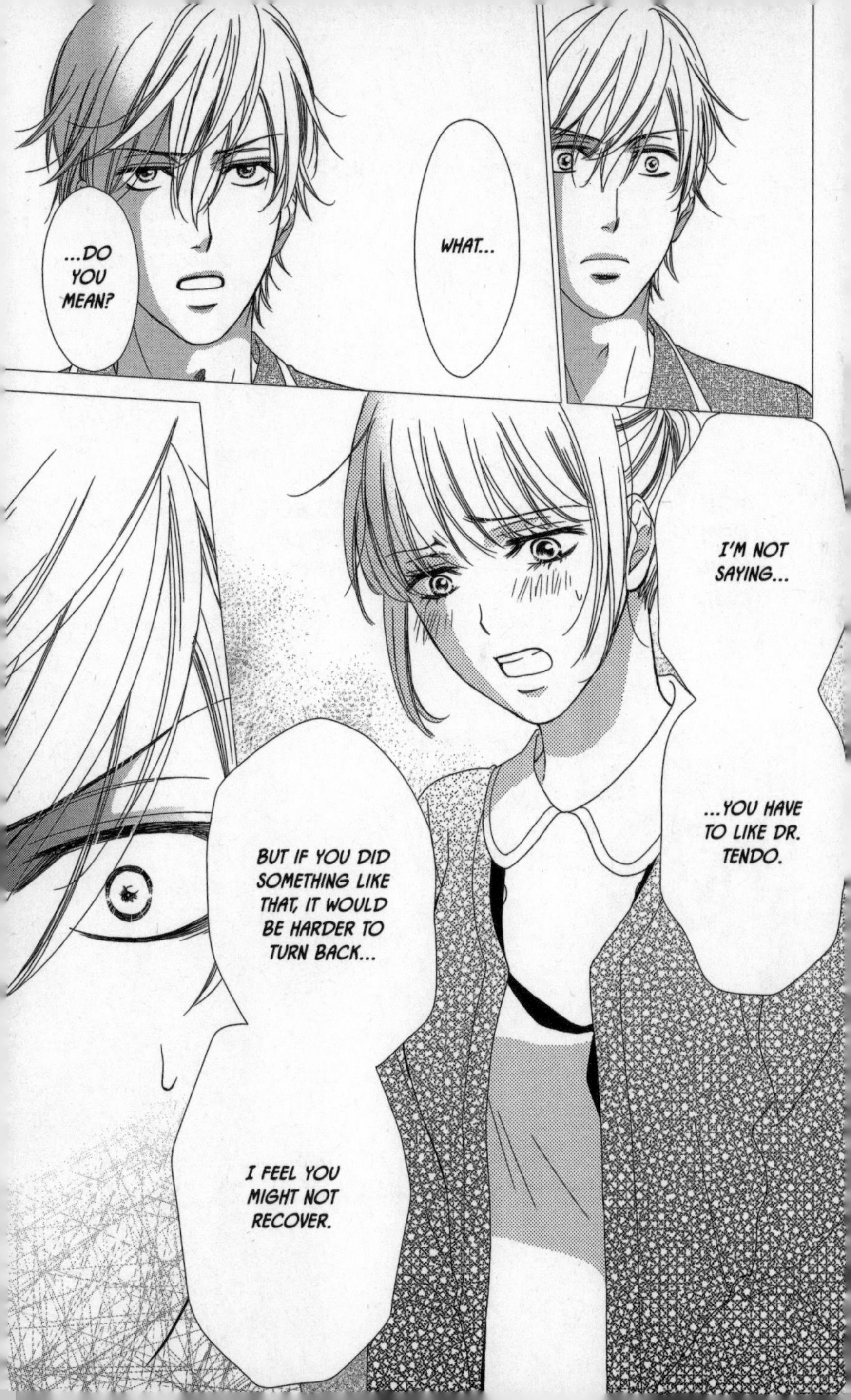
WHAT...
...DO YOU MEAN?
I'M NOT SAYING...
...YOU HAVE TO LIKE DR. TENDO.
BUT IF YOU DID SOMETHING LIKE THAT, IT WOULD BE HARDER TO TURN BACK...
I FEEL YOU MIGHT NOT RECOVER.

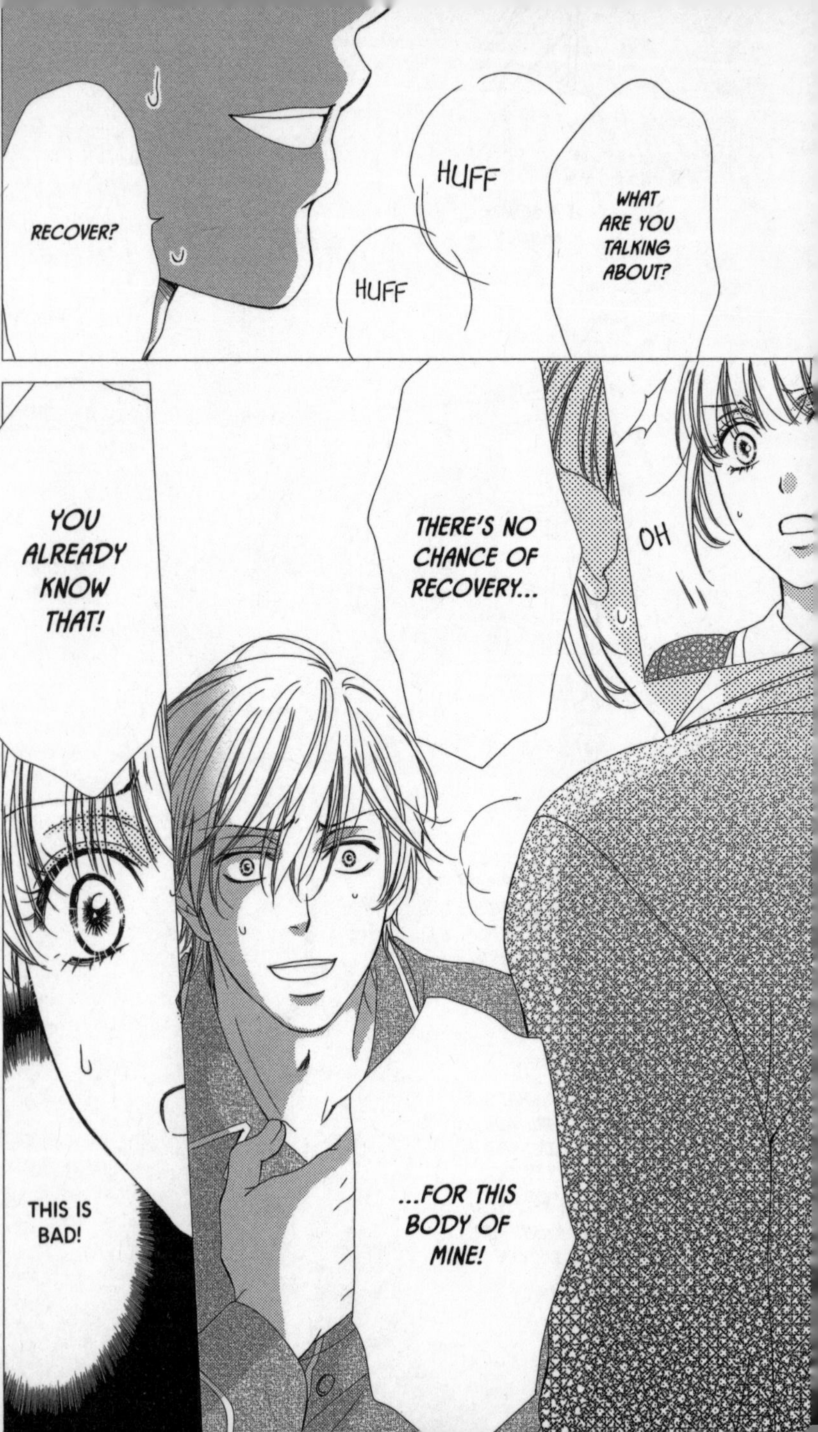
WHAT ARE YOU TALKING ABOUT?
HUFF
HUFF
RECOVER?
OH
THERE'S NO CHANCE OF RECOVERY...
...FOR THIS BODY OF MINE!
YOU ALREADY KNOW THAT!
THIS IS BAD!

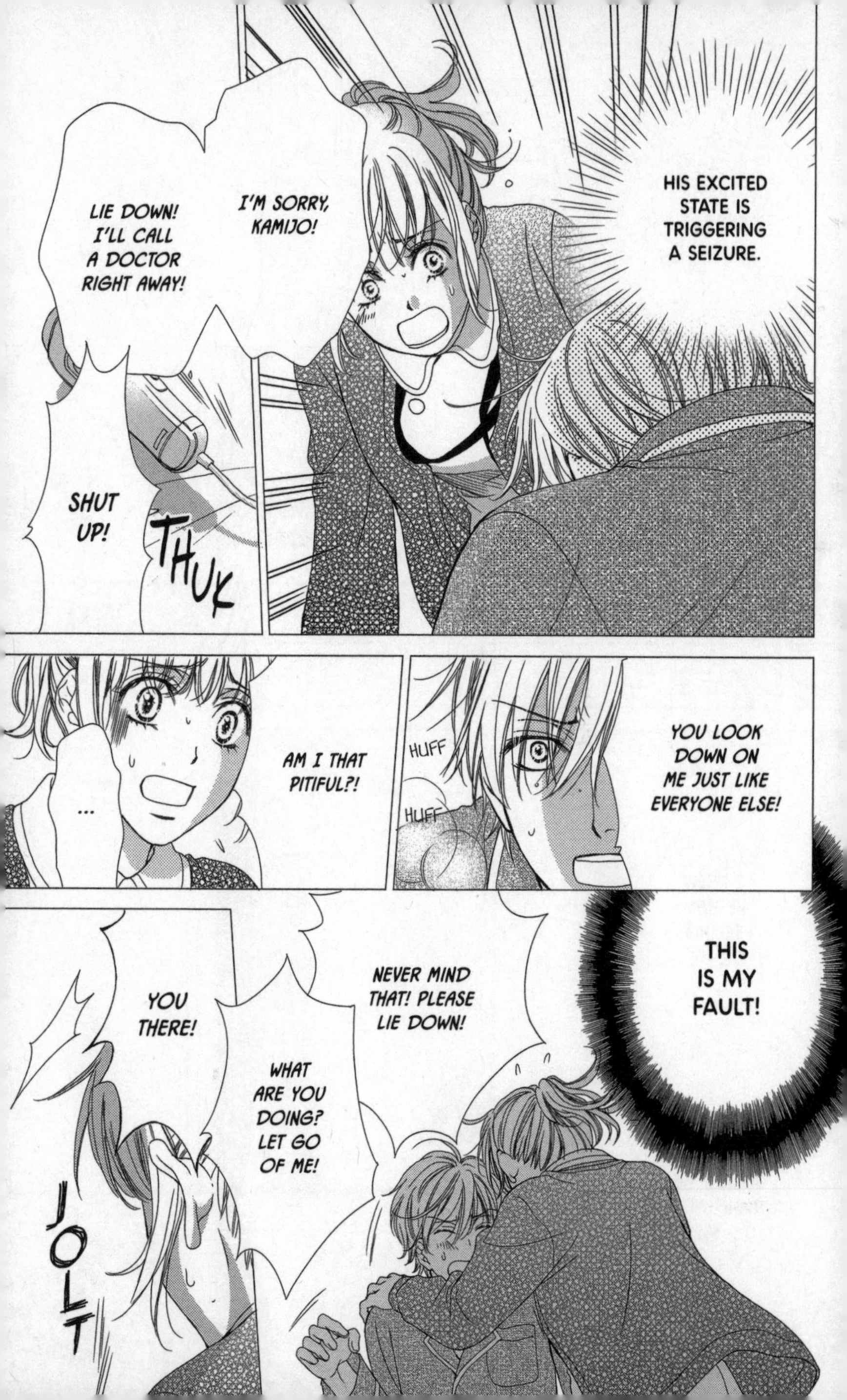
HIS EXCITED STATE IS TRIGGERING A SEIZURE.
I'M SORRY, KAMIJO!
LIE DOWN! I'LL CALL A DOCTOR RIGHT AWAY!
SHUT UP!
THUK
YOU LOOK DOWN ON ME JUST LIKE EVERYONE ELSE!
HUFF
HUFF
AM I THAT PITIFUL?!
...
THIS IS MY FAULT!
NEVER MIND THAT! PLEASE LIE DOWN!
YOU THERE!
WHAT ARE YOU DOING? LET GO OF ME!
JOLT

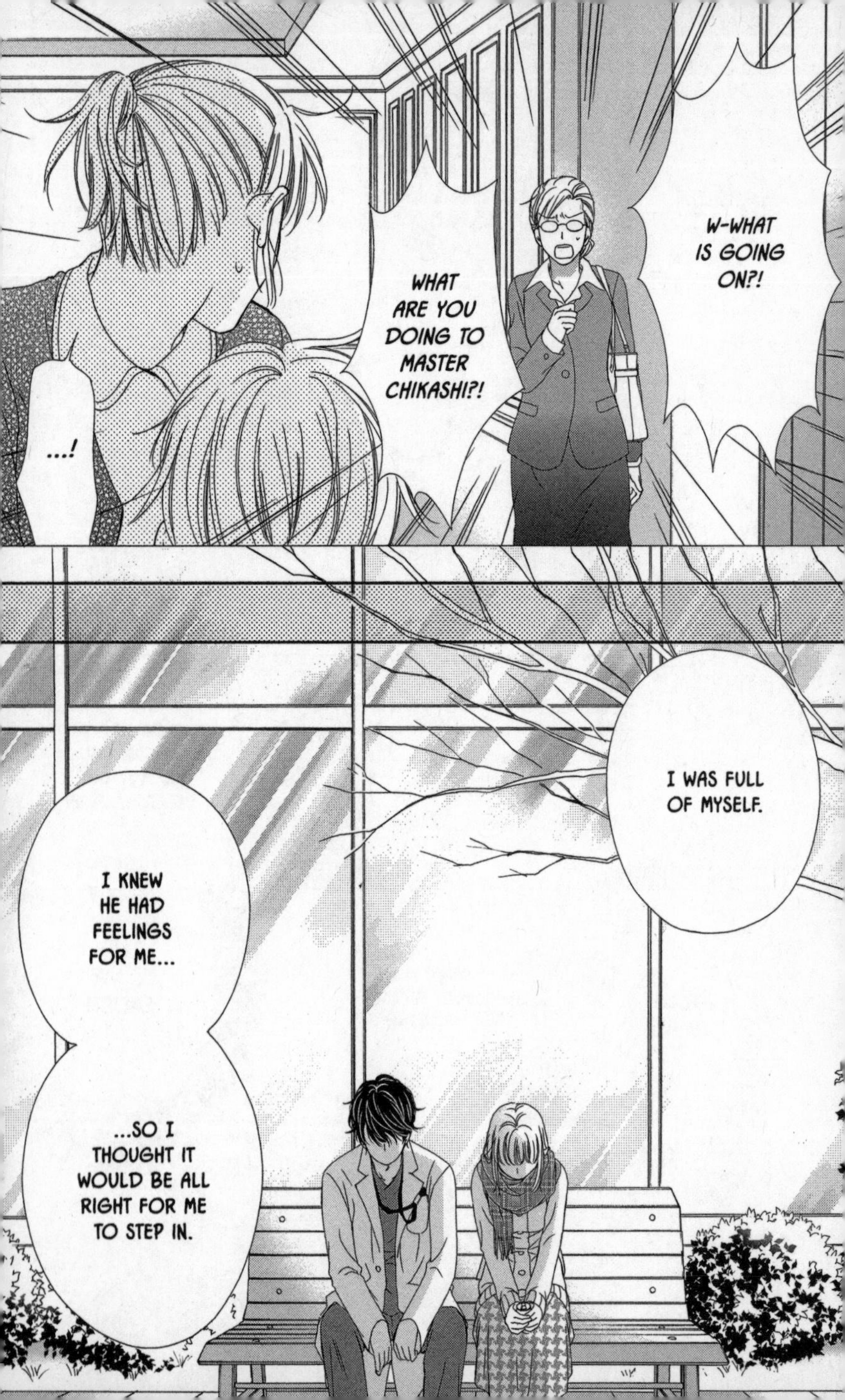
W-WHAT IS GOING ON?!
WHAT ARE YOU DOING TO MASTER CHIKASHI?!
...!
I WAS FULL OF MYSELF.
I KNEW HE HAD FEELINGS FOR ME...
...SO I THOUGHT IT WOULD BE ALL RIGHT FOR ME TO STEP IN.

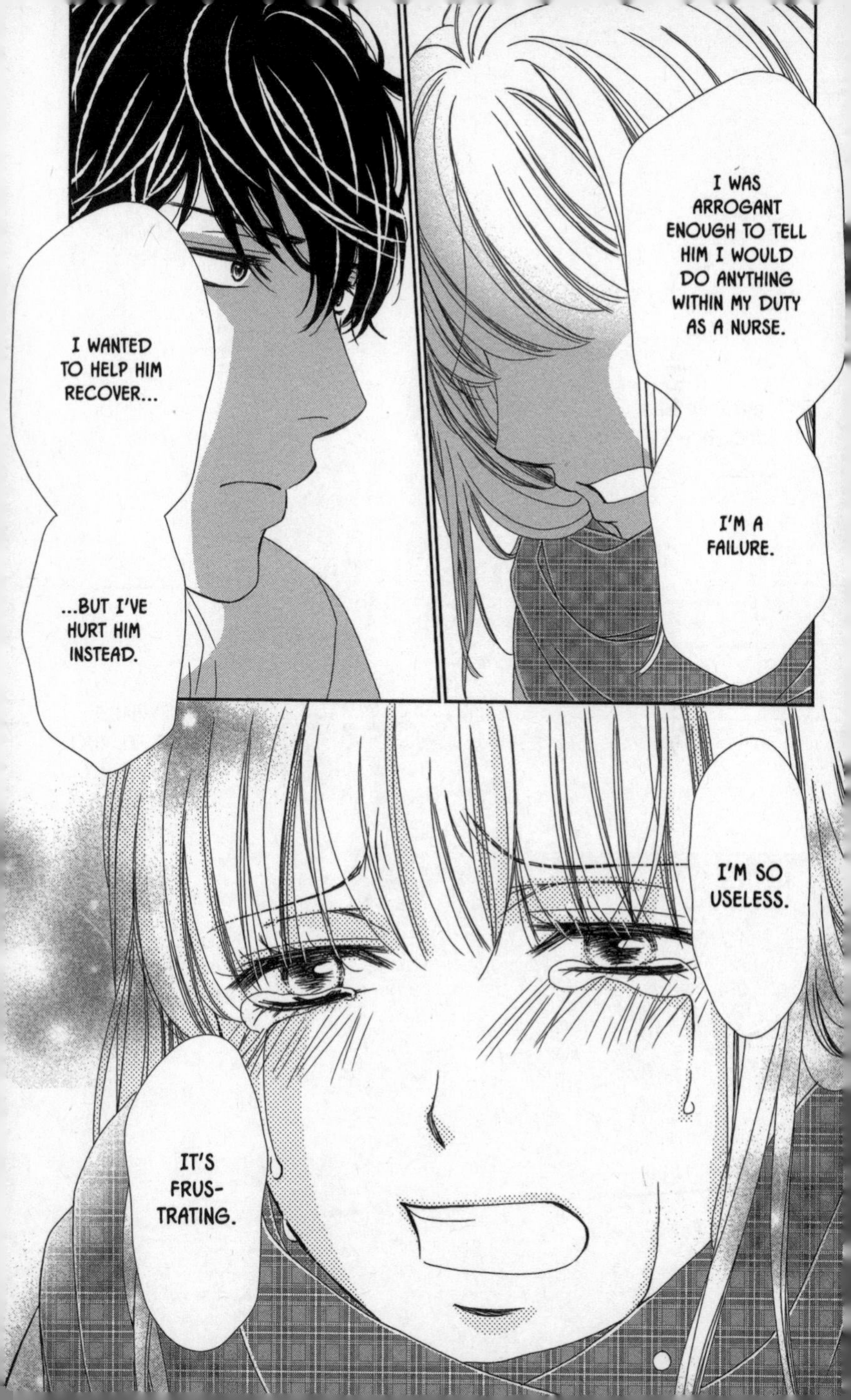
I WAS ARROGANT ENOUGH TO TELL HIM I WOULD DO ANYTHING WITHIN MY DUTY AS A NURSE.
I'M A FAILURE.
I WANTED TO HELP HIM RECOVER...
...BUT I'VE HURT HIM INSTEAD.
I'M SO USELESS.
IT'S FRUS-TRATING.

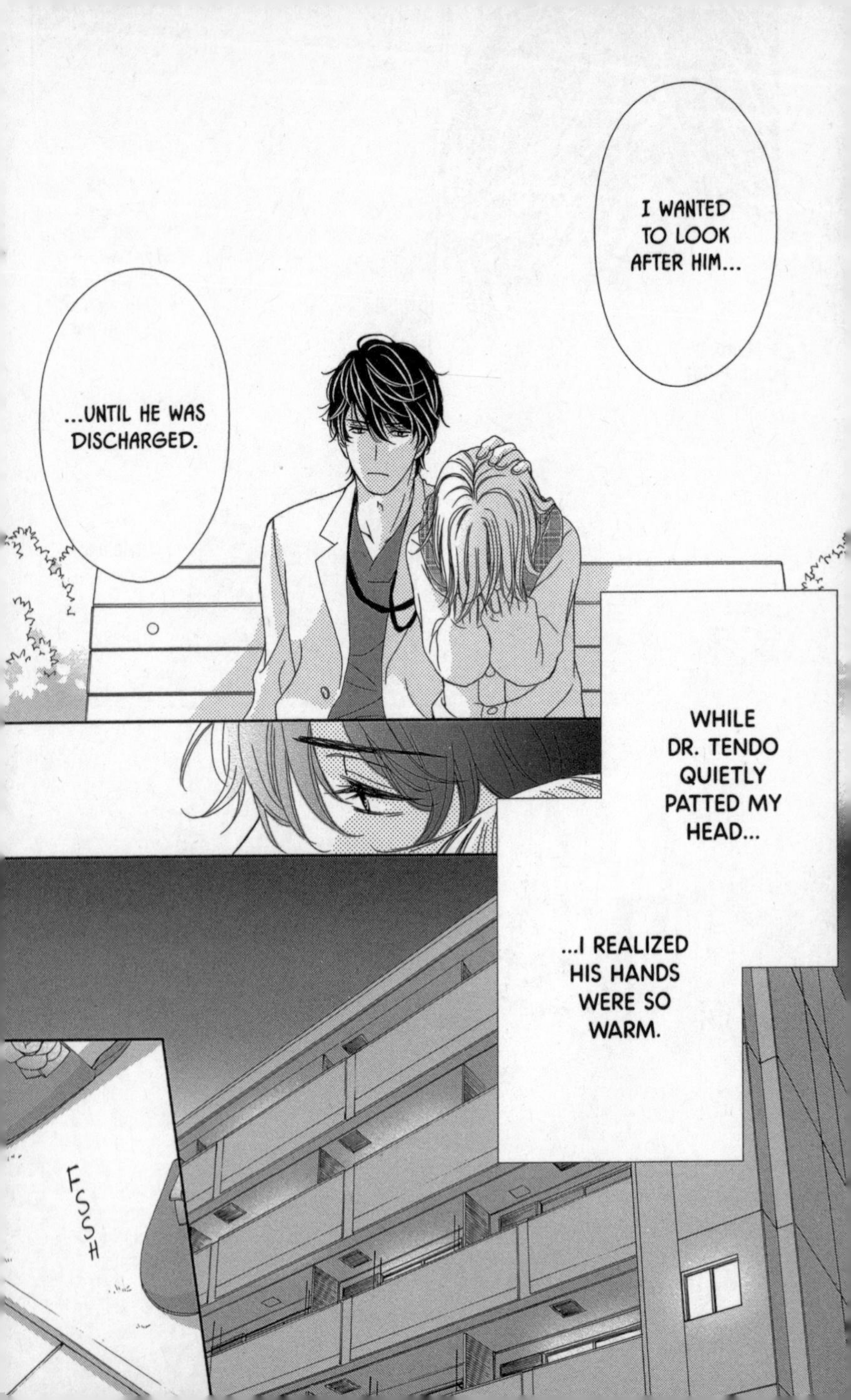
I WANTED TO LOOK AFTER HIM...
...UNTIL HE WAS DISCHARGED.
WHILE DR. TENDO QUIETLY PATTED MY HEAD...
...I REALIZED HIS HANDS WERE SO WARM.
FSSH

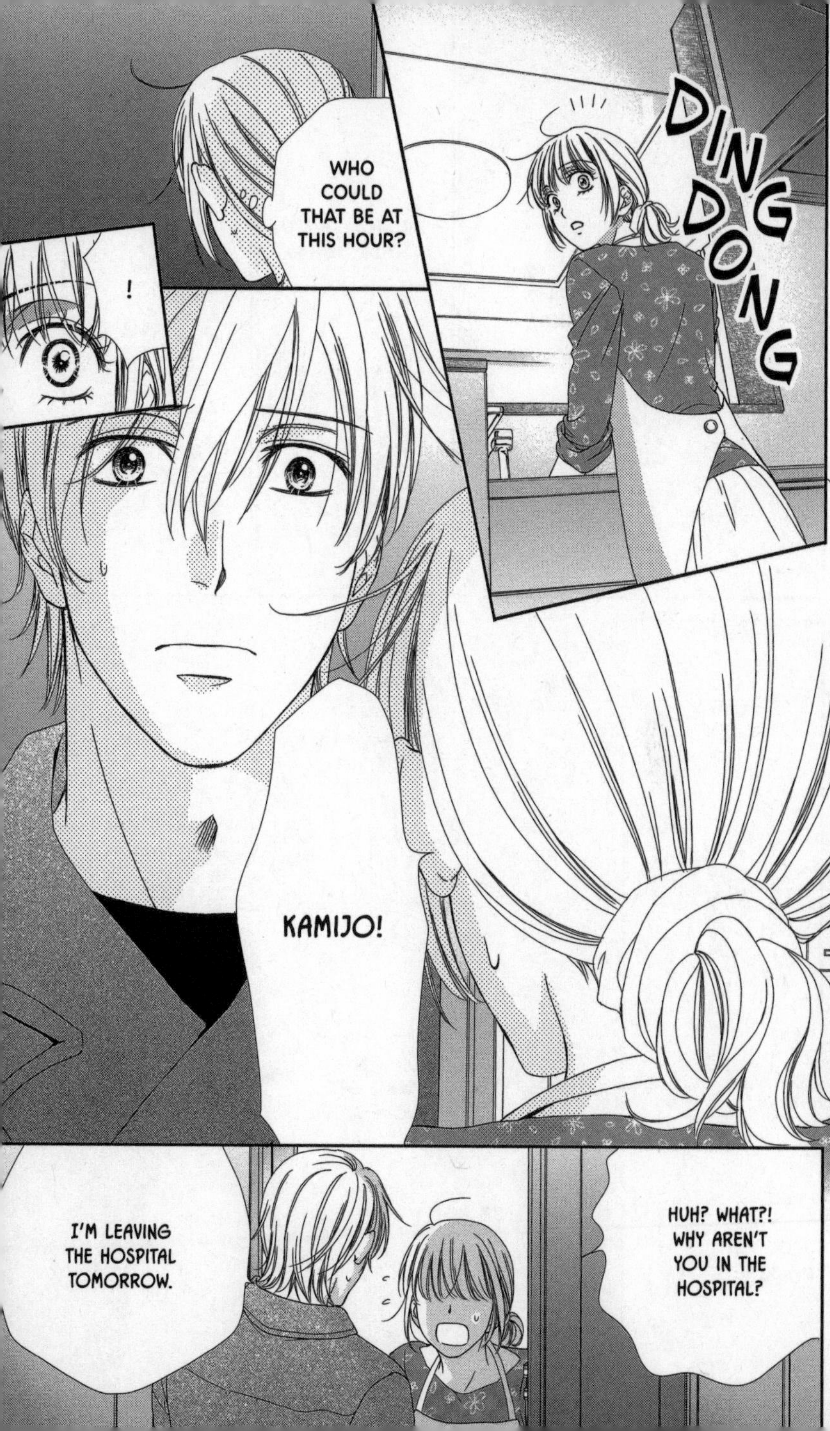
DING DONG
WHO COULD THAT BE AT THIS HOUR?
!
KAMIJO!
HUH? WHAT?! WHY AREN'T YOU IN THE HOSPITAL?
I'M LEAVING THE HOSPITAL TOMORROW.

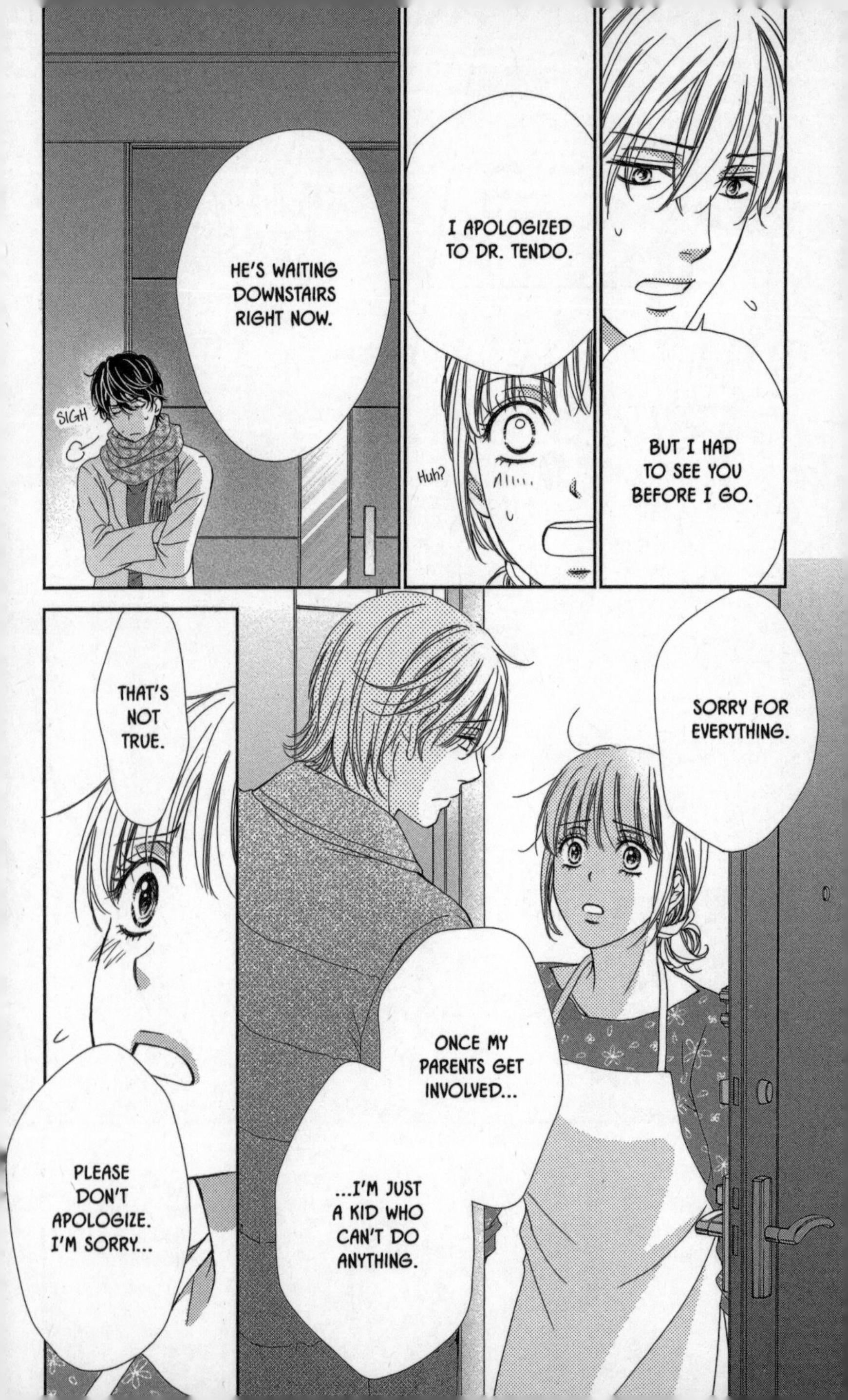
BUT I HAD TO SEE YOU BEFORE I GO.
I APOLOGIZED TO DR. TENDO.
Huh?
HE'S WAITING DOWNSTAIRS RIGHT NOW.
SIGH
SORRY FOR EVERYTHING.
ONCE MY PARENTS GET INVOLVED...
...I'M JUST A KID WHO CAN'T DO ANYTHING.
THAT'S NOT TRUE.
PLEASE DON'T APOLOGIZE. I'M SORRY...

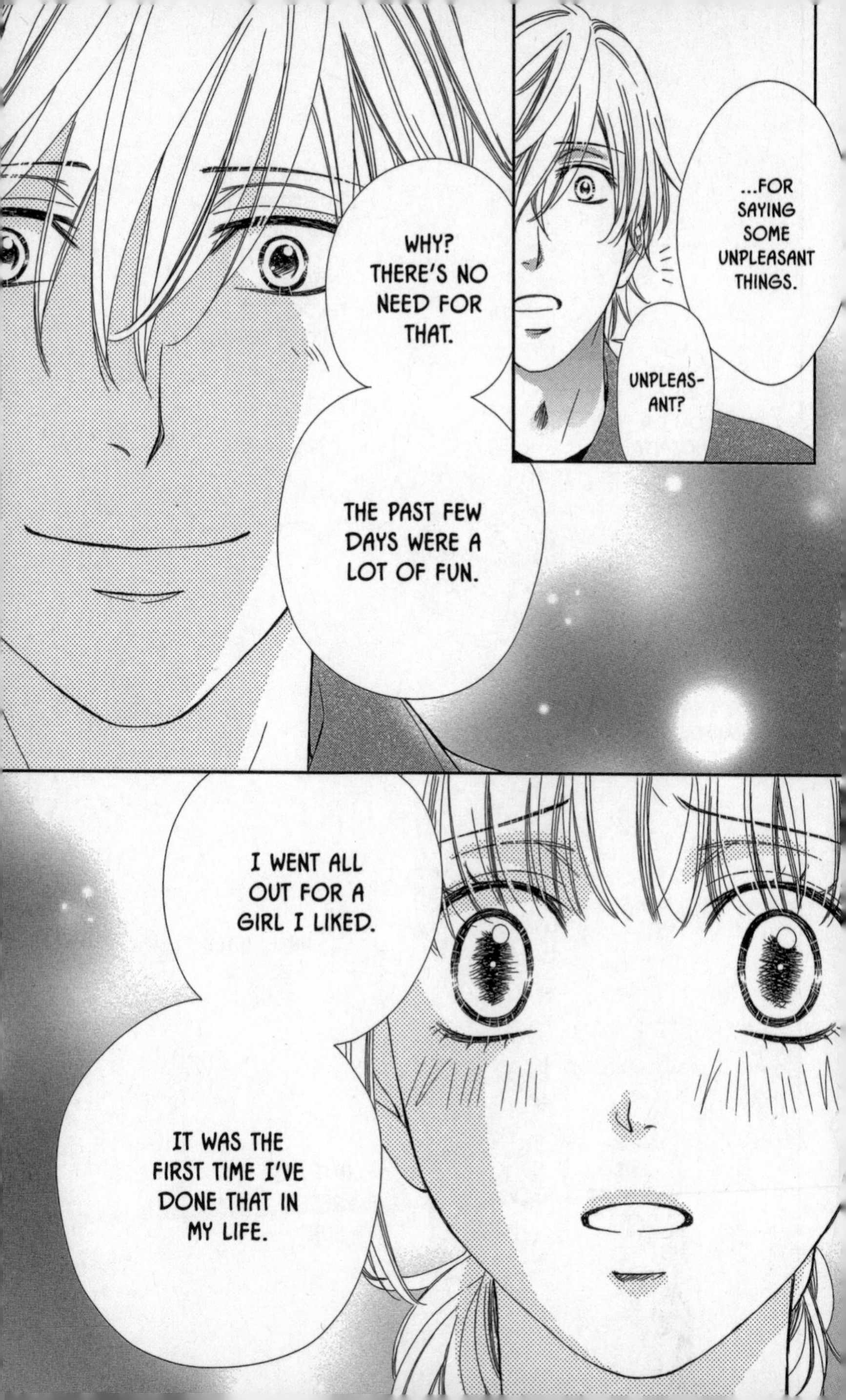
...FOR SAYING SOME UNPLEASANT THINGS.
UNPLEAS-ANT?
WHY? THERE'S NO NEED FOR THAT.
THE PAST FEW DAYS WERE A LOT OF FUN.
I WENT ALL OUT FOR A GIRL I LIKED.
IT WAS THE FIRST TIME I'VE DONE THAT IN MY LIFE.

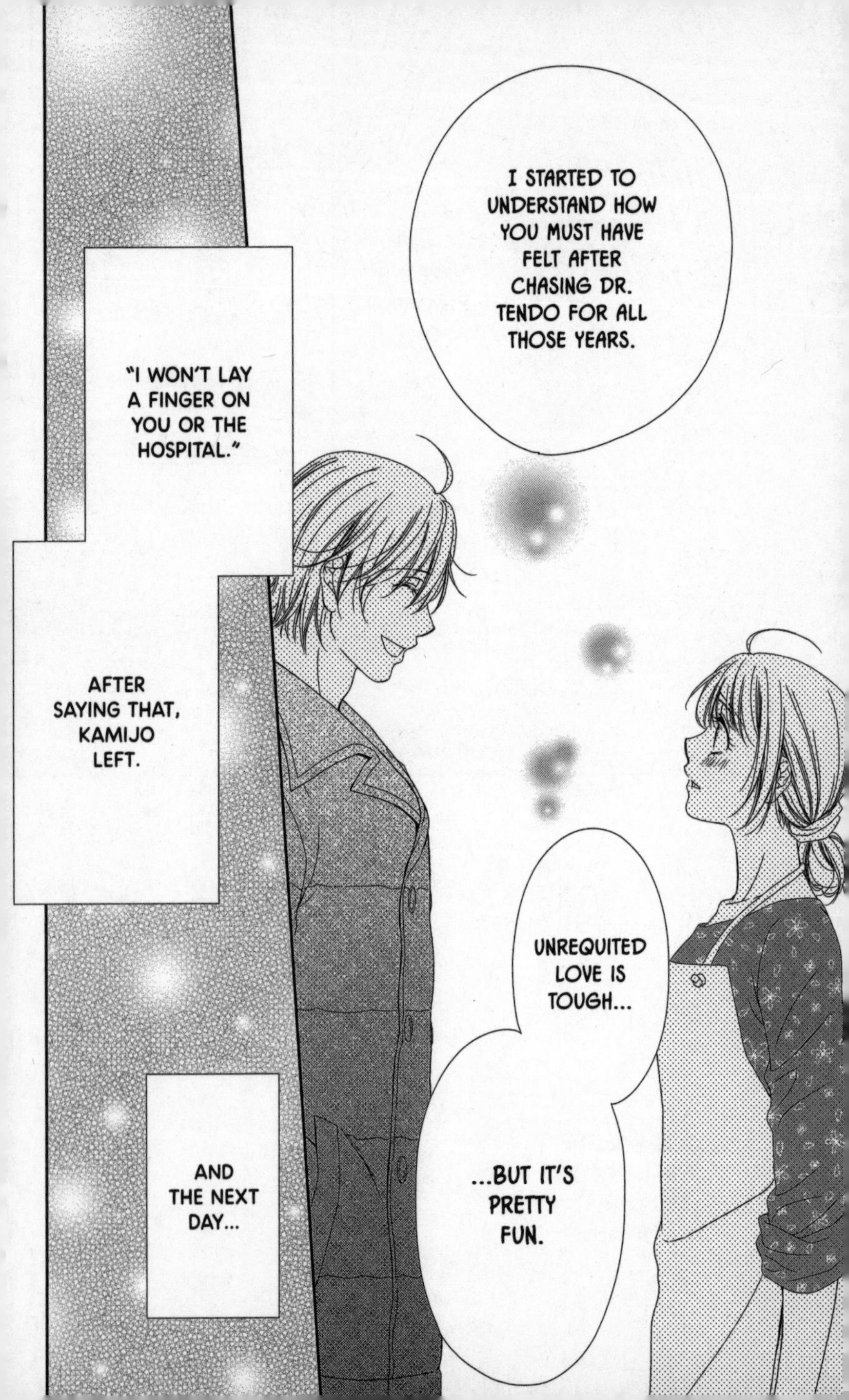
I STARTED TO UNDERSTAND HOW YOU MUST HAVE FELT AFTER CHASING DR. TENDO FOR ALL THOSE YEARS.
UNREQUITED LOVE IS TOUGH...
...BUT IT'S PRETTY FUN.
"I WON'T LAY A FINGER ON YOU OR THE HOSPITAL."
AFTER SAYING THAT, KAMIJO LEFT.
AND THE NEXT DAY...

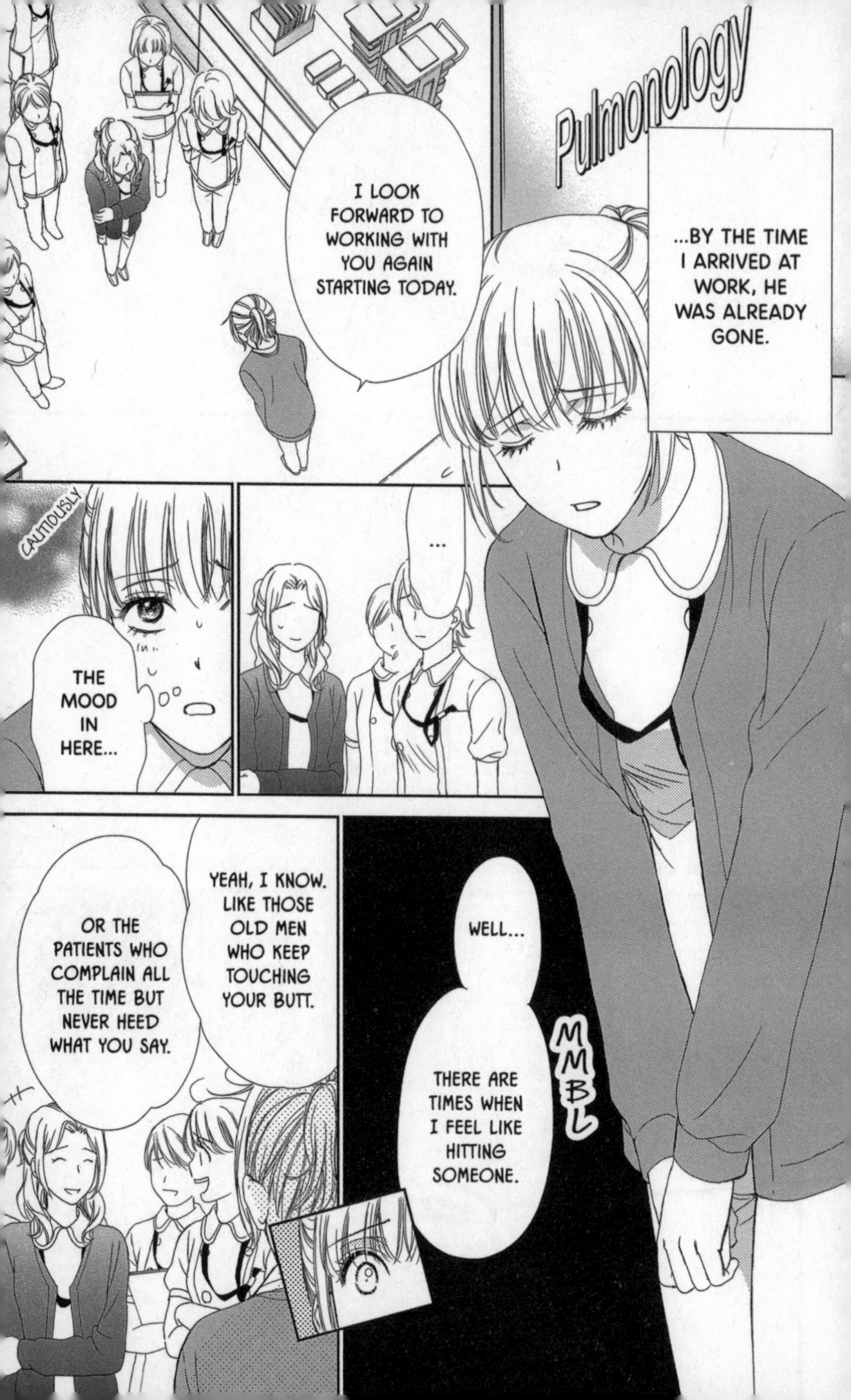
Pulmonology
...BY THE TIME I ARRIVED AT WORK, HE WAS ALREADY GONE.
I LOOK FORWARD TO WORKING WITH YOU AGAIN STARTING TODAY.
...
CAUTIOUSLY
THE MOOD IN HERE...
WELL...
THERE ARE TIMES WHEN I FEEL LIKE HITTING SOMEONE.
MMBL
YEAH, I KNOW. LIKE THOSE OLD MEN WHO KEEP TOUCHING YOUR BUTT.
OR THE PATIENTS WHO COMPLAIN ALL THE TIME BUT NEVER HEED WHAT YOU SAY.

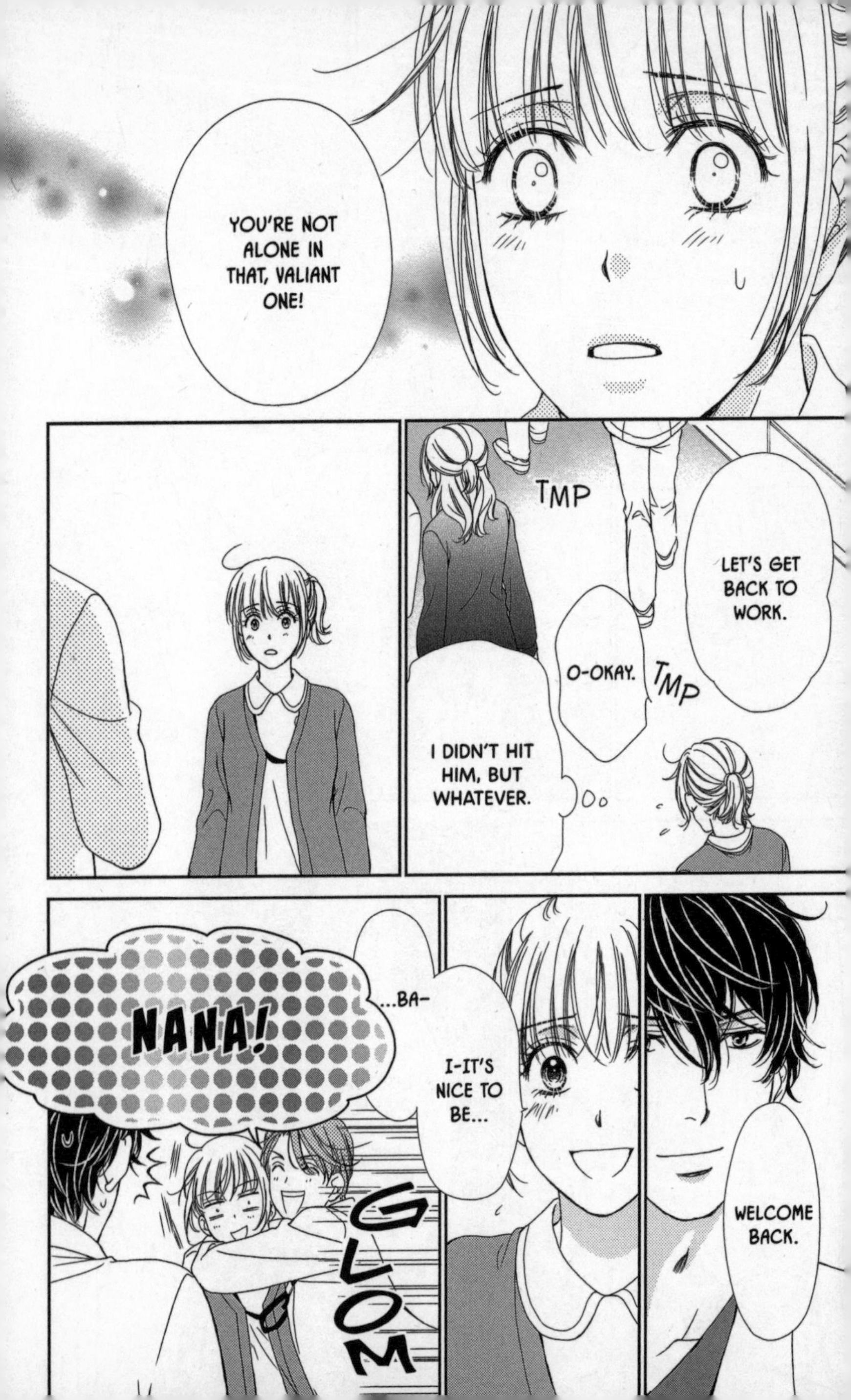
YOU'RE NOT ALONE IN THAT, VALIANT ONE!
TMP
LET'S GET BACK TO WORK.
TMP
O-OKAY.
I DIDN'T HIT HIM, BUT WHATEVER.
WELCOME BACK.
I-IT'S NICE TO BE...
...BA-
NANA!
GLOM

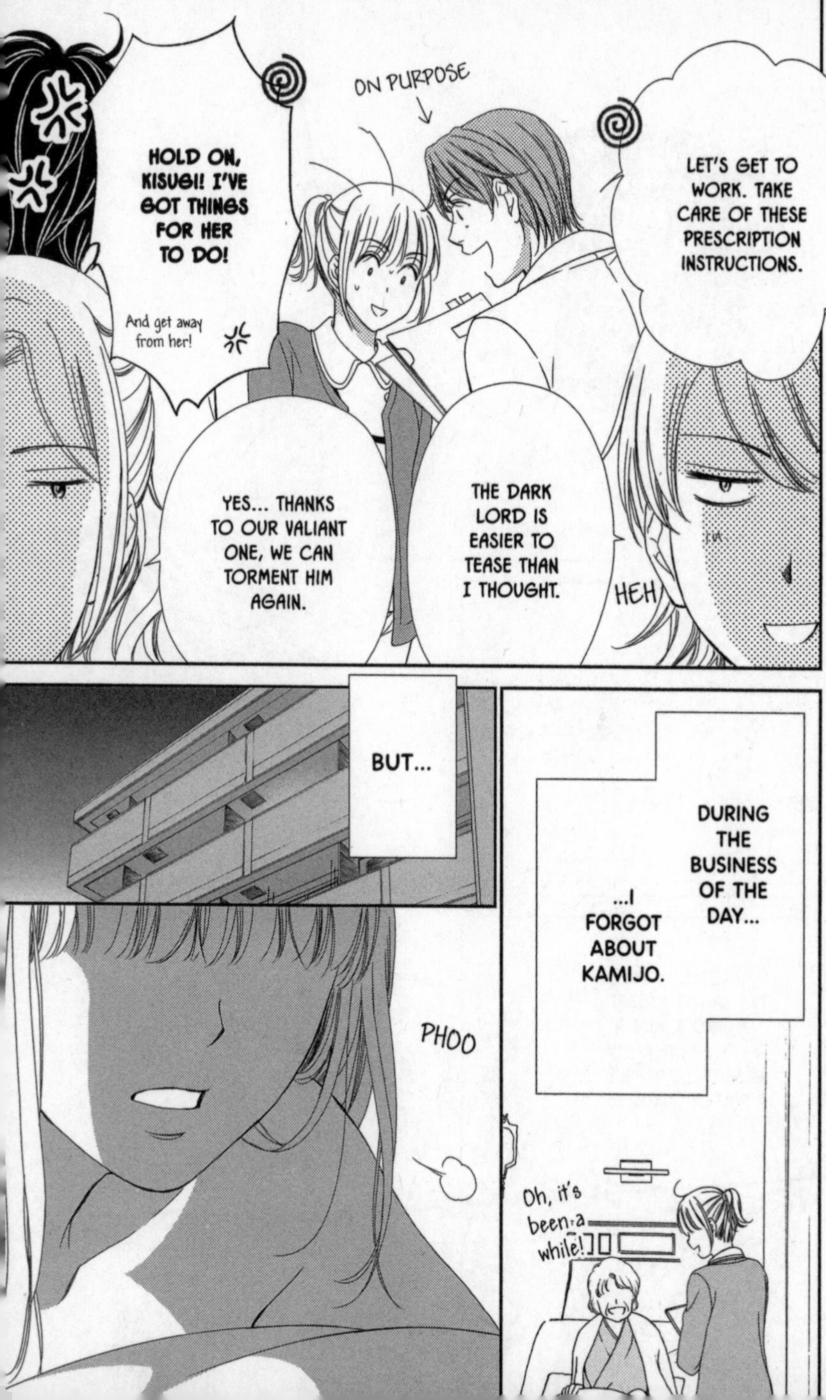
LET'S GET TO WORK. TAKE CARE OF THESE PRESCRIPTION INSTRUCTIONS.
ON PURPOSE
HOLD ON, KISUGI! I'VE GOT THINGS FOR HER TO DO!
And get away from her!
HEH
THE DARK LORD IS EASIER TO TEASE THAN I THOUGHT.
YES... THANKS TO OUR VALIANT ONE, WE CAN TORMENT HIM AGAIN.
BUT...
DURING THE BUSINESS OF THE DAY...
...I FORGOT ABOUT KAMIJO.
Oh, it's been a while!
PHOO

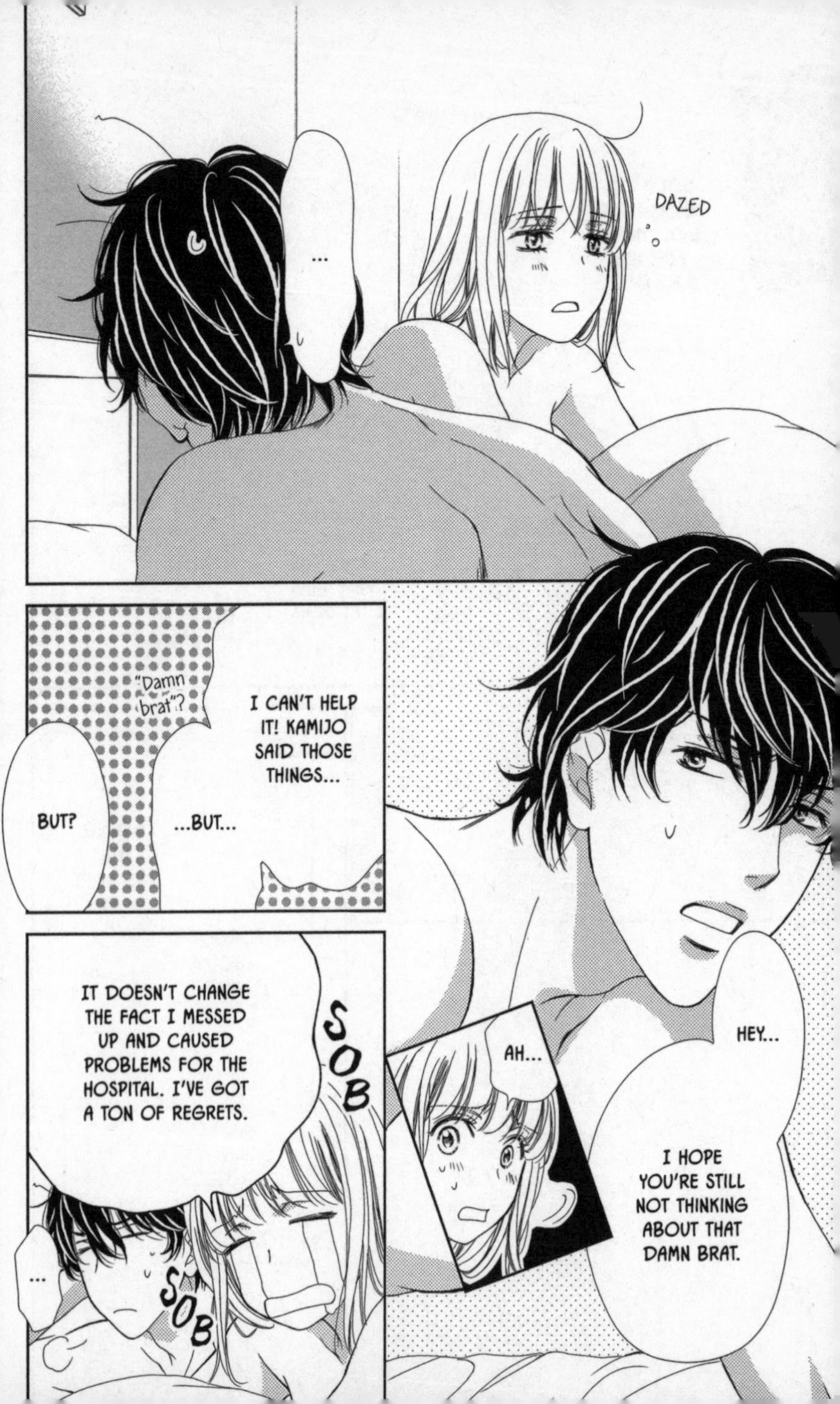

DAZED
...
HEY...
I HOPE YOU'RE STILL NOT THINKING ABOUT THAT DAMN BRAT.
AH...
I CAN'T HELP IT! KAMIJO SAID THOSE THINGS...
"Damn brat"?
...BUT...
BUT?
IT DOESN'T CHANGE THE FACT I MESSED UP AND CAUSED PROBLEMS FOR THE HOSPITAL. I'VE GOT A TON OF REGRETS.
SOB
SOB
...

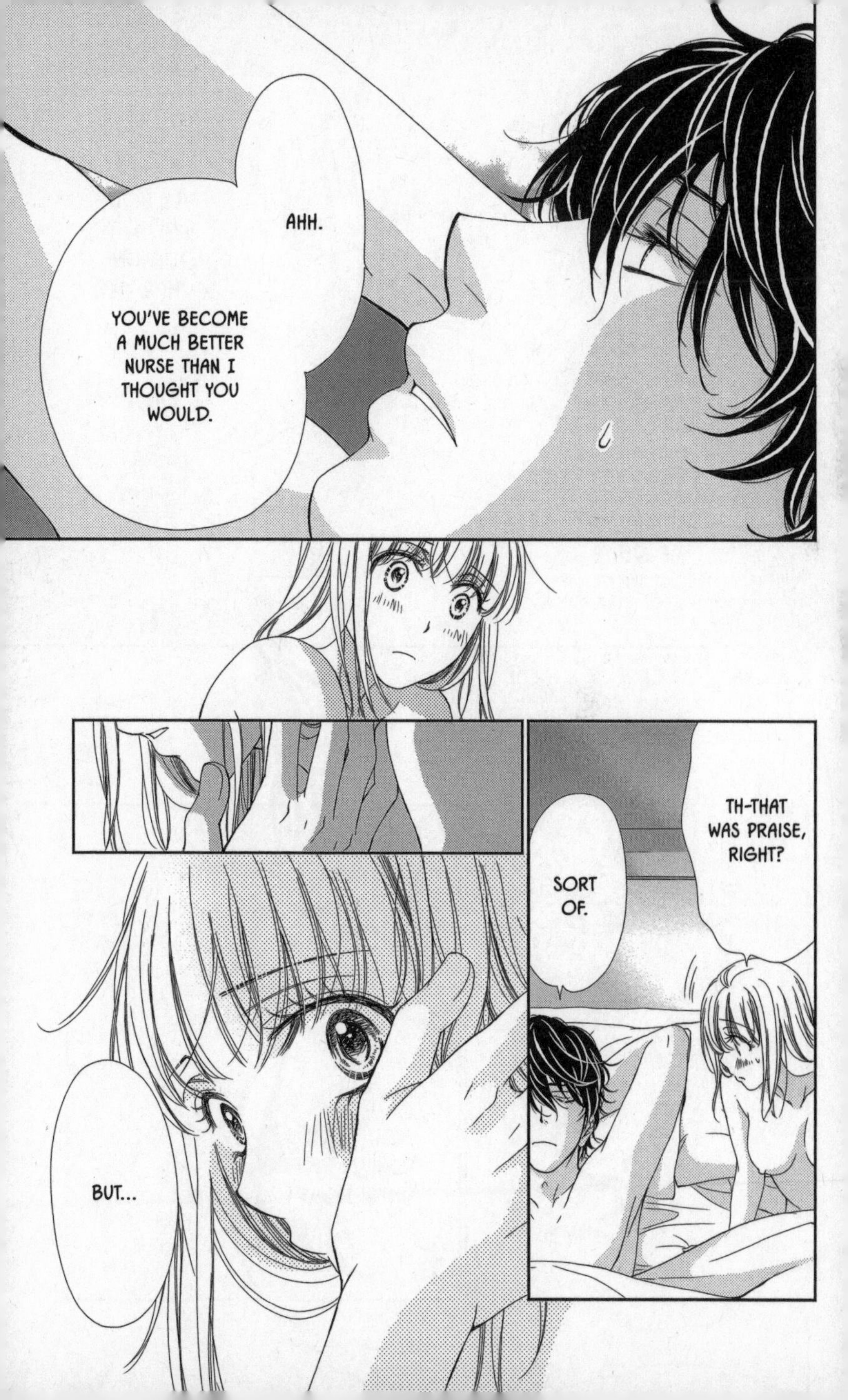
AHH.
YOU'VE BECOME A MUCH BETTER NURSE THAN I THOUGHT YOU WOULD.
TH-THAT WAS PRAISE, RIGHT?
SORT OF.
BUT...

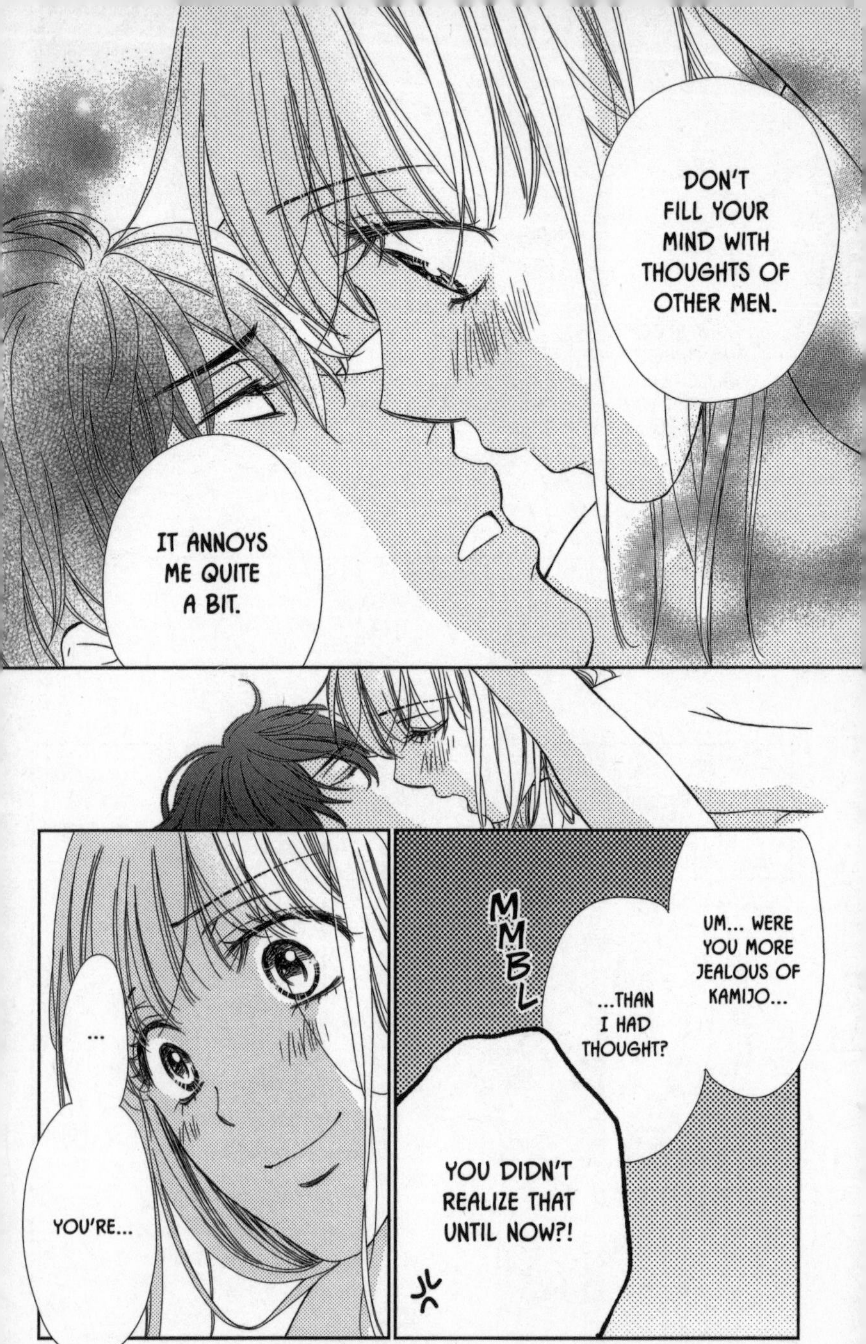
DON'T FILL YOUR MIND WITH THOUGHTS OF OTHER MEN.
IT ANNOYS ME QUITE A BIT.
UM... WERE YOU MORE JEALOUS OF KAMIJO...
...THAN I HAD THOUGHT?
MMBL
YOU DIDN'T REALIZE THAT UNTIL NOW?!
...
YOU'RE...

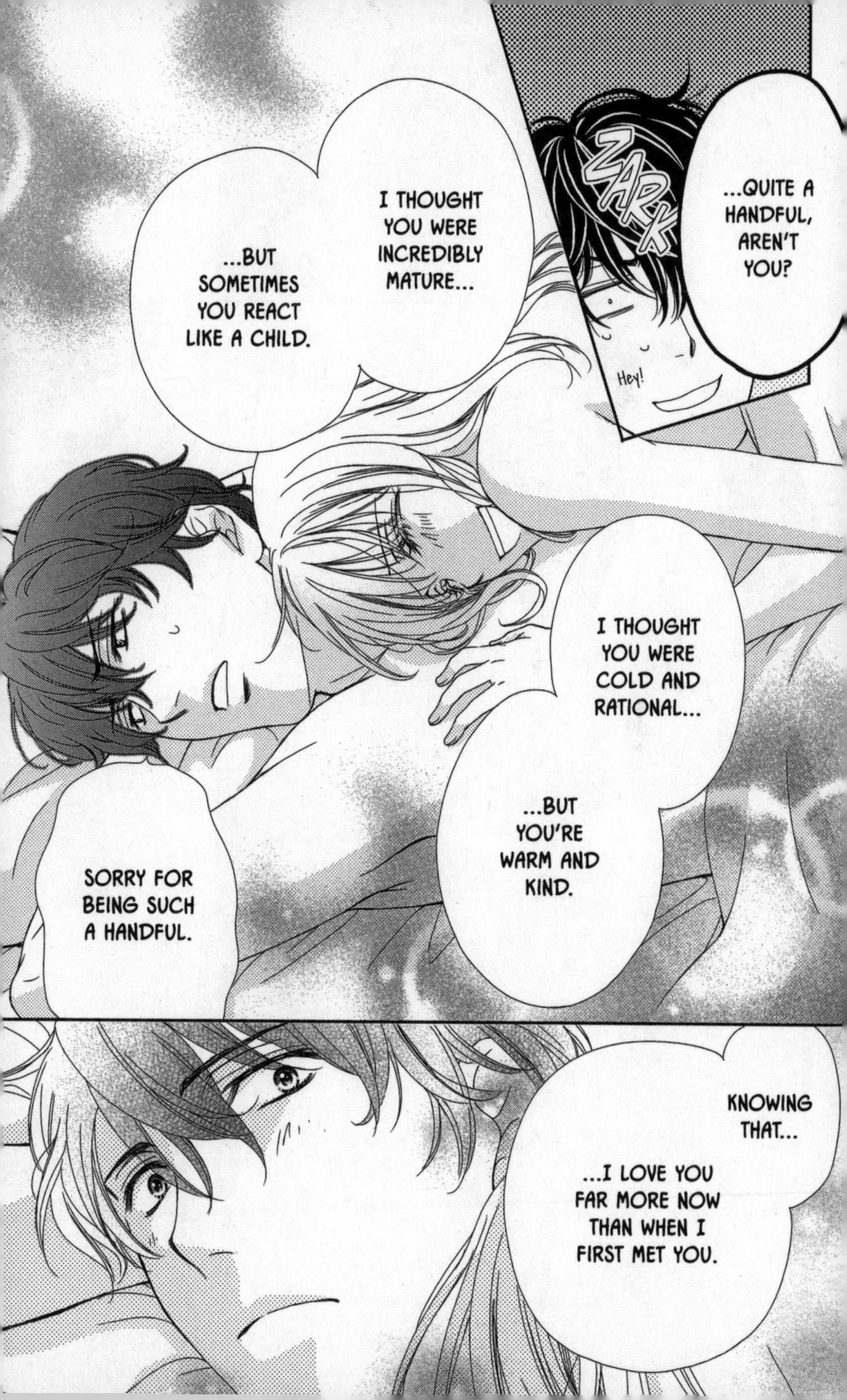
I THOUGHT YOU WERE INCREDIBLY MATURE...
...BUT SOMETIMES YOU REACT LIKE A CHILD.
ZARK
Hey!
...QUITE A HANDFUL, AREN'T YOU?
I THOUGHT YOU WERE COLD AND RATIONAL...
...BUT YOU'RE WARM AND KIND.
SORRY FOR BEING SUCH A HANDFUL.
KNOWING THAT...
...I LOVE YOU FAR MORE NOW THAN WHEN I FIRST MET YOU.

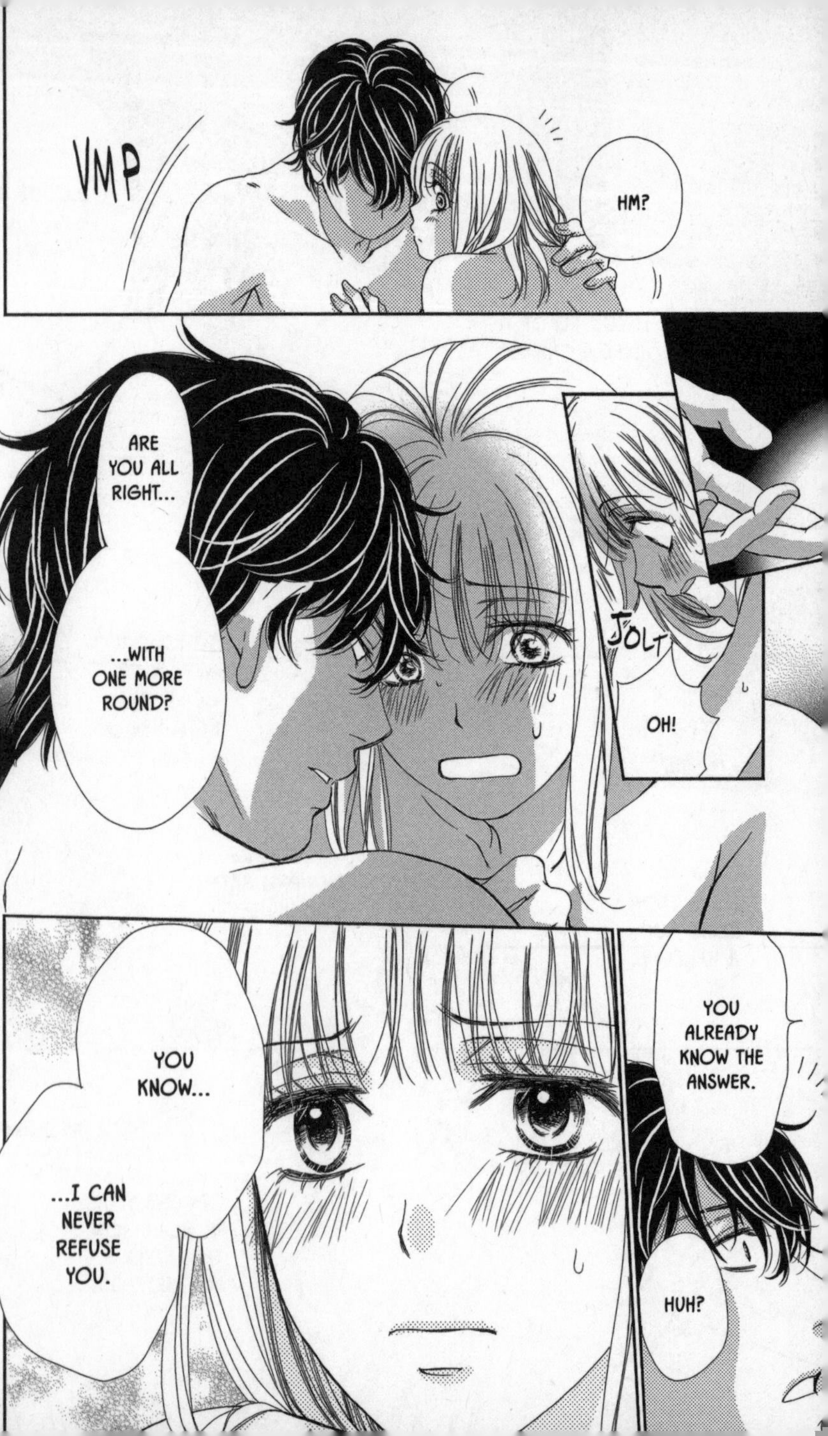
HM?
VMP
JOLT
OH!
ARE YOU ALL RIGHT...
...WITH ONE MORE ROUND?
YOU ALREADY KNOW THE ANSWER.
HUH?
YOU KNOW...
...I CAN NEVER REFUSE YOU.

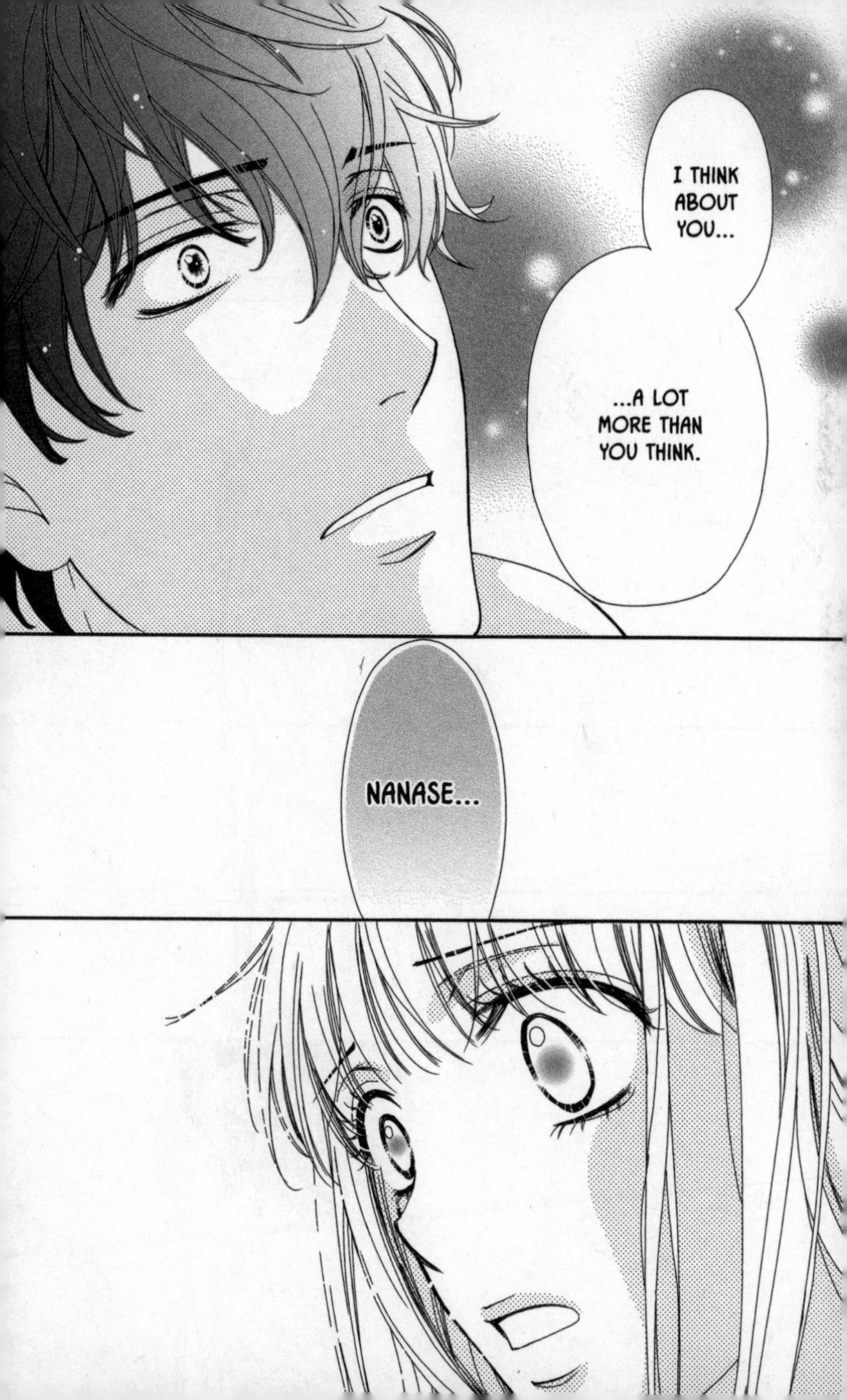
I THINK ABOUT YOU...
...A LOT MORE THAN YOU THINK.
NANASE...

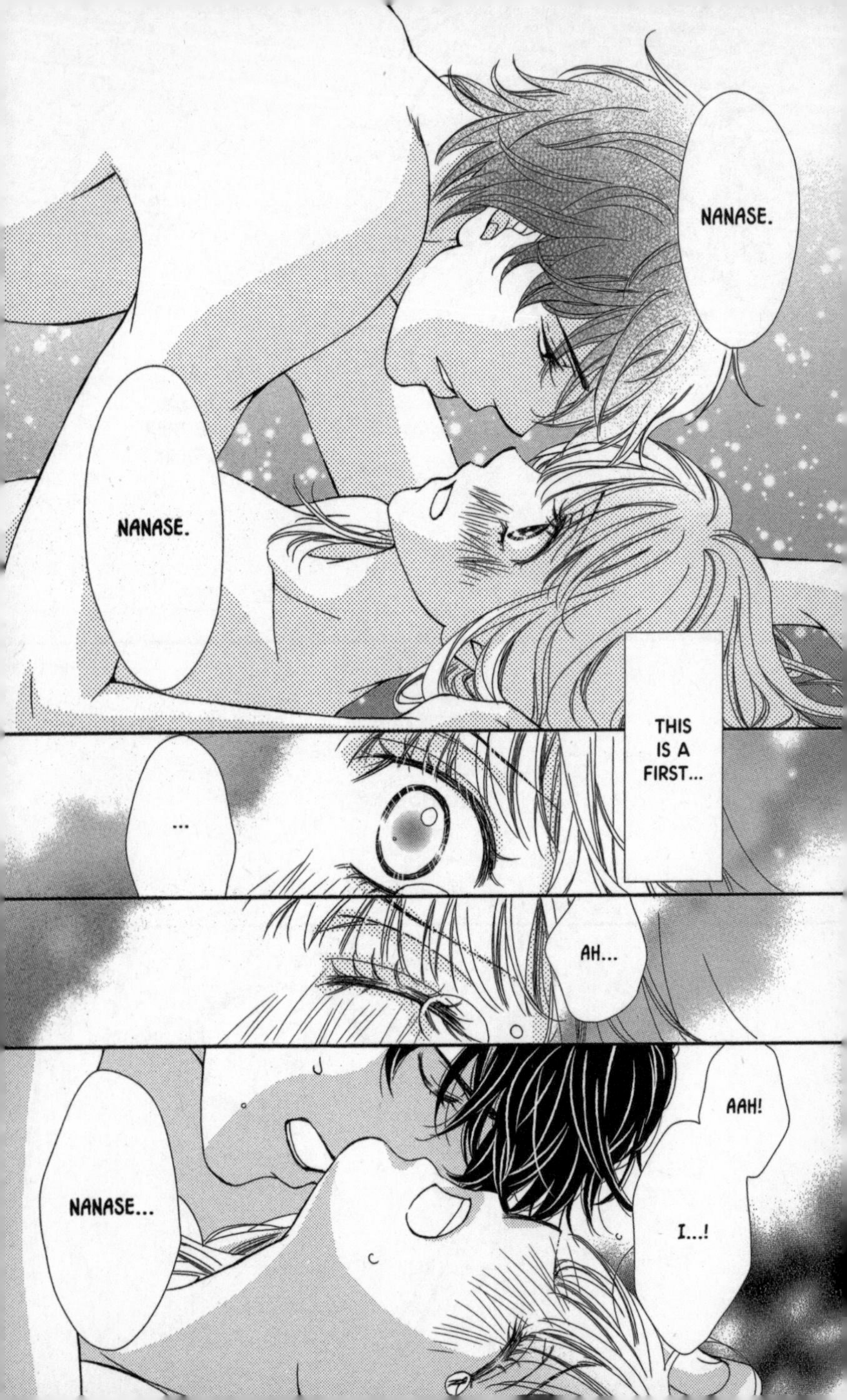
NANASE.
NANASE.
THIS IS A FIRST...
...
AH...
AAH!
I...!
NANASE...

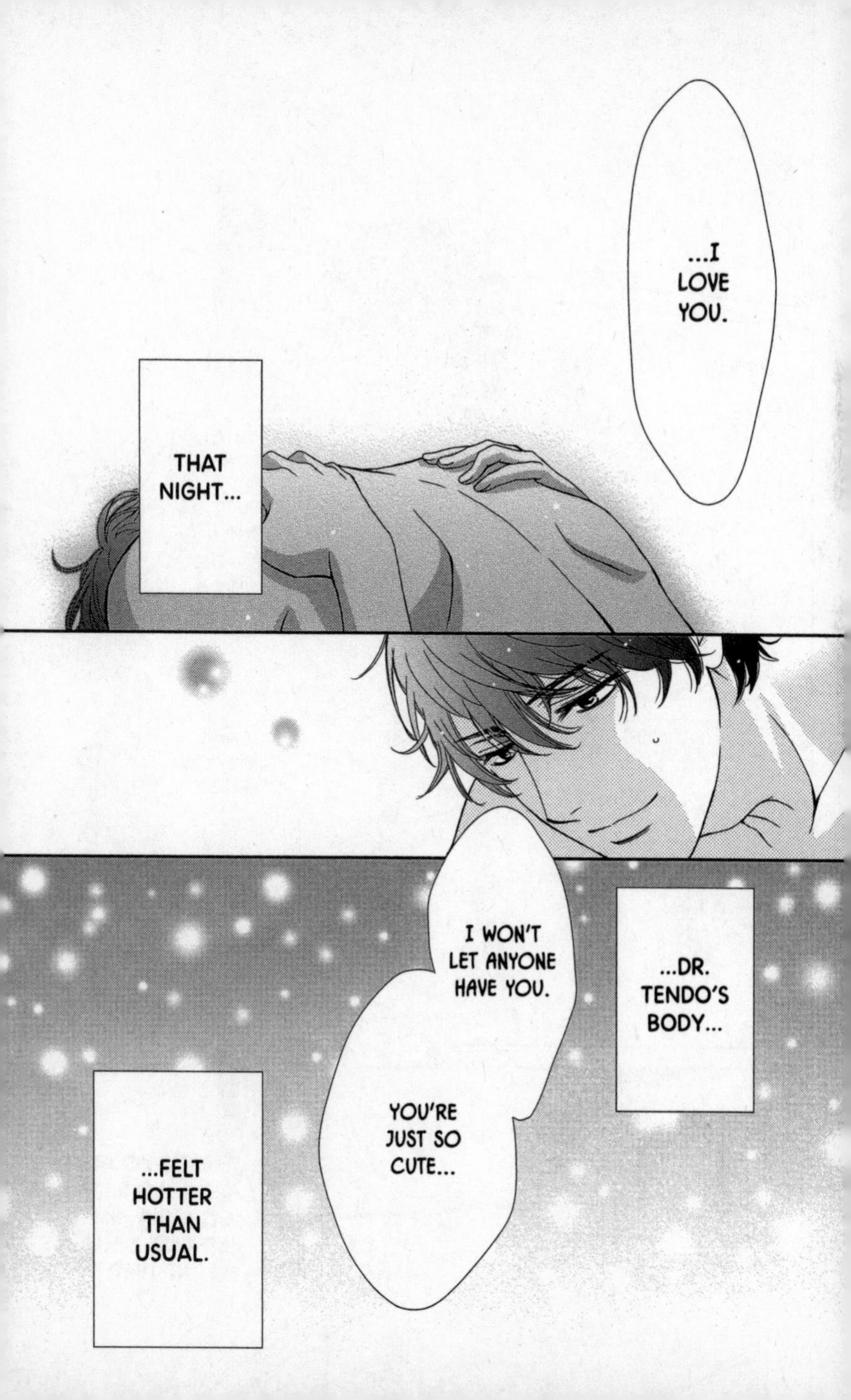
...I LOVE YOU.
THAT NIGHT...
...DR. TENDO'S BODY...
I WON'T LET ANYONE HAVE YOU.
YOU'RE JUST SO CUTE...
...FELT HOTTER THAN USUAL.

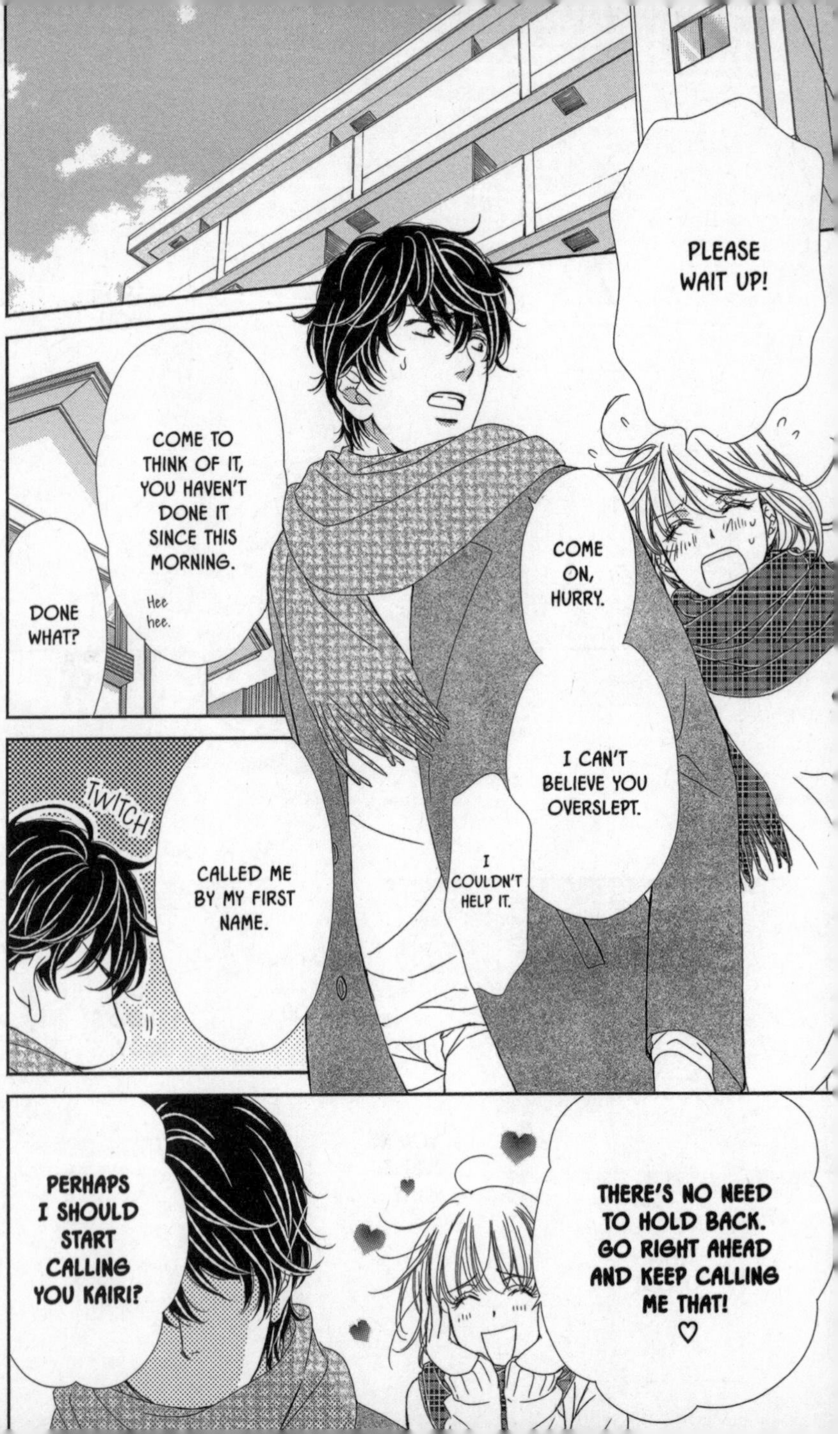
PLEASE WAIT UP!
COME ON, HURRY.
I CAN'T BELIEVE YOU OVERSLEPT.
I COULDN'T HELP IT.
COME TO THINK OF IT, YOU HAVEN'T DONE IT SINCE THIS MORNING.
Hee hee.
DONE WHAT?
TWITCH
CALLED ME BY MY FIRST NAME.
THERE'S NO NEED TO HOLD BACK. GO RIGHT AHEAD AND KEEP CALLING ME THAT! ♡
PERHAPS I SHOULD START CALLING YOU KAIRI?

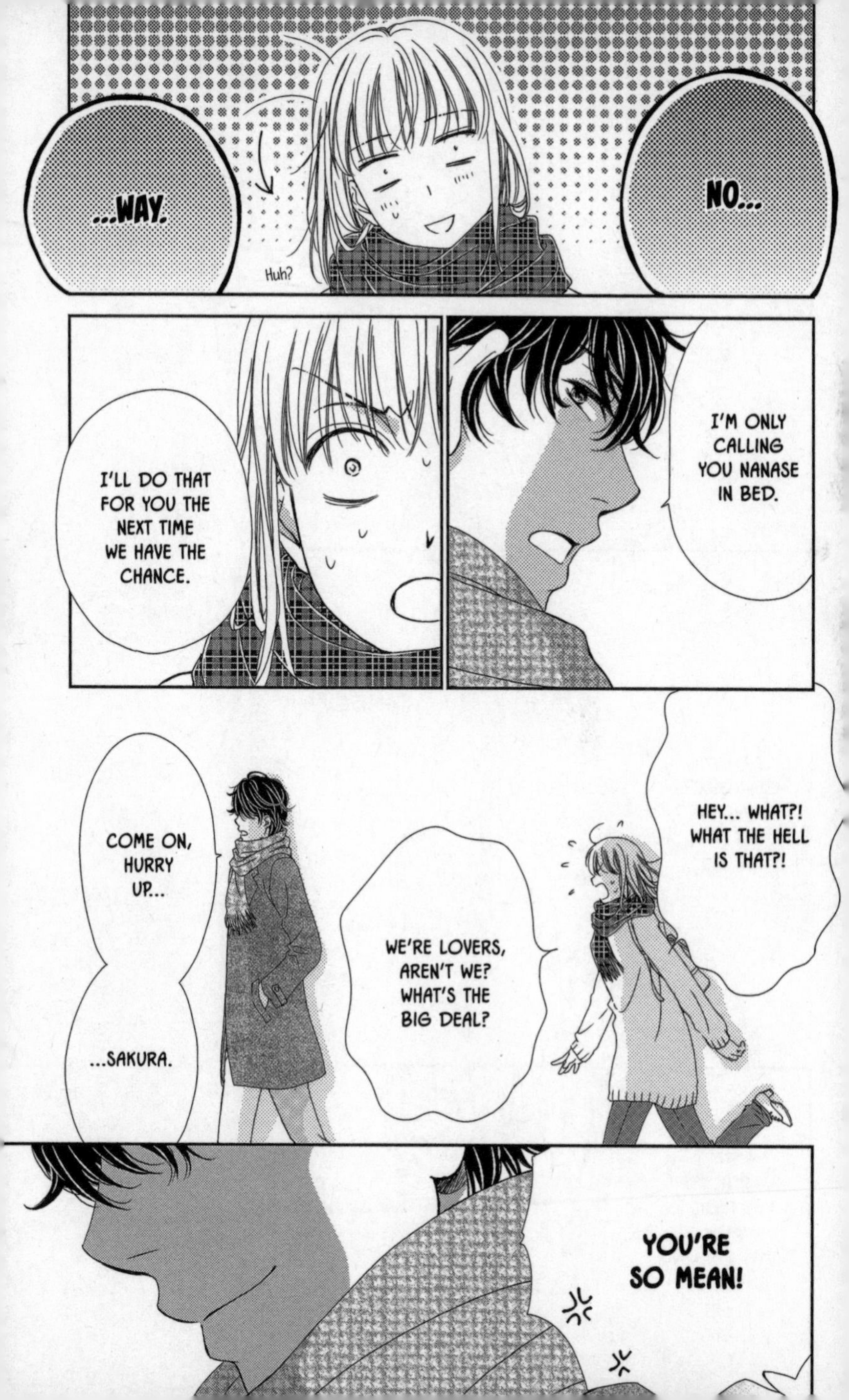
NO...
...WAY.
Huh?
I'M ONLY CALLING YOU NANASE IN BED.
I'LL DO THAT FOR YOU THE NEXT TIME WE HAVE THE CHANCE.
HEY... WHAT?! WHAT THE HELL IS THAT?!
WE'RE LOVERS, AREN'T WE? WHAT'S THE BIG DEAL?
COME ON, HURRY UP...
...SAKURA.
YOU'RE SO MEAN!

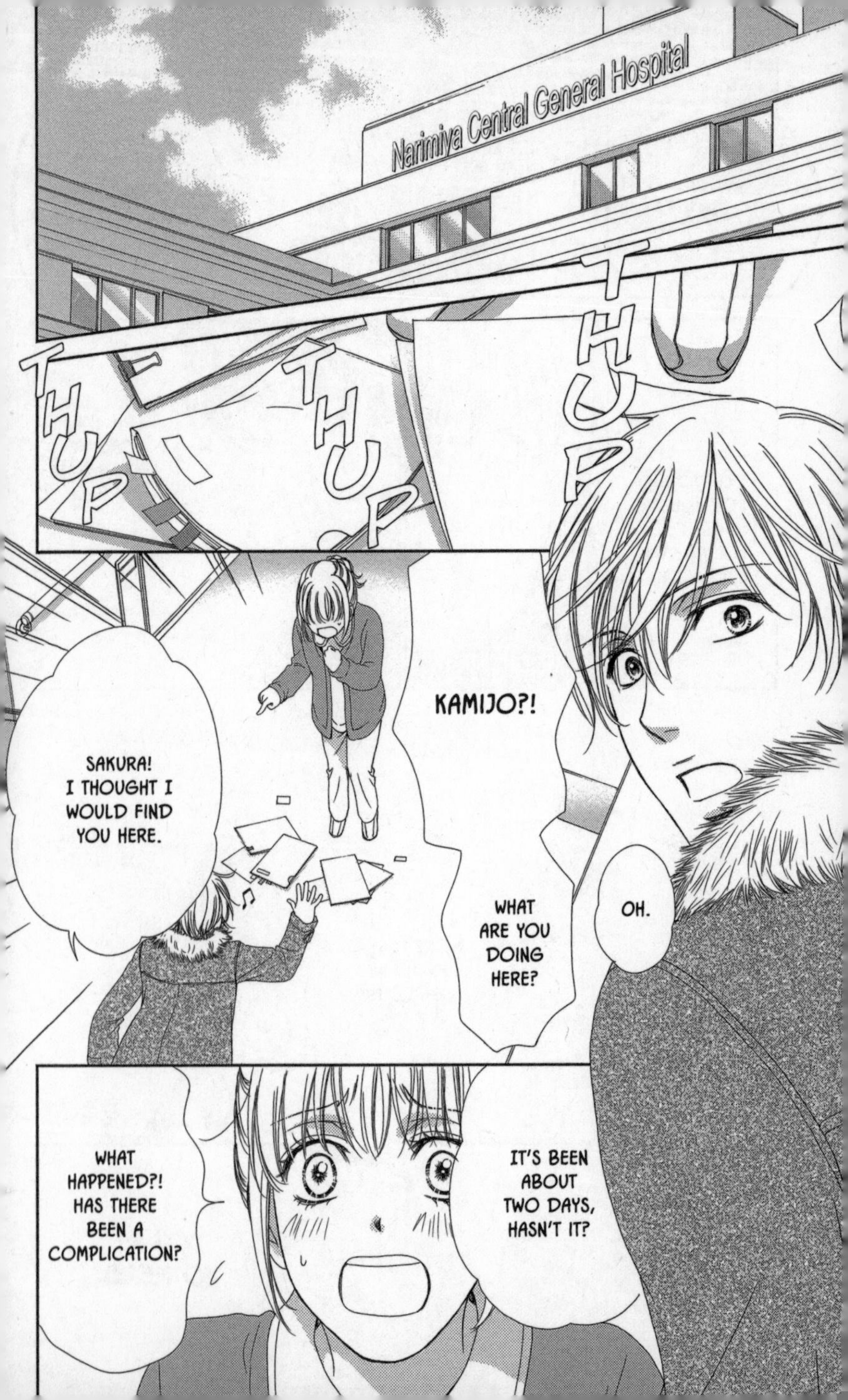
Narimiya Central General Hospital
THUP
THUP
THUP
OH.
KAMIJO?!
WHAT ARE YOU DOING HERE?
SAKURA! I THOUGHT I WOULD FIND YOU HERE.
IT'S BEEN ABOUT TWO DAYS, HASN'T IT?
WHAT HAPPENED?! HAS THERE BEEN A COMPLICATION?

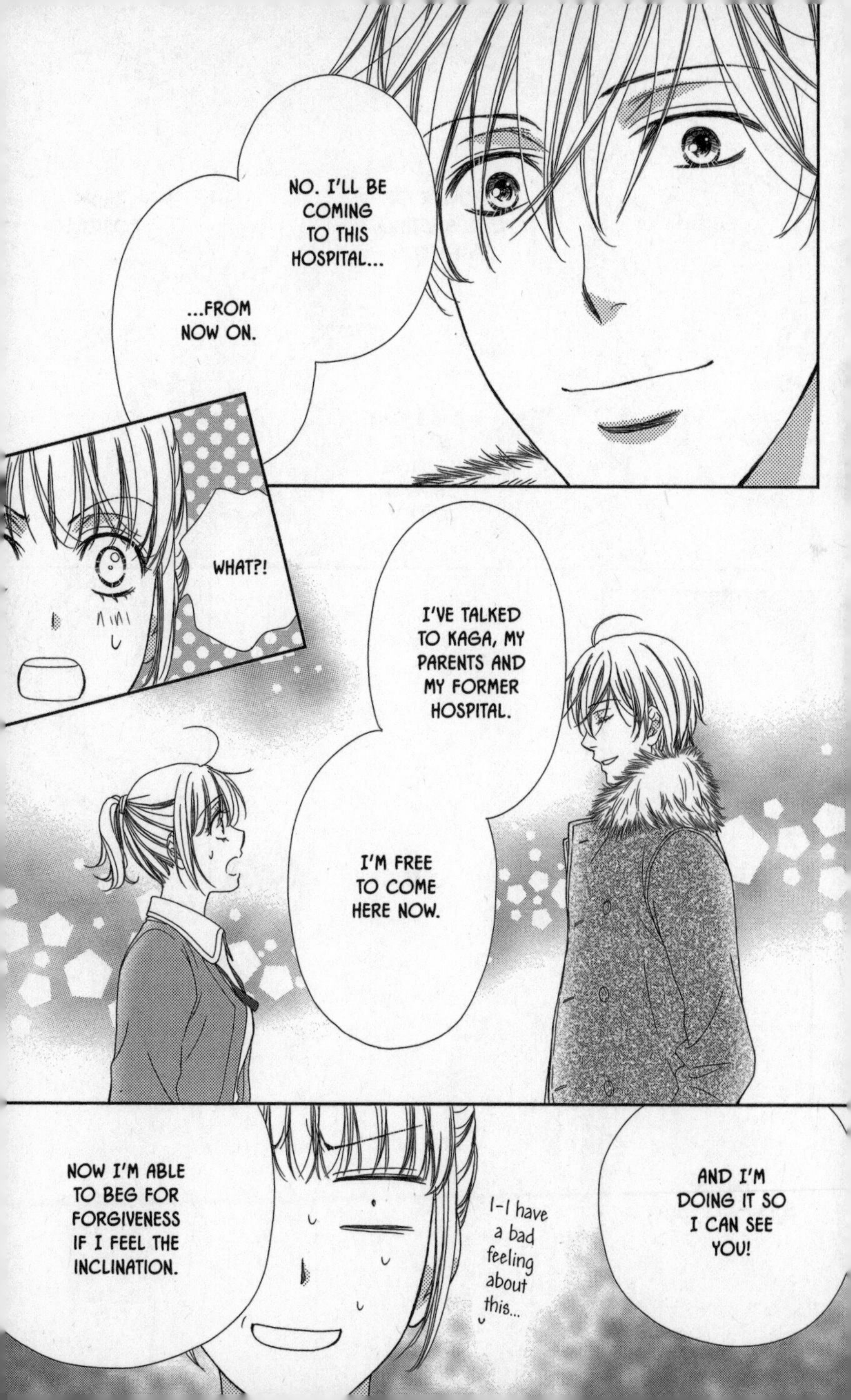
NO. I'LL BE COMING TO THIS HOSPITAL...
...FROM NOW ON.
WHAT?!
I'VE TALKED TO KAGA, MY PARENTS AND MY FORMER HOSPITAL.
I'M FREE TO COME HERE NOW.
AND I'M DOING IT SO I CAN SEE YOU!
I-I have a bad feeling about this...
NOW I'M ABLE TO BEG FOR FORGIVENESS IF I FEEL THE INCLINATION.

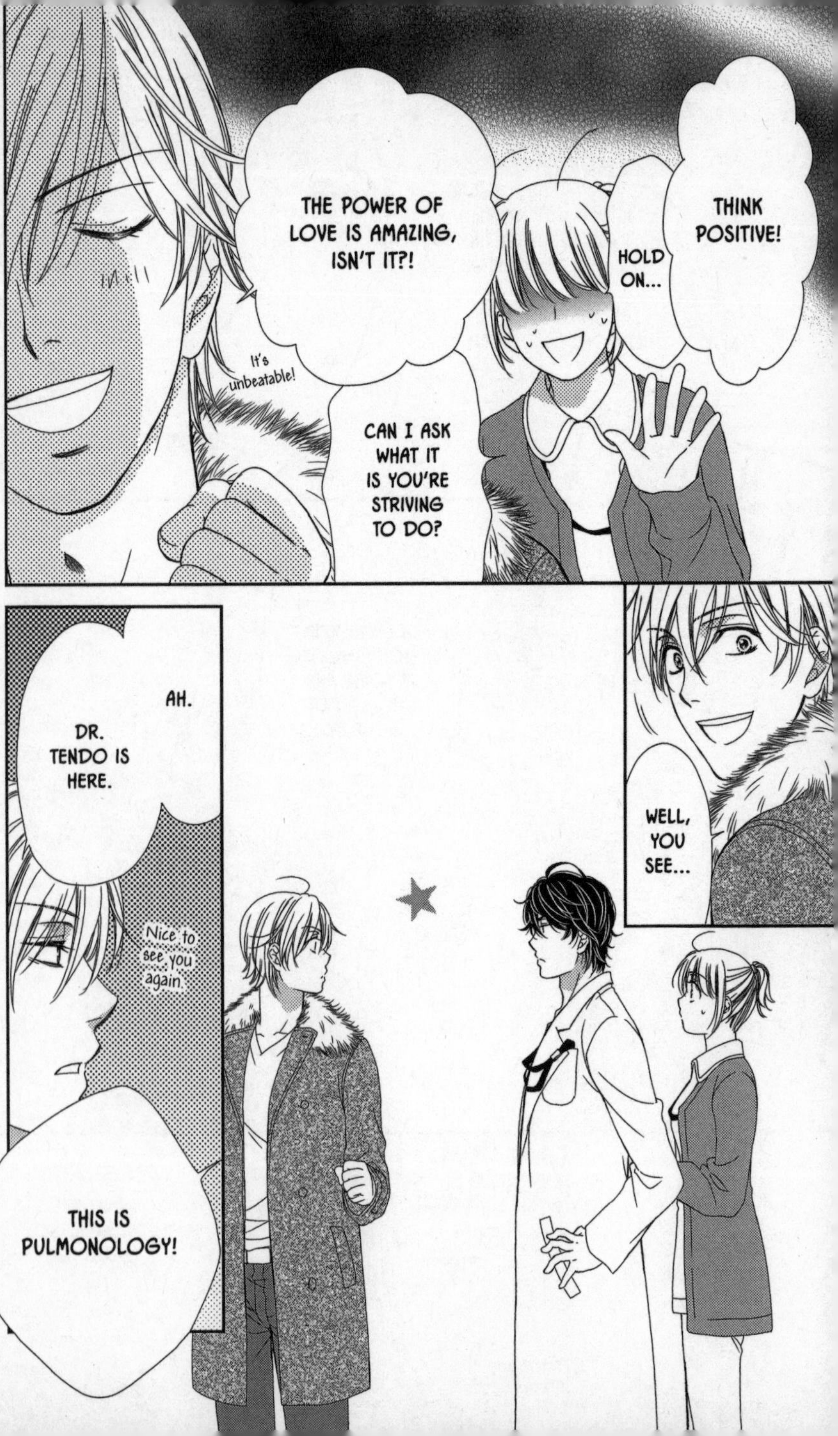
THINK POSITIVE!
HOLD ON...
THE POWER OF LOVE IS AMAZING, ISN'T IT?!
It's unbeatable!
CAN I ASK WHAT IT IS YOU'RE STRIVING TO DO?
WELL, YOU SEE...
AH.
DR. TENDO IS HERE.
Nice to see you again.
THIS IS PULMONOLOGY!

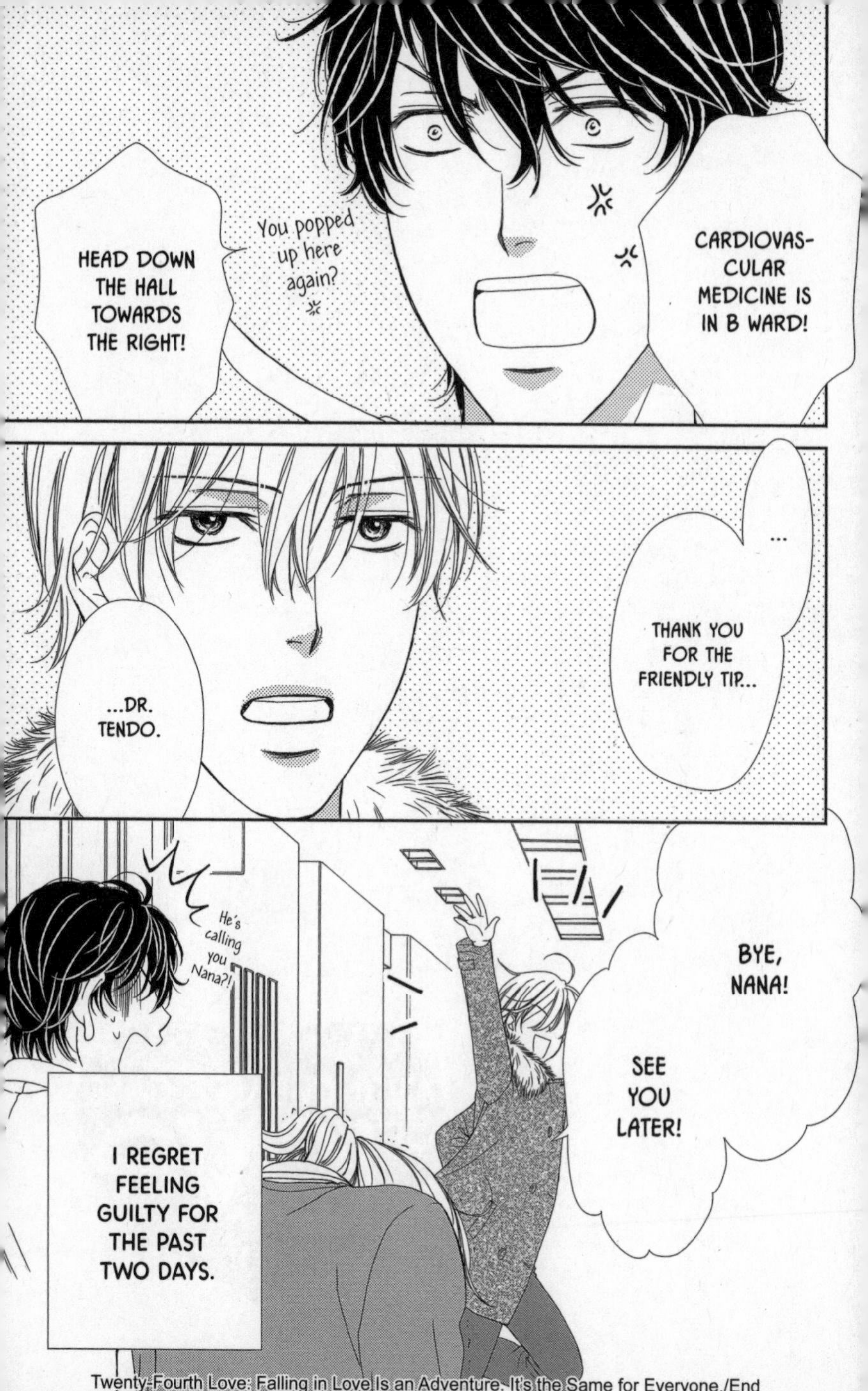
CARDIOVAS-CULAR MEDICINE IS IN B WARD!
You popped up here again?
HEAD DOWN THE HALL TOWARDS THE RIGHT!
...
THANK YOU FOR THE FRIENDLY TIP...
...DR. TENDO.
BYE, NANA!
SEE YOU LATER!
He's calling you Nana?!
I REGRET FEELING GUILTY FOR THE PAST TWO DAYS.

Twenty-Fourth Love: Falling in Love Is an Adventure. It's the Same for Everyone./End

AN INCURABLE CASE OF LOVE

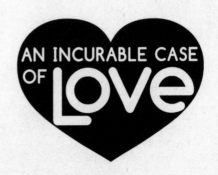

## Twenty-Fifth Love

# Are You Beautiful or Not? That's the Question!

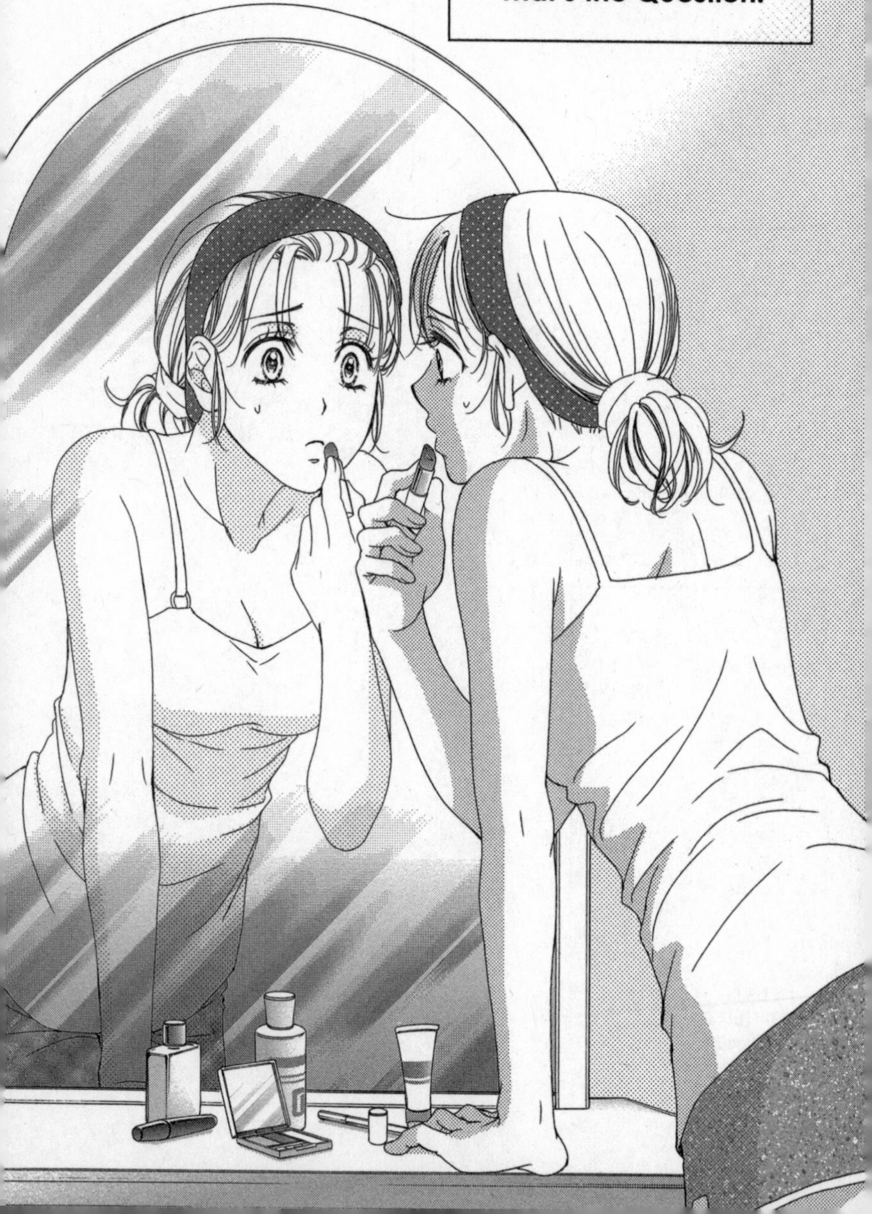

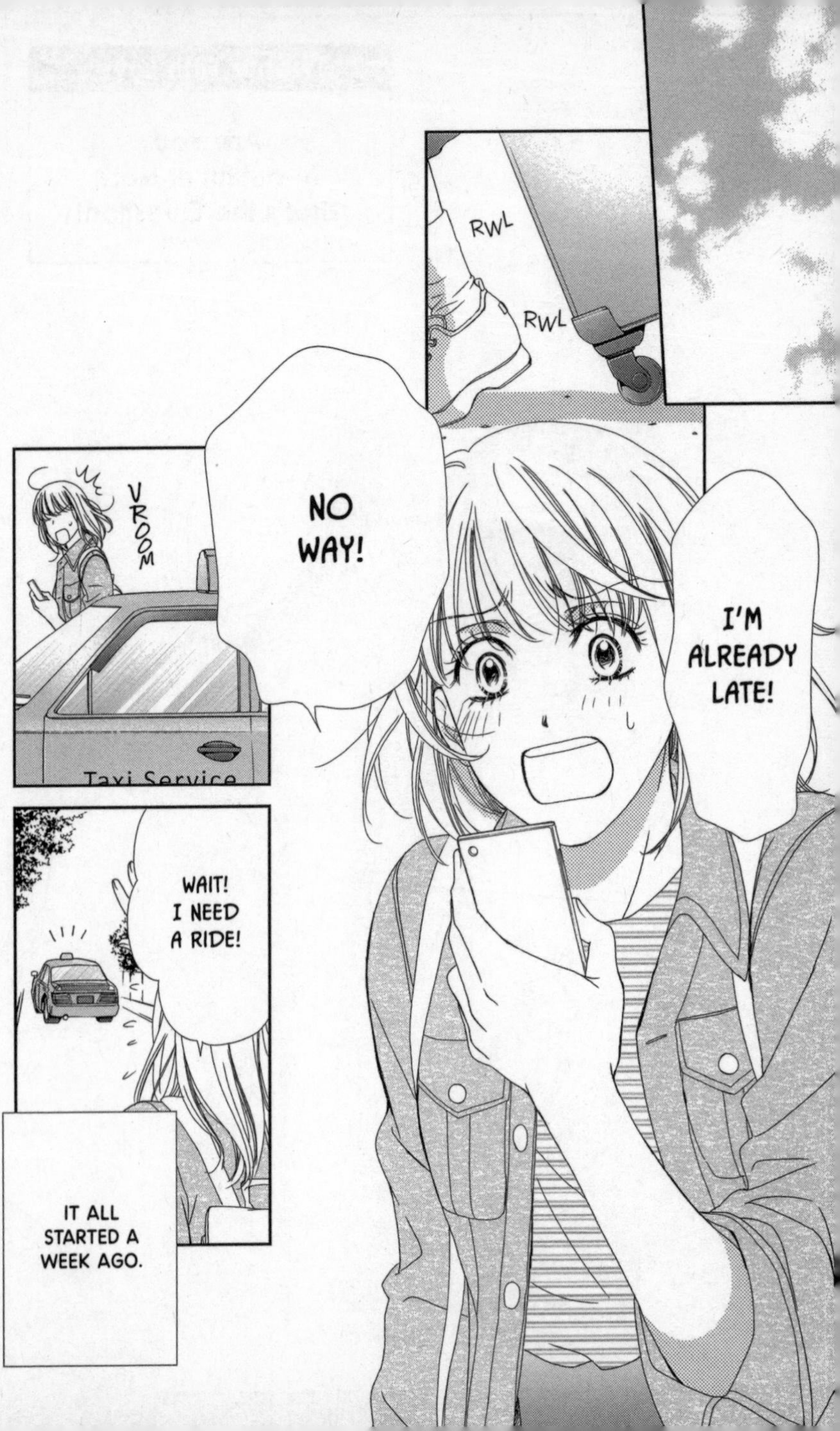
RWL
RWL
NO WAY!
I'M ALREADY LATE!
VROOM
Taxi Service
WAIT! I NEED A RIDE!
IT ALL STARTED A WEEK AGO.

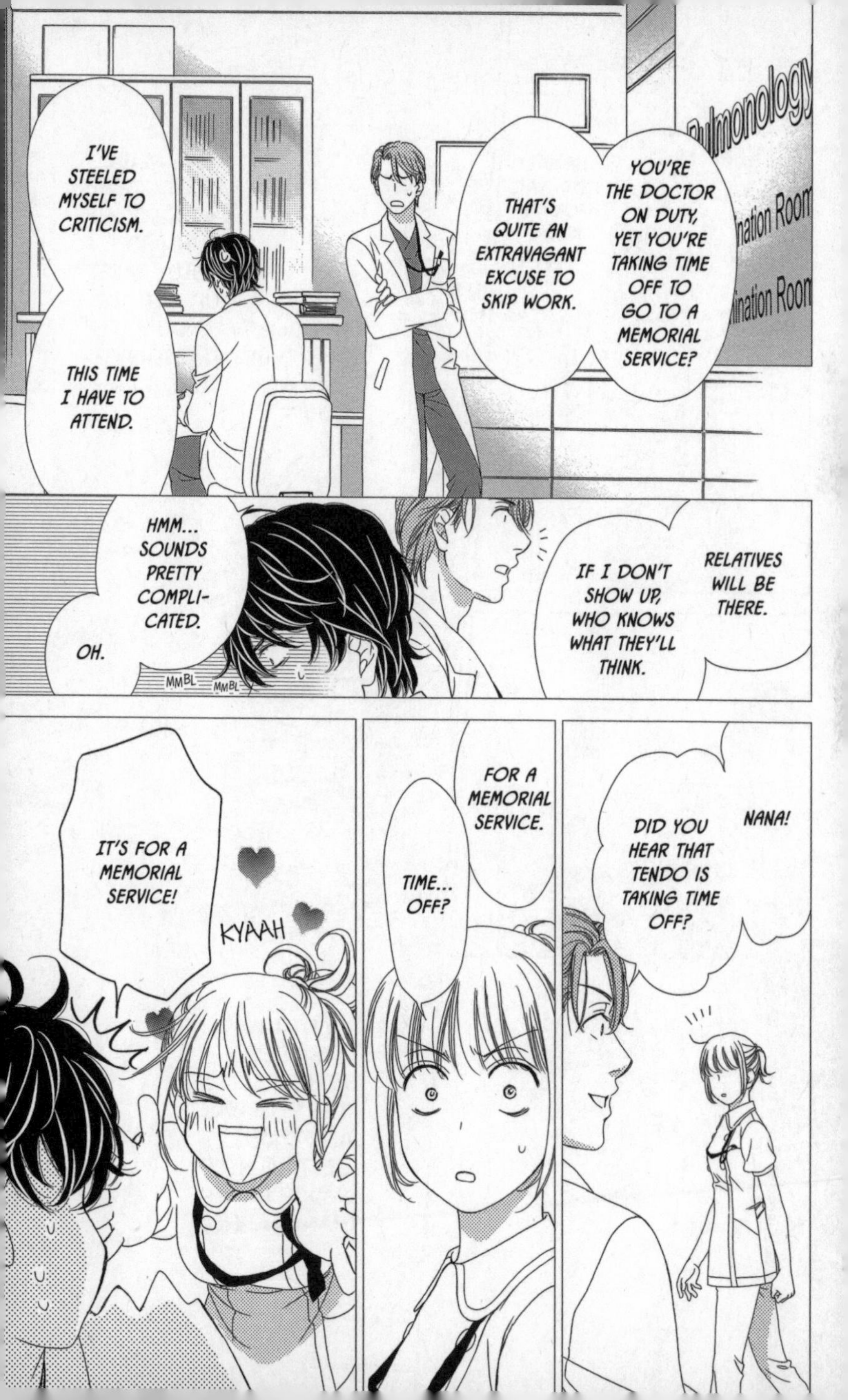
YOU'RE THE DOCTOR ON DUTY, YET YOU'RE TAKING TIME OFF TO GO TO A MEMORIAL SERVICE?
THAT'S QUITE AN EXTRAVAGANT EXCUSE TO SKIP WORK.
I'VE STEELED MYSELF TO CRITICISM.
THIS TIME I HAVE TO ATTEND.
RELATIVES WILL BE THERE.
IF I DON'T SHOW UP, WHO KNOWS WHAT THEY'LL THINK.
HMM... SOUNDS PRETTY COMPLI-CATED.
OH.
MMBL MMBL
NANA!
DID YOU HEAR THAT TENDO IS TAKING TIME OFF?
FOR A MEMORIAL SERVICE.
TIME... OFF?
IT'S FOR A MEMORIAL SERVICE!
KYAAH

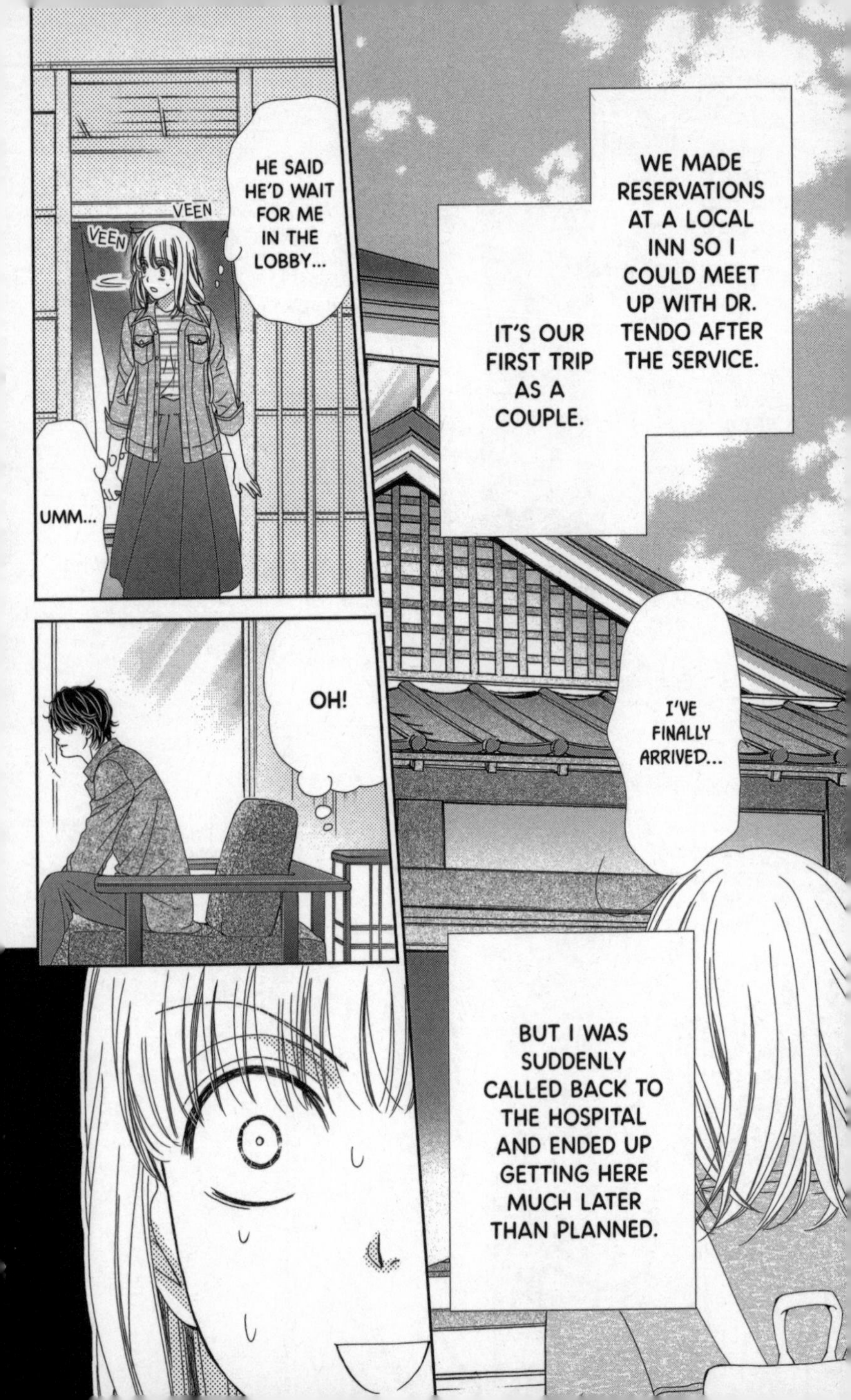
WE MADE RESERVATIONS AT A LOCAL INN SO I COULD MEET UP WITH DR. TENDO AFTER THE SERVICE.
IT'S OUR FIRST TRIP AS A COUPLE.
I'VE FINALLY ARRIVED...
BUT I WAS SUDDENLY CALLED BACK TO THE HOSPITAL AND ENDED UP GETTING HERE MUCH LATER THAN PLANNED.
HE SAID HE'D WAIT FOR ME IN THE LOBBY...
VEEN
VEEN
UMM...
OH!

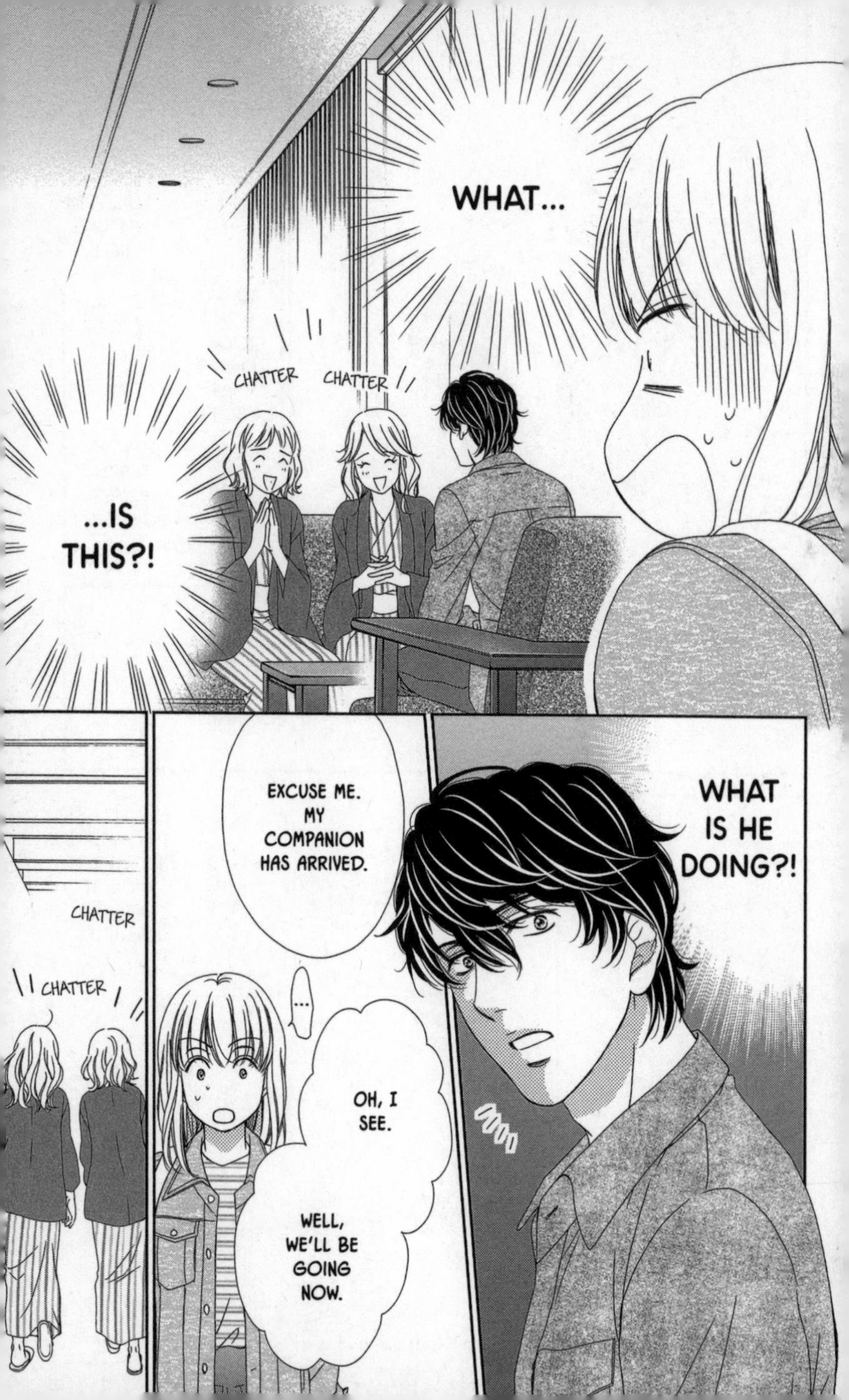
WHAT...
CHATTER CHATTER
...IS THIS?!
WHAT IS HE DOING?!
EXCUSE ME. MY COMPANION HAS ARRIVED.
...
OH, I SEE.
WELL, WE'LL BE GOING NOW.
CHATTER
CHATTER

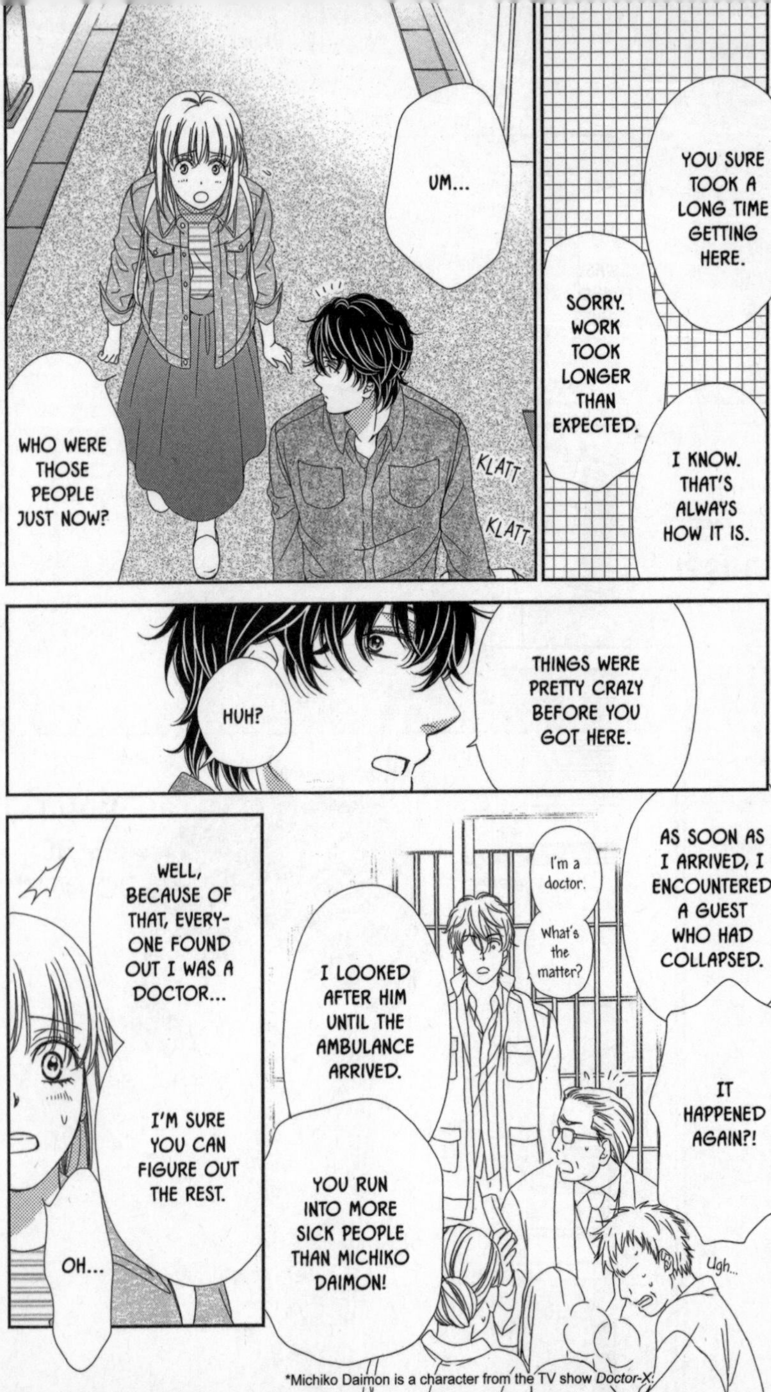
YOU SURE TOOK A LONG TIME GETTING HERE.
SORRY. WORK TOOK LONGER THAN EXPECTED.
I KNOW. THAT'S ALWAYS HOW IT IS.
UM...
KLATT
KLATT
WHO WERE THOSE PEOPLE JUST NOW?
THINGS WERE PRETTY CRAZY BEFORE YOU GOT HERE.
HUH?
AS SOON AS I ARRIVED, I ENCOUNTERED A GUEST WHO HAD COLLAPSED.
I'm a doctor.
What's the matter?
IT HAPPENED AGAIN?!
I LOOKED AFTER HIM UNTIL THE AMBULANCE ARRIVED.
Ugh...
YOU RUN INTO MORE SICK PEOPLE THAN MICHIKO DAIMON!
WELL, BECAUSE OF THAT, EVERY-ONE FOUND OUT I WAS A DOCTOR...
I'M SURE YOU CAN FIGURE OUT THE REST.
OH...

*Michiko Daimon is a character from the TV show *Doctor-X*.

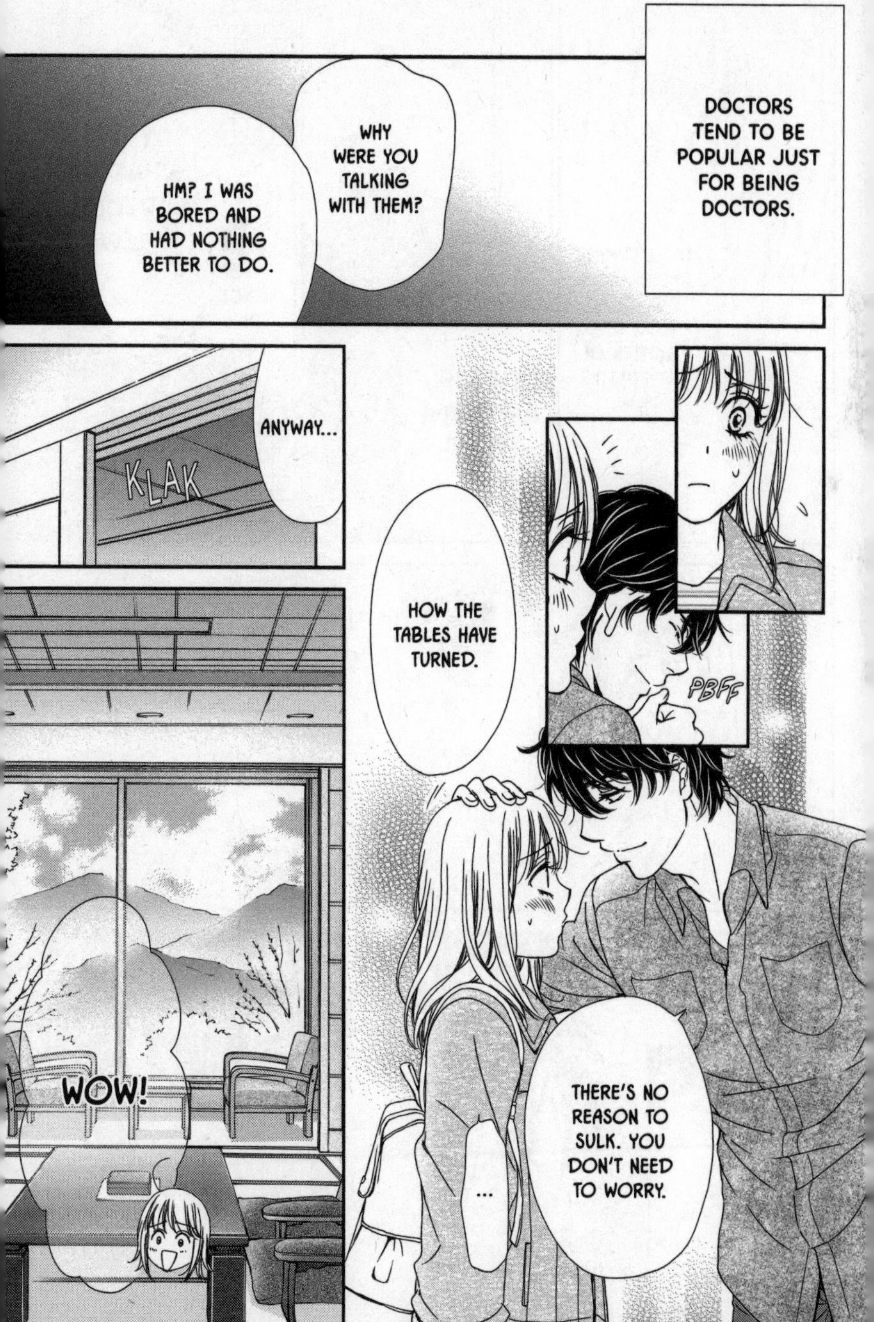
DOCTORS TEND TO BE POPULAR JUST FOR BEING DOCTORS.
WHY WERE YOU TALKING WITH THEM?
HM? I WAS BORED AND HAD NOTHING BETTER TO DO.
PBFF
HOW THE TABLES HAVE TURNED.
THERE'S NO REASON TO SULK. YOU DON'T NEED TO WORRY.
...
KLAK
ANYWAY...
WOW!

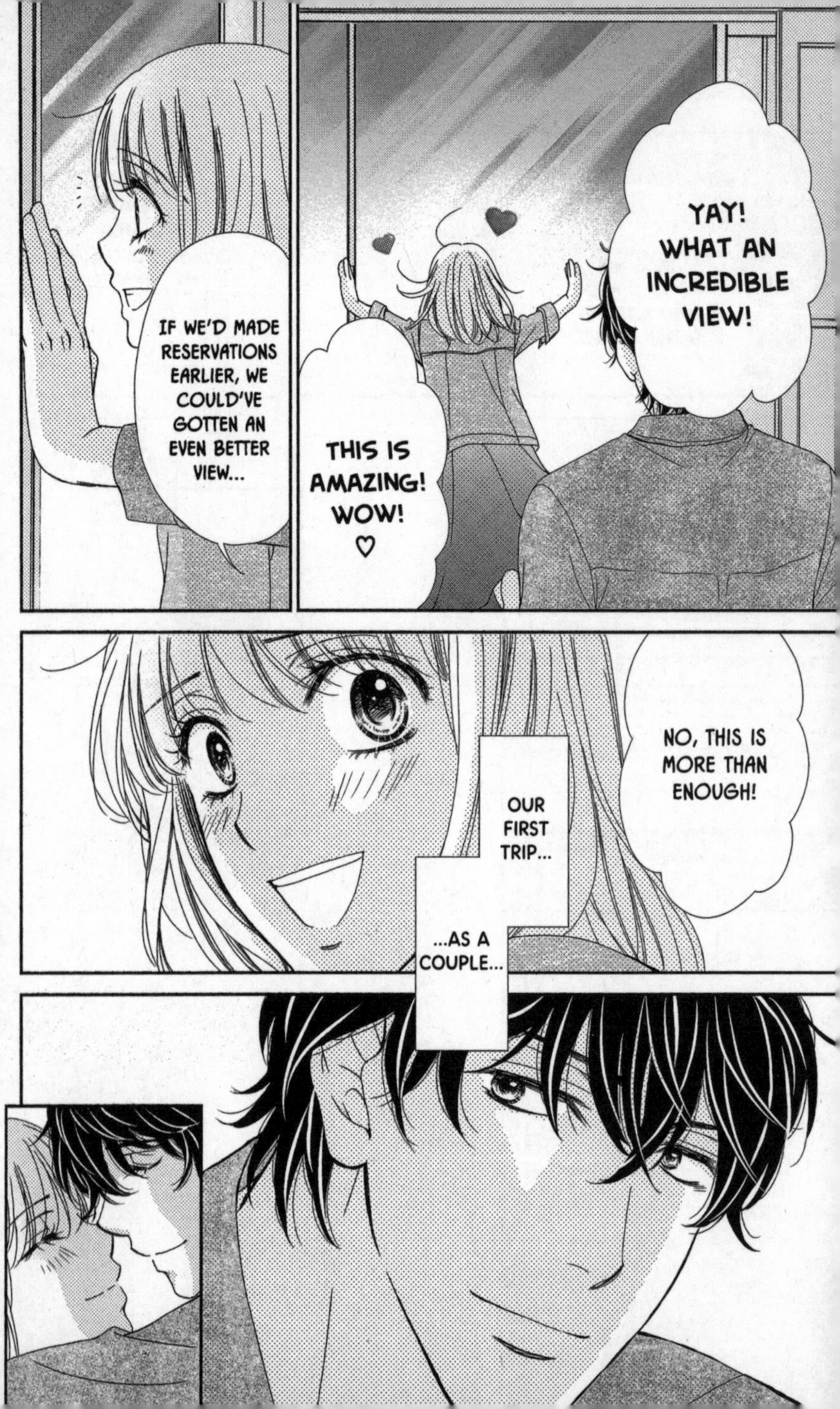
YAY! WHAT AN INCREDIBLE VIEW!
THIS IS AMAZING! WOW! ♡
IF WE'D MADE RESERVATIONS EARLIER, WE COULD'VE GOTTEN AN EVEN BETTER VIEW...
NO, THIS IS MORE THAN ENOUGH!
OUR FIRST TRIP...
...AS A COUPLE...

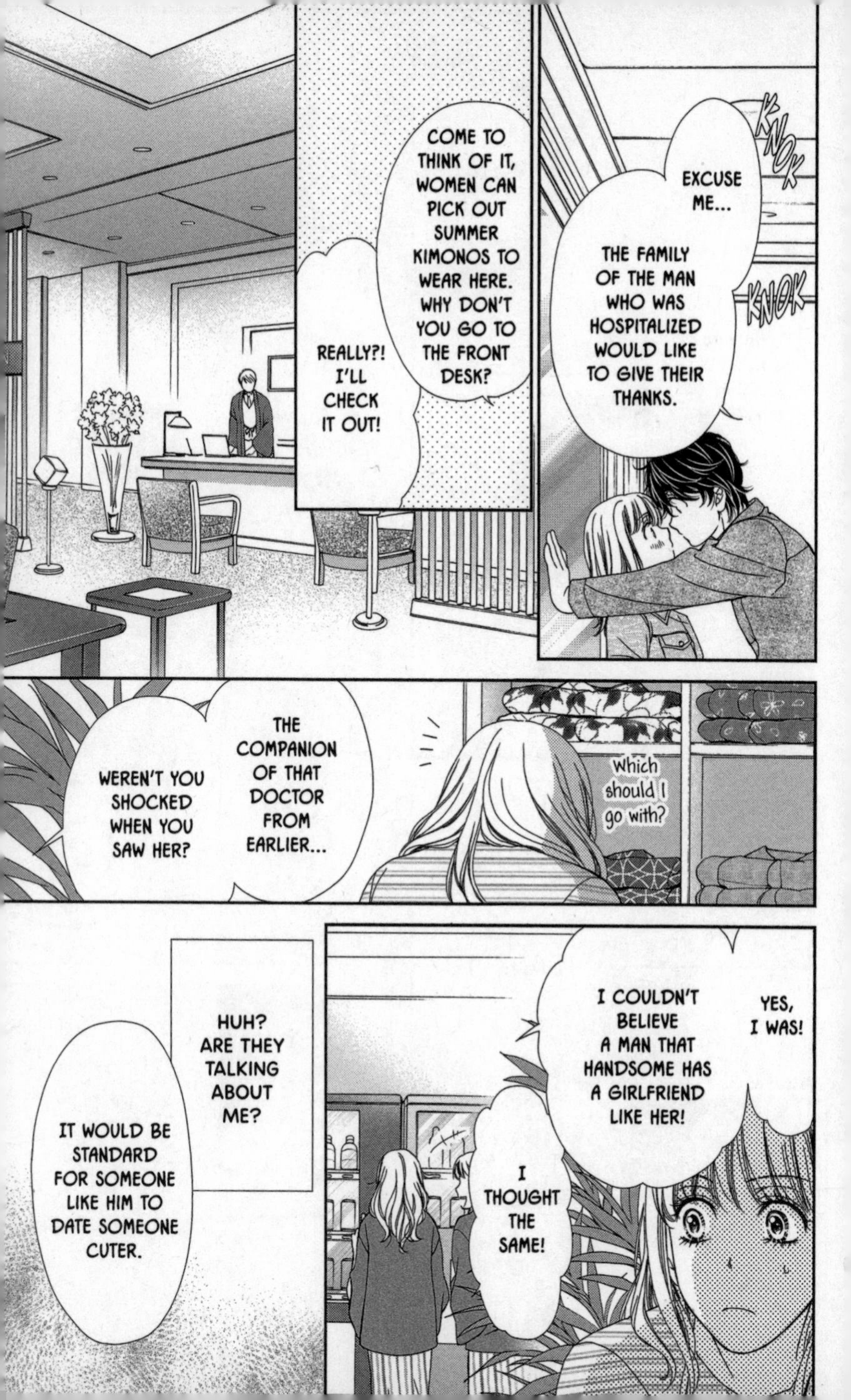
KNOK
EXCUSE ME...
THE FAMILY OF THE MAN WHO WAS HOSPITALIZED WOULD LIKE TO GIVE THEIR THANKS.
KNOK
COME TO THINK OF IT, WOMEN CAN PICK OUT SUMMER KIMONOS TO WEAR HERE. WHY DON'T YOU GO TO THE FRONT DESK?
REALLY?! I'LL CHECK IT OUT!
Which should I go with?
THE COMPANION OF THAT DOCTOR FROM EARLIER...
WEREN'T YOU SHOCKED WHEN YOU SAW HER?
YES, I WAS!
I COULDN'T BELIEVE A MAN THAT HANDSOME HAS A GIRLFRIEND LIKE HER!
I THOUGHT THE SAME!
HUH? ARE THEY TALKING ABOUT ME?
IT WOULD BE STANDARD FOR SOMEONE LIKE HIM TO DATE SOMEONE CUTER.

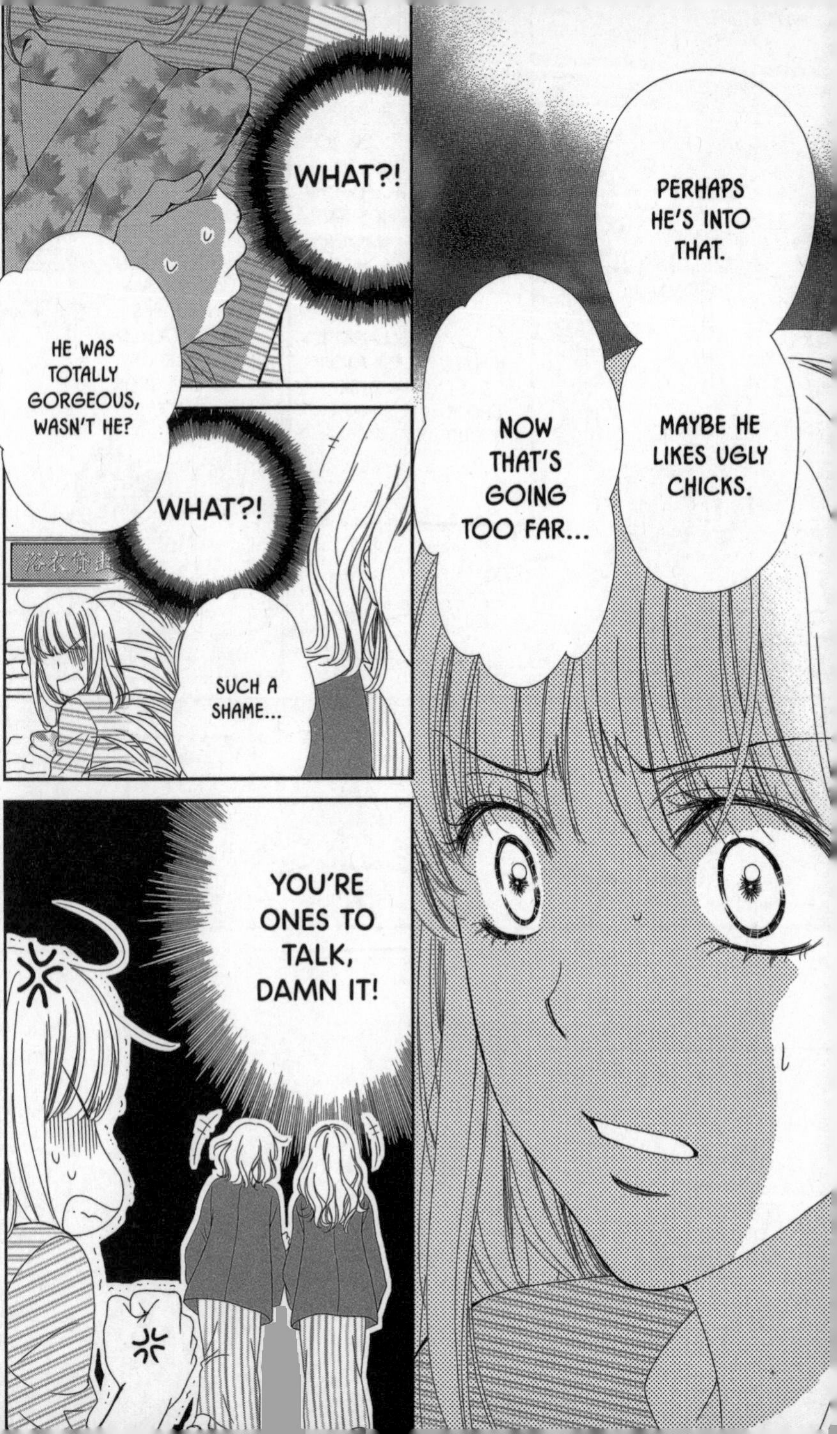
PERHAPS HE'S INTO THAT.
MAYBE HE LIKES UGLY CHICKS.
NOW THAT'S GOING TOO FAR...
WHAT?!
HE WAS TOTALLY GORGEOUS, WASN'T HE?
WHAT?!
SUCH A SHAME...
YOU'RE ONES TO TALK, DAMN IT!

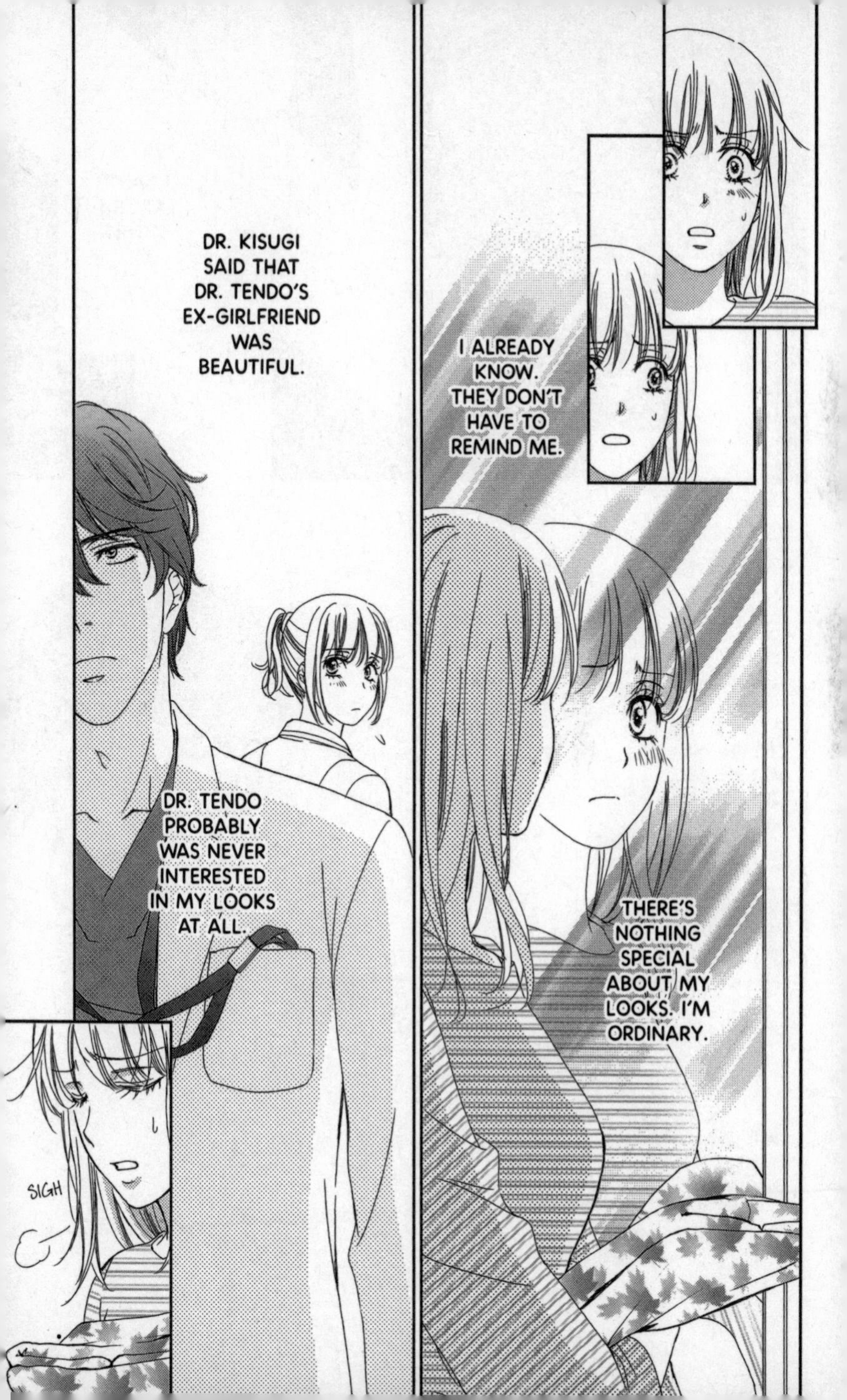
I ALREADY KNOW. THEY DON'T HAVE TO REMIND ME.
THERE'S NOTHING SPECIAL ABOUT MY LOOKS. I'M ORDINARY.
DR. KISUGI SAID THAT DR. TENDO'S EX-GIRLFRIEND WAS BEAUTIFUL.
DR. TENDO PROBABLY WAS NEVER INTERESTED IN MY LOOKS AT ALL.
SIGH

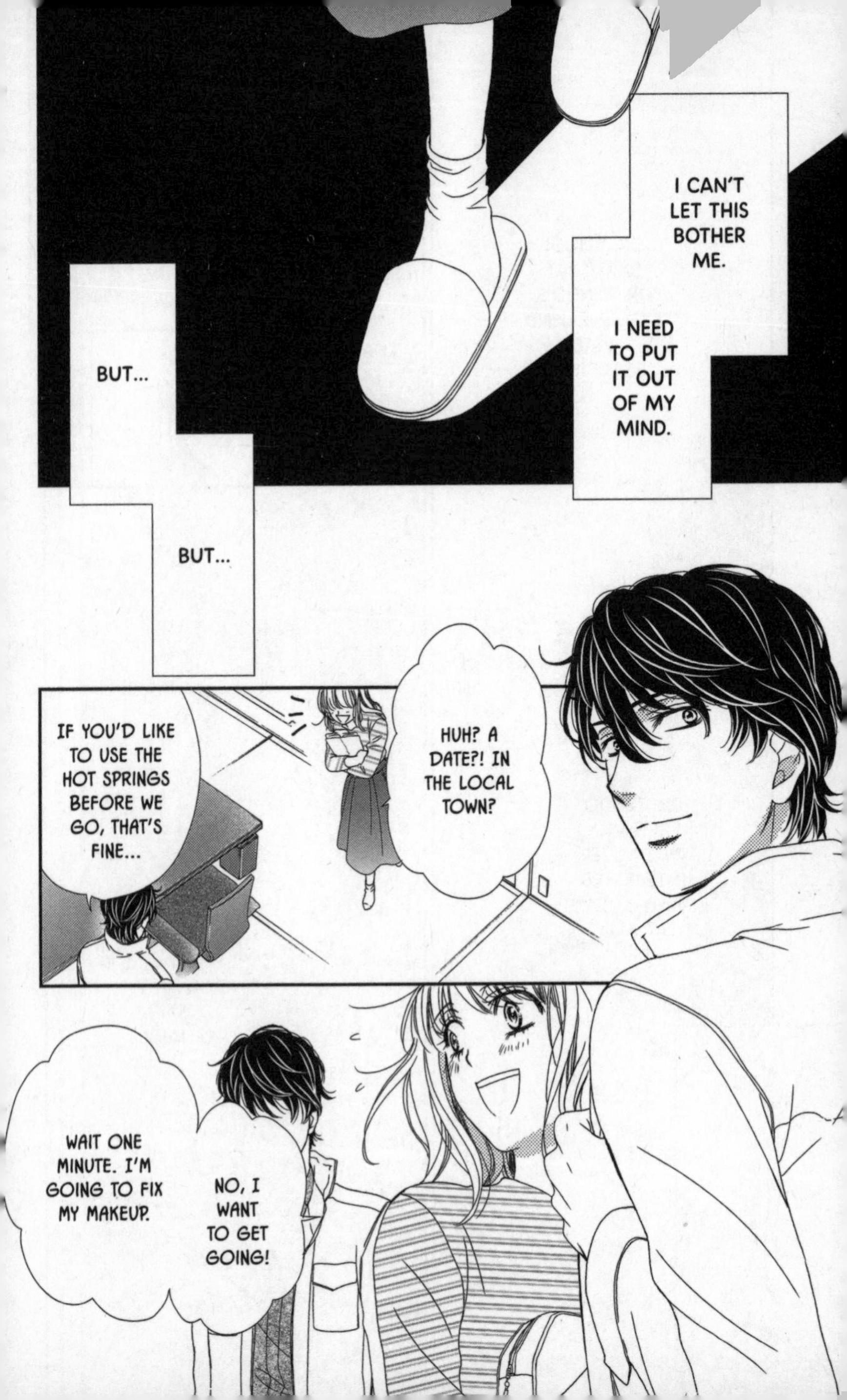
I CAN'T LET THIS BOTHER ME.
I NEED TO PUT IT OUT OF MY MIND.
BUT...
BUT...
HUH? A DATE?! IN THE LOCAL TOWN?
IF YOU'D LIKE TO USE THE HOT SPRINGS BEFORE WE GO, THAT'S FINE...
WAIT ONE MINUTE. I'M GOING TO FIX MY MAKEUP.
NO, I WANT TO GET GOING!

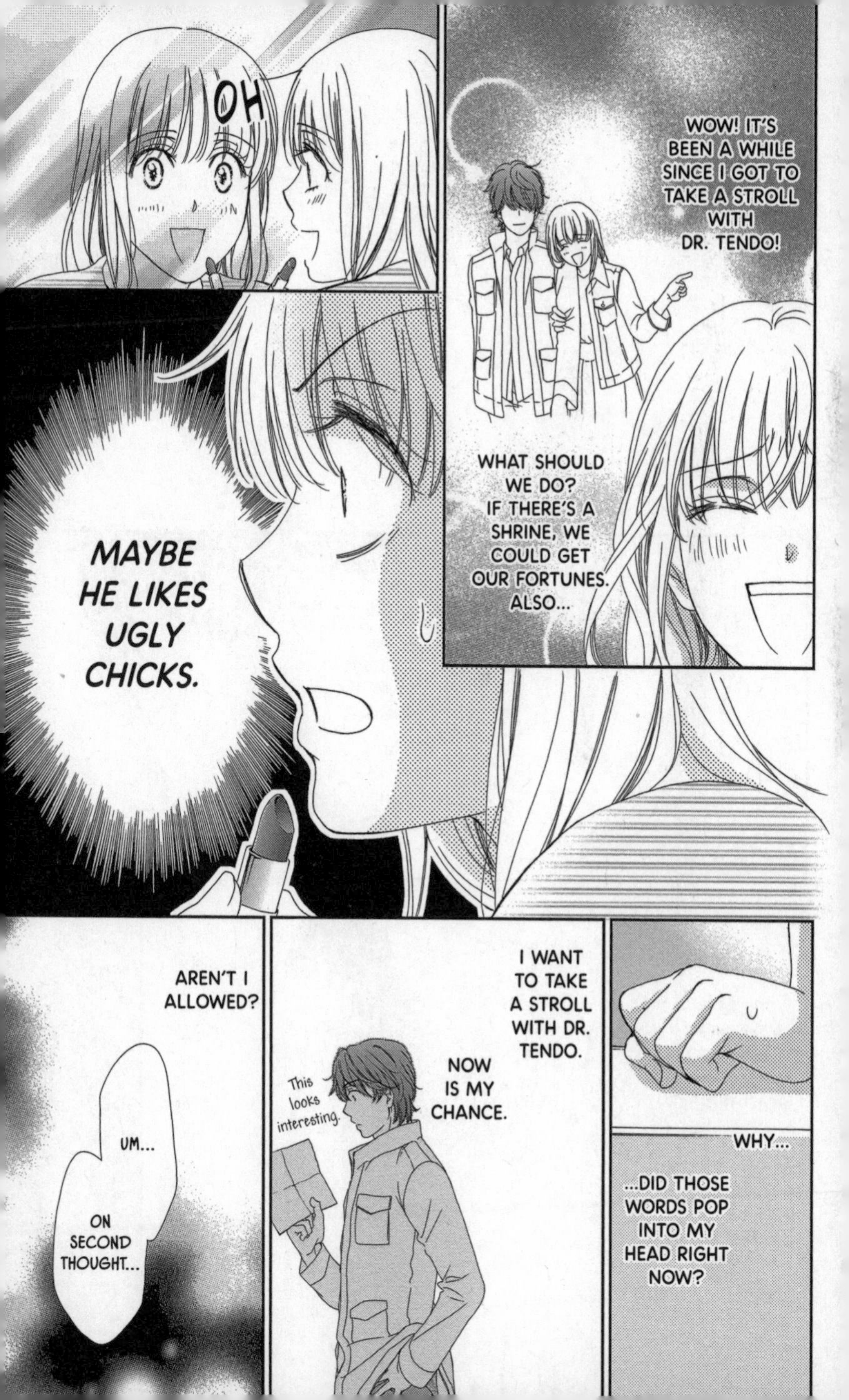
WOW! IT'S BEEN A WHILE SINCE I GOT TO TAKE A STROLL WITH DR. TENDO!
WHAT SHOULD WE DO? IF THERE'S A SHRINE, WE COULD GET OUR FORTUNES. ALSO...
OH
MAYBE HE LIKES UGLY CHICKS.
WHY...
...DID THOSE WORDS POP INTO MY HEAD RIGHT NOW?
I WANT TO TAKE A STROLL WITH DR. TENDO.
NOW IS MY CHANCE.
This looks interesting.
AREN'T I ALLOWED?
UM...
ON SECOND THOUGHT...

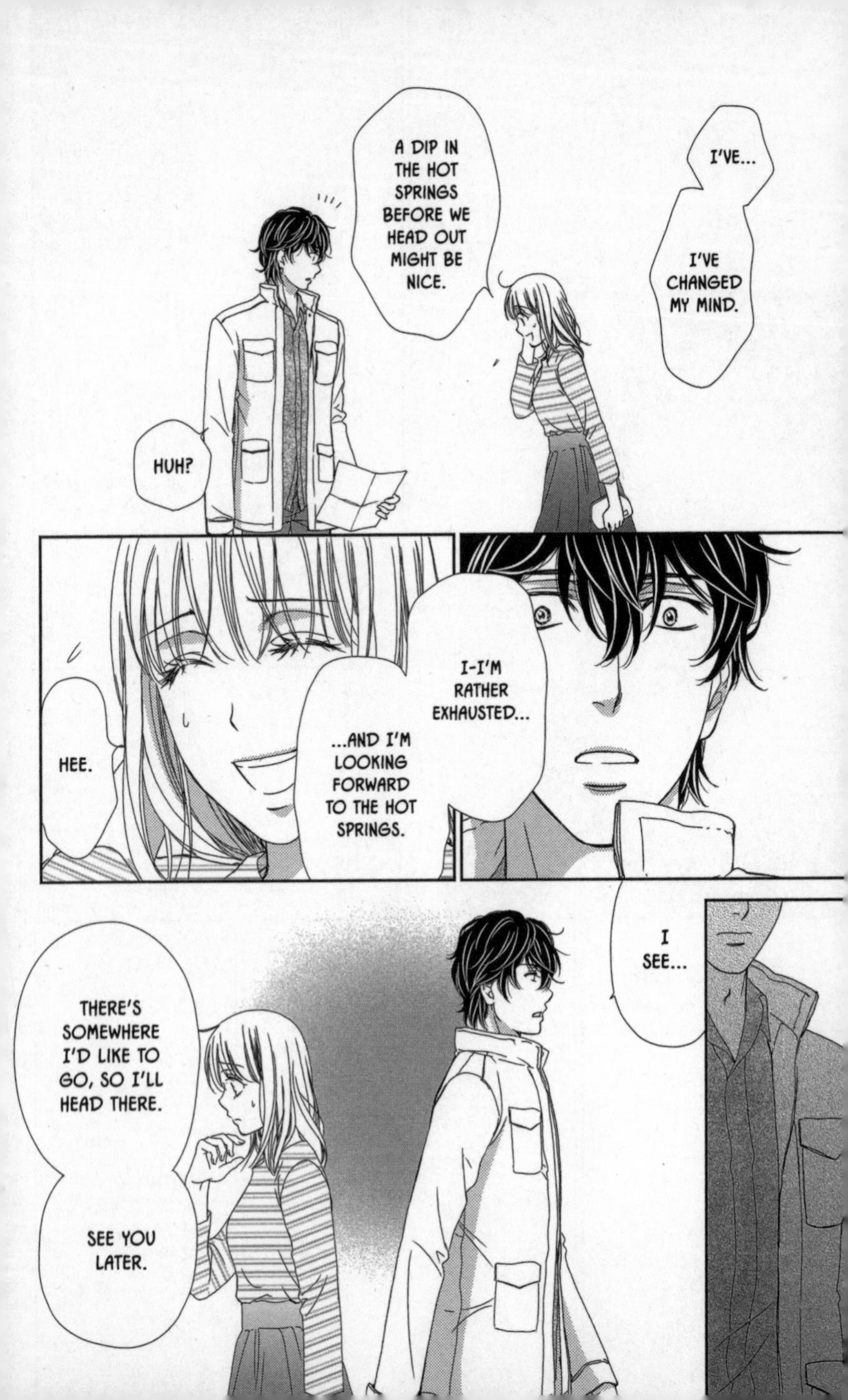
I'VE...
I'VE CHANGED MY MIND.
A DIP IN THE HOT SPRINGS BEFORE WE HEAD OUT MIGHT BE NICE.
HUH?
I-I'M RATHER EXHAUSTED...
...AND I'M LOOKING FORWARD TO THE HOT SPRINGS.
HEE.
I SEE...
THERE'S SOMEWHERE I'D LIKE TO GO, SO I'LL HEAD THERE.
SEE YOU LATER.

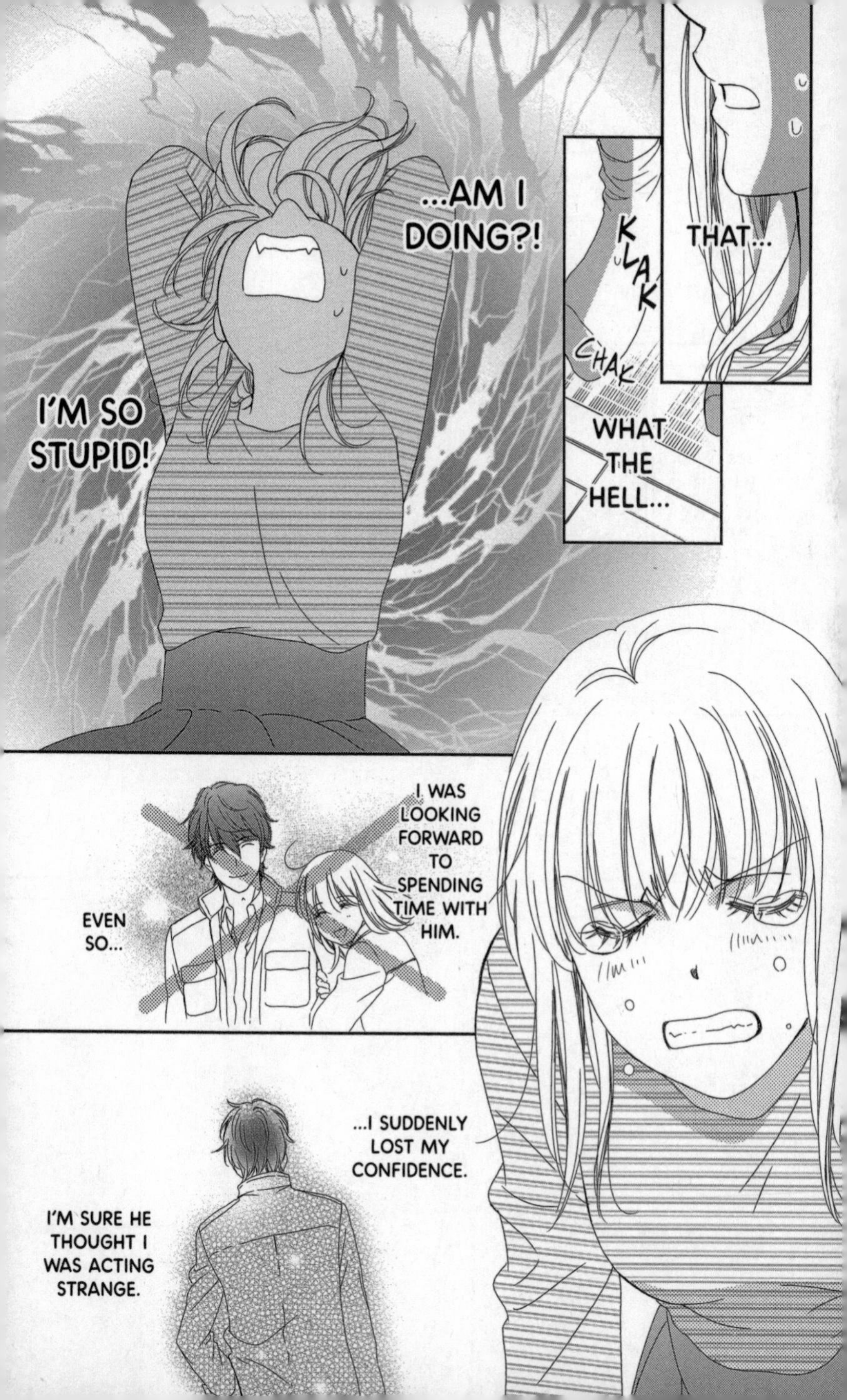
THAT...
KLAK
CHAK
WHAT THE HELL...
...AM I DOING?!
I'M SO STUPID!
I WAS LOOKING FORWARD TO SPENDING TIME WITH HIM.
EVEN SO...
...I SUDDENLY LOST MY CONFIDENCE.
I'M SURE HE THOUGHT I WAS ACTING STRANGE.

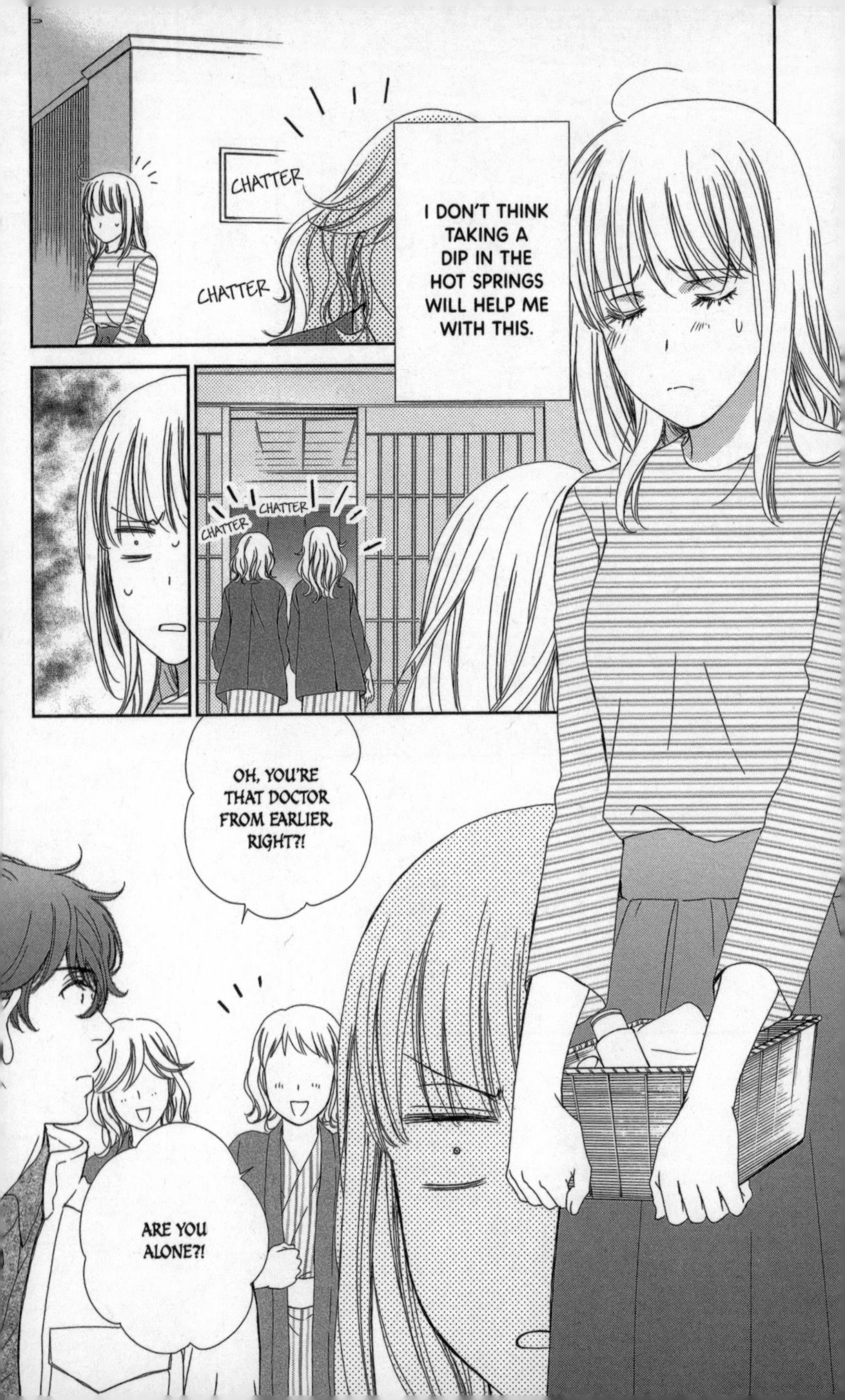
I DON'T THINK TAKING A DIP IN THE HOT SPRINGS WILL HELP ME WITH THIS.
CHATTER
CHATTER
CHATTER
CHATTER
OH, YOU'RE THAT DOCTOR FROM EARLIER, RIGHT?!
ARE YOU ALONE?!

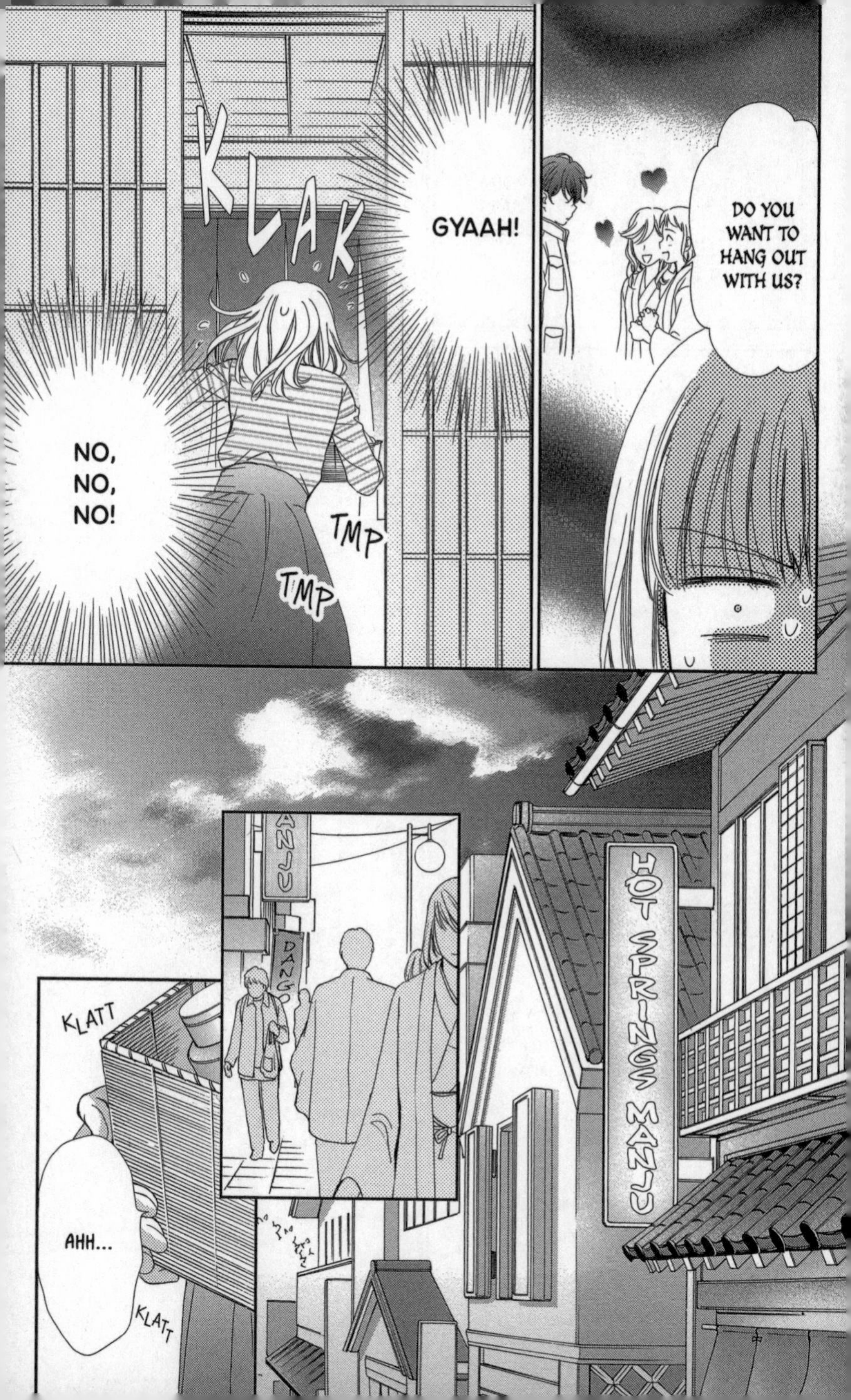

DO YOU WANT TO HANG OUT WITH US?
GYAAH!
KLAK
NO, NO, NO!
TMP
TMP
HOT SPRINGS MANJU
MANJU
DANGO
KLATT
AHH...
KLATT

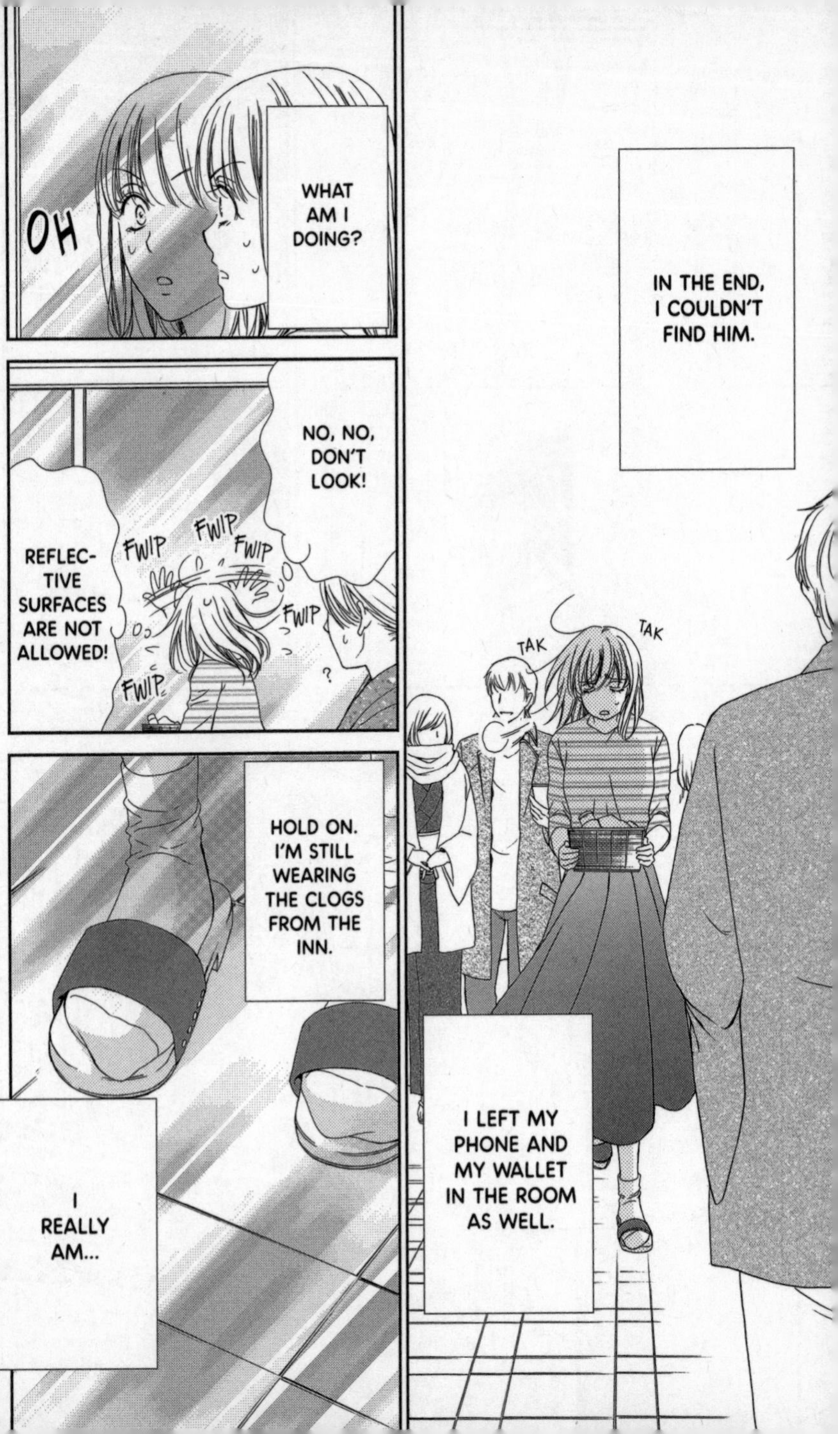
IN THE END, I COULDN'T FIND HIM.
TAK
TAK
I LEFT MY PHONE AND MY WALLET IN THE ROOM AS WELL.
WHAT AM I DOING?
OH
NO, NO, DON'T LOOK!
FWIP
FWIP
FWIP
FWIP
REFLEC-TIVE SURFACES ARE NOT ALLOWED!
FWIP
?
HOLD ON. I'M STILL WEARING THE CLOGS FROM THE INN.
I REALLY AM...

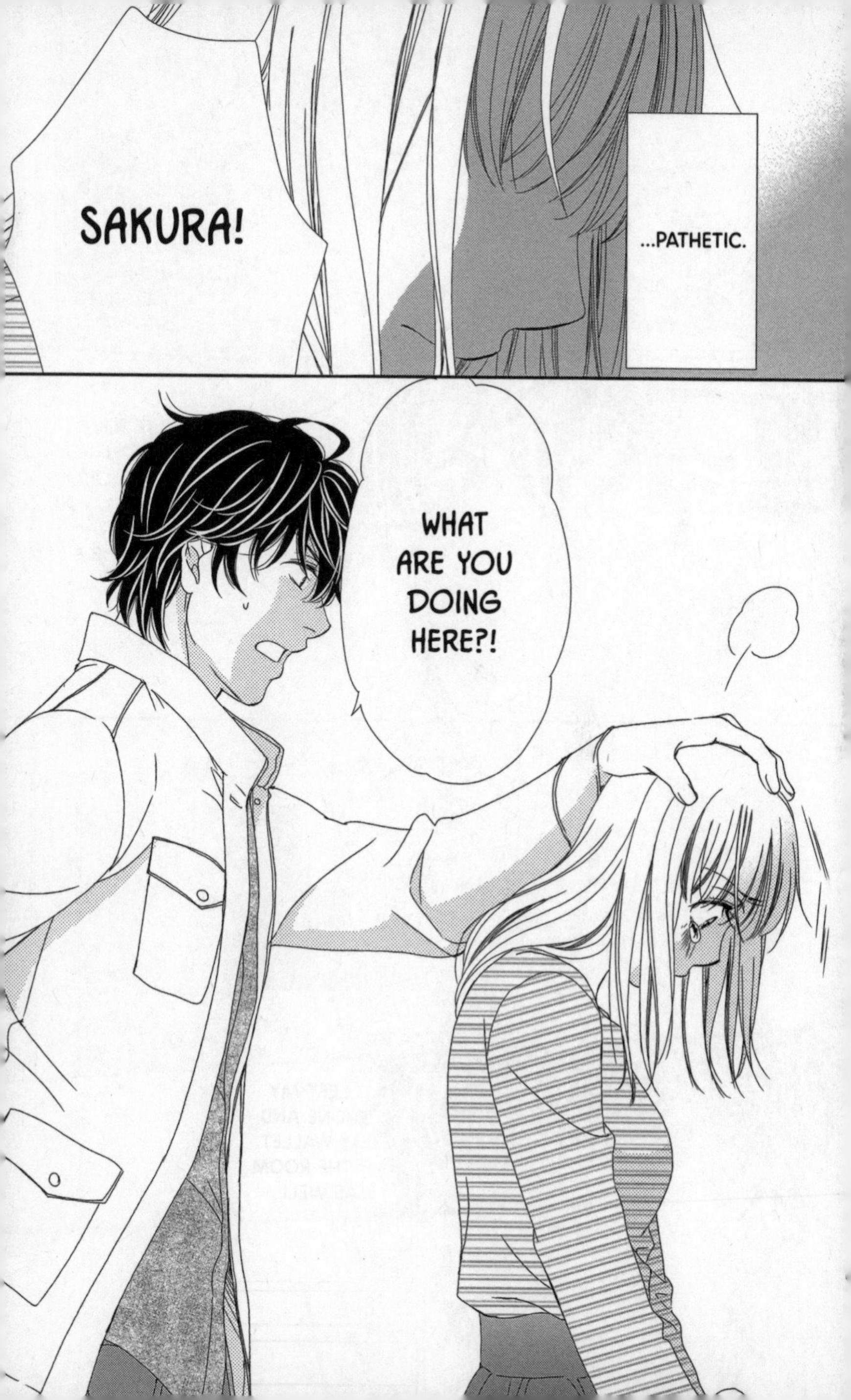
...PATHETIC.
SAKURA!
WHAT ARE YOU DOING HERE?!

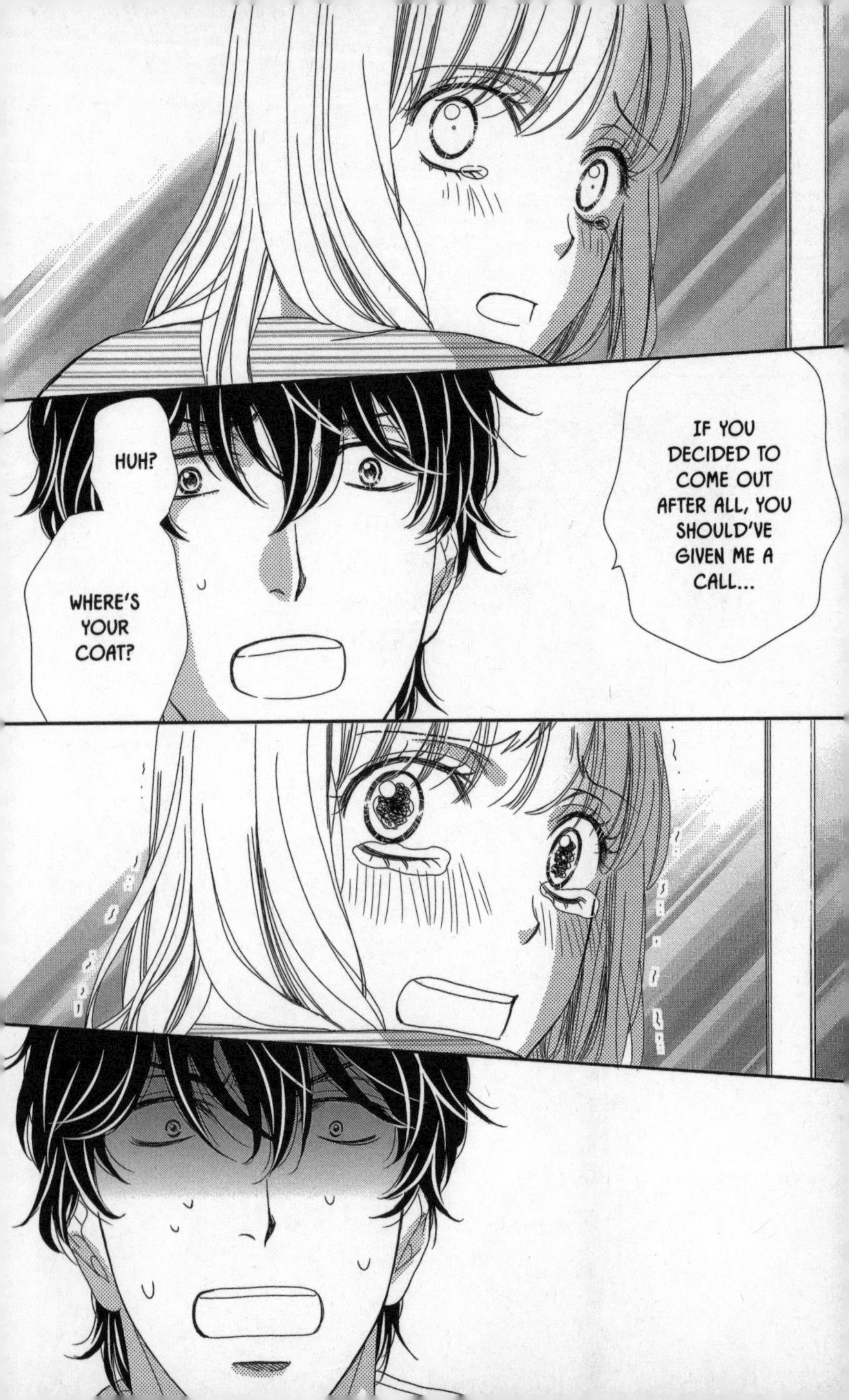
IF YOU DECIDED TO COME OUT AFTER ALL, YOU SHOULD'VE GIVEN ME A CALL...
HUH?
WHERE'S YOUR COAT?

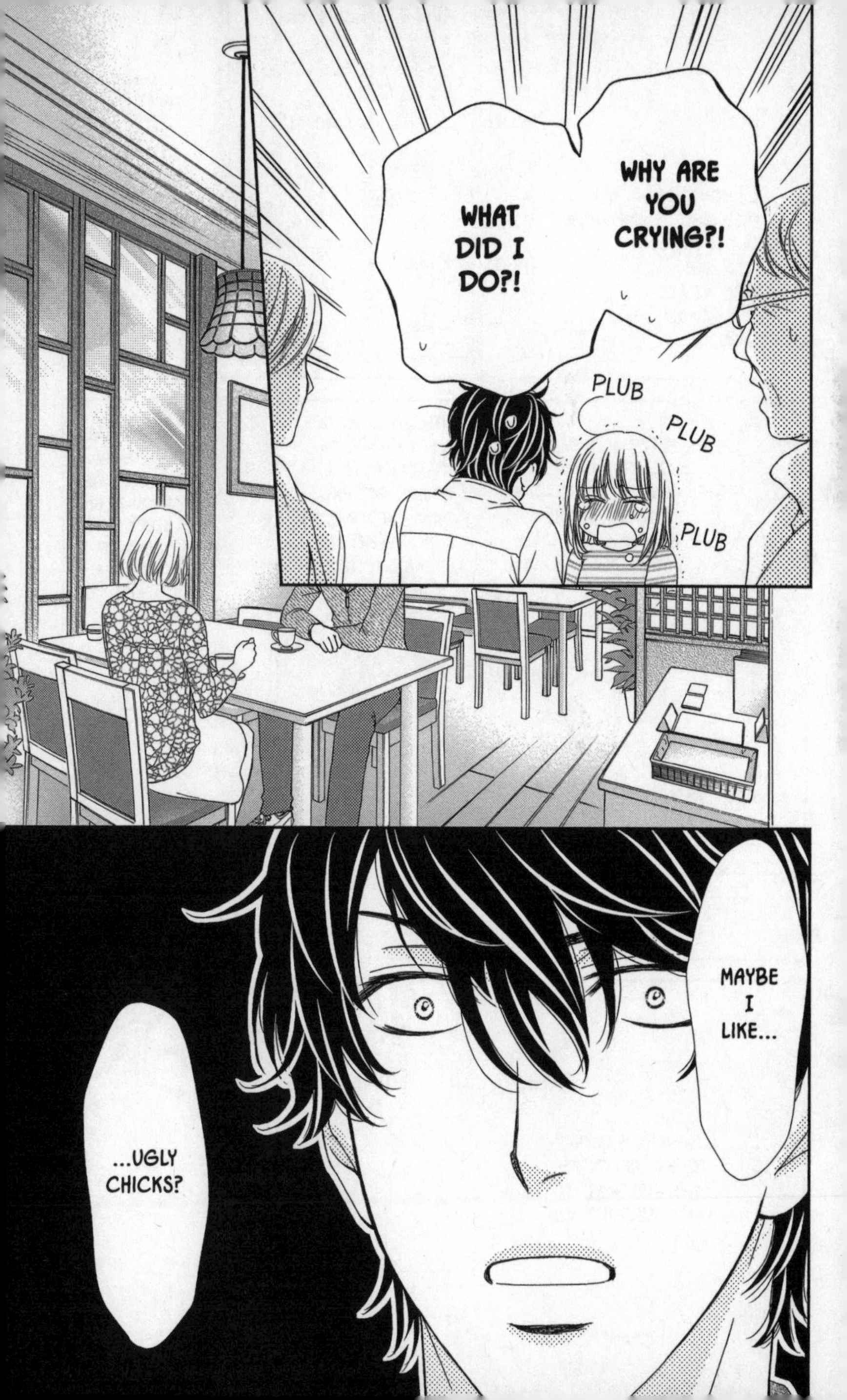
WHY ARE YOU CRYING?!
WHAT DID I DO?!
PLUB
PLUB
PLUB
MAYBE I LIKE...
...UGLY CHICKS?

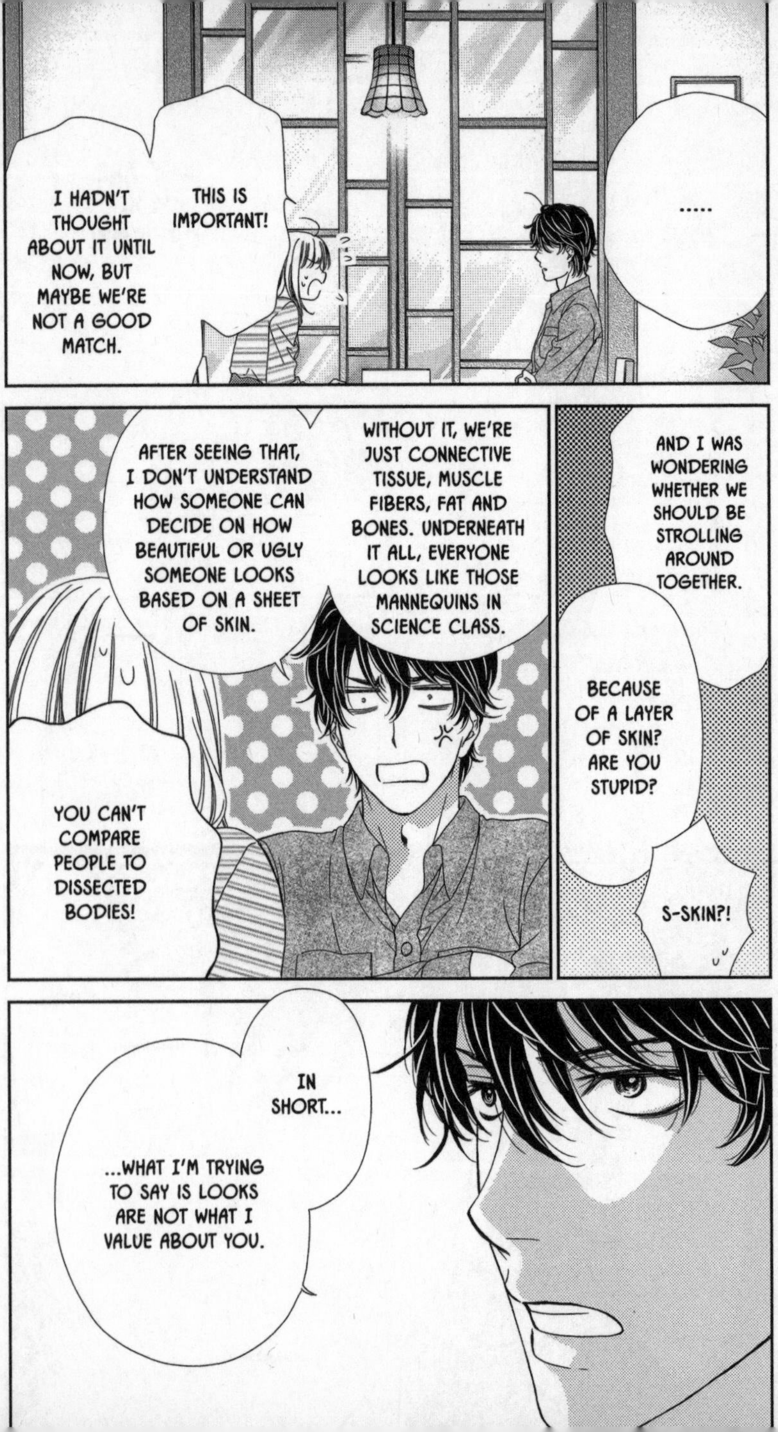
.....
I HADN'T THOUGHT ABOUT IT UNTIL NOW, BUT MAYBE WE'RE NOT A GOOD MATCH.
THIS IS IMPORTANT!
AND I WAS WONDERING WHETHER WE SHOULD BE STROLLING AROUND TOGETHER.
BECAUSE OF A LAYER OF SKIN? ARE YOU STUPID?
S-SKIN?!
AFTER SEEING THAT, I DON'T UNDERSTAND HOW SOMEONE CAN DECIDE ON HOW BEAUTIFUL OR UGLY SOMEONE LOOKS BASED ON A SHEET OF SKIN.
WITHOUT IT, WE'RE JUST CONNECTIVE TISSUE, MUSCLE FIBERS, FAT AND BONES. UNDERNEATH IT ALL, EVERYONE LOOKS LIKE THOSE MANNEQUINS IN SCIENCE CLASS.
YOU CAN'T COMPARE PEOPLE TO DISSECTED BODIES!
IN SHORT...
...WHAT I'M TRYING TO SAY IS LOOKS ARE NOT WHAT I VALUE ABOUT YOU.

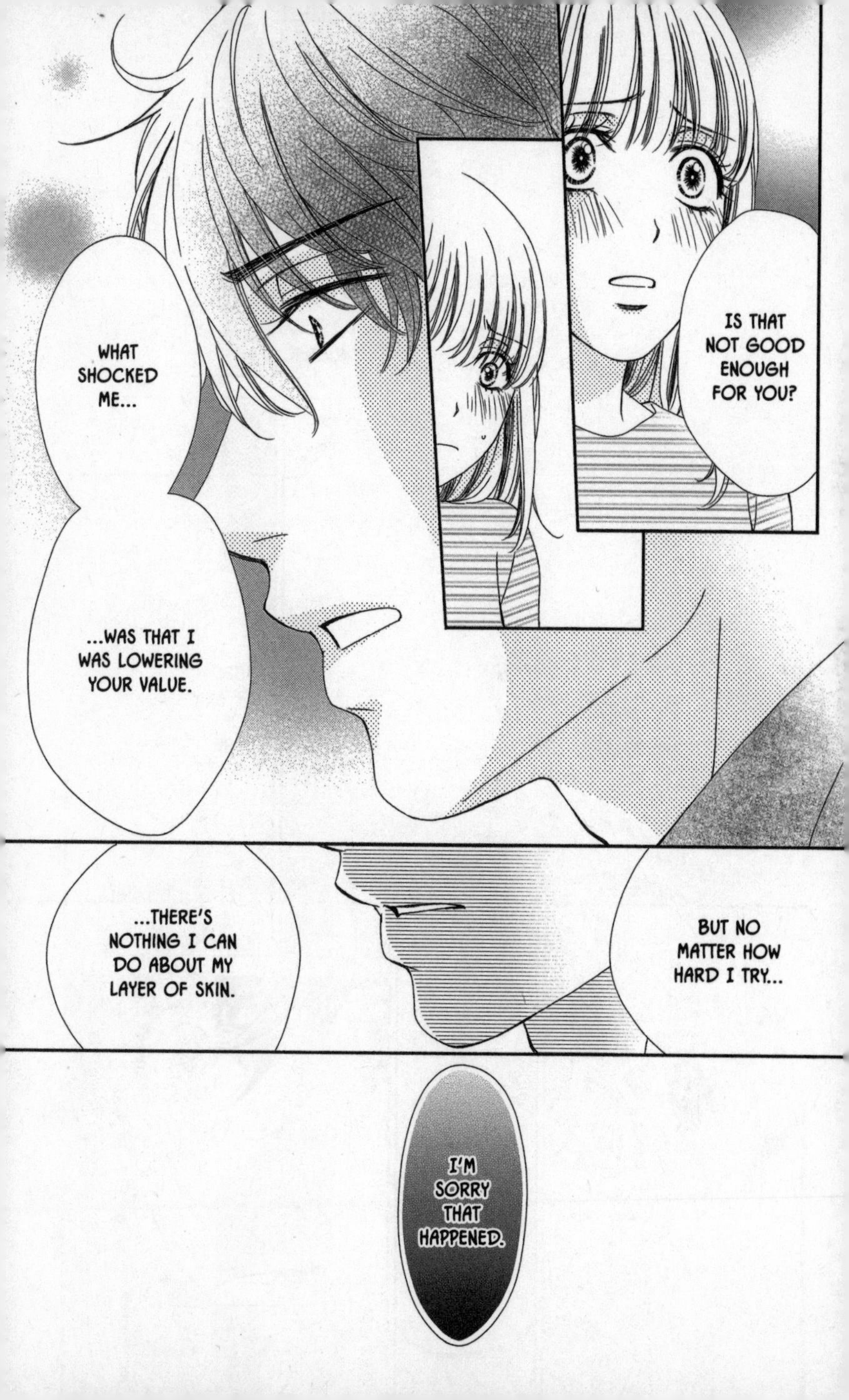
IS THAT NOT GOOD ENOUGH FOR YOU?
WHAT SHOCKED ME...
...WAS THAT I WAS LOWERING YOUR VALUE.
BUT NO MATTER HOW HARD I TRY...
...THERE'S NOTHING I CAN DO ABOUT MY LAYER OF SKIN.
I'M SORRY THAT HAPPENED.

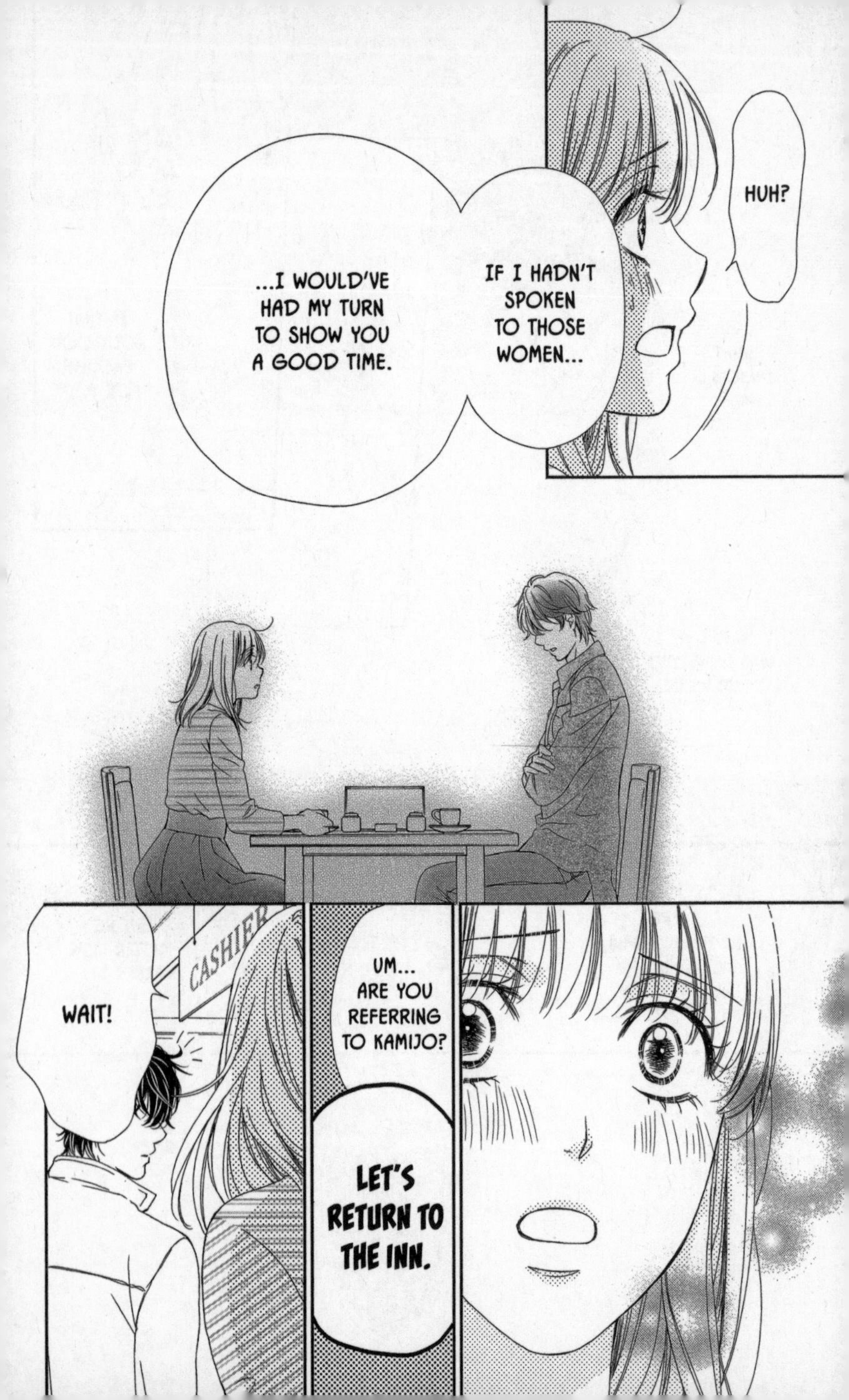
HUH?
IF I HADN'T SPOKEN TO THOSE WOMEN...
...I WOULD'VE HAD MY TURN TO SHOW YOU A GOOD TIME.
UM... ARE YOU REFERRING TO KAMIJO?
LET'S RETURN TO THE INN.
CASHIER
WAIT!

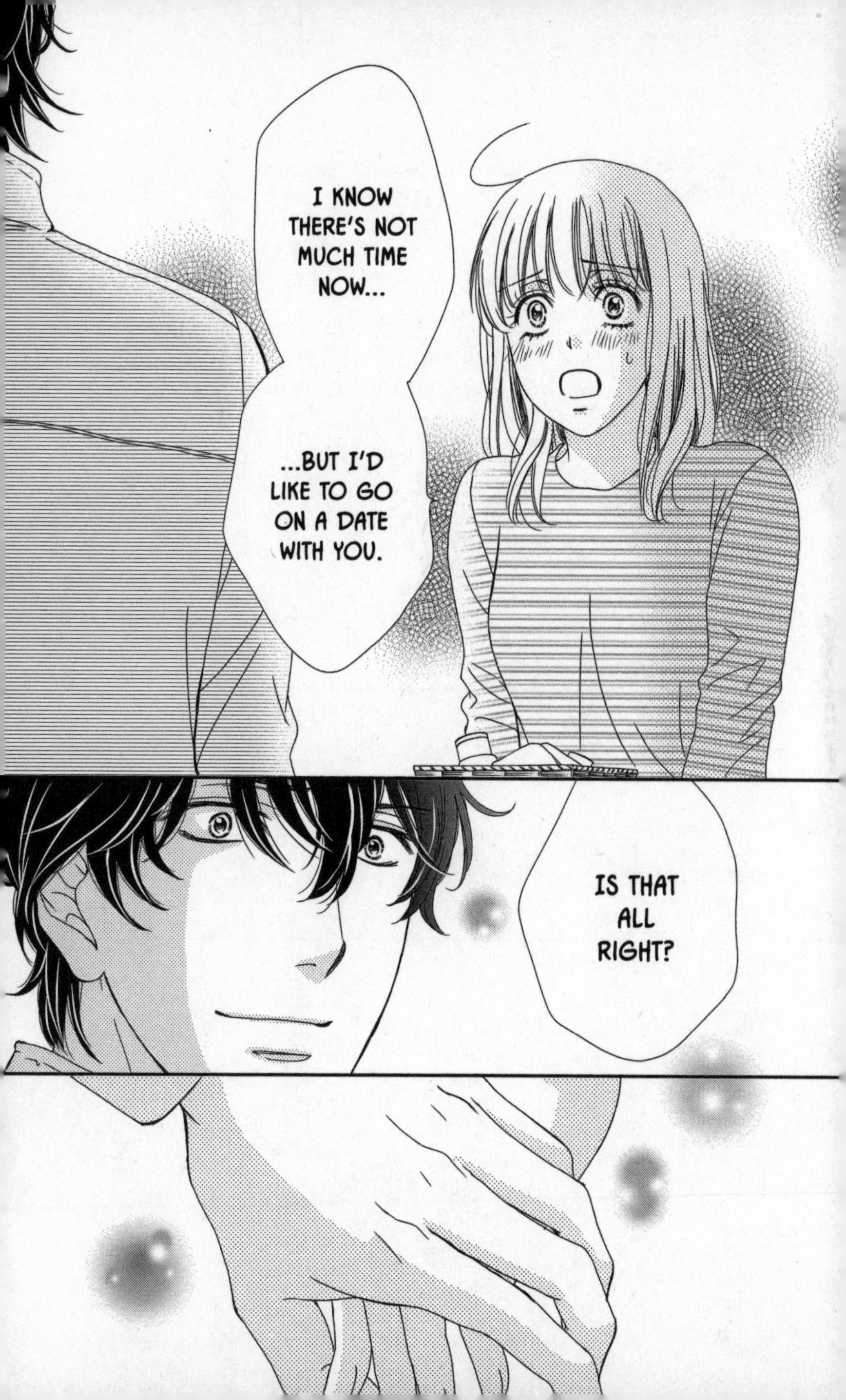
I KNOW THERE'S NOT MUCH TIME NOW...
...BUT I'D LIKE TO GO ON A DATE WITH YOU.
IS THAT ALL RIGHT?

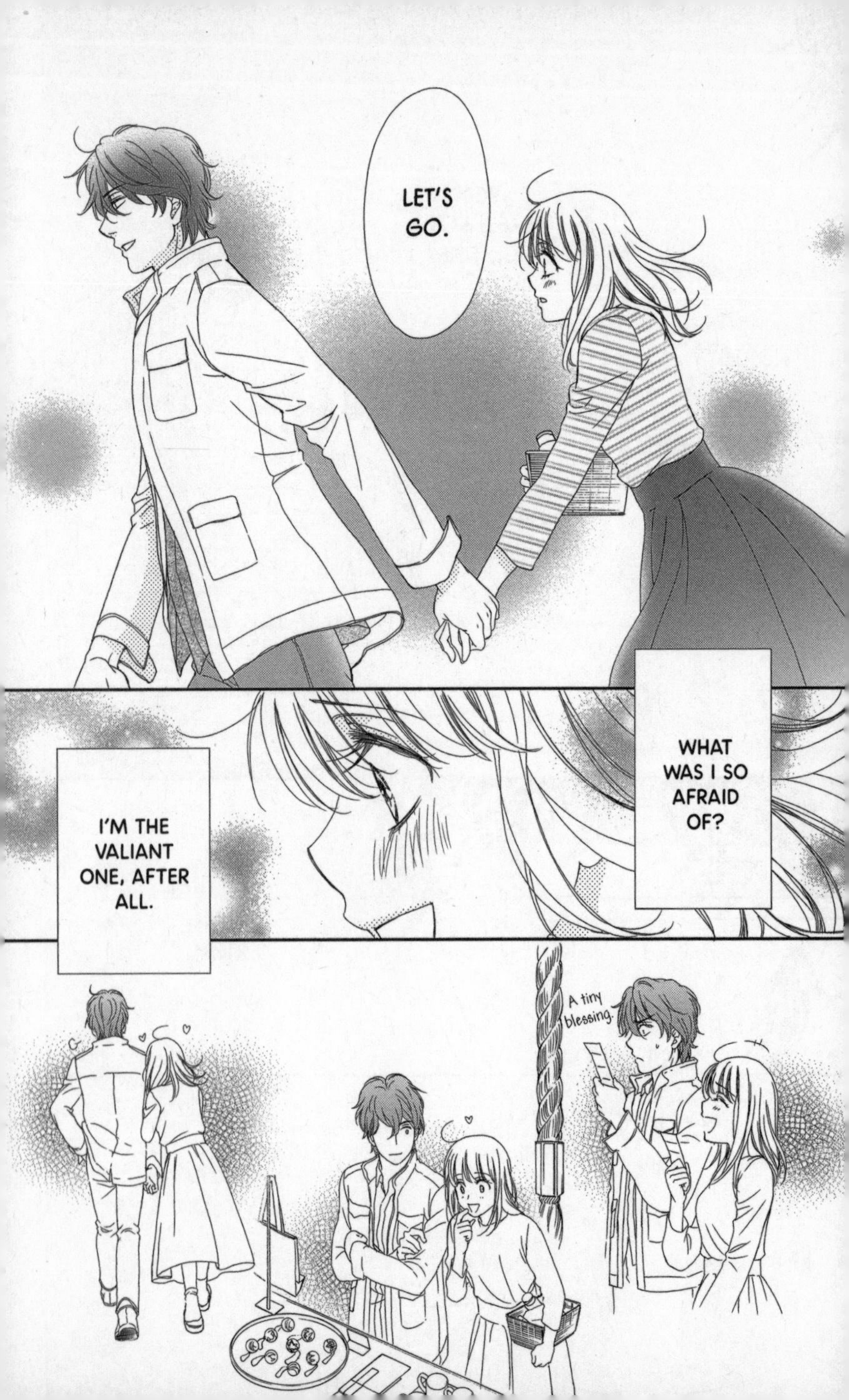
LET'S GO.
WHAT WAS I SO AFRAID OF?
I'M THE VALIANT ONE, AFTER ALL.
A tiny blessing.

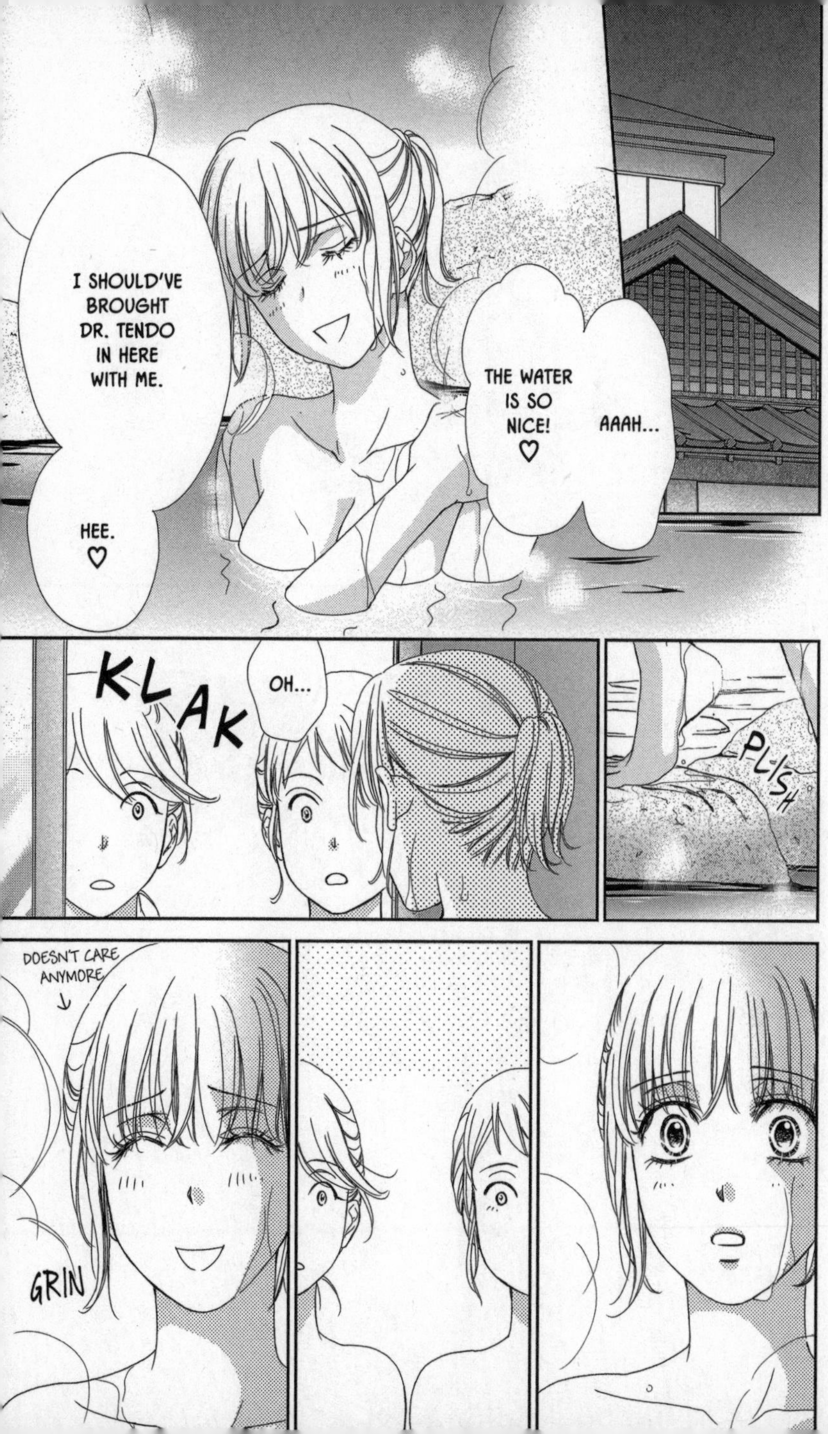
AAAH...
THE WATER IS SO NICE! ♡
I SHOULD'VE BROUGHT DR. TENDO IN HERE WITH ME.
HEE. ♡
PLISH
OH...
KLAK
DOESN'T CARE ANYMORE
GRIN

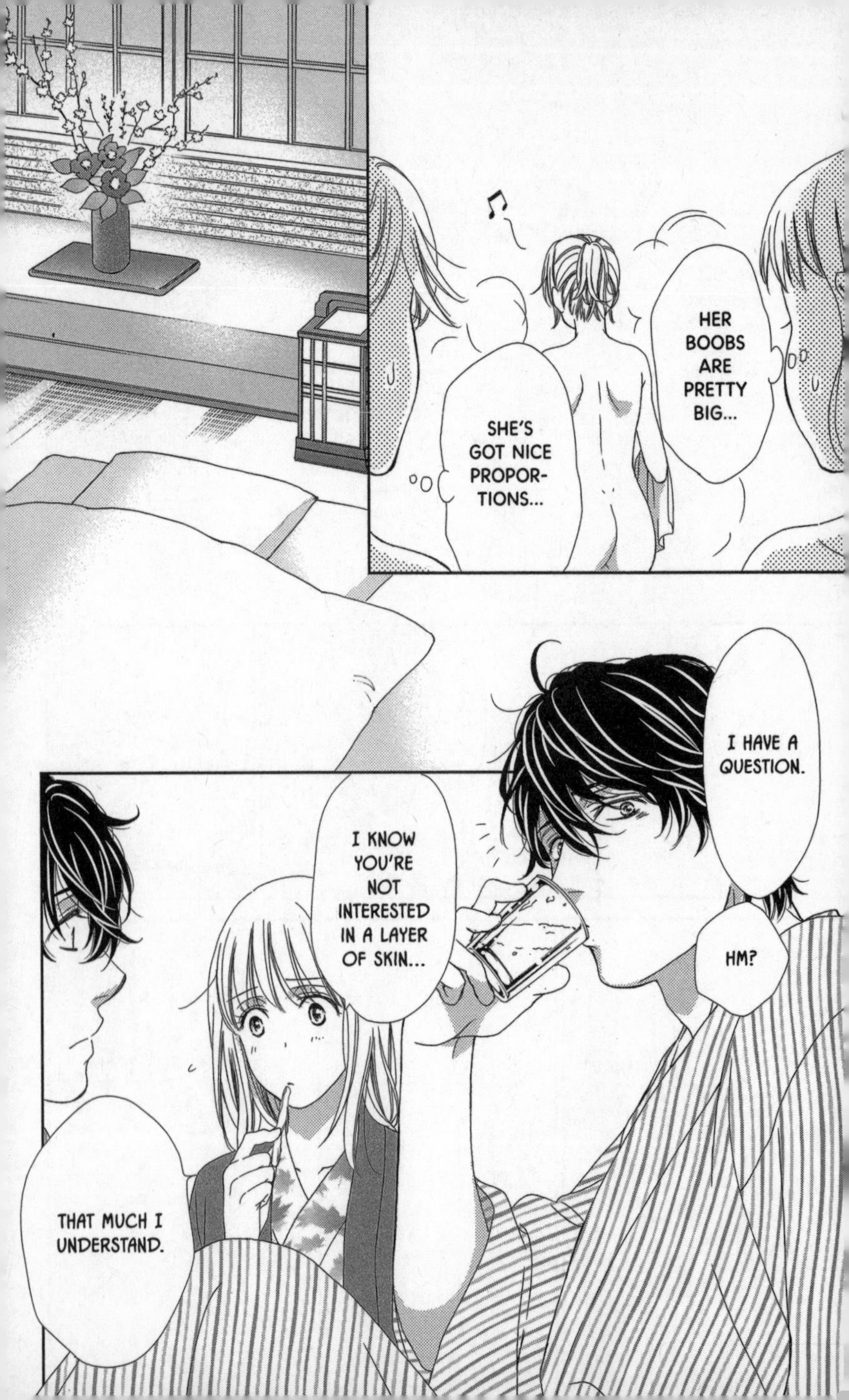

HER BOOBS ARE PRETTY BIG...
SHE'S GOT NICE PROPOR-TIONS...
I HAVE A QUESTION.
HM?
I KNOW YOU'RE NOT INTERESTED IN A LAYER OF SKIN...
THAT MUCH I UNDERSTAND.

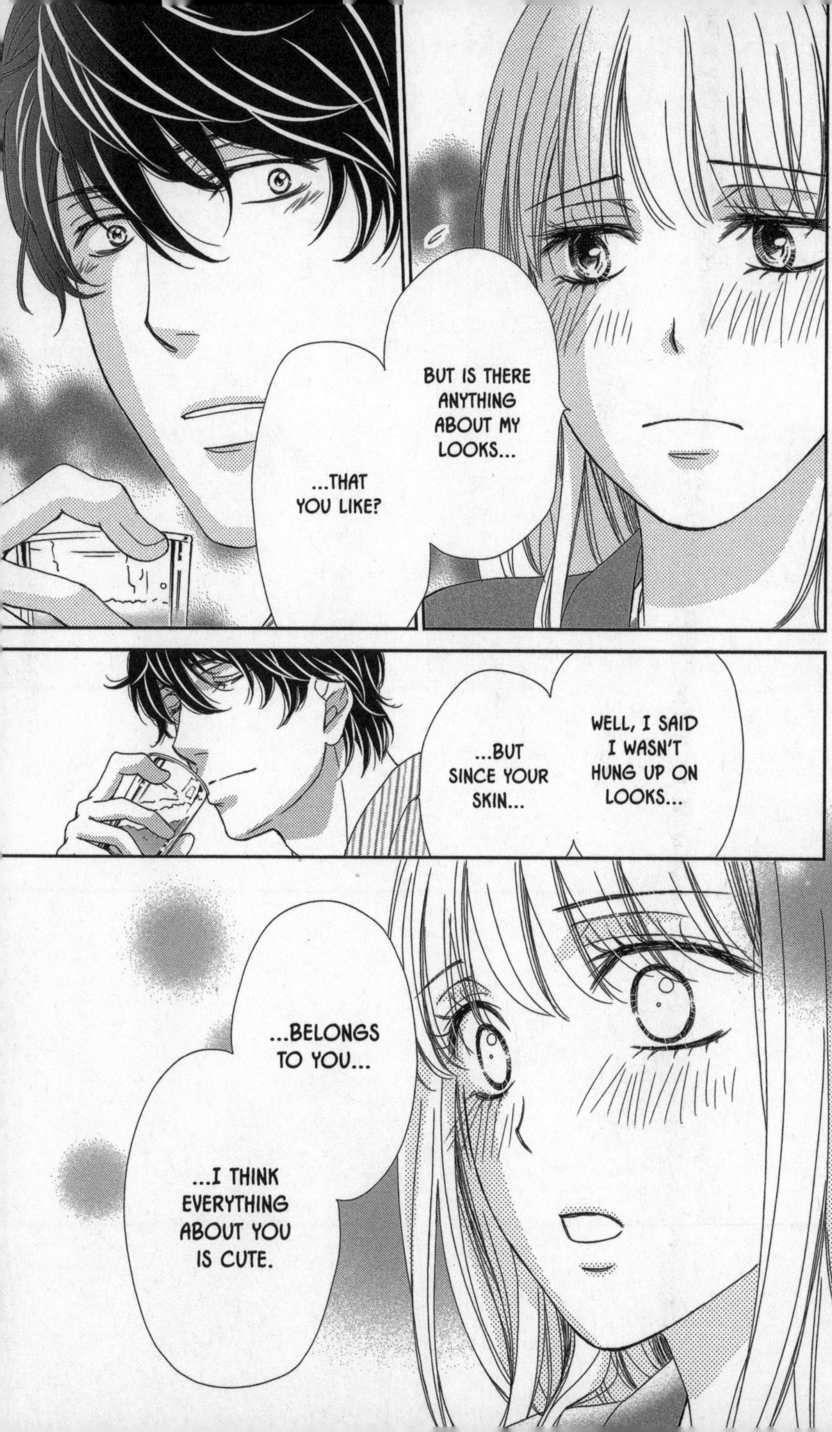
BUT IS THERE ANYTHING ABOUT MY LOOKS...
...THAT YOU LIKE?
WELL, I SAID I WASN'T HUNG UP ON LOOKS...
...BUT SINCE YOUR SKIN...
...BELONGS TO YOU...
...I THINK EVERYTHING ABOUT YOU IS CUTE.

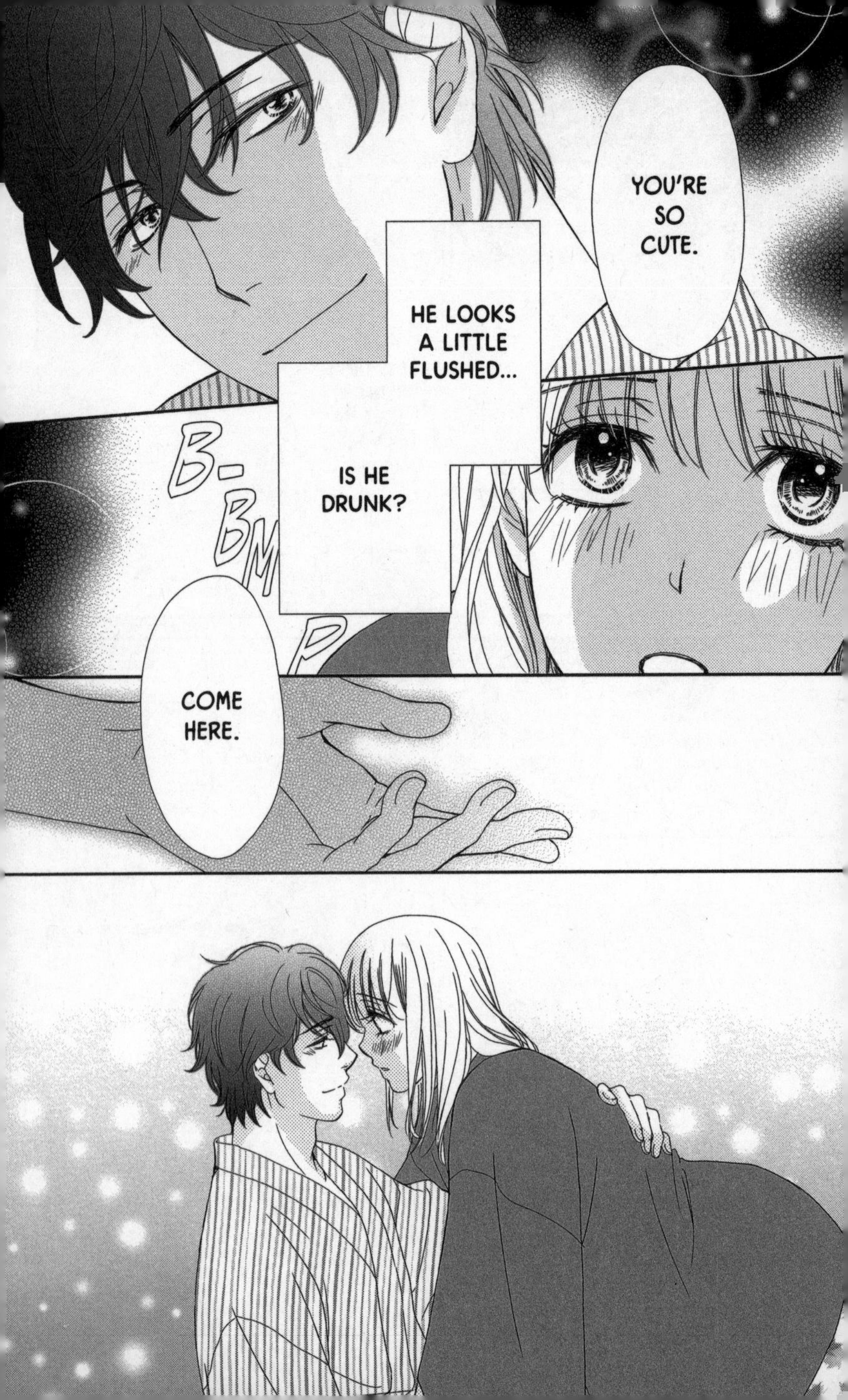
YOU'RE SO CUTE.
HE LOOKS A LITTLE FLUSHED...
IS HE DRUNK?
B-BMP
COME HERE.

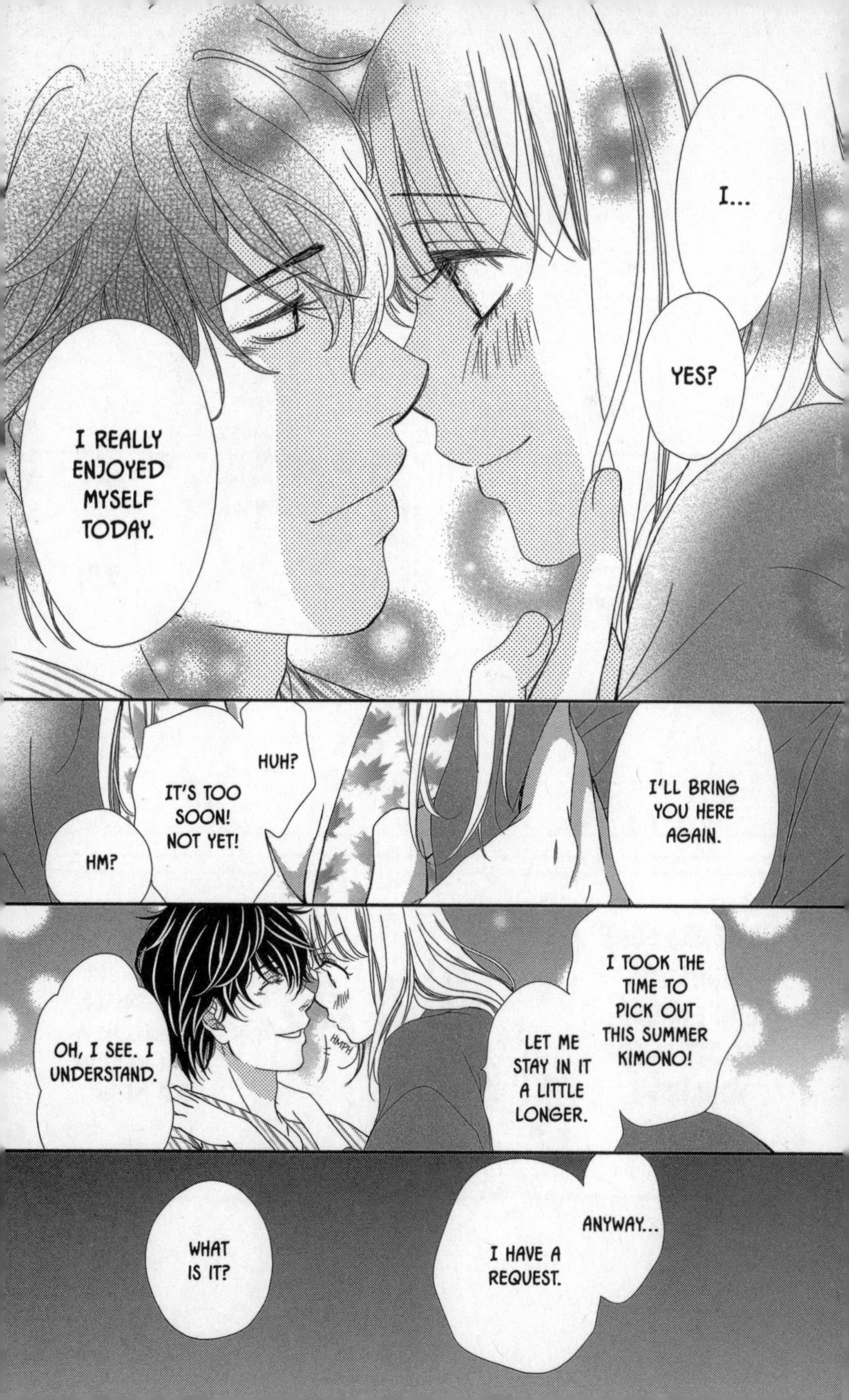
I...
YES?
I REALLY ENJOYED MYSELF TODAY.
I'LL BRING YOU HERE AGAIN.
HUH?
IT'S TOO SOON! NOT YET!
HM?
I TOOK THE TIME TO PICK OUT THIS SUMMER KIMONO!
LET ME STAY IN IT A LITTLE LONGER.
HMPH
OH, I SEE. I UNDERSTAND.
ANYWAY...
I HAVE A REQUEST.
WHAT IS IT?

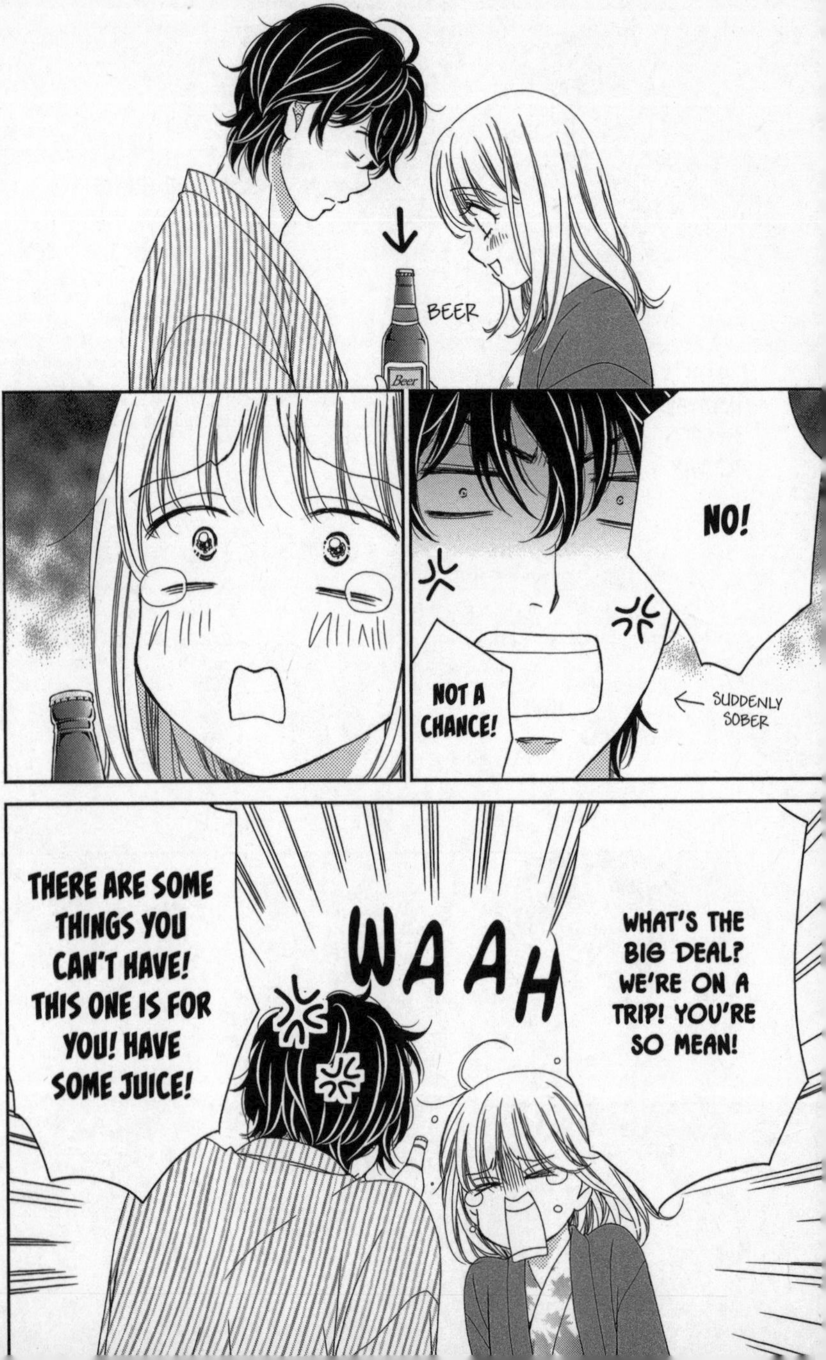
BEER
Beer
NO!
NOT A CHANCE!
SUDDENLY SOBER
WHAT'S THE BIG DEAL? WE'RE ON A TRIP! YOU'RE SO MEAN!
WAAH
THERE ARE SOME THINGS YOU CAN'T HAVE! THIS ONE IS FOR YOU! HAVE SOME JUICE!

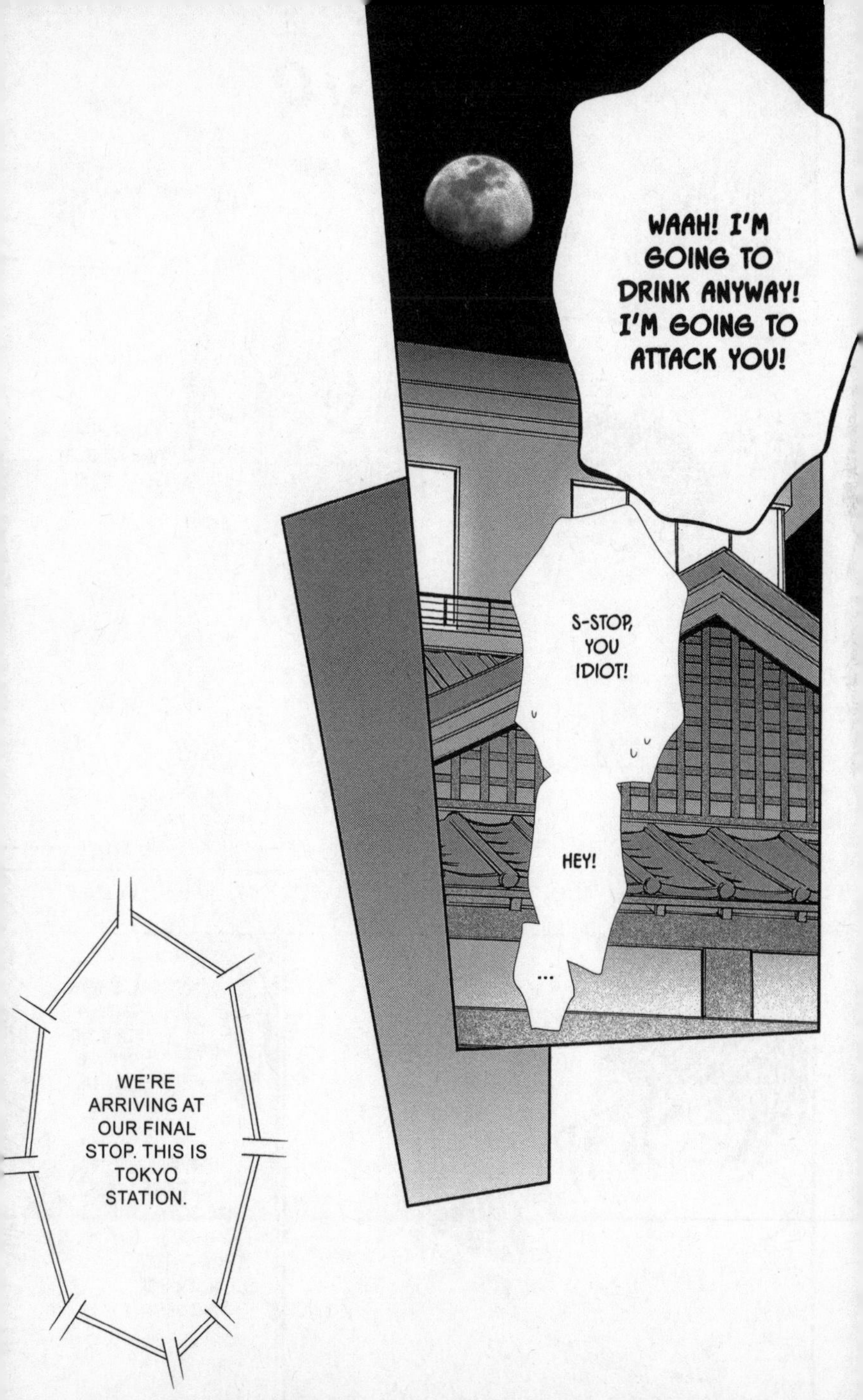
WAAH! I'M GOING TO DRINK ANYWAY! I'M GOING TO ATTACK YOU!
S-STOP, YOU IDIOT!
HEY!
...
WE'RE ARRIVING AT OUR FINAL STOP. THIS IS TOKYO STATION.

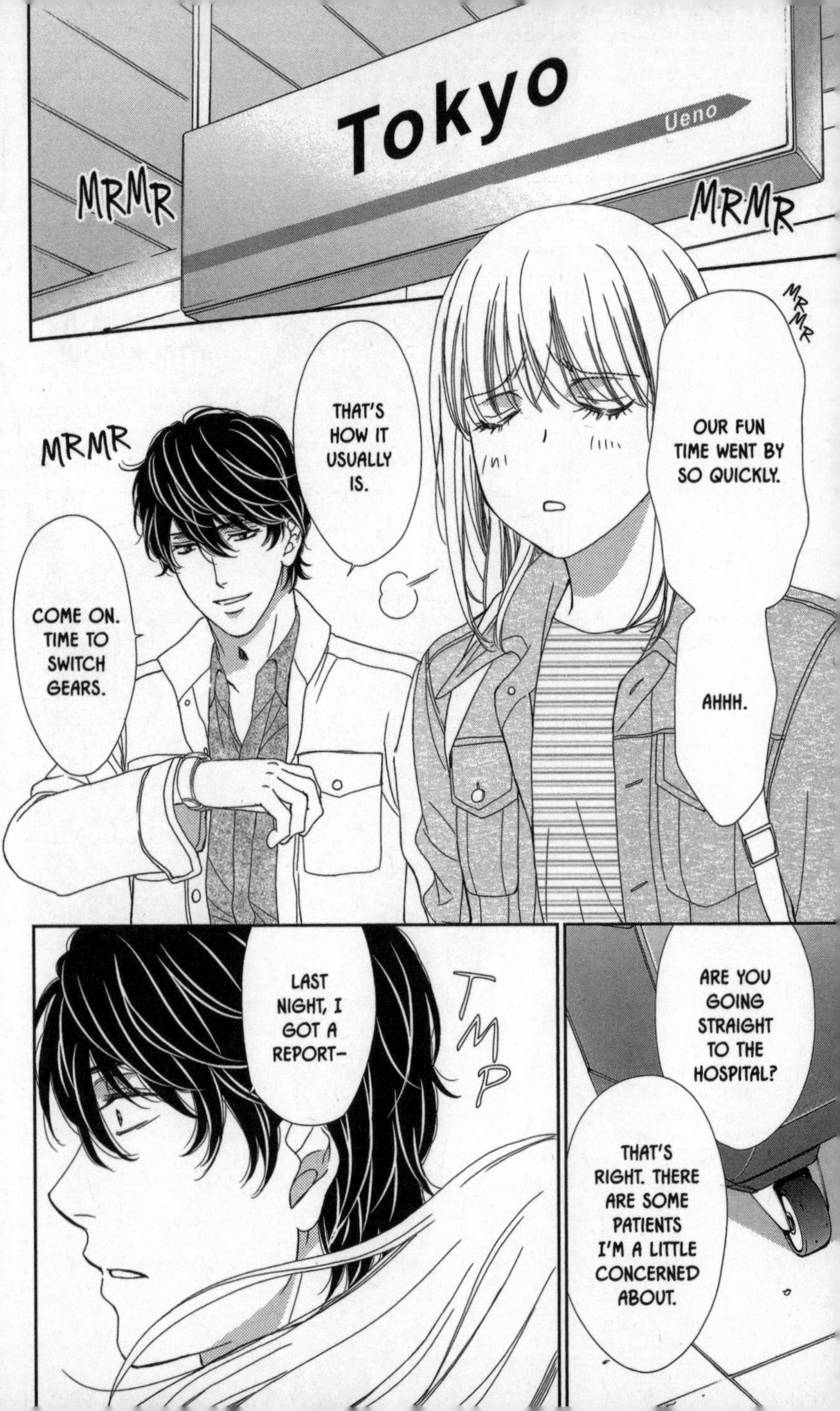
Tokyo
Ueno
MRMR
MRMR
MRMR
OUR FUN TIME WENT BY SO QUICKLY.
AHHH.
THAT'S HOW IT USUALLY IS.
MRMR
COME ON. TIME TO SWITCH GEARS.
ARE YOU GOING STRAIGHT TO THE HOSPITAL?
THAT'S RIGHT. THERE ARE SOME PATIENTS I'M A LITTLE CONCERNED ABOUT.
TMP
LAST NIGHT, I GOT A REPORT—

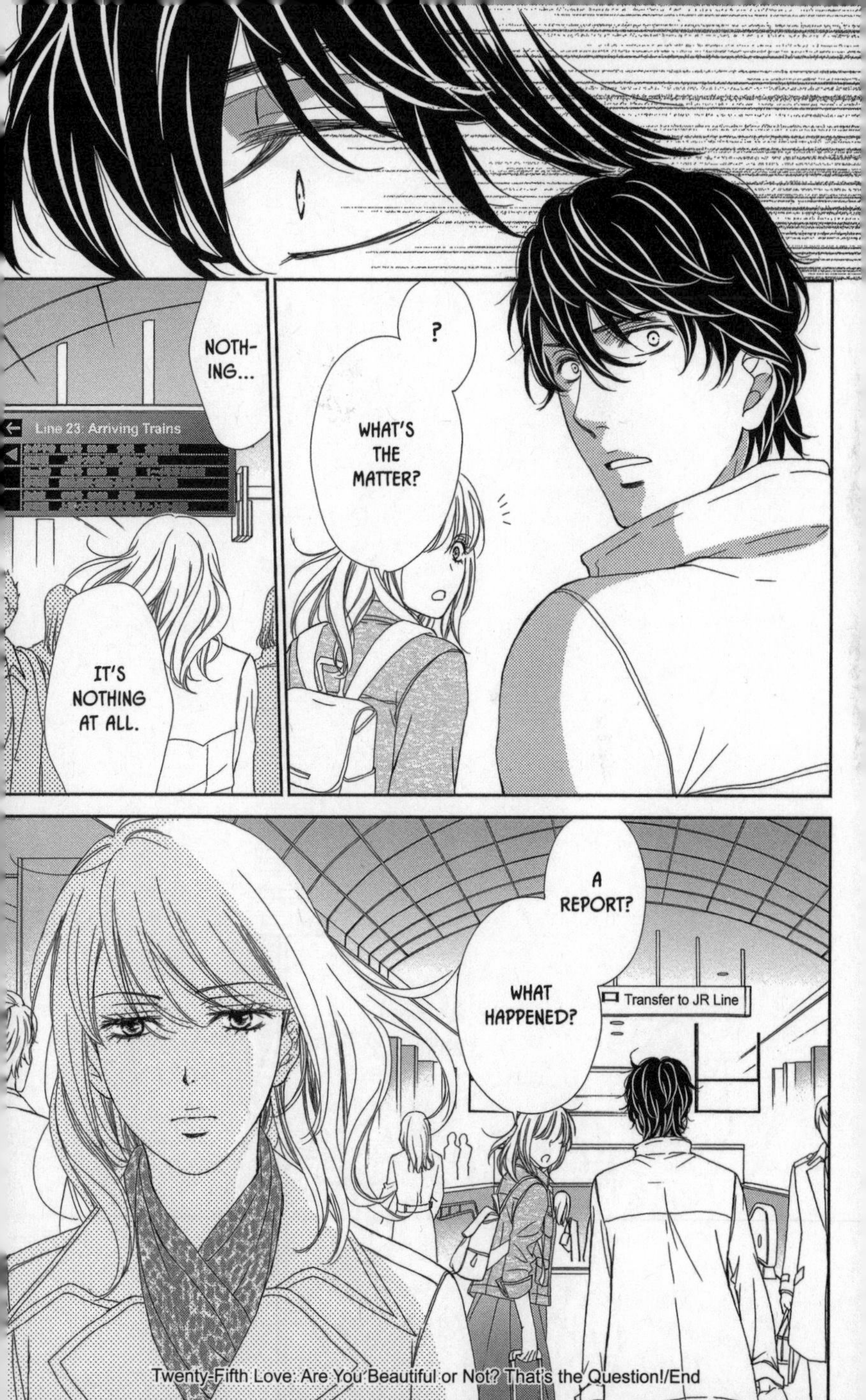
?
WHAT'S THE MATTER?
NOTH-ING...
Line 23: Arriving Trains
IT'S NOTHING AT ALL.
A REPORT?
WHAT HAPPENED?
Transfer to JR Line

Twenty-Fifth Love: Are You Beautiful or Not? That's the Question!/End

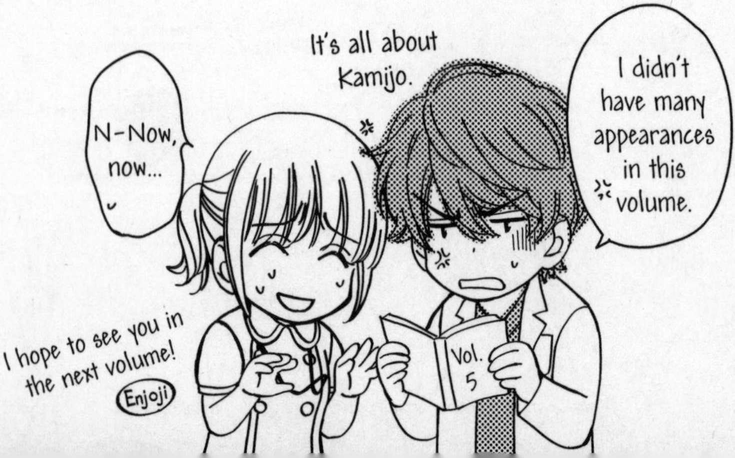
I didn't have many appearances in this volume.
It's all about Kamijo.
N-Now, now...
Vol. 5
I hope to see you in the next volume!
Enjoji

They don't wear this nowadays.

It's been 15 years since I made my debut as a manga artist. I'm amazed I haven't gotten any better at creating manga even though I've been doing this for over 15 years! What in the world is going on? (*sob*)

—Maki Enjoji

Maki Enjoji was born on December 8 in Tokyo. She made her debut with *Fu Junai* (Wicked Pure Love). Her series *Happy Marriage?!*, also published by VIZ Media's Shojo Beat imprint, was made into a live-action drama.

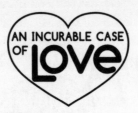

# AN INCURABLE CASE OF LOVE

Volume 5

SHOJO BEAT EDITION

STORY & ART BY
**Maki Enjoji**

TRANSLATION
**JN Productions**

TOUCH-UP ART & LETTERING
**Inori Fukuda Trant**

DESIGN
**Alice Lewis**

EDITOR
**Nancy Thistlethwaite**

KOI WA TSUZUKU YO DOKOMADEMO Vol. 5
by Maki ENJOJI

Original Japanese edition published by SHOGAKUKAN.
English translation rights in the United States of America, Canada, the United Kingdom, Ireland, Australia and New Zealand arranged with SHOGAKUKAN.

Original Cover Design: Erika ADACHI



Printed in the U.S.A.

Published by VIZ Media, LLC
P.O. Box 77010
San Francisco, CA 94107

10 9 8 7 6 5 4 3 2 1
First printing, October 2020

ratings.viz.com RATED M MATURE

**PARENTAL ADVISORY**
AN INCURABLE CASE OF LOVE is rated M for Mature and is recommended for ages 18 and up. This series contains sexual themes.

VIZ MEDIA
viz.com

Shojo Beat
shojobeat.com

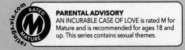

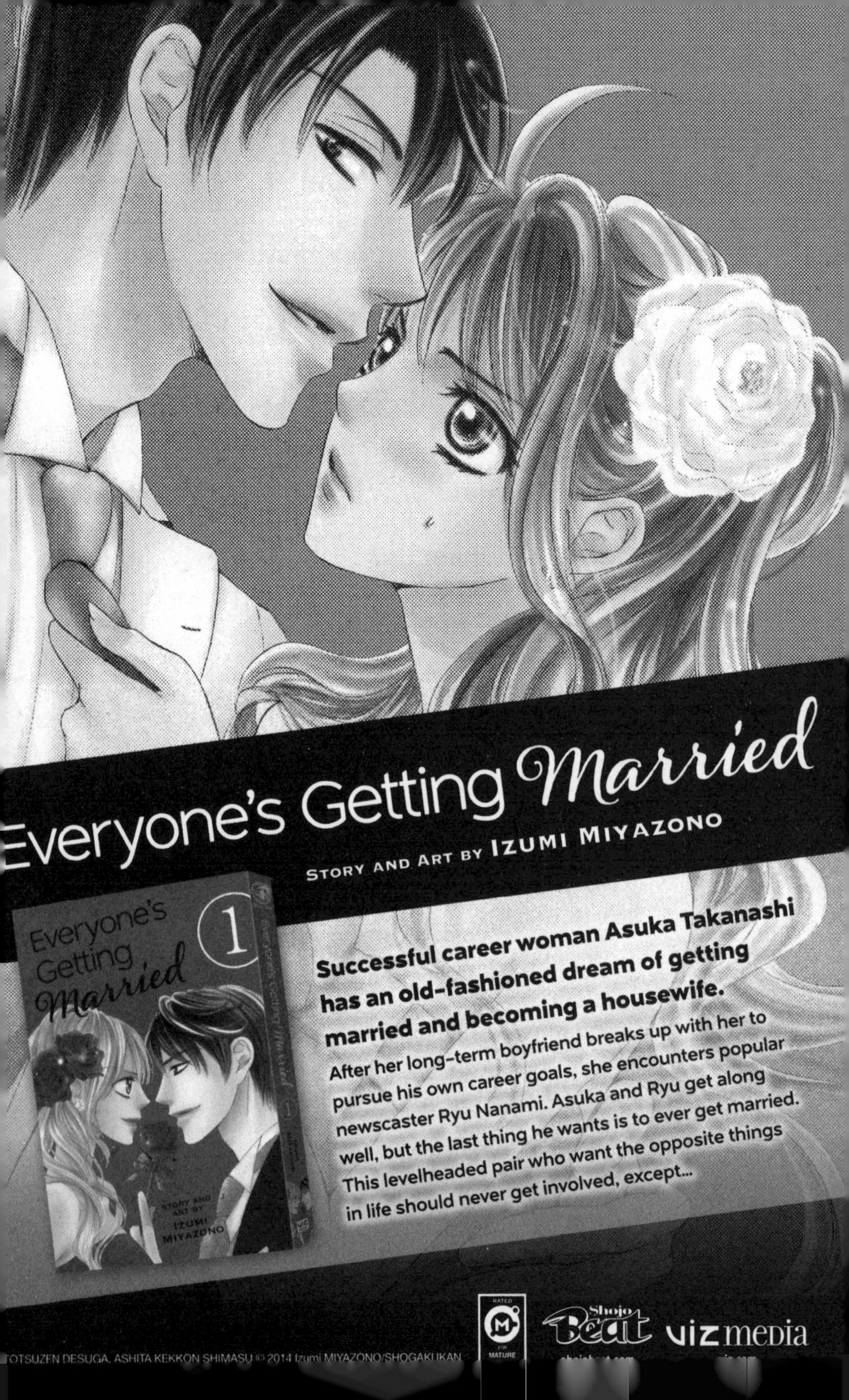
Everyone's Getting Married
STORY AND ART BY IZUMI MIYAZONO
Everyone's Getting Married
1
Successful career woman Asuka Takanashi has an old-fashioned dream of getting married and becoming a housewife.
After her long-term boyfriend breaks up with her to pursue his own career goals, she encounters popular newscaster Ryu Nanami. Asuka and Ryu get along well, but the last thing he wants is to ever get married. This levelheaded pair who want the opposite things in life should never get involved, except...
RATED
FOR MATURE
Shojo Beat
VIZ media
TOTSUZEN DESUGA, ASHITA KEKKON SHIMASU © 2014 Izumi MIYAZONO/SHOGAKUKAN

lolololol

# So Cute It Hurts!!

### Story and Art by Go Ikeyamada

The Kobayashi twins, Megumu and Mitsuru, were named after historical figures, but only Megumu has grown up with a taste for history. So when Mitsuru is in danger of losing his weekends to extra history classes, he convinces his sister to swap clothes with him and ace his tests! After all, how hard can it be for them to play each other?

But Megumu can't rely on just her book smarts in Mitsuru's all-boys, delinquents' paradise of a high school. And Mitsuru finds life as a high school girl to be much more complicated than he expected!

Shojo Beat

RATED M MATURE
ratings.viz.com

VIZ media
viz.com

lolololol

So Cute It Hurts!!

Story and Art by Go Ikeyamada

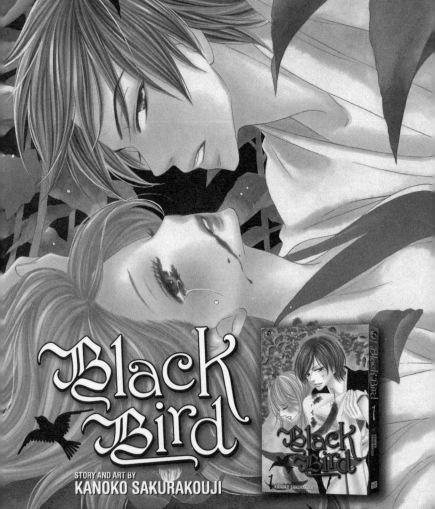

# Black Bird

**STORY AND ART BY**
**KANOKO SAKURAKOUJI**

There is a world of myth and magic that intersects ours, and only a special few can see it. Misao Harada is one such person, and she wants nothing to do with magical realms. She just wants to have a normal high school life and maybe get a boyfriend.

But she is the bride of demon prophecy, and her blood grants incredible powers, her flesh immortality. Now the demon realm is fighting over the right to her hand...or her life!

BLACK BIRD © 2007 Kanoko SAKURAKOUJI/SHOGAKUKAN

Kaya is accustomed to scheduling his "dinner dates" and working odd hours, but can she handle it when Kyohei's gaze turns her way?

# Midnight Secretary

### Story & Art by Tomu Ohmi

Kaya Satozuka prides herself on being an excellent secretary and a consummate professional, so she doesn't even bat an eye when she's reassigned to the office of her company's difficult director, Kyohei Tohma. He's as prickly—and hot—as rumors paint him, but Kaya is unfazed...until she discovers that he's a vampire!!

footer

footer

footer

footer

footer

footer

footer

footer

footer

footer

footer





RATED **M** FOR MATURE

**VIZ** media

www.viz.com

Shojo **BEAT**

copyright

copyright

copyright

copyright

copyright

copyright

MIDNIGHT SECRETARY © 2007 Tomu OHMI/SHOGAKUKAN

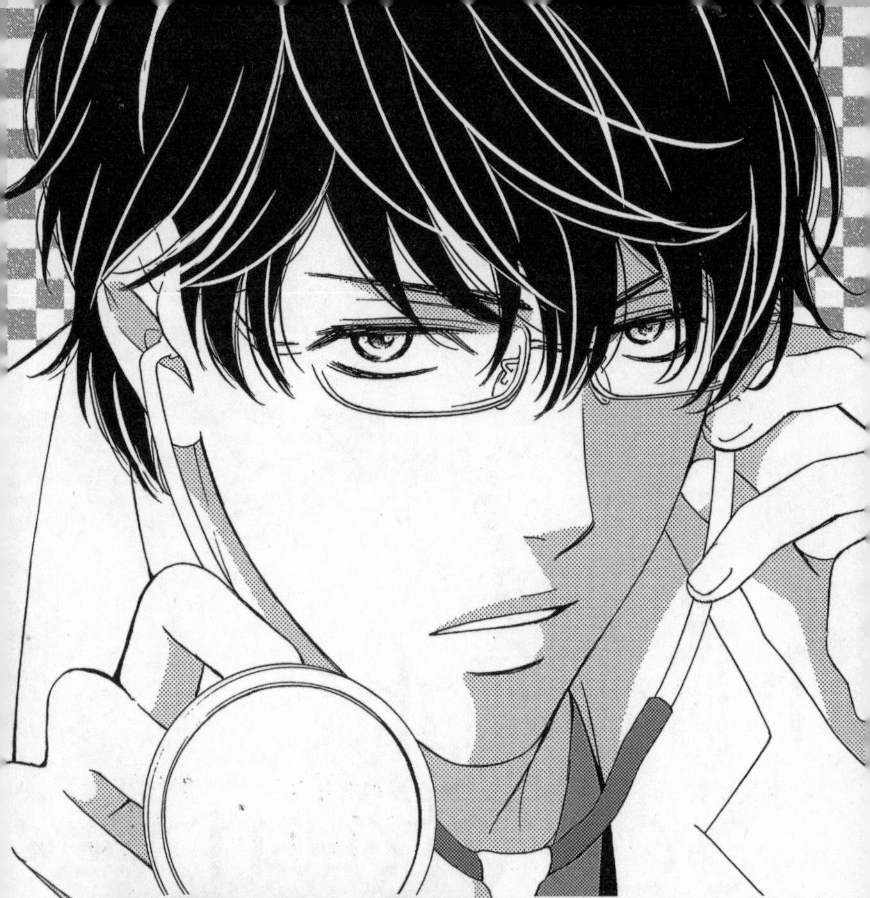

# STOP!

## You may be reading the wrong way!

In keeping with the original Japanese comic format, this book reads from right to left—so action, sound effects and word balloons are completely reversed to preserve the orientation of the original artwork.

Check out the diagram shown here to get the hang of things, and then turn to the other side of the book to get started!

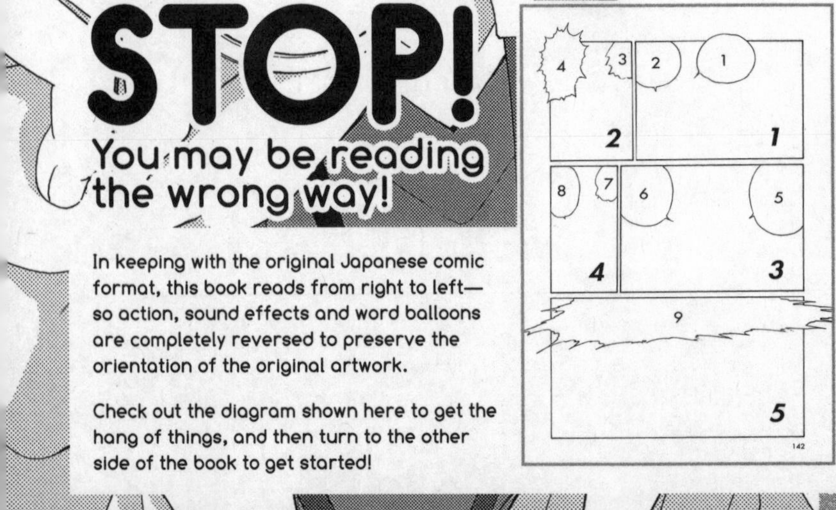
1
2
3
4
1
2
5
6
7
8
3
4
9
5
142